K

EASTERN SEABOARD

ya ●

Chanthaburi ●

Trat ●

Khlong Yai ●

of Thailand

Eastern Seaboard

Lower Western Gulf Coast

Upper Western Gulf Coast

Deep South

ongkhla

DEEP SOUTH

0 km   50

0 miles   50

EYEWITNESS TRAVEL

THAILAND'S
BEACHES & ISLANDS

EYEWITNESS TRAVEL

THAILAND'S
BEACHES & ISLANDS

DK | Penguin Random House

Managing Editor Aruna Ghose

Senior Editorial Manager Savitha Kumar

Senior Design Manager Priyanka Thakur

Project Designer Amisha Gupta

Editors Smita Khanna Bajaj, Diya Kohli

Designer Shruti Bahl

Senior Cartographer Suresh Kumar

Cartographer Jasneet Arora

DTP Designers Azeem Siddique, Rakesh Pal

Senior Picture Research Coordinator Taiyaba Khatoon

Picture Researcher Sumita Khatwani

Contributors Andrew Forbes, David Henley, Peter Holmshaw

Photographer David Henley

Illustrators Surat Kumar Mantoo, Arun Pottirayil

Printed and bound in China

First American Edition, 2010

16 17 18 19 10 9 8 7 6 5 4 3 2 1

Published in the US by
DK Publishing, 345 Hudson Street
New York, New York 10014

Reprinted with revisions 2012, 2014, 2016

Copyright © 2010, 2016 Dorling Kindersley Limited, London

A Penguin Random House Company

Published in the UK by Dorling Kindersley Limited.

A catalog record for this book is available from the Library of Congress.

ISSN 1542-1554

ISBN 978-1-4654-4132-4

MIX
Paper from
responsible sources
FSC™ C018179
www.fsc.org

Front cover main image: Boat at anchor, Lower Andaman Coast

◀ Limestone crags tower over clear turquoise waters, Krabi Coast

Longtail tour boats at idyllic Hat Tham Phra Nang, Krabi

Contents

How to Use This Guide **6**

Introducing Thailand's Beaches and Islands

Discovering Thailand's Beaches and Islands **10**

Putting Thailand's Beaches and Islands on the Map **16**

A Portrait of Thailand's Beaches and Islands **18**

Thailand's Beaches and Islands Through the Year **38**

The History of Thailand **42**

Devotees outside San Chao Chui Tui Temple in Phuket

Kayaking into limestone caves,
Than Bok Koranee National Park

Thailand's Beaches and Islands Area by Area

Diver exploring coral reefs rich in
marine life, Ko Chang

Nang talung puppet

Travelers' Needs

Survival Guide

Wat Phra Mahathat Woramahawihan,
Nakhon Si Thammarat

HOW TO USE THIS GUIDE

This guide helps you get the most from your visit to Thailand's Beaches and Islands. It provides detailed practical information and expert recommendations. *Introducing Thailand's Beaches and Islands* maps the region and sets it in its historical and cultural context. The six regional chapters, plus *Bangkok*, describe important sights, using maps, pictures, and illustrations. Hotel and restaurant listings and information about watersports and other outdoor activities are found in *Travelers' Needs*. The *Survival Guide* has information on everything from transportation to personal safety.

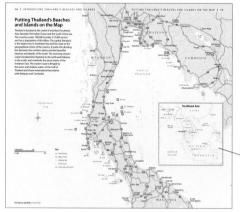

Putting Thailand's Beaches and Islands on the Map

The orientation map shows the location of coastal Thailand in relation to its neighboring countries. The guide specifically covers the beaches and islands of Thailand. These are divided into seven areas, including Bangkok which is covered as a separate section.

A locator map shows where you are in relation to other Southeast Asian countries.

Thailand's Beaches and Islands Area by Area

Each of the seven areas in the guide has its own chapter. The most interesting places to visit have been numbered on a *Regional Map*. The key to the map symbols is on the back flap.

A suggested route for a walk around the Street-by-Street area is shown in red.

1 Introduction
The landscape and character of each area is outlined here, showing how the area has developed and what it has to offer the visitor today.

Each area of the book can be identified by its color coding, shown on the inside front cover.

Story boxes explore related topics.

Stars indicate the sights that no visitor should miss.

2 Street-by-Street Map This gives a bird's-eye view of a key area in each chapter.

3 Regional Map This shows the main road network and gives an illustrated overview of the whole region. All entries are numbered; there are also useful tips on getting around.

Sights at a Glance lists the chapter's sights by category: Towns, Cities, and Villages; National Parks; Theme Parks; Historical Buildings and Religious Sites; Beaches, Islands, and Bays.

4 Information with Map Some beaches and islands have illustrated maps with additional information. The map shows the main towns, beaches, and road networks.

5 Detailed Information All important places are described individually. They follow the numbering on the Regional Map.

The information block provides details needed to visit each sight. Map references locate sights on the road map on the inside back cover.

A feature deals with a topic related to that region or place.

For all the top sights, a Visitors' Checklist provides the practical information needed to plan a visit.

6 Thailand's Beaches and Islands' Top Sights These are given two or more full pages. An illustrated map shows the layout and landscape of the sight. Areas good for diving and watersports are marked along with other information.

INTRODUCING THAILAND'S BEACHES AND ISLANDS

DISCOVERING THAILAND'S BEACHES AND ISLANDS

The following tours have been designed to cover three prime areas for experiencing the delights of coastal Thailand and the capital city of Bangkok, while keeping long-distance travel to a minimum. The two-day tour introduces modern and ancient Bangkok. Next, a ten-day itinerary moving south from

Phuket island showcases the beauty of the Andaman Sea. The following one-week tour covers island-hopping along the Gulf of Thailand. These two tours could be combined to form a three-week beach itinerary. Finally, there is a week-long tour on the Eastern Seaboard, within easy reach of Bangkok.

Ko Lanta beach
The Ko Lanta archipelago boasts miles and miles of golden sands. Much of it falls under the protection of the Marine National Park designation, so that both the beaches and waters remain beautifully unspoiled.

Ten Days on the Andaman Coast

- Wander old **Phuket** town, with its fine Sino-Portuguese architecture, Chinese Taoist shrines, and eclectic shops.
- Unwind on **Hat Nai Yang**, a quiet beach at the north end of Phuket's west coast.
- Take a longtail boat to the dramatic limestone stacks and sea caves of **Phang Nga Bay**.
- Jump into the pulsating nightlife of **Patong** or just enjoy a tranquil seafood dinner overlooking the sea.
- Savor the laid-back seaside town of **Krabi**, and take a boat to its offshore islands.
- Watch the rock climbers at **Rai Leh beach** and give sea-kayaking a try.
- Catch the ferry to **Ko Phi Phi** for some snorkeling and fresh, tasty seafood.
- Explore **Ko Lanta**'s western beaches and its old Chinese trading port in the east.
- Let nature restore you in the splendor of **Ko Tarutao Marine National Park**.

A Week on the Gulf of Thailand

- Savor fine dining after a day of sunbathing and watersports on blissful **Chaweng beach**.
- Explore **Ko Samui**'s interior jungles, mountains, and caves.
- Admire the sunset at the **Big Buddha** statue on Ko Samui's Bangrak beach.
- Board the ferry to **Ko Pha Ngan,** then relax with a massage under the palm trees on the beach.
- Bathe in the clear waters of **Than Sadet Falls** on Ko Phangan, visited by Thai kings.
- Admire the magnificent coral reefs of **Ko Tao** – either with a mask and fins or in a glass-bottomed boat.
- Enjoy kayaking, hiking, or snorkeling in the pristine wilds and waters of **Ang Thong Marine National Park**.

Chumphon

Ranong

Surin Islands

Surat Thani

THAILAND

Phang Nga Bay
Hat Nai
Patong
Phuket
Ko Yao
Yai
Krabi
Ko Phi Phi
Ko Lanta

Andaman Sea

Ko Libong

Ko Tarutao Marine National Park

◀ Celestial deities depicted in a temple mural from the Ayutthaya period

Ko Chang
At fishing villages such as Ban Salak Phet, colorfully painted boats moor at bamboo-thatched jetties with huts on stilts.

A Week on the Eastern Seaboard

- Sample the nightlife of **Pattaya** – discos, cabarets, and dinners of delicious, great-value seafood.

- Walk the entire east coast of **Ko Samet** and discover each bay's unique character.

- Try some fresh spring rolls in the Vietnamese Quarter of **Chanthaburi** after a stroll in the nearby riverside **gem market**.

- Visit lively **Hat Sai Khao** on the island of Ko Chang – offering beach games and trendy restaurants.

- Dive into dense jungle to reach **Khlong Phlu**, Ko Chang's highest waterfall.

- Discover paradise on **Ko Wai** – one of numerous pristine islands south of Ko Chang – boasting white sands, palm trees, and coral reefs.

Key

— Andaman Coast tour
— Gulf of Thailand tour
— Eastern Seaboard tour

0 kilometers 100
0 miles 100

Big Buddha statue, Ko Samui
An imposing staircase flanked by undulating serpents leads to this towering statue. Despite crowds of visitors, food stands, and souvenir stalls clustered around it, the Buddha himself remains serene.

Two Days in Bangkok

Thailand's vibrant capital dazzles visitors with its array of contrasts – serene temples, gardens, and royal palaces amid Western modernity in both luxurious and raucous guises.

- **Arriving** Bangkok's Suvarnabhumi International Airport lies 16 miles (26 km) east of the city. A high speed rail link reaches various parts of the city, and taxis abound. Don Muang Airport, 12 miles (19 km) north of Bangkok, is used by budget carriers.

- **Moving on** Flights to Phuket, Ko Samui, Krabi, and Trat (near Ko Chang) leave from both airports. Buses to Pattaya and points beyond on the Eastern Seaboard leave from the Eastern Bus Terminal, and southbound trains leave from Hua Lampong railway station.

Day 1
Morning Bangkok is a huge city, but its best sights are found within a fairly small area along the breezy Chao Phraya River. **Wat Phra Kaeo** (pp60–63) houses one of Thailand's most esteemed cultural artifacts, a small jade Buddha image. Ornate pavilions and *chedi* (pagodas) fill the compound, which is surrounded by a covered walkway decorated with superb murals depicting scenes from the Ramakien, Thailand's version of the Indian epic Ramayana. Adjacent to the *wat* is the **Grand Palace** (pp64–5), home to the first six kings of the current Chakri Dynasty, displaying a mix of traditional Thai and European Neo-Classical architecture. Most impressive is the Dusit Throne Hall, containing the original teak throne of the dynasty's founder.

Afternoon As an excellent counterpoint to the intense atmosphere of Wat Phra Kaeo, explore sprawling, peaceful, and tree-filled **Wat Pho** (pp68–9).

The magnificent central *bot* (chapel) contains a bronze Buddha image salvaged from the former capital Ayutthaya; another houses the immense **Reclining Buddha**, which exudes calm. End the day by experiencing a therapeutic massage in the temple's school of traditional medicine.

Day 2
Morning Head to **The Jim Thompson House** (pp80–81), the former home of an American entrepreneur who revitalized the Thai silk industry after World War II. The six traditional Thai teak houses contain superb collections of Asian art, including sculpture from the 7th century, antique Thai ceramics, Burmese wood carvings, and Ming porcelain. Stop for lunch at the on-site restaurant.

Afternoon Near The Jim Thompson House lies a wide choice of modern shopping malls (pp84–5), from the elegant **Siam Paragon** to the bazaar-like atmosphere at **Mahboonkrong**, offering electronics and clothing at bargain prices. More shopping on nearby Phoenchit Road can be followed by a visit to the **Erawan Shrine** (p79), where traditional Thai dancers perform in honor of the Hindu god Indra, held holy by Thai Buddhists.

To extend your trip…
Take a tour out of the city to huge, chaotic **Chatuchak Market** (p82) or to the colorful **Damnoen Saduak Floating Market** (p83).

Ten Days on the Andaman Coast

- **Airports** Arrive at Phuket International Airport (direct flights from abroad) and depart from Krabi Airport (domestic only).

- **Transport** Scheduled ferries travel to and from Phuket and Krabi to all destinations in this tour. Buses run between Phuket and Krabi.

Day 1: Phuket
Spend a morning wandering the streets of charming Phuket old town (pp226–8) and visit two Chinese temples, **San Chao Chui Tui** and **San Chao Put Jaw** (p226). Both shrines were established by Chinese immigrants who flocked here in the 19th century to work in the tin mines. They celebrate the Taoist tradition and the ambience is less serene than the tranquillity that pervades Thai temples. Nearby, the **Chinese Mansions** (pp230–31), once the homes of tin barons, are a fascinating mixture of Asian and Western architecture. After lunch, head for the secluded beaches of **Hat Nai Yang** or **Hat Nai Thon** (pp236–7) at the northern end of the island's west coast.

Day 2: Phang Nga Bay
A day trip to **Phang Nga Bay** (pp220–21) is a must, to see the spectacular limestone stacks and hidden sea caves that create a home for the marine and avian life for which it is famous. For the best views, hire a long-tail boat or join a sea-kayaking tour for some cave paddling.

The huge Reclining Buddha at Wat Pho, Bangkok

Longtail boats lining the beach at Hat Tham Phra Nang

> **To extend your trip…**
> Spend a night (or more) on the placid and pristine island of **Ko Yao Yai** in Phang Nga Bay (p242).

Day 3: Phuket
Back on the island of Phuket, head to bustling **Hat Patong** (p233). Every seaside diversion is offered here, from sailing to jet-skiing to late-night discos. **Kata** and **Karon** beaches to the south, while still offering good facilities, are more relaxing.

> **To extend your trip…**
> The **Surin Islands Marine National Park** (pp208–9) off the coast of Ranong Province, north of Phuket, is home to the world-famous Burma Banks diving site – the waters are crystal clear. All accommodations here are in National Park bungalows, giving a non-commercial feel to the park.

Day 4: Krabi and Rai Leh
Stroll along the riverside walkway in **Krabi** (p248) to the fishing port, and enjoy the views of mangrove forests and islands. Take a longtail boat to the nearby beach of **Hat Rai Leh East** (p252), famed for limestone cliffs that attract climbers from around the world. Sea-kayaking is a good alternative for sufferers from vertigo. A walk over the headland leads to the beautiful white sands of **Hat Rai Leh West** (p252).

Day 5: Hat Tham Phra Nang
From either of the Rai Leh beaches, take a longtail boat to the picturesque **Hat Tham Phra Nang** beach (p253) and its large cave, **Tham Phra Nang** (p253), dedicated to an Indian princess lost in the Andaman Sea, whose spirit is now revered by fishermen and by women hoping for a child.

Day 6: Ko Phi Phi
Take a morning boat from Ao Nang near Hat Tham Phra Nang for a day trip to the spectacular island of **Ko Phi Phi** (pp256–9). Cool off in one of the hip cafés in **Ban Ton Sai** village, and then walk across the isthmus to **Ao Dalam**, a lovely bay bounded by coconut palms and limestone crags. A steep but short walk leads to a viewpoint with fantastic vistas of this island jewel. Alternatively, walk along the level trail to **Hat Yao** and go snorkeling on the reef, where iridescent fish dart among the vivid corals. Return to Krabi as the sun sets.

Day 7: Ko Lanta
Either from Krabi or directly from Ko Phi Phi island, take a speedboat to Ban Sala Dan on the north end of the island of **Ko Lanta Yai** (pp264–7). From here, a rented vehicle provides the flexibility to pick and choose among the many beaches along the west coast of the island. For budget travelers, **Hat Khlong Khong** offers cheap accommodations, while **Ao Kantiang** provides more upscale resorts.

Day 8: Ko Lanta
Cross to the island's eastern coast, stopping for lunch on **Viewpoint Hill** (p265) to see both coasts and the surrounding islets simultaneously. Visit the village of **Ban Si Raya** (p267), also known as Old Lanta Town, the original settlement on Ko Lanta, where old Chinese shophouses and mosques tell of days gone by.

> **To extend your trip…**
> Explore some of the less-visited islands lying off the coast of Trang Province. **Ko Libong** (p271) is particularly peaceful.

Day 9: Ko Tarutao Marine National Park
Take the ferry (or choose a speedboat to whisk you in comfort) to **Ko Lipe** (p279), the best known island (and one of the smallest) in this archipelago. The main beach, **Hat Pattaya**, has incredibly white sands and sumptuous resorts, perfect for sea-kayaking by day and candlelit dinners on the beach after sunset.

Day 10: Ko Tarutao Marine National Park
From Ko Lipe, catch a boat to the larger islands of **Ko Adang** and **Ko Rawi** (p278). Go snorkeling on the reefs offshore, bask on the deserted beaches, and listen to the birds that inhabit the jungle interior.

Busy Patong street lined with "little red vans" – the Phuket tuk-tuk – for hire

A Week on the Gulf of Thailand

- **Airports** Fly to and from Ko Samui via Bangkok or Phuket.

- **Transport** Ko Samui is big enough to make a rental car worth considering, but public transport is best on Ko Phangan and Ko Tao, due to poor road conditions. Both car and passenger ferries serve Ko Samui and Ko Phangan from the mainland, and the three islands in this tour are all connected by a variety of passenger boat services. On Ko Phangan and Ko Tao, traveling from one beach to another is sometimes easier and faster by boat, rather than dealing with the often hazardous roads here.

Day 1: Ko Samui

Spend the day on one of the two finest beaches on Ko Samui's east coast – **Hat Chaweng** (p170) is longer and has more entertainment options, while **Hat Lamai** (p170) is better for families. Both are great for swimming and water sports, from windsurfing to parasailing. At sunset, visit the Big Buddha statue near **Hat Bangrak** (p169), on the island's quieter north coast, and dine at one of the excellent restaurants in the nearby Fisherman's Village at **Hat Bophut** (p169).

Day 2: Ko Samui

Head inland to the **Na Muang waterfalls** (p171) – walk to the falls, and cool off in the clear pool at the falls' base. Enjoy the eclectic statuary of the **Secret Buddha Garden** (pp170-71) and check out the coconut-collecting simians at a **monkey training school** (p175). Alternatively, play a round at one of the island's world-class golf courses, or learn to make real Thai food at one several good cooking schools.

Day 3: Ang Thong Marine National Park

Catch a speedboat from Ko Samui to **Ang Thong Marine National Park** (pp184–5), a group of 12 unspoiled islands. Explore via kayak, go snorkeling, or hike to the spectacular Ko Wua Talab viewpoint.

Day 4: Ko Phangan

A quick boat ride from Ko Samui takes you to **Thong Sala** (p176), the main village on this island. Hop on a *songtaew* to **Ao Si Thanu** (p176), an impossibly beautiful bay with a fishing village at the western end.

Day 5: Ko Phangan

Visit the island's lush interior, best seen at the **Than Sadet Falls** (p179), visited by Thailand's adventurous King Rama V in 1889, and continue down to the idyllic bay of **Ao Thong Nai Pan** (p179).

Kayaking under natural rock archways, Ang Thong Marine National Park

> **To extend your trip…**
> Go on a meditation retreat at **Wat Khao Tham** (p181), or take in a **Full Moon Party** (p181). These wild parties now occur at half-moon as well. Best to go with friends and leave fairly early.

Day 6: Ko Tao

Another quick hop by boat from Thong Sala leads to **Ko Tao** (pp186–9), famed for the best diving on the Gulf of Thailand. Charter a longtail boat from **Ban Mae Hat** village (p186) and circumnavigate this small island in a day, with stops for snorkeling and refreshments at the numerous bays – the most spectacular are on the east and northern coasts.

Day 7: Ko Tao

Spend a couple of hours wandering around Ban Mae Hat, then make the short trip by jeep northeast across the island to isolated **Ao Hinwong** (p187), where huge boulders surround a bay with excellent reefs for snorkeling. **Ao Mamuang** (Mango Bay) on the north coast is also lovely, and offers upscale accommodations plus a few restaurants and bars, but is best reached by longtail boat.

> **To extend your trip…**
> Take an introductory scuba diving course from one of Ko Tao's many diving schools.

Hillside bungalows overlooking turquoise seas, Ko Samui

For practical information on traveling around Thailand, see pp346–53

A Week on the Eastern Seaboard

- **Airports** There are flights between Bangkok and Trat, a town close to the ferry port serving Ko Chang.

- **Transport** Regular bus services serve the area from Bangkok's Eastern Bus Terminal and directly from Suvarnabhumi International Airport. A passenger ferry runs to Ko Samet from the village of Ban Phe. Both car and passenger ferries go from Laem Ngop to Ko Chang.

Thai dance cabaret-style, part of Pattaya's lively nightlife

Day 1: Pattaya

Walk along **Pattaya's** (pp108–11) Beach Road admiring the colorful fishing boats in this wide bay. Less busy than Pattaya beach is the adjacent bay of **Ao Naklua** (pp108-9), where excellent seafood can be had for a fraction of the price. Visit the nearby **Sanctuary of Truth** (p108) to absorb the serene atmosphere and view the superb collection of Buddhist statuary in this teakwood mansion. In the evening, head to South Pattaya's **Walking Street** (p111), a brightly lit throng of go-go bars, discos and open-air beer bars. If you prefer a quieter beach scene, North Pattaya is slightly more restrained, notwithstanding that the most famous transvestite cabaret shows are here.

Day 2: Ko Samet

A journey of a few hours from Pattaya, by road, ferry, then *songtaew*, will take you far from the bright lights of Pattaya to the powdery white sands of **Ko Samet** (pp114–15). From the

Traditional shophouses in Chanthaburi's Vietnamese Quarter

busy **Hat Sai Kaew** beach you can walk to the calmer (by day) sands of **Ao Phai** (p115).

Day 3: Ko Samet

Put on some solid footwear and take the walking trail toward the southern tip of the island – deserted Ao Toei – stopping to rest in the leafy shade on each headland, which heralds a new and different bay with its own character. Fresh coconuts provide excellent refreshment en route, or make a pitstop at the ultra-luxurious Paradee Resort for high tea.

Day 4: Chanthaburi

Back on the mainland, between islands, spend a night in the charming provincial town of **Chanthaburi** (pp118–19). Take a stroll along the river, visit the **gem market**, and try the fresh (uncooked) spring rolls in the town's **Vietnamese Quarter**.

Day 5: Ko Chang

Much bigger than Ko Samet, **Ko Chang** (pp122–9) offers a wide variety of experiences including kayaking. Take the short ferry ride from Laem Ngop on the mainland and catch a *songtaew* either to **Hat Sai Khao** beach (p126) for beach barbecues, live music, and fire juggling shows or a bit farther to quieter **Hat Khlong Phrao** (p126) for the best seafood on the island. The short walk to the three-tiered **Khlong Phlu Waterfall** reveals some of the island's dense jungle.

Day 6: Ko Wai

From Bang Bao village on a bay in southern Ko Chang, catch a boat to **Ko Wai** (p130), a pristine islet with excellent snorkeling and views of the surrounding islands of the Ko Chang archipelago.

> **To extend your trip…**
> Visit **Ko Mak, Ko Kut**, or any of the other islets off the southern tip of Ko Chang.

Day 7: Ko Chang

Returning from Ko Wai, take a boat around the coast to **Hat Sai Yao** (p129) on the southern tip of Ko Chang. Its splendidly isolated long white beach is perfect for walks and swimming. From nearby Tha Tantawan, you can catch a ferry directly back to the mainland.

Busy Hat Sai Khao beach on Ko Chang, lined with bars and restaurants

Putting Thailand's Beaches and Islands on the Map

Thailand is located at the center of mainland Southeast Asia, between the Indian Ocean and the South China Sea. The country covers 198,000 sq miles (513,000 sq km) and has a population of 68 million. The capital, Bangkok, is the largest city in Southeast Asia and lies close to the geographical center of the country. It marks the dividing line between the northern plains and the beautiful beaches and islands of the south. The stunning western coast is bordered by Myanmar in the north and Malaysia in the south, and overlooks the azure waters of the Andaman Sea. The eastern coast is fringed by the warm and shallow waters of the Gulf of Thailand and shares international boundaries with Malaysia and Cambodia.

Andaman Sea

| 0 kilometers | 100 |
| 0 miles | 100 |

Key

━━ Expressway
━━ Major road
— Railway line
- - Ferry route
▧▧▧ International border

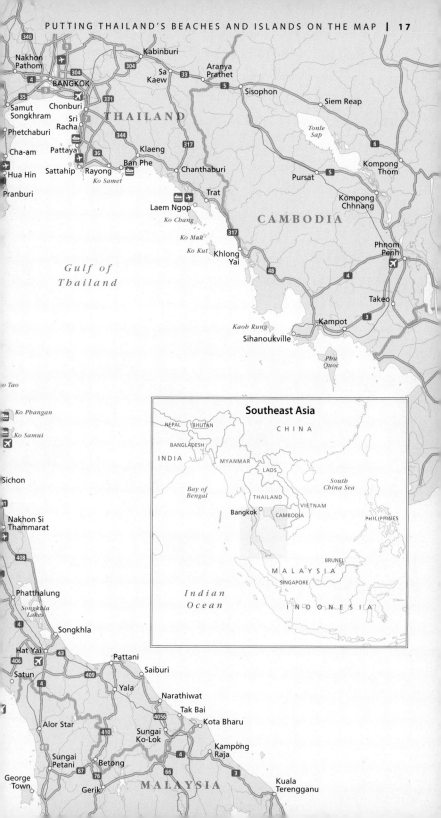

340
Nakhon
Pathom
9
Kabinburi
304
304
Sa
Kaew
33
Aranya
Prathet
BANGKOK
4
5
Sisophon
Siem Reap
35
9
331
Chonburi
THAILAND
Tonle
Sap
Samut
Songkhram
Sri
Racha
Phetchaburi
344
6
Cha-am
Pattaya
Klaeng
317
Kompong
Thom
36
Ban Phe
Pursat
5
Hua Hin
Sattahip
Rayong
Chanthaburi
Kompong
Chhnang
Pranburi
Ko Samet
Trat
CAMBODIA
Laem Ngop
Ko Chang
Phnom
Penh
Ko Mak
317
Ko Kut
Khlong
Yai
48
Takeo
Gulf of
Thailand
3
Kaoh Rung
Kampot
Sihanoukville
Phu
Quoc

o Tao
Ko Phangan
Ko Samui
Sichon
Nakhon Si
Thammarat
408
Phatthalung
Songkhla
Lake
4
Songkhla
Hat Yai
43
406
Satun
409
Pattani
Saiburi
Yala
Narathiwat
4056
Tak Bai
Alor Star
410
Kota Bharu
Sungai
Ko-Lok
Sungai
Petani
4
Kampong
Raja
George
Town
Betong
67
76
MALAYSIA
66
3
Gerik
Kuala
Terengganu

Southeast Asia

NEPAL BHUTAN
CHINA
BANGLADESH
INDIA
MYANMAR
LAOS
Bay of
Bengal
THAILAND
South
China Sea
Bangkok
VIETNAM
CAMBODIA
PHILIPPINES
BRUNEI
MALAYSIA
SINGAPORE
Indian
Ocean
INDONESIA

A PORTRAIT OF THAILAND'S BEACHES AND ISLANDS

The outstanding natural beauty of south Thailand's beaches and islands, with miles of white sand lapped by azure waters, lush national parks, and teeming coral reefs, attracts millions of visitors. The cultural heritage of the region seen in its grand temples, palaces, and vibrant festivals further magnifies its appeal.

Southern Thailand's coastline, located in a fertile monsoon zone, extends for more than 2,000 miles (3,200 km) and encompasses parts of the Indian and Pacific Oceans. It is set midway between India and China, the two great countries that have influenced Southeast Asia. Yet, this region has a distinct identity that derives from a number of factors. These include an uninterrupted history of independence while at some point all its neighbors were under colonial rule; a rich Buddhist heritage; and a strong monarchical system. Coastal Thailand is politically linked to, but culturally distinct from, the rest of the country.

The population is a diverse ethnic mix, which although predominantly Thai, has a strong Chinese, Myanmar, Malay, Vietnamese, and Muslim influence. Bangkok, the nation's capital and gateway to the coast, is a pulsating megacity of more than 12 million people, celebrated for its palaces, temples, colorful street markets, glittering malls, and unrestrained nightlife. Tourism is the mainstay of the economy and Ko Samui, Phuket, as well as smaller islands such as the Surin archipelago, are world-famous holiday retreats. Bangkok aside, there are no major cities along the coast and the region is overwhelmingly rural in aspect.

Bustling thoroughfare in the heart of colorful Pattaya

◀ Traditionally painted door leading to the beach, Thanya Resort, Ko Hai

Offices and shopping malls towering over the lake at Lumphini Park, Bangkok

Economic Development

Rice, rubber, fishing, coconut farming, and tin mining have long been the mainstay of coastal Thailand's economy. Over the past 25 years, however, this traditional sector has been outstripped by light industrial and technologically advanced manufacturing, especially along the eastern coast. An offshore oil and natural gas industry is also being developed in the Gulf of Thailand. Regarded as one of Asia's "tiger" economies since the mid-1980s, it suffered greatly due to financial speculation in the late 1990s. The country has recovered

Rice-farming, a major occupation in the coastal region

since, and has weathered the 2008 global financial crisis quite well, suffering only a temporary slowdown. Tourism continues to be the region's largest foreign exchange earner, especially at internationally renowned beach resorts such as Phuket, Krabi, Ko Samui, Hua Hin, and Pattaya.

The Indian Ocean tsunami of 2004 had a terrible but relatively brief impact on Thailand's Andaman Coast, causing great loss of life and property and also severely hitting the tourism industry. However, Thailand was self-sufficient enough to rebuild and bounce back from this calamity. Today, with a tsunami warning system in place, the travel sector is well on its way to recovery.

Ecology and Conservation

Unfortunately, the environment in this region has suffered from overdevelopment in the last 50 years and forest cover has been severely depleted. However, increasing awareness has led to the implementation of conservation measures by the government. Logging of forests is now illegal across Thailand, and emphasis is being placed on the preservation of rich and fragile ecosystems such as mangrove forests and coral reefs. Threatened marine animals such as turtles, dolphins, and dugongs are officially protected, as are endangered mammals such as tigers, gibbons, and tapirs.

Society and Politics

In spite of the pressures of change, Thai society is quite cohesive. There is a growing and powerful middle class in Bangkok. Rural poverty is quite rare, as the coastal regions, rich in natural resources, are among the most prosperous in the country, with a high standard of living. Thai women are estimated to control 62 percent of all small and medium-sized businesses nationwide. The traditional family structures, however, have become increasingly fragmented owing to modernization and urbanization.

The Buddhist clergy and the king are the most venerated figures in the country. In contrast, politicians are less respected, and are often criticized by the liberal Thai press. Prime Minister Thaksin Shinawatra was overthrown in a bloodless coup in 2006. Since then the Thai political scene has been plagued by protests and violence under successive governments led by Abhisit Vejjajiva and Yingluck Shinawatra (Thaksin's sister). A military coup in 2014 resulted in General Prayut Chan-o-cha establishing himself as prime minister.

Preparing for a bout at a Thai kickboxing match

Ceremonial dragon steps leading to Big Buddha statue, Ko Samui

Culture and the Arts

Southern Thailand's traditional culture and arts are greatly influenced by Theravada Buddhism (*see pp28–9*). The best showcase is the *wat* (temple), distinguished by sweeping, multitiered roofs, countless Buddha images, detailed murals, and varied architectural flourishes. The literary tradition is confined to the classics, the most important being the Ramakien (*see p63*), an ancient moral epic. This tale provides the narrative content for many performing arts, including the stylized *khon* and *lakhon* (*see pp30–31*). To this tradition the south has added its own style of Islamic and Malay-influenced dance, music, and shadow puppetry (*see p195*). Thailand's most notable literary figure, the 19th-century poet Sunthorn Phu, was inspired by the beauty of southern Thailand and based his poetry in this region. On the sports front, *muay thai* (Thai kickboxing) draws big crowds. Other traditional pastimes range from *takraw* (kick-volleyball) to kite flying. Many colorful festivals are also celebrated with fanfare. Whatever the activity, Thais believe that life should comprise *sanuk* (fun) and *sabai* (well-being) and visitors should embrace this spirit to get the most from their stay.

Landscape and Wildlife

Thailand stretches from south of the Tropic of Cancer to 620 miles (1,000 km) north of the equator; its tropical climate is affected by two monsoons. Varied topography and a gentle climate have led to a rich diversity of flora and fauna. Limestone hills in the north are clad in dense tropical forest. Open forest is more usual in the northeast and central plains while the south and Gulf have superb coastlines and pockets of rain forest. Many habitats are threatened by industry and tourism; deforestation is rife, and some animal species face extinction. As a result, many national parks have been established. The largest among these is Kaeng Krachan National Park *(see p143)*.

Coconut palms on the island of Ko Samui in the Gulf of Thailand

Montane Tropical Forest

This type of forest is made up mostly of broad-leaf evergreens and some deciduous trees such as laurel, oak, and chestnut. Mosses, ferns, and epiphytic orchids growing on host plants are common.

Atlas moths are the world's largest species. The female is larger than the male.

Sun bear, also known as honey bear or dog bear, is the smallest and most agile of all bear species.

Palm civets are nocturnal omnivores found in tropical forests and occasionally near human settlements.

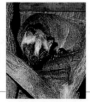

Open Forest

The most common trees in the open forest, also called savanna forest, are dipterocarps, a family of trees native to Southeast Asia. The ground around them is often carpeted by coarse scrub.

Sambar, Thailand's largest deer, can be seen in the central plains and in the northeast.

Pig-tailed macaques are found in Southeast Asia. They eat mainly fruit, storing it in their cheek pouches.

Wild boar have been heavily hunted in the past. They feed mainly on grass.

Thai Flowers

The diversity of Thailand's flowers reflects its range of natural habitats. Most famous are its orchids; there are some 1,300 different varieties. Unfortunately, illegal picking has made them rare in the wild. Other flowers are used as spices and for medicinal purposes.

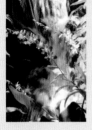

The mallow flower, a relative of the hibiscus, is common throughout Southeast Asia.

Mountain pitchers are insectivorous plants. Their prey falls into the "pitcher" where the plant's juices slowly dissolve it.

Lotus lilies' seed pods and stems are edible. Other lilies are grown for decoration.

Orchids come mainly from northern Thailand; they are prized for their beauty.

Wetlands

Freshwater swamp forests have been decimated by farming, although some survive in the south. River basins and man-made lakes and ponds can be found all over Thailand.

Dusky leaf monkeys are found in the Thai-Malay peninsula. Three other species of leaf monkey also live in Thailand.

Painted storks migrate to Thailand's swamps to breed. During this time the pigment in their face turns pink.

Purple swamp hens are common. Long-toed feet allow them to walk on floating vegetation.

Coastal Forest

The seeds of trees such as pines and Indian almond are transported by sea currents; thus ribbons of coastal forest are found all over Southeast Asia. Thailand's coastal forests are now threatened by farming and tourism.

Green turtles are the only herbivorous sea turtles. They feed on sea grass and algae and are nocturnal.

Lizards are common in island forests. Most eat insects, although some species also eat mice and small birds.

Crested wood partridges are found in areas of coastal, lowland forest.

Coral Reef Ecosystems

Thailand's many coral reefs support a complex biodiversity with more than 1,000 species of fish, 30 types of sea snake, crustaceans, invertebrates, millions of microscopic organisms, and birds. With enough warm water and sunlight, these flourishing and fragile ecosystems are made up of at least 300 different species of coral. Unfortunately, the reefs are under threat from industrial and human pollution, dynamite fishing, and irresponsible tourist activities. Several government and private initiatives are now attempting to protect and conserve this marine habitat.

Many types of seabirds gather around coral reefs to feed on the abundant fish life. The great egret, a large wading bird, feeds by stabbing small fish with its razor-sharp bill.

Colorful clown fish come in over 20 varieties and live protected amid poisonous sea anemones. They stay in small groups and share a symbiotic relationship with their predatory host.

A Typical Reef

Thailand's coral reefs are found in a variety of formations. The fringing reef develops off the coastline and slopes into the sea. The reef flat curves away from the beach, rises to a crest, then drops to the seabed in a sharp incline or reef slope.

Shoals of colorful fish swarm in and around the coral reefs. Smaller fish derive many benefits from this grouping, including some protection against predators and greater success in breeding. Swimming in shoals also makes foraging more efficient.

Leopard sharks, also known as zebra sharks, are usually found around sandy bays. With cylindrical bodies and elongated tail fins, leopard sharks are fast swimmers that mostly stay at the bottom of the reef. These docile nocturnal creatures feed on mollusks and crustaceans.

Five species of sea turtle are found in Thai waters, including olive ridleys, green turtles, hawksbills, loggerheads, and leatherbacks. Unfortunately, all of these are listed as endangered species, and sightings even in the nesting season – between November and February – have become increasingly rare.

Octopuses are intelligent and skilled hunters that defend themselves against attack by hiding, changing their body color, and ejecting ink. They can also quickly squeeze into narrow gaps in the reef by means of their flexible structure, which lacks any skeleton.

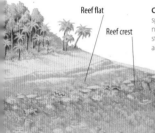

Reef flat

Reef crest

Cabbage patch corals share space on the reefs with a number of species including stagshorn, columna, sea anemones, and starfish.

The squid is an elusive decapod that hunts and hides in gaps within the coral. Like the octopus, it changes its color to blend with the surroundings.

Manta ray found in tropical waters is the largest of the rays and can grow up to 25 ft (8 m).

Reef slope

Starfish

Giant hermit crabs are soft-bodied crustaceans. They protect their bodies by living and moving around the seabed in the empty shells of mollusks such as whelks.

Coral: The Reef's Building Block

Coral is made of the skeletons of polyps, small animals related to sea anemones and jellyfish. Polyps are unusual in that they build their skeleton on the outside of their body. As they divide, the coral colony gradually builds up. There may be as many as 200 different species of coral in a reef, divided into hard corals such as brain coral, and colorful soft corals, which have no stony outer skeleton.

Hard, textured brain coral

Soft coral

Diving and Snorkeling

Thailand's clear waters and rich marine life draw diving enthusiasts from all over the world. All three of the country's major coastal regions – the Andaman Coast, the Western Gulf Coast, and the area around Ko Chang (see pp122–30) on the Eastern Seaboard – are popular diving and snorkeling destinations. The best and most advanced diving is available on the Andaman Coast, but this region is generally inaccessible during the southwest monsoon from June to September. Along the east coast, diving is a year-long activity. Over 50 dive schools operate around Thailand offering courses for all levels. Most offer PADI (Professional Association of Diving Instructors) certification to enrolled members.

Waterproof dive bags and other equipment on sale, Ko Chang

Boats take divers back and forth from the jumping-off points or dive areas. It is possible to hire them locally at most dive-oriented beaches, but visitors must ensure that the operators are PADI licensed. These boats should be specially fitted for diving with enough space for diving gear.

Wet suits are worn by divers to protect against the cold or other underwater hazards.

Coral reefs swarm with a wide variety of brightly colored tropical fish.

Scuba divers must check the diving equipment carefully, as any malfunction can be dangerous – even fatal. Divers should ensure that the oxygen tank is full and that the fins are in good condition. It is also useful to learn basic sign language to enable underwater communication.

Dive instructors are responsible for planning the dive and training groups according to the difficulty level. They usually explain the diving location, depth, currents, timing, and any hazards before setting off on the dive.

The shallow waters above coral reefs are generally clear and teeming with small fish and crustaceans. These stretches near the shore are great for snorkeling. Visitors uncomfortable with heavy equipment and deep dives can enjoy the underwater landscape with just a snorkeling mask.

Top 10 Dive Sites

① Chumphon Pinnacle *(see p186)*
② Hin Bai *(see p178)*
③ Ko Chang *(see pp122–30)*
④ Richelieu Rock *(see p209)*
⑤ Surin Islands *(see pp208–9)*
⑥ Similan Islands *(see pp214–15)*
⑦ Ko Phi Phi *(see pp256–9)*
⑧ Ko Rok *(see p267)*
⑨ Hin Daeng *(see p267)*
⑩ Hin Muang *(see p267)*

Diving at a Coral Reef

Thailand's coral reefs offer unparalleled opportunities for snorkeling and scuba diving. It is essential to hire the best equipment available, as diving in the coral reefs can be hazardous for the unprepared. Divers should also be careful not to damage the corals in any way.

Coral heads shelter a host of tiny marine creatures that are important to the reef building process.

Sea anemones are colorful creatures that attach themselves to the coral and feed on fish and crustaceans.

Diving tips

Never go diving if feeling sick or even a little under the weather.
Carry a safety balloon while ascending or diving in shallow waters. It is also a useful signaling device for divers in open waters.
Hire or buy equipment only from certified places.
Dive with a companion and also have backup and first aid on the boat at the surface.
Look for PADI-certified trainers and courses.
Beginners should head for the safer Gulf of Thailand, and leave the deeper Andaman Sea for experienced divers.

Snorkeling for beginners is safer and more enjoyable in groups where a guide can identify the marine life forms. It is also possible to undertake a PADI snorkeling course. First-timers should avoid going out alone unless accompanied by an experienced diver with proper qualifications and familiarity with the site.

Instructor checking equipment prior to a dive, Ko Phi Phi

Thai Buddhism

At least 90 percent of Thais practice Theravada Buddhism. It was first brought to the region from India around the 3rd century BC and is based on the ancient Pali canon of Buddha's teachings, the Tripitaka. However, Thai practice incorporates many Hindu, Tantric, and Mahayana Buddhist influences. The worship of Buddha images, for example, is a Mahayana Buddhist practice. Thais are of the view that Buddhism is one of the three forces that give their kingdom its strength, the other two being monarchy and nationhood. Religious rituals color daily life, especially in the form of merit-making, the performance of good deeds as laid out in Buddhist doctrine.

Rama IX (b.1927), like other Thai rulers, spent time as a monk. For Thais, this act reinforces the notion that Buddhism and the monarchy are unified powers.

Siddhartha sets out to attain enlightenment.

Most Thai males are ordained as monks in adolescence, a major rite of passage. They usually spend at least a few months as monks, earning merit for themselves and their families. Few Thai women become nuns.

Applying gold leaf to Buddha images is a popular act of merit-making. Books of gold leaf can be readily purchased at temples, and the thin leaves are applied in profusion to Buddha statues, decoration of the *wat* or temple, and murals.

Story of the Buddha

The Buddha was born Prince Siddhartha Gautama in India in the 6th century BC. He gave up his riches to seek enlightenment, and later taught the way to nirvana or perfect peace. Statues of the Buddha and murals depicting his previous lives, as told in the jataka *stories, abound in Thailand.*

Buddhism infuses family life in Thailand. Senior monks are asked by the family to give blessings at child-naming ceremonies, weddings, to a new house or car, or simply after a donation to the *wat* has been made. Children are taught the simple moral codes of Buddhism from an early age.

Walking meditation is practiced by most monks. The most senior monk leads the line walking around the temple clockwise. Meditation on the nature of existence is a major way in which Buddhists progress toward enlightenment – Buddha literally means "One who is Enlightened".

Vishnu, with four arms, is part of the Hindu holy trinity.

Thai folding book painting, c.1900

A garland of jasmine symbolizes the beauty of the Buddha's teachings and, as it perishes, the impermanence of all life. Vendors offer garlands of jasmine to be hung in cars and shrines.

Devas (heavenly beings) bear Prince Siddhartha through the air.

Ritualistic tattooing is an ancient Hindu-Buddhist custom. Such tattoos are believed to act as powerful talismans against negative forces.

Inscriptions in the ancient Pali script

Buddhist monks collect alms from lay people every morning. Thais believe that giving alms is a way to make merit and improve their *karma* (destiny) in this life as well as the next.

Islam

Thailand's second religion is Islam. Thai-speaking Muslims are well integrated into Thai society, tracing their origins to a variety of ancestries – Arab, Persian, South Asian, and Chinese – all of which are followers of the moderate Sunni Hanafi school. The only exception is in the far southern provinces of Satun (see pp272–3), Yala, Pattani (see p288), and Narathiwat (see p289), where most Muslims speak Malay and remain outside the mainstream. They are a rural people, generally working as farmers or by catching fish, studying their faith in *pondok* (religious schools), and traveling on *hajj* (pilgrimage) to Mecca. However, they are not overly rigorous or fundamentalist and, although women cover their heads, they go unveiled.

Thai Muslim women covering their heads

Thai Theater and Music

The two principal forms of classical Thai drama are *khon* and *lakhon*. *Khon* was first performed in the royal court in the 15th century, with storylines taken from the Ramakien *(see p63)*. The more graceful *lakhon*, which also features elements from *jataka* tales of the Buddha, is of two kinds – *lakhon nai* (inside *lakhon*) and *lakhon nok* (outside *lakhon*). *Khon* and *lakhon* involve slow, highly stylized, angular dance movements set to the music of a *piphat mon* ensemble.

Finger extensions, emphasizing the graceful curves of a dancer's hands, are seen in *lakhon* performances and "nail dances."

Natural-looking makeup enhances the features of characters who do not wear masks.

Students learn by imitating their teacher. Training begins at an early age (when limbs are still supple) and includes a sequence of moves known as *mae bot* (mastery of dancing).

A *Khon* Performance

In khon *drama, demons and monkeys wear masks, while human heroes and celestial beings sport crowns. As the story is told mainly through gestures,* khon *can be enjoyed by non-Thais too. Visitors are most likely to see performances at restaurants catering to tourists.*

Khon and **lakhon renditions** are often staged at outdoor shrines. Dancers are hired to perform to the resident god by supplicants whose wishes have been granted.

Instruments of Classical Thai Music

A mahori *ensemble shown in a mural*

Thailand's classical music originated in the Sukhothai era *(see p44)*. The basic melody is set by the composer, but, as no notation is used, each musician varies the tune and adopts the character of the instrument. A *piphat* (tuned percussion ensemble) accompanies theater performances and boxing matches *(see p287)*. A *mahori* ensemble includes stringed instruments.

Ranat (xylophone)

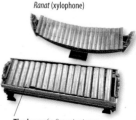

The keys of a flat xylophone produce a different tone from those of a curved one.

Likay, by far the most popular type of dance-drama, is a satirical form of *khon* and *lakhon*. The actors wear gaudy costumes and the plot derives from ancient tales laced with improvised jokes and puns.

Khon and **lakhon** troupes, employed by the royal palace until the early 20th century, are now based at the Fine Arts Department *(see p337).*

Khon masks, adorned with gold and jewelry, are treated as sacred, with supernatural powers.

This mural at Wat Benchamabophit *(see p72)* depicts a scene from a *khon* performance. In it, Erawan, the elephant mount of Indra, descends from heaven.

Lavish costumes, made of heavy brocade and adorned with jewelry, are modeled on traditional court garments.

Hun krabok are rodded marionettes operated by hidden threads pulled from under the costumes. *Hun krabok* puppets are very rare today.

Khong wong lek (small gong circle)

Chake (crocodile zither)

The hollowed hardwood body is inlaid with ivory.

Small gongs are struck by the player to give the tune's basic melody.

The strings of a *chake* are plucked. It accompanies fiddles and flutes in a string ensemble.

A *piphat mon* ensemble, including a vertical gong circle, also plays at funerals because their music is slow.

Vernacular Architecture

Southern Thailand's architecture is very diverse. Traditionally, rural Thai, Cambodian, and Malay houses are built on stilts and their grandeur and size reflect the wealth and status of the occupying family. Thailand's location along important trade routes brought seafaring people such as Chinese and Portuguese merchants to this region. They built houses that differed from indigenous Thai and Malay styles and, over time, these evolved into Sino-Portuguese shophouses and mansions *(see pp230–31)*. The best examples of this type of architecture can be found in Phuket town.

Village on stilts, Chonburi province

Traditional Thai Houses

In the humid coastal regions, a large, centrally situated veranda, which also acts as an outdoor living area, is the dominant feature of many traditional houses. Some houses have covered verandas running alongside the main structure. In an extended family setup, a communal veranda will have several houses clustered around it. Traditionally, domestic animals were sheltered beneath the houses, and this practice still continues in some villages.

Wood-paneled gable

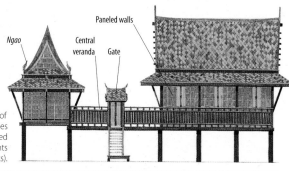

Paneled walls

Ngao

Central veranda

Gate

Gabled roofs of southern Thai houses are often decorated with curved ornaments called *ngaos* (hooks).

Sino-Portuguese Shophouses

Known as *tiem chu* (row houses) in Cantonese, shophouses have a unique architectural style. The ground floor facing the street is a commercial space with living quarters and a courtyard further inside. A partially covered veranda or five-foot way connects the shophouses and protects pedestrians from the rain and sun.

Characteristic gabled roof

Wooden window frame

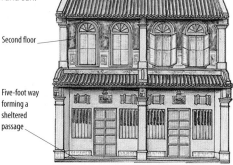

Second floor

Five-foot way forming a sheltered passage

Shophouses are low-rise buildings that can extend up to three stories in crowded areas. These quaint structures usually have tiled roofs and brightly colored façades.

Sino-Portuguese Mansions

These grand mansions, also known as *ang mor lau* (red hair buildings), were built in the early 20th century and were regarded as status symbols for nouveau riche merchants and traders. Greco-Roman pilasters and columns were added to embellish the existing structures. At the time these mansions must have seemed showy, but today, after restoration, they reflect a distinct old-world charm.

Gold painted stucco

Tiled roof

Grand exterior of a mansion

Elaborate pillars and pediments are used to decorate Phuket's Western-style mansions, blending aspects of Classical and Oriental architectural design.

Traditional Malay Houses

Found mainly in the Deep South, these houses are raised and centered around a main living room or covered by a pitched roof with gables to protect them from high winds. Shuttered windows, a suspended veranda in front, and an enclosed one at the back, enable ventilation and keep the house cool. The kitchen is usually built separately at the back of the house.

The interior is carefully designed, keeping the privacy of its inhabitants in mind, and there are many carved openings, slatted panels, and windows to keep it cool.

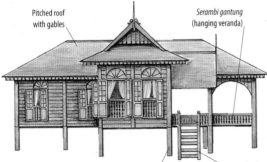

Pitched roof with gables

Serambi gantung (hanging veranda)

Stilts to protect the house from floods

Stairs leading to the house

Spirit house in the garden of The Jim Thompson House, Bangkok

Spirit Houses

Traditionally constructed within the grounds of many Thai homes, these houses shelter the guardian spirit of the property, and are usually elevated on a pole. Spirit houses come in a variety of styles that range from simple replicas of the homes to which they belong, to elaborate models of religious buildings. Erected to placate the spirits of the land, usually before the construction of the main building begins, they are worshiped daily with incense, flowers, and food. These miniature temples are placed in the grounds after consultation with a priest and the style depends upon the spirit that will inhabit it. Built out of wood or concrete, the spirit house can range in size from a small dollhouse to a big walk-in space.

Arts and Crafts

While the center of arts and handicrafts production in Thailand lies in and around Chiang Mai in the north, the coastal regions also have distinct art forms. Basket-making in Pattani, Benjarongware in Samut Songkhram, stoneware in Ang Sila, and woodcarving are all part of the traditional arts and crafts of coastal Thailand. The gemstones of Chanthaburi *(see pp118–9)* and pewterware and cultured pearls of Phuket *(see p243)* are especially highly coveted. *Nang talung (see p195)* of Nakhon Si Thammarat, among the most authentic of southern crafts, are a popular art form. The town is also the best producer of nielloware in the country.

Rattan vines being made into baskets and furniture

Shadow puppets

Among the most ancient art and theater forms in South Asia, shadow puppets date back to 400 BC, but are still very popular in the Nakhon province. Their most opulent version – nang yai – performed with the help of life-sized puppets, depicts stories from the Ramakien. These puppets are maneuvered by a puppet master, accompanied by a band of musicians.

Nang talung puppet

Niello, a black metallic alloy, is used as an inlay on engraved metal. Nielloware, which belongs to the Ayutthaya period *(see pp44–5)*, usually features intricate patterns on items such as rings, bowls, knife handles, and trays.

Nang talung theater troupes usually consist of five to 10 puppeteers and musicians.

Benjarongware, a five-colored ceramic ware, has long been popular at the royal court and celebrated throughout the kingdom. Although it is made in several southern localities, the best-known producer is Ban Benjarong (Benjarong Village) in Samut Songkhram province.

Locally sourced granite is used to make finely handcrafted kitchen tools such as pestles and mortars, as well as small figures of animals. The most renowned producer of stoneware is the fishing village of Ang Sila in Chonburi province.

Batik is a method of dyeing cloth in which portions are covered with wax and dipped in color to create patterns. Made into sarongs, tablecloths, mats, curtains, and picture frames, its patterns feature palms, fish, dolphins, and flowers. Batik sarongs are popular in the Deep South.

Pearl culture has emerged as a profitable business, making pearls an important export product. Fine, handmade silver and gold jewelry featuring locally produced pearls is sold in the many bazaars and malls of Phuket.

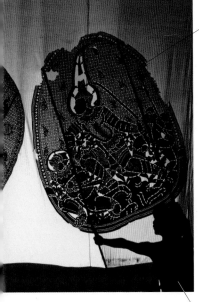

Nang talung **puppets**, carved from buffalo skin.

Orchid jewelry

Yellow and blue sapphire ring

A selection of sapphires

Gemstones are usually bought and sold uncut and later fashioned into exquisite rings and pendants set in gold. Today, most gems come from across the Cambodian border in Pailin, but Si Chan Road in Chanthaburi remains the main gem market area in southern Thailand.

Nai nag (puppet master)

Pewter is an easily worked metal alloy of tin, with small quantities of copper and antimony that act as hardeners. Mostly manufactured in Phuket, it is used to make decorative objects such as statuettes and figurines, goblets, cups, plates, and pendants.

Basketry and rattan work products are mostly made in Pattani, which has a predominantly Malay-Muslim population. These materials are woven into geometric designs, typical of the non-representational art forms associated with Islam.

Best Beaches

Blessed with clean white sands and clear blue waters, Thailand is home to some of the most stunning beaches in the world. These are also popular destinations for vacationers seeking active outdoor recreation and exciting watersports. Visitors expecting the luxuries of upscale resorts and spas will not be disappointed either. Thailand has holiday options for every kind of traveler. Visitors can head to the secluded coves of Ko Phangan and Ko Chang, partake in the glittering nightlife at the lively, but crowded beaches of Phuket and Ko Samui, go diving and snorkeling in the waters surrounding Ko Tao, or spend some family time at the royals' favorite resort – Hat Hua Hin.

Visitors enjoying a game of volleyball on the beach at Ko Lipe

Ao Yai, or Big Bay *(see p204)*, Ko Chang, has a 2-mile (3-km) stretch of beach, with a selection of beach bungalows and restaurants.

Hat Kata Yai *(see p232)*, Phuket, may be quiet but it has the advantage of being close to Hat Patong and its exciting nightlife. A great place for the young and adventurous, Hat Kata Yai is also excellent for windsurfing.

Bang Saphan

Chumphon

Ranong

Chaiya

Chiaw Lan Lake

Khao Lak

Wang Sa

Phang Nga

Krabi

Phuket

Khlong Thom

Ko Phi Phi

Ko Lanta

Trang

Andaman Sea

Hat Tham Phra Nang *(see p253)*, Krabi, is perhaps the loveliest beach in Thailand with beautiful offshore coral reefs, coconut groves, and craggy limestone outcrops. Tham Phra Nang and Sa Phra Nang, popular sights located on the beach, are also worth a visit.

| 0 kilometers | 100 |
| 0 miles | 100 |

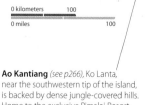

Ao Kantiang *(see p266)*, Ko Lanta, near the southwestern tip of the island, is backed by dense jungle-covered hills. Home to the exclusive Pimalai Resort and Spa *(see p301)*, the beach here is also known for the beautiful coral reefs at its northern end. Ao Kantiang is a popular spot for snorkeling and swimming.

Hat Sai Kaew *(see p116)*, Ko Samet, also known as Diamond Beach, is among the busiest beaches on the island. A range of exciting watersports such as snorkeling and jet-skiing is on offer, along with a vibrant nightlife.

Hat Khlong Phrao *(see pp126-7)*, Ko Chang, is isolated by the rocky cape of Laem Chaichet. There are some breathtaking views across the bay.

Hat Hua Hin *(see p144)*, Hua Hin, was made popular by the Thai royal family in the early 20th century. The best stretch of beach is opposite the famous Centara Grand Resort and Villas *(see p144)*. Visitors can enjoy pony rides or a round of golf, as well as indulging in the usual watersports.

Hat Sai Ri *(see p186)*, Ko Tao, is the longest stretch of beach on the island. This long curve of crisp, white sand is ideal for diving and snorkeling and popular throughout the year. There are some good restaurants as well as shops selling diving equipment lining the beach.

Ao Thong Nai Pan *(see p179)*, Ko Phangan, is for those travelers who can brave the 8-mile (13-km) long rough road to reach its beautiful beaches. Lack of facilities ensures the bay's continued isolation.

THAILAND'S BEACHES AND ISLANDS THROUGH THE YEAR

The traditional Thai year revolves around the two monsoons – southwest and northeast – which dictate the year's farming activities and the religious calendar. Most festivals are Buddhist, and often observed on significant days of the lunar cycle, especially during full moons. Festivals may also mark a seasonal change, such as the end of the rains or a related agricultural event, such as the beginning of the rice-planting season. The three main seasons are rainy, cool, and hot. Farmers plant rice-seedlings at the start of the rainy season. After tending the crop as it matures, they then harvest it during the cool season. During most weeks a festival is held somewhere in the country.

Hot Season

High temperatures combined with high humidity make this an uncomfortable time inland, although cooling sea breezes help bring the temperature down nearer the shore. With fields fallow and rivers running low, the landscape appears dull. Considering the heat during this time, it is not surprising that Thailand's traditional New Year, Songkran, is celebrated with water.

March

ASEAN Barred Ground Dove Fair *(1st week)*, Yala. Dove-singing contest that attracts bird lovers from as far away as Cambodia, Malaysia, Singapore, and Indonesia.
Thao Thep Kasatri and Thao Si Sunthorn Festival *(Mar 13)*, Phuket. This festival is held annually to commemorate the two courageous heroines of Phuket – the sisters Khun Chan and Khun Muk – who had rallied the people of the island to defeat the Burmese invaders in 1785 *(see p238)*.
Pattaya International Music Festival *(variable)*, Pattaya. Three evenings of pop, rock, hip-hop, and jazz performed on several different stages by Thai and international musicians.
Trang Food Festival *(Mar 30– Apr 3)*, Trang. Held at Somdet Phra Srinakharin Park to promote the local cuisine. A variety of delicious food, including southern Thai, Chinese, and seafood is available, along with local Trang specialities.

April

Chakri Day *(Apr 6)*, Bangkok, nationwide. Commemorates the founding of the ruling Chakri Dynasty by Rama I (r.1782–1809). The Royal Pantheon at Wat Phra Kaeo, Bangkok, which displays statues of former kings, is open to the public on this day only.
Songkran *(Apr 13–15)*, nationwide. Traditional Thai New Year, celebrated with the pouring of fragrant water on revered Buddha images and a great deal of boisterous fun, which includes throwing water over all and sundry.
Wan Lai Festival *(mid-Apr)*, Pattaya. The Pattaya Wan Lai, or Water-Flowing Festival, is generally held a week after the Songkran celebrations. It features floral floats, colorful parades, and plenty of water-throwing.
Pak Lat Festival *(mid-Apr)*, Phra Pradaeng. The ethnic Mon people hold their New Year celebrations a week after

A religious procession during Songkran, the traditional Thai New Year

Average Daily Hours of Sunshine

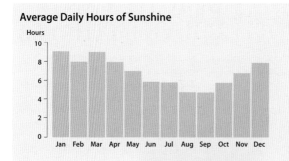

Sunshine Chart
Even during the rainy season, most days have some sunshine. The tropical sun can be very fierce, and adequate precautions against sunburn and sunstroke should be taken. Sunscreen, a sun hat, and sunglasses are highly recommended.

Songkran. The emphasis is on entertainment, with a Miss Songkran procession, and traditional Mon games.

May

Coronation Day *(May 5)*, Bangkok, nationwide. This ceremony marks the crowning of Rama IX (b.1927).

Visakha Bucha *(May full moon)*, nationwide. Most important date on the Buddhist calendar. Celebrates the birth, enlightenment, and passing of the Buddha. Sermons and candle-lit processions at temples.

World Durian Festival *(mid-May for 2 weeks)*, Chanthaburi. Highlights include fruit-decorated floats and beauty queens.

Rainy Season

The rural scene comes alive with the advent of the rains, which soften the soil, readying it for plowing. Once the rice has been planted, there is a lull in farming activity which coincides with the annual three-month Buddhist Rains Retreat (also referred to as Buddhist Lent). It is a period when young men traditionally enter monkhood for a brief period. It is a good time to observe the ordination ceremonies held throughout Thailand – a joyous blend of festivities accompanied by deep religious feelings.

June

Hua Hin Jazz Festival *(variable)*, Hua Hin. Jazz festival featuring large numbers of Thai and international performers, generally held by the seaside at Hua Hin.

Monks chanting in front of golden Buddha on Asanha Bucha day

Sunthorn Phu Day *(Jun 26)*, Rayong. Festival in honor of Thailand's greatest poet, Sunthorn Phu (see p115). Held at Sunthorn Phu Monument, Klaeng District.

July

Asanha Bucha *(Jul full moon)*, nationwide. The second of the year's three major Buddhist festivals commemorates the anniversary of the Buddha's first sermon after he had achieved enlightenment.

Khao Pansa *(Jul full moon)*, nationwide. Marks the start of the Buddhist Rains Retreat. Monks remain in temples to devote themselves to study and meditation.

August

Rambutan and Thai Fruit Festival *(early Aug)*, Surat Thani. Annual rambutan fair held to celebrate the local fruit produce.

Her Majesty the Queen's Birthday *(Aug 12)*, nationwide. Buildings and streets are lavishly decorated in honor of Queen Sirikit's birthday. Bangkok is elaborately decorated, especially along Ratchadamnoen Avenue and the Grand Palace.

King's Cup and Princess' Cup Boat Races *(variable)*, Chumphon. Beautifully decorated boats from all over the south compete at Nong Yai, Tambon Na Cha-ang, and other places.

Lively performance by a jazz group during the Hua Hin Jazz Festival

Average Monthly Rainfall (Bangkok)

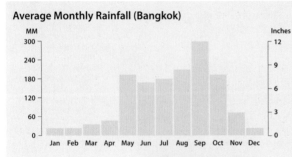

Rainfall Chart
The southern peninsula has the highest rainfall, some 95 inches (240 cm) annually; the north and central regions receive 51 inches (130 cm). In many places, torrential rain falls almost daily in the rainy season, from June to September.

September

Festival of the 10th Lunar Month *(1st waning moon–15th waning moon)*, Nakhon Si Thammarat. Deceased sinners are permitted to rise and meet their relatives, but must return to the underworld before the 15th day. There is merrymaking at temples on the 15th day, accompanied by a magnificent procession along the central Ratchadamnoen Road.

Trang Pork Festival *(variable)*, Trang. A celebration of Trang's special roast pork recipe featuring pork fermented with herbs and spit-roasted on a special grill.

Trang Moon Festival *(late Sep/ early Oct full moon)*, Trang. The ethnic Chinese of Thung Yao County, Palian District, commemorate the victory of the Chinese Ming Dynasty over the mighty Mongols in 1368.

Narathiwat Fair *(last week of Sep)*, Narathiwat. A good opportunity

Dancers in Isan dress perform during the festival of Ok Phansa

to experience the mixed Thai-Malay culture of the Deep South.

Vegetarian Festival *(late Sep/ early Oct)*, *(see p229)* Phuket, Trang. Self-mortification rituals accompanied by strict abstinence from meat. One of the most revered, spectacular, and unusual festivals in southern Thailand.

October

Traditional Boat Procession and Races *(variable)*, Chumphon. Elaborately decorated boats carrying Buddha images from local temples progress along the Lang Suan River in a local ceremony dating back to the reign of Rama III (r.1824–51).

Ok Phansa *(Oct full moon)*, nationwide. Celebration of the Buddha's reappearance on earth after a season spent preaching in heaven. This period marks the end of the Buddhist Rains Retreat.

Chak Phra Festival *(Oct full moon)*, Surat Thani. Local southern festival celebrating the end of the Rains Retreat. Illuminated images of the Buddha are erected all over town, splendidly adorned floats are pulled by hand, and images of the Buddha are carried on a beautifully decorated barge across the river, accompanied by boat racing and traditional games.

Cool Season

After the rains, the skies are clear and the air cools to a comfortable warmth. The countryside looks its finest during this time – lush and green from the rains. It is the best time to visit Thailand, especially during the coolest months of December and January. Numerous festivals are held in December and January to celebrate the end of the rice harvest, which lasts from November to early December. This allows the hardworking Thais a period of relaxation.

Spectacular street procession during the Vegetarian Festival, Phuket

Average Monthly Temperature (Bangkok)

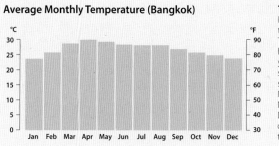

Temperature Chart
For visitors from temperate climes, Thailand feels hot and humid throughout the year, especially in the south. It is uncomfortably so during April and May but pleasant in November and December. It can be chilly at night during the coolest months.

November
Golden Mount Fair *(1st week of Nov)*, Bangkok. Thailand's largest temple fair, held at the foot of the Golden Mount in Bangkok.

Loy Krathong *(Nov full moon)*, nationwide. Perhaps Thailand's loveliest national festival. Pays homage to Mae Khongkha, goddess of rivers and waterways. In the evenings, people gather at rivers, lakes, and ponds to float *krathongs*, or rafts, decorated with flowers, candles, and incense.

Thot Pah Pa Klang Nam *(Nov full moon)*, Rayong. Yellow robes offered to the monks on the occasion of Loy Krathong at the pier of the Prasae River in the middle of Rayong.

December
Trooping of the Colors *(Dec 3)*, Bangkok. A spectacular ceremony showcasing the regal pageantry, presided over by the king and queen.

His Majesty the King's Birthday *(Dec 5)*, Bangkok, nationwide. Government and private buildings are elaborately decorated, and the area around the Grand Palace is illuminated. In the evening, excited crowds gather around Sanam Luang for the celebrations. This occasion shows the deep respect Thais have for their king.

King's Cup Regatta *(variable)*, Phuket. Phuket's Kata Beach Resort hosts international yachtsmen, who compete furiously in the neighboring Andaman Sea for trophies.

Chanthaburi Gemstone Fair *(Dec 8–12)*, Chanthaburi. The largest gemstone fair in Thailand, held annually at Chanthaburi Gems Center on Tri Rat and Chanthanimit Roads.

January
King Taksin the Great's Commemoration Day *(Dec 28– Jan 4)*, Chanthaburi. Fairs and beauty pageants celebrating King Taksin the Great's expulsion of the Burmese invaders in 1767.

Chinese New Year *(Jan/Feb full moon)*, nationwide. This three-day festival is widely observed by Thais of Chinese ethnic origin with the lighting of firecrackers.

February
Phra Nakhon Khiri Fair *(late Feb)*, Phetchaburi. A five-day celebration of Phetchaburi's cultural heritage and royal rulers.

Makha Bucha *(Feb/March full moon)*, nationwide. Third annual Buddhist festival, marking Buddha's revelation of the *dhamma* (teachings of Buddha) to a gathering of 1,250 disciples. Temples host candle-lit processions and offerings are made.

Public Holidays

International New Year's Day (Jan 1)

Makha Bucha (Feb/Mar full moon)

Chakri Day (Apr 6)

Songkran/Thai New Year (Apr 13–15)

Labor Day (May 1)

Coronation Day (May 5)

Royal Plowing Ceremony (early May)

Visakha Bucha (May full moon)

Asanha Bucha and Khao Pansa (Jul full moon)

Queen's Birthday (Aug 12)

Chulalongkorn Day (Oct 23)

King's Birthday (Dec 5)

Constitution Day (Dec 10)

International New Year's Eve (Dec 31)

Beautiful fireworks at Wat Mahathat during the Loy Krathong festival

THE HISTORY OF THAILAND

The story of Thailand is that of an area of Southeast Asia, rather than of a single nation. From small regional kingdoms to a single unified nation, the country's past is a tumultuous history of conquests, rebellions, and coups, as well as a resilient monarchy that has time and again steered the nation away from danger and anarchy, and continues to do so even today.

The earliest civilization in Thailand dates from around 3600 BC, when the people of Ban Chiang in the northeastern region developed bronze tools and pottery, and began rice cultivation. By 2000 BC, the Malay people were already settled in the peninsula along the Andaman and Gulf coasts. Inland, in the hills and jungles, lived small groups of Negrito hunter-gatherers, the ancestors of today's Mani people. Influenced by Indian and Chinese cultures, the first civilizations to develop along Thailand's coasts were Malay, Mon, and Khmer.

The Indic Kingdoms

As early as 250 BC, the Malay region, including peninsular Thailand, was strongly influenced by Indian traders, who called the region Suvarnabhumi, meaning Golden Land. At this time, three separate and powerful kingdoms were established – Dvaravati (6th–11th centuries AD), in what is now the heart of Thailand; the Sumatra-based Srivijaya Empire (7th–13th centuries) in the peninsula; and the Khmer Empire (9th–13th centuries) based at Angkor.

All three were heavily influenced by Indian culture and religion. The Tai, from southern China, migrated to the area from the 11th century onward.

The Srivijaya Empire, ruled by Hindu maharajas, prospered through trade with India and China. However, its power began to decline from the 10th century onward due to a series of wars with Java, and the advent of Muslim traders and teachers who spread Islam in Sumatra and along the Malay coast. At the same time, the Dvaravati kingdom of the Mons played a significant role in the spread of Buddhism in Thailand.

The third powerful kingdom – that of the Khmers – was established by Jayavarman I. Although its capital was moved to Angkor between AD 889 and 915 by Yasovarman I (r.889–910), the empire reached its zenith under Suryavarman II (r.1113–50). The greatest Khmer ruler was Jayavarman VII (r.1181–1219), who unified the empire and constructed Angkor Thom, probably the greatest city in the world at that time. However, all three kingdoms eventually fell victim to the emerging power that was to become Siam.

Srivijaya-style Buddha

250 BC Maritime trade established between India and Southeast Asia

500 Srivijaya Empire spreads to Sumatra and peninsular Thailand; Hindu-Buddhist culture dominates

790 Khmer kingdom of Cambodia established by Jayavarman I

1113 Suryavarman II orders the construction of Angkor Wat

| 4000 BC | AD 1 | AD 300 | AD 600 | AD 900 |

3600 BC Cultivation of rice in Ban Chiang

200 Chen La civilization established in lower Mekong region is influenced by Indo-Chinese cultures

550 Mon kingdom of Dvaravati flourishes; promotes Buddhism

889 Yasovarman I founds new capital at Angkor

1289 City of Angkor Thom is completed

Dvaravati coin

◀ One of the oldest murals at Buddhaisawan Chapel, National Museum, Bangkok

Stone engraving of the illustrious King Ramkhamhaeng

The Kingdom of Sukhothai

In 1238, two Tai chieftains seceded from the Khmer Empire, establishing the first notable Tai kingdom – Sukhothai. It was the Khmers who referred to the Tai as Siam, a name that came to be used for this and subsequent Tai kingdoms. Sukhothai expanded by forming alliances with other Tai kingdoms and Theravada Buddhism was adopted as the state religion. Under King Ramkhamhaeng (r.1279–98), the kingdom enjoyed an era of prosperity. The Thai alphabet evolved during his reign, and the political and cultural foundations of Thailand were secured. Indeed, most Thai people today are descendants of the Tai. Ramkhamhaeng conquered the Mon and Khmer territories in the south as far as the Andaman Sea and Nakhon Si Thammarat, as well as over the Chao Phraya Valley and along the southeastern coast, to what is now Cambodia. In 1378, the capital was moved from Sukhothai to the city of Phitsanulok. Among the most prosperous of the ancient kingdoms, Sukhothai was peaceful and stable, lasting 200 years with only nine rulers.

The Kingdom of Ayutthaya

As the power of Sukhothai waned, a rival Tai kingdom began to develop in the early 14th century, in the lower Chao Phraya Valley, centered on the ancient Khmer city of Lopburi, not far from present-day Bangkok. In 1350, the ambitious ruler U Thong moved his capital from Lopburi to Ayutthaya and proclaimed himself King Ramathibodi (r.1351–69). He propagated Theravada Buddhism as the state religion, inviting monks from nearby Sri Lanka to preach its doctrine. He even compiled a legal code based on the highly respected Indian text, *Dharmasastra*.

In AD 1369, the last year of his reign, Ramathibodi seized Angkor in the first of a series of successful attacks by the Tais on the Khmer Empire. The weakened Khmer Empire eventually had to submit to Ayutthaya's overlordship, as did Sukhothai, which was finally conquered in 1438. The 15th century saw Ayutthaya become the strongest power in Southeast Asia.

Much of Ayutthaya's energies were also directed toward the Malay peninsula in the south, where Melaka, a great trading port, was opposing its claims to sovereignty. Melaka and other Malay states to the south of Nakhon Si Thammarat had converted to Islam in the early 15th century, and Islam served as a unifying symbol of Malay solidarity against the Tais. Although it failed to conquer Melaka, Ayutthaya gained control over much of the peninsular region, extending Tai authority over Pattani, Kedah, and Kelantan. However, the kingdom met its nemesis in the rise of Burma during the 16th century. The first Burmese attack

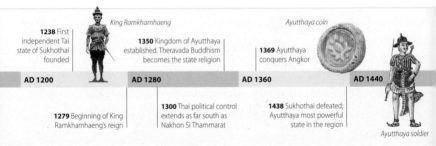

King Ramkhamhaeng

Ayutthaya coin

1238 First independent Tai state of Sukhothai founded

1350 Kingdom of Ayutthaya established. Theravada Buddhism becomes the state religion

1369 Ayutthaya conquers Angkor

AD 1200   AD 1280   AD 1360   AD 1440

1279 Beginning of King Ramkhamhaeng's reign

1300 Thai political control extends as far south as Nakhon Si Thammarat

1438 Sukhothai defeated; Ayutthaya most powerful state in the region

Ayutthaya soldier

came in 1569. A vassal ruler, King Maha Thammaracha (r.1569–90), was appointed king, and his successor, King Naresuan the Great (r.1590–1605), later succeeded in regaining some of Ayutthaya's lost glory after defeating Burma in the Battle of Nong Sarai (1593). Soon after, Europeans found their way to the kingdom for trade. The Dutch arrived in 1604, followed by the French and the English.

A 17th-century Dutch map of Ayutthaya

In 1767, Burmese armies invaded once again, destroying Ayutthaya, scattering Tai forces, and laying the capital to ruin. Despite this disaster, Siam rapidly recovered under Taksin, a noble of Chinese descent. From Chanthaburi in the south-east, he defeated the Burmese and set up a new Siamese state with its capital at Thonburi, on the west bank of the Chao Phraya river, opposite modern-day Bangkok. Crowned King Taksin in 1768, he soon reunited the central Tai heartlands under his rule, and conquered Cambodia in

1769. He then marched south, establishing Siamese rule over all of the southern as well as the Malay States.

Yet by 1779, Taksin was in trouble. He alienated the Buddhist establishment by claiming supernatural powers and attacking the powerful Chinese merchant class. In 1782, while his army was invading Cambodia, a rebellion broke out in Thonburi. The rebels, who enjoyed popular support, offered the throne to General Chakri, who accepted. King Taksin was later executed, although rumors persist that he eventually became a monk.

King Naresuan fighting the Burmese, a 19th-century depiction of the Battle of Nong Sarai

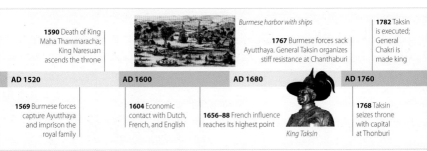

1590 Death of King Maha Thammaracha; King Naresuan ascends the throne

Burmese harbor with ships

1767 Burmese forces sack Ayutthaya. General Taksin organizes stiff resistance at Chanthaburi

1782 Taksin is executed; General Chakri is made king

AD 1520

AD 1600

AD 1680

AD 1760

1569 Burmese forces capture Ayutthaya and imprison the royal family

1604 Economic contact with Dutch, French, and English

1656–88 French influence reaches its highest point

King Taksin

1768 Taksin seizes throne with capital at Thonburi

The Chakri Dynasty

General Chakri replaced the vanquished Taksin as king in 1782, and took the title of Rama I. With him began the Chakri Dynasty, which continues to this day. Successive rulers, who also took the title of Rama, shaped present-day Thailand. The Chakri kings consolidated their power through treaties with the Europeans, expanded trade, built *wats* and canals, opened universities, patronized art and architecture, and modernized the country. Their policies and diplomacy kept colonial powers at bay. However, political turmoil and several coups forced the monarchy to become a constitutional entity in 1932.

Grand Palace and Wat Phra Kaeo, constructed by Rama I in 1782

Early Chakri Dynasty

The early Chakri kings, Rama I, II, and III, reconstituted the Thai state and promoted Thai culture, following the model of the erstwhile kingdom of Ayutthaya. Patrons of art, literature, and poetry, they ushered in an era of stability in Thailand.

Rama I (r.1782–1809)
Rama I moved the capital from Thonburi to Bang Makok. Having defeated the Burmese, he expanded and strengthened the kingdom.

Court ceremonies until the reign of Rama V were formal affairs with courtiers prostrating before the king.

Early Bangkok
Known as Bang Makok (Place of Olive Plums), early Bangkok had waterways and canals, but hardly any paved roads.

Sunthorn Phu (1786–1855)
Court poet of Rama II, III, and IV, Sunthorn Phu is the most celebrated bard in Thailand.

Buddhism
The early Chakri kings were great proponents of Theravada Buddhism. They built beautiful *wats* to house magnificent images of the Buddha.

1782 Rama I moves his capital to Bangkok and begins a massive building program on Rattanakosin Island

1785 Rama I defeats the Burmese near Kanchanaburi; Thai authority re-established

1809–24 Reign of Rama II; Wat Arun is built in Bangkok; ties strengthened with European powers, notably Great Britain

1824–51 Reign of Rama III; rivalry with Vietnam for control of Cambodia

Wat Arun

1851 Rama IV, the first great reformer, ascends the Chakri throne

1868 Reign of Rama V, Father of Modern Thailand, begins

| 1790 | 1805 | 1820 | 1835 | 1850 | 1865 |

Rama IV (r.1851–68)
Also known as King Mongkut, he was the first reforming monarch of the Chakri Dynasty. Besides being a skilled linguist, Rama IV was also interested in science.

European diplomats were permitted to stand in the king's presence, but had to make a low bow.

Modernization
Bangkok's first surfaced motor road, called Charoen Krung or New Road, was opened in 1861 during the reign of Rama IV.

Reign of Rama IV and Rama V

Rama IV and Rama V were both far-sighted and wise rulers who chose to learn from the West and modernize Siam, thus avoiding colonization.

French Attacks (1893–1907)
The French attempted to assert their authority over Indochina and, during the reign of Rama V, took over the Siam-controlled region of Laos.

Rama V (r.1868–1910)
Christened King Chulalongkorn, Rama V assiduously safeguarded the kingdom's independence from Colonial powers.

Rama IX (b.1927)
King Bhumibol Adulyadej, the reigning monarch, and Queen Sirikit are very popular with Thais.

Constitutional Monarchs

A military coup in 1932 transformed Thailand from an absolute to a constitutional monarchy. As a result, the king today holds no formal political power.

Chulalongkorn University
The University, named after Rama V, was founded in 1917. It is the most prestigious institute of higher learning in Thailand.

1893 The French with their gunboats become a huge threat to Bangkok, leading to a confrontation in Pak Nam

Rama V

1917 Thailand's flag is officially adopted

1939 Siam is officially renamed Thailand

1942 Japanese invasion compels Thailand to enter World War II as Japanese ally

| 1880 | 1895 | 1910 | 1925 | 1940 |

Chakri coin

1897 Rama V visits Europe for the first time

1932 Coup by Phibun Songkram establishes a constitutional monarchy

1945 Thailand on losing side in World War II

1946 Rama IX, the present king, ascends to the throne

Student protest slogan, "You must return my people to me", 1973

An Era of Uncertainty

After World War II, the left-leaning Seni Pramoj became prime minister and re-established Thailand's fledgling democracy. He was succeeded in 1946 by the democratically elected Pridi Phanomyong. In 1947, the wartime leader, Phibun Songkram, staged another coup and set the country on a path of military dictatorships that would mark Thailand's politics for much of the remainder of the 20th century. Phibun's return to power coincided with the start of the Cold War, for the duration of which Thailand remained a loyal anti-communist ally of the United States, taking part in the Vietnam War on behalf of Washington and the Saigon regime, and also fighting and eventually defeating a home-grown communist insurgency.

In 1973, a student uprising in Bangkok forced the retirement of military strongman Thanom Kittikachorn, and for a brief period, democratic government was reinstated. In 1976, however, the army once again seized power, with right-wing general Thanin

Kraivixien (1976–7) being succeeded by Kriangsak Chomanand (1977–80) and then Prem Tinsulanond (1980–88). The latter, a firm royalist with a reputation for being incorruptible, stepped down voluntarily in 1988, paving the path for democracy. The army intervened in 1991, with Suchinda Kraprayoon seizing power in the 17th coup since 1932. However, on this occasion, the current king, Rama IX, used his unchallenged moral authority to bring a swift end to military rule. A series of more-or-less corrupt or incompetent civilian governments followed, leading to the election of Thaksin Shinawatra in 2001.

The Crisis Deepens

A devastating tsunami wreaked havoc in Phuket and the Andaman Coast in 2004. Thaksin was re-elected as Prime Minister in 2005. He adopted a carrot-and-stick policy in the Deep South in an attempt to end the insurgency which began at the beginning of the 21st century, with the aim of establishing an independent Pattani Republic.

Military dictator
Phibun Songkram

His rule was marked by corruption, nepotism, and brutality – more than 2,500 suspected drug dealers suffered extrajudicial execution at the hands of the police, and hundreds of local Muslims suffocated to death after being arrested and packed into trucks. While Thaksin managed to reinforce his power base in the rural north and northeast through a mixture of vote-buying and populist policies, he made the mistake of alienating major elements of the army and, most disastrously of all, the royal court.

SEATO military units in Bangkok

1979 Elections take place once again and parliamentary democracy is re-established

1975 End of Vietnam War; US troops begin to leave Thailand

| 1950 | 1960 | 1970 | 1980 |

1954 The South East Asia Treaty Organization (SEATO) is formed

1947 Phibun Songkram stages coup to topple Pridi Phanomyong

1973 Student uprising against military dictator Thanom Kittikachorn

1976 Power seized by the army; Thanin Kraivixien, is succeeded by Chomanand

Thousands of protesters demanding Prime Minister Thaksin Shinawatra's resignation in 2006

Troubled Times

Thaksin was overthrown in 2006 in another bloodless military coup. The military authorities appointed General Surayud Chulanont as prime minister. Thaksin was convicted for corruption and sentenced to two years' imprisonment. Remaining in exile abroad, he formed the People's Power Party (PPP) to contest elections in December 2007. The PPP won a majority and assumed office.

For most of 2008, Thaksin effectively governed indirectly, infuriating not only the south, but also important elements of the Bangkok establishment and the middle classes, represented by the People's Alliance for Democracy (PAD), a political group better known as the Yellow Shirts. The PAD and its supporters used non-violent civic action to bring down the PPP, culminating in the illegal occupation of Bangkok's international airport in November 2008.

The PPP was eventually dissolved for electoral fraud and Abhisit Vejjajiva, leader of the opposition Democratic Party, was sworn in as prime minister. A new movement, the Red Shirts United Front for Democracy against Dictatorship (UDD), took to the streets in support of Thaksin. Violence escalated between the Red Shirts and the police. Elections in 2011 saw Thaksin's sister Yingluck Shinawatra's party elected to government, igniting a storm of protest from those who saw her as simply her brother's mouthpiece. In 2014, the military staged another coup, and General Prayut Chan-o-cha became prime minister.

General Prayut Chan-o-cha (right), Thailand's prime minister

1992 Coup by General Suchinda fails; period of increasing democracy and growth

2001 Thaksin Shinawatra is elected as the Prime Minister

2006 Thaksin overthrown, while out of the country, in a bloodless coup

2007 New constitution announced; PPP is established

2011 Elections held – Thaksin's sister elected

1990   2000   2010   2020

1997 Thai economy suffers serious setback in Asian financial crisis

2004 Indian Ocean tsunami devastates Phuket and Thailand's Andaman Coast

2005 Thaksin re-elected; situation in Deep South deteriorates; rising communal violence

2014 General Prayut Chan-o-cha becomes prime minister after a military coup

Former Prime Minister Thaksin

THAILAND'S BEACHES AND ISLANDS AREA BY AREA

Thailand's Beaches and Islands at a Glance

The southern peninsula of Thailand is dominated by the Andaman Sea to the west and the Gulf of Thailand to the east. A central spine of jungle-covered mountains to the north marks the frontier with Myanmar. While the capital, Bangkok, influences the whole country, the old Buddhist city of Nakhon Si Thammarat is the political and cultural capital of the south. Hat Yai, newer and vibrant, is the south's economic stronghold. Major resorts include Phuket, Krabi, and Ko Samui, while the seaside resort of Pattaya offers an eclectic mix of family entertainment alongside its risqué go-go bars. The region is also well-known for the astounding beauty of its national parks and wildlife sanctuaries.

White *prangs* of Wat Mahathat Worawihan in Phetchaburi

Ang Thong Marine National Park *(see pp184–5)* is among the most pristine areas in Thailand, offering a variety of activities ranging from snorkeling, trekking, and caving to simply enjoying breathtaking views of sunsets.

0 kilometers   100

0 miles   100

UPPER
WESTERN
GULF COAS
(see pp134–5S

Chumphon

Lang Su

Ranong

UPPER
ANDAMAN
COAST
(see pp200–43)

Sura
Tha

Similan Islands
(see pp214–15) is
an isolated archipelago
of tiny granitic islands
set in the midst of the
Andaman Sea. They offer
some of the best diving
and snorkeling sites in
southern Thailand.

Phang Nga

Phuket

LOWER
ANDAMA
COAST
(see pp244–7

Hat Rai Leh *(see p252)* is perhaps one of southern Thailand's most popular beaches, with the best swimming and rock-climbing opportunities. The large number of resorts and restaurants here cater to varied tastes and budgets.

Pak Khlong Market *(see p76)*, located in the heart of Bangkok, is the kingdom's single largest flower market. On sale are local orchids, fragrant imported roses, hyacinths, and tulips from Europe, as well as many varieties of lovely tropical blooms.

BANGKOK
(see pp54–99)

Phetchaburi

EASTERN SEABOARD
(see pp100–33)

Pattaya

Gulf of Thailand

Chanthaburi

Pranburi

Trat

Khao Sam Roi Yot National Park *(see pp148–9)* was the country's first coastal national park. Its varied landscape is home to hundreds of species of migratory birds.

Sichon

Pattaya *(see pp108–11)* is one of the most popular destinations in Thailand. It is known for its decadent but vibrant nightlife, discos, and go-go bars.

OWER WESTERN
GULF COAST
(see pp160–99)

Songkhla

Hat Yai

Pattani

DEEP SOUTH
(see pp280–89)

atun

Narathiwat

Betong

Songkhla Lakes *(see p286)* form the largest natural lake system in Thailand. Divided into three distinct parts, it is home to the Thale Noi Waterfowl Park, a haven for native species and migratory birds from Siberia and China.

BANGKOK

Founded at the end of the 18th century, Thailand's capital is a young city, yet it has prospered and grown into a megalopolis of more than 12 million people in just two centuries. Straddling the Chao Phraya River, Bangkok is a thriving modern city which combines old world culture with urban delights. It offers visitors options ranging from ornate Buddhist temples to magnificent palaces, and trendy restaurants and nightclubs to bustling street markets.

Established in 1782 by Rama I (r.1782–1809), Bangkok was the "new" capital built on a readily defensible site along a bend in the Chao Phraya River. Set up at the small village and trading settlement of Bang Makok – literally, "Place of Olive Plums" after the fruit trees growing in the area – it was formally consecrated and given a new royal title extending over 150 letters, which soon became abbreviated to Krung Thep, meaning "City of Angels".

There is an absence of any single center in Bangkok. The old Royal City, built within three concentric canals on Rattanakosin Island, is the cultural and historical heart of the city, home to the Grand Palace and the much-revered Wat Phra Kaeo. Downtown Bangkok's Silom Road and the surrounding area is the cornerstone of the financial district with all the major banking and trading institutions. The notorious Patpong Road near the eastern end is famous for its neon lights and go-go bars. Just outside central Bangkok lies Sukhumvit Road, a shopper's paradise and the choice for many foreign visitors. Diverse ethnic groups such as the Chinese and Portuguese have left an indelible imprint across different quarters of the city.

With gleaming and futuristic skyscrapers dominating the cityscape, and floating markets crowding the river, Bangkok juggles many worlds. It is intersected and linked by a network of canals branching off from the Chao Phraya River. A vibrant city that never sleeps, Bangkok is truly global in its dimensions.

The Bangkok skyline at night dominated by soaring skyscrapers

◀ The Temple of the Emerald Buddha in Bangkok's Grand Palace

Exploring Bangkok

The country's capital, Bangkok is an exhilarating metropolis. It is also the center of most Thai commercial and cultural activity. Dotted with some of the most magnificent palaces and *wats* (temples) in Asia, and laced by the mighty Chao Phraya River, it boasts such glorious sights as the Grand Palace and Wat Phra Kaeo in the heart of royal Bangkok. Southeast of the center lies Chinatown, a bustling commercial quarter. Dusit area is the bureaucratic stronghold, dominated by government offices, broad avenues, and Wat Benchamabophit, where the ashes of Rama V (r.1868–1910) lie. Silom Road houses the city's financial center, while the main shopping hub is along Sukhumvit Road.

Busy waters of the Chao Phraya River

Sights at a Glance

Temples and Shrines

❶ *Grand Palace and Wat Phra Kaeo pp60–65*
❷ *Wat Pho pp68–9*
❹ Wat Ratchapradit
❺ Wat Mahathat
❽ Wat Rakhang
❾ Wat Arun
❿ Wat Kalayanimit
⓫ Wat Ratchabophit
⓬ Wat Suthat and the Giant Swing
⓭ Wat Bowonniwet
⓮ Wat Benchamabophit
⓱ Wat Saket and the Golden Mount
㉒ Wat Traimit
㉗ Erawan Shrine

Museums and Palaces

❸ Museum of Siam
❻ National Museum
❼ Royal Barge Museum
㉘ *The Jim Thompson House pp80–81*
㉙ Suan Pakkad Palace

Neighborhoods and Markets

⓲ Monk's Bowl Village
⓳ Phahurat Market
⓴ Pak Khlong Market
㉑ Chinatown
㉓ Hua Lampong Station
㉕ Patpong

Parks and Gardens

⓯ *Dusit Park pp74–5*
⓰ Dusit Zoo
㉖ Lumphini Park

Hotels

㉔ Mandarin Oriental

Getting Around

Bangkok is a large city which is consistently hot and humid for most of the year – not the best place for those who prefer exploring a city on foot. Fortunately, Bangkok has an excellent local transport system comprising taxis, buses, ferries, the metro, and Skytrain. Getting around by taxi is simple and relatively cheap. Buses are even cheaper, but require some knowledge of the city's routes. The Skytrain and metro offer easy, fast, and reliable access to most downtown areas. Finally, the ferries and other crafts operating on the Chao Phraya River, as well as on several major *khlongs* (canals), are reasonably priced and a remarkably picturesque way of exploring the city.

Serene grounds of Wat Phra Kaeo, Thailand's holiest shrine

Key

- Major sight
- Skytrain route
- Railway line
- Expressway
- Airport rail link

For keys to symbols *see back flap*

Street-by-Street: Around Sanam Luang

สนามหลวง

One of the few large open spaces in Bangkok, Sanam Luang, meaning Field of Kings, is the traditional site for royal cremations. The annual Kite Flying Festival and the Royal Plowing Ceremony, an ancient festival marking the beginning of the rice-growing season, are also held here. Bordered by the Grand Palace, the Lak Muang shrine, and the Amulet Market, this is regarded as one of the holiest areas in the city. The streets overflow with salesmen hawking potions and amulets for luck, love, or protection from evil spirits, and astrologers who read palms. Notable sights include Wat Mahathat, Thailand's revered center of Buddhist studies, and the National Museum, which traces the country's fascinating history.

Colorful and intricately designed gable at Lak Muang

Phra Chan Pier

Maharaj Chao Praya Express Pier

Amulet Market

❹ Wat Mahathat
Dating from the 18th century, this *wat* is known more for its bustling ambience than its architecture. Meditation classes are held at the Buddhist university within the temple compound.

0 meters 100
0 yards 100

Chang Chao Phraya Express Pier

MAHATHAT

TROK SILLAPAKORN

NA PHRA LAN

To Grand Palace and Wat Phra Kaeo (see pp60–65)

Western edge of Sanam Luang

To Lak Muang (City Pillar)

Silpakorn University of Fine Arts
Thailand's most famous art school, the Silpakorn University of Fine Arts, regularly hosts excellent art shows in its exhibition hall. The signs outside the entrance have more details and opening times.

Key
— Suggested route

For hotels and restaurants in this area see pp294–301 and pp308–17

Amulets

The Thais are a highly superstitious people – those who do not wear some protective charm or lucky amulet are a minority. Amulets come in myriad forms and are sold in specialty markets, often near auspicious spiritual sites. Although many are religious in nature – such as miniature Buddhas and copies of sacred statues – others are created for more worldly purposes, such as model phalluses to ensure sexual potency. Amulets are such a big business that they even have magazines dedicated to them.

A selection of charms sold at stalls around Sanam Luang

Thammasat University, noted for its law and political science departments, was the site of violently suppressed student riots in the 1970s.

To Phra Pin-Klao Bridge

❺ ★ National Museum
A magnificent range of arts and crafts from every period of Thai history are displayed in this huge museum.

The Gallery of Thai History at the National Museum provides a good introduction to the country.

Fortune Teller at Sanam Luang
Thai people set great store by the predictions of fortune tellers, many of whom are found at Sanam Luang near Wat Phra Kaeo.

★ Kite Flying at Sanam Luang
Rama V was an avid kite flyer and allowed Sanam Luang to be used for the sport. Even today, fiercely contested kite-flying matches are regularly held between February and April.

❶ Grand Palace and Wat Phra Kaeo

พระบรมมหาราชวังและวัดพระแก้ว

Construction of this site began in Rattanakosin island in 1782, to mark the founding of the new capital and provide a resting place for the sacred Phra Kaeo, or the Emerald Buddha, and a residence for the king. Surrounded by walls stretching for 6,234 ft (1,900 m), the complex was once a self-sufficient city within a city. Visitors must cover their knees and heels before entering. Note that the complex is always open; if you are told otherwise it's an attempted scam.

Wat Phra Kaeo's skyline, as seen from Sanam Luang

★ Bot of the Emerald Buddha
Devotees make offerings to the Emerald Buddha at the entrance to the *bot*, the most important building in the *wat*.

Chapel of the Gandharara Buddha

★ Ramakien Gallery
Extending all around the cloisters are 178 panels depicting the complete story of the Ramakien *(see p63)*.

1750	1800	1850	1900	1950

1783 Work begins on Wat Phra Kaeo, Dusit Throne Hall, and Phra Maha Monthien

1855 New buildings epitomize fusion of Eastern and Western styles

1925 Rama VII (r.1925–35) chooses to live in the Chitrlada Palace at Dusit. Grand Palace reserved for special occasions

1782 Official founding of new capital

1809 Rama II (r.1809–24) introduces Chinese details

1840s Women's quarter laid out as a city within a city

1880 Rama V (r.1868–1910), the last king to make major additions, involves 26 of his half-brothers in the renovation of the *wat*

1932 Chakri Dynasty's 150th year celebrated at palace

1982 Renovation of the complex

KEY

① **Emerald Buddha**

② **The Phra Si Rattana Chedi** contains a piece of the Buddha's breastbone.

③ **The Upper Terrace** houses several important buildings, some of which are open to the public on special occasions such as Chakri Day.

④ **Ho Phra Monthien Tham** is the auxiliary library.

Phra Mondop (library)
Green and blue glass mosaic adorns the exterior of the library. The original building was destroyed in the fireworks display celebrating its completion.

Decorative Gilt Figures
Encircling the exterior of the *bot* are 112 *garudas* (mythical beasts – half-man, half-bird) holding *nagas* (serpents). They are typical of the *wat's* decorative details.

Ho Phra Nak (royal mausoleum)

Wihan Yot

The Royal Pantheon

Wat Phra Kaeo

Wat Phra Kaeo is a sub-complex within the greater Grand Palace complex. The temple is Thailand's holiest shrine, but unlike other Thai wats, has no resident monks.

Grand Palace and Wat Phra Kaeo

1 Entrance
2 Wat Phra Kaeo complex
3 Dusit Throne Hall
4 Aphonphimok Pavilion
5 Chakri Throne Hall
6 Inner Palace
7 Phra Maha Monthien Buildings
8 Siwalai Gardens
9 Rama IV Chapel
10 Boromphiman Mansion
11 Audience Chamber

Key

▨ Wat Phra Kaeo complex
▢ Buildings
▢ Lawns

Exploring Wat Phra Kaeo

When Rama I established the new capital of Bangkok in 1782, his ambition was to construct a royal temple along the lines of the grand *wats* in previous Thai capitals. Symbolizing the simultaneous founding of the Chakri Dynasty, this temple would surpass its Sukhothai and Ayutthaya predecessors in both design and decor. The result of his vision was Wat Phra Kaeo, or Temple of the Emerald Buddha, officially known as Wat Phra Si Rattana Sasadaram. It is so called because the *bot* (ordination hall) houses the Emerald Buddha, brought from Wat Arun *(see p70)* in 1785.

Fine decorations adorning the façade at Chapel of the Gandharara Buddha

The Bot and Peripheral Buildings

The most sacred building within the palace complex, the *bot* or *ubosot* of Wat Phra Kaeo was erected to house the most revered image of the Buddha in Thailand – the Emerald Buddha.

The doors and windows in the exterior of the *bot* are inlaid with delicate mother-of-pearl. There are a series of gilded *garudas* along the marble base supporting the structure. The staircase leading to the main entrance is guarded by Cambodian-style *singhas* or lions.

Inside, the surprisingly small image of the Emerald Buddha sits in a glass case high above a golden altar. Carved from a single piece of jade (not emerald), it is 26 in (66 cm) tall and has a lap span of 19 in (48 cm). The Buddha has been attributed to the late Lanna style of the 15th century. It is dressed in one of three costumes – a crown and jewelry for the summer season, a golden shawl in winter, and a gilded monastic robe and headdress in the rainy season. The reigning monarch or a prince appointed by him presides over each changing of the Buddha's attire in a deeply symbolic ceremony. Inside the *bot* are murals from the reign of Rama III (r.1824–51). They depict themes from the Traiphum, texts based on Buddhist cosmology; the Buddha's victory over Mara, the god of death; and scenes from the *jatakas* (tales from the previous lives of the Buddha). Around the temple are 12 open-sided *salas* (small pavilions) built as contemplative shelters.

To the southeast of the *bot* is the 19th-century **Chapel of the Gandharara Buddha** with a bronze Buddha image. The figure is depicted calling the rains and is used in the Royal Plowing Ceremony *(see p58)*. The bell in the nearby belfry is rung only on special occasions such as New Year's Day.

The Upper Terrace

Of the four structures on this elevated terrace, the **Phra Si Rattana Chedi** is the most striking. Located at the western end, this was built by Rama IV (r.1851–68) as a shrine for a portion of the Buddha's breastbone. The golden tiles that decorate the exterior were later added by Rama V.

The adjacent **Phra Mondop**, used as a library, was built by Rama I as a hall to house Buddhist scriptures. Although the library is closed to the public, the exterior is splendid in itself. The Javanese Buddha images on the four outer corners are copies of early 9th-century originals, which are preserved in the museum near the entrance to the palace complex. Outside the building

Entrance to the Phra Mondop guarded by a pair of gold *yakshas*

Mural depicting a scene from the Ramakien in the Ramakien Gallery

The Prangs, Yakshas, and Ramakien Gallery

Surrounding the temple complex is the cloister-like Ramakien Gallery, decorated with lavishly painted and meticulously restored murals. This is Thailand's most extensive depiction of the ancient legend of the Ramakien, the Thai version of the Indian epic Ramayana. This is a tale of the triumph of good over evil with the virtuous hero, Rama, as the central character. The 178 panels were painted in the late 18th century, but damage from humidity means that frequent renovation is necessary. The murals are divided by marble pillars inscribed with verses relating the story, which begin opposite the Wihan Yot and proceed in a clockwise direction.

Guarding each gateway to the gallery is a pair of *yakshas* (nature spirits). Placed here during the reign of Rama II, they are said to protect the Emerald Buddha from evil spirits. Each *yaksha* represents a different character from the Ramakien myth.

The eight *prangs* (conical towers) at the edge of the temple complex, representing the eight elements of Buddhism, are painted in different colors and decorated with delicate Chinese porcelain.

are memorials to the kings of the Chakri Dynasty, as well as bronze elephant statues that represent the royal white elephants *(see p73)* from the first five reigns of the dynasty.

To the north of the *mondop* is a model of Angkor Wat in Cambodia, which was commissioned by Rama IV to show his people the scale and splendor of 12th-century Khmer architecture.

The **Royal Pantheon**, which houses statues of the Chakri kings, was built to commemorate the founding of the Chakri Dynasty. Rama IV built the hall to house the Emerald Buddha but later decided it was too small. The pantheon is open to the public only on Chakri Day *(see p38)*.

The Northern Terrace

Ho Phra Nak was originally constructed by Rama I in the late 18th century to enshrine a *nak* (alloy of gold, silver, and copper) Buddha image that had been rescued from Ayutthaya. Rama III, however, demolished the original hall, preferring to build the present brick and mortar structure to house the ashes of minor members of the

royal family. The Nak Buddha was moved into the neighboring **Wihan Yot**, which is shaped like a Greek cross and decorated with Chinese porcelain.

The Northern Terrace housing the **Ho Phra Monthien Tham**, or Auxiliary Library, was built by Rama I's brother. The door panels inlaid with mother-of-pearl were salvaged from Ayutthaya's Wat Borom Buddharam. Inside, Buddhist scriptures are stored in fine cabinets.

Ramakien figure outside *chedi*

The Legend of the Emerald Buddha

The most sacred image in Thailand, the Emerald Buddha is revered by kings and commoners alike. In 1434, lightning struck the *chedi* of Wat Phra Kaeo in Chiang Rai in northern Thailand, revealing a stucco image. The abbot of the temple kept it in his residence until the flaking plaster exposed a jade statue beneath. Learning about the discovery, the king of Chiang Mai sent an army of elephants to bring the image to him. The elephant bearing the Emerald Buddha, however, refused to take the road to Chiang Mai, and, treating this as an auspicious sign, the entourage rerouted to Lampang. The image was moved over the next century and taken to Laos in 1552. It was not until Rama I captured Vientiane in 1778 that the Emerald Buddha was returned to Thailand. It was kept in Wat Arun for six years, before a grand river procession brought it to its current resting place in March 1784.

The small Emerald Buddha inside the *bot*

Exploring the Grand Palace

Built at the same time as Wat Phra Kaeo, the Grand Palace was the king's official residence from 1782 to 1946, although Rama V (1853–1910) was the last monarch to live here. Today, the royal family resides at Chitrlada Palace, Dusit. Throughout the palace's history, many structures have wbeen altered. Within the complex there are still a few functioning government offices, but most buildings are unused. Important ceremonies are still held in the Dusit Throne Hall and the Amarin Winichai Hall.

Dusit Throne Hall

This cross-shaped throne hall was originally built in 1784 as a reproduction of one of Ayutthaya's grandest buildings, the Sanphet Maha Prasat. Five years later, the hall was struck by lightning and rebuilt on a smaller scale. Crowned with a sumptuously decorated, tiered spire, it is one of the finest examples of early Rattanakosin architecture. Inside is a master-piece of Thai art – the original Rama I teak throne, inlaid with beautiful mother-of-pearl. In the south wing is a window in the form of a throne. The hall is used for the annual Coronation Day celebrations (see p39).

Aphonphimok Pavilion

Rama IV built this small wooden structure as a royal changing room for when he was giving audience at the Dusit Throne Hall. The king would be carried on a palanquin to the pavilion's shoulder-high first step. Inside the

building he would change into the appropriate apparel for the occasion. The pavilion's simple structure, complemented by its elaborate decoration, makes it a building of perfect proportions – a glory of Thai architecture. It inspired Rama V so much that he had a replica built at Bang Pa-in, in northern Thailand.

Chakri Throne Hall

Also known as the Grand Palace Throne Hall, the Chakri Throne Hall was built in Neo-Classical style by the British architect John Chinitz. Rama V commissioned the building in 1882 to mark the centenary of the Chakri Dynasty, a fact reflected in the theme of its elaborate decoration. The structure was originally intended to have a domed roof, but the royal court decided that, in the interest of maintaining aesthetic harmony with

the surrounding buildings, a Thai-style roof would be more appropriate.

Housed on the top floor of the Central Hall are the ashes of royal monarchs. The first floor functions as the main audience hall where the king receives ambassadors and entertains foreign monarchs.

Behind the Niello Throne in the Chakri Throne Room is the emblem of the dynasty – a discus and trident. The paintings in the room depict diplomatic missions, including Queen Victoria welcoming Rama IV's ambassador in London. The East Wing is used as a reception room for royal guests. Although most of the Chakri Throne Hall is restricted for use by the royal family and VIPs, an impressive exhibit of ancient arms and armor is open to the public. Entering this exhibit also gives visitors a close-up look at this unique and impressive 19th-century building.

Elephant statue by Chakri Throne Hall

Phra Maha Monthien Buildings

This cluster of connected buildings, located to the east of the Chakri Throne Hall, is the Grand Residence of the palace complex.

The focal point of the 18th-century **Amarin Winichai Hall**, the northernmost building of the group, is Rama I's boat-shaped Busabok Mala Throne. When an audience was present, two curtains hid the throne as the king ascended, and the curtains were drawn back with elaborate fanfare to reveal the king wearing a loose, golden gown and seeming to float on the prow-like part of the throne. In the 19th century, two British ambassadors were received in such manner here, John Crawford by Rama II and Sir John Bowring by Rama IV. The hall is now used for some important state ceremonies.

Connected to the hall by a gateway through which only the king, queen, and royal

Exterior of the Dusit Throne Hall, with its elegant multitiered roof

Visitors taking a tour of the exquisite Phaisan Thaksin Hall

children may walk is the **Phaisan Thaksin Hall**. This was used by Rama I as a private hall when dining with family, friends, and members of the royal court. In 1809, a Borom Rachaphisek Ceremony was performed in this hall to mark the coronation of Rama II. On the high altar is the Phra Siam Thewathirat, a highly venerated guardian figure, placed here by Rama IV.

The third building is the **Chakraphat Phiman Hall**. It served as a residence for the first three Chakri kings. It is still the custom for a newly crowned king to spend a night here as part of his coronation ceremony.

Inner Palace

Behind a gateway to the left of the Chakri Throne Hall is the entrance to the Inner Palace, which is closed to the public. Until the time of Rama VII, the palace was inhabited solely by wives and daughters of the royal family. Apart from sons, who had to leave the palace on reaching puberty, the king was the only male allowed to live within its walls. The palace functioned as a small city, with its own government and laws, complete with prison cells. Under the strict eye of a Directress of the Inside, a small army of uniformed officers policed the area.

Rama III renovated the overcrowded and precarious wooden structures, and, in the late 19th century, Rama V built small, fantastical Victorian-style palaces here for his favorite consorts. Since his successor, Rama VI, had only one wife, the complex was left virtually empty, and it eventually fell into disrepair.

One of the palace buildings continues to function as a finishing school for daughters of high-society Thai families. They are taught a variety of grooming skills such as flower weaving, Thai royal cuisine, and social etiquette.

Siwalai Gardens

These beautiful gardens, closed to the public, lie east of the Inner Palace and contain the **Phra Buddha Ratana Sathan**, a personal chapel built by Rama IV. The pavilion is covered in gray marble and decorated with white and blue glass mosaics. The marble *bai sema* (boundary stones) are inlaid with the insignia of Rama V, who placed the stones here, Rama II, who had the gardens laid out, and Rama IV.

A Neo-Classical palace, **Boromphiman Mansion** in the gardens was built by Rama V, in 1903, as a residence for the Crown Prince (later Rama VI). The building served as a temporary residence for several kings including the present monarch Rama IX. Today, it is used as a guesthouse for visiting dignitaries.

Audience Chamber

Visible from outside the palace walls, this chamber – Phra Thinang Sutthaisawan Prasat – is located between Thewaphithak and Sakchaisit gates. It was built by Rama I to grant audiences during royal ceremonies and to watch the training of his elephants. Rama III strengthened the wooden structure with brick, and decorative features were added later. These include the crowning spire and ornamental cast-iron motifs.

The grand Boromphiman Mansion, designed by Hercules Manfredi

❷ Wat Pho
วัดโพธิ์

See pp68–9.

❸ Museum of Siam
พิพิธภัณฑ์สยาม

Sanam Chai Rd. **City Map** 5 C1.
Tel 0-2225-2777. 🚌 12, 47; AC: 3, 82.
🚤 Tien. **Open** 10am–6pm Tue–Sun.
Closed Songkran Holiday, 31 Dec,
1 Jan. 🏛 🌐 **museumsiam.org**

This museum is housed in a
handsome Italianate building
designed by the Milanese
architect Mario Tamagno, and
completed in 1922. Permanent
interactive exhibits spread over
three floors explore what it means
to be Thai throughout ancient
and modern history. Buddhism,
village life, politics, and
communication are some of
the themes that are examined.

❹ Wat Ratchapradit
วัดราชประดิษฐ์

Saran Rom Rd. **City Map** 2 D5.
Tel 0-2223-8215. 🚌 42; AC: 503.
🚤 Tien. **Open** 5am–10pm daily.

This small temple was built in
the mid-19th century by Rama
IV and the Western flourish in
his architecture is apparent in
the choice of building materials.
The main *wihan* (assembly hall),
for instance, is in forbidding
gray marble. The murals in its
interior were painted in the late
19th century and depict festivals
from the Thai lunar calendar.

The grounds contain graceful
pavilions, Khmer-style *prangs*,
and a marble *chedi* (stupa).

Entrance to the Buddhist University within
Wat Mahathat

❺ Wat Mahathat
วัดมหาธาตุ

Na Phra That Rd. **City Map** 1 C4.
Tel 0-2221-5999. 🚌 AC: 203, 506.
🚤 Chang, Maharaj. **Open** daily.

This is a large, busy temple
complex, which is interesting
because of its atmosphere
rather than its architecture.
Dating back to the 1700s,
the *wihan* and *bot* were
both rebuilt between
1844 and 1851. The
mondop gives the
temple its name –
Temple of the
Great Relic – and
has a cruciform
roof, a rare feature
in Bangkok.

The *wat* is the
national center for
the Mahanikai monastic sect,
and it has one of Bangkok's
two Buddhist universities
(meditation classes are offered
at 1pm and 6pm, near the
monks' quarters). A traditional
herbal medicine market and a
weekend market with stalls are
also found here.

Sukhothai Buddha Image,
National Museum

❻ National Museum
พิพิธภัณฑสถานแห่งชาติ

1 Na Phra That Rd. **City Map** 1 C4.
Tel 0-2224-1333. 🚌 15, 19, 32, 39,
53, 59, 70; AC: 3, 6, 7. 🚤 Phra Athit.
Open 9am–4pm Wed–Sun. 🏛 🎫
📷 🚫 📷

The National Museum has one
of the most comprehensive
collections in Southeast Asia
and provides an excellent
introduction to the art and
history of Thailand. This building
was originally the residence of
the King's viceroy, which was
then turned into a museum by
Rama V in 1887 in order to
showcase the country's rich
past and cultural heritage.

Two of the buildings in the
museum – the 18th-century
Wang Na Palace, and the
Buddhaisawan Chapel – are
works of art in themselves. The
chapel, constructed in 1787,
is decorated with some of
the best murals of the
Rattanakosin period. It
also houses the sacred
Phra Sihing Buddha
image, which is one of
Thailand's holiest
images after the
Emerald Buddha.
It claims to be the
original of the three
extant pieces and
is crafted in the
Sukhothai style. The Wang Na
Palace has an eclectic selection
of artifacts, from ancient
weaponry to shadow puppets.

Two wings of the museum,
set around Wang Na Palace, are
devoted to art and sculpture.
This section includes several
important exhibits such as the
Dvaravati Wheel of Law, an
8th-century stone wheel set
above a deer, representing
the Buddha's first sermon
at Sarnath. There is also a
handcrafted 14th-century
Sukhothai Buddha image in
bronze with a red lacquer and
gold finish. The works of art in
this museum are historically
significant, as they represent
the styles of the Rattanakosin,
Sukhothai, Lanna, and
Ayutthaya periods. Other

Mural depicting a festival in the main *wihan* at Wat Ratchapradit

Interior of Buddhaisawan Chapel at National Museum

interesting places include the Gallery of Thai History, which takes visitors right through the annals of Thai history from the ancient period to the modern era.

The Royal Funeral Chariots Gallery, with its display of ornate carriages, is also worth a visit. Taking one of the museum's guided tours, at 9:30am on Wednesdays and Thursdays, is highly recommended.

❼ Royal Barge Museum
พิพิธภัณฑ์เรือพระที่นั่ง

Khlong Bangkok Noi. **City Map** 1 B3. **Tel** 0-2424-0004. 🚤 from Chang to Wang Lang. **Open** 9am–5pm daily. 🚷 🖼

This is a massive warehouse-like structure that houses a collection of royal barges which once comprised Thailand's naval fleet. The museum also contains paintings of Ayutthaya barges engaged in battles and stately processions, as well as photographs of royal barge ceremonies in Bangkok over the past 150 years. These have often provided representative images for Thailand in postcards and brochures. The vessels are rarely used and have been kept in this museum since 1967. They are reproductions of Ayutthaya-style barges built over 200 years ago by Rama I (r.1782–1809).

In 1981, most of the royal barges underwent a face-lift and have ever since appeared in all their glory for auspicious occasions such as the 1982 Bangkok Bicentennial celebrations and the present king Rama IX's 60th birthday, among others. On such occasions, more than 50 barges sail down the Chao Phraya River with a crew of about 2,000 sea cadets dressed in traditional uniforms.

The central vessel in the museum, Supphanahongsa, meaning "Golden Swan", is the most important royal barge. Made from a single piece of teak, it is 165 ft (50 m) long, weighs 15 tons, and requires a trained crew of 64. The prow is fashioned as the mythical bird Hongsa. Anantanagaraj, another barge, bearing a multiheaded *naga* (snake) and a Buddha image on its prow, is used for conveying monks' robes. Narai Song Suban Rama IX is the first new barge built during Rama IX's reign.

❽ Wat Rakhang
วัดระฆัง

Soi Wat Rakhang. **City Map** 1 B5. 🚌 42, 82. 🚤 Chang to Wat Rakhang. **Open** daily.

Wat Rakhang was among the last major temples to be constructed by Rama I in the early 19th century. The fine murals in the main *wihan* were painted between 1922 and 1923 by a monk, Phra Wanawatwichit, and depict recognizable scenes of life in Bangkok. Although the capital has changed much, the Grand Palace, which stands just across the river, is easy to identify. One mural shows the Grand Palace in the middle of an imaginary attack, while another one is a portrayal of an elaborate procession of royal barges.

Rama I used to live in the *ho trai* (wooden library) of Wat Rakhang, in the west of the compound, before he became king. The building's eaves support delicately carved bookcases, and the gold and black doors are period masterpieces. Inside the library are murals depicting scenes from the Ramakien *(see p63)* as well as a portrait of Rama I.

Façade of the raised wooden library at Wat Rakhang

❷ Wat Pho

วัดโพธิ์

Officially known as Wat Phra Chetuphon, Wat Pho is not only Bangkok's oldest and largest temple, but also Thailand's foremost center for public education. Unlike the Grand Palace *(see pp60–65)*, it has a lived-in, dilapidated grandeur. In the 1780s, Rama I rebuilt the original 16th-century temple on this site and enlarged the complex. In 1832, Rama III built the Chapel of the Reclining Buddha, and turned the temple into a place of learning. Today, Wat Pho is a traditional medicine center which includes the famous Institute of Massage. Nearby, on Chetuphon Road, is the temple monastery, home to some 300 monks.

Wihan
The western *wihan* is one of four around the main *bot*.

★ Medicine Pavilion
Embedded in the inner walls of this pavilion are stone plaques showing massage points. The pavilion is now a souvenir shop.

★ Reclining Buddha
The 150-ft (46-m) long, gilded plaster-and-brick image fills the whole *wihan*.

Visitors' entrance

③

②

①

Visitors' entrance

KEY

① **Small buildings** at this end of the *wat* are reserved for children.

② **The feet of the Reclining Buddha** have images representing the 108 *lakshanas*, signs of the true Buddha.

③ **The Phra Si Sanphet Chedi** encases the remains of a sacred Buddha image.

④ ***Farang* guards** stand at the compound's inner gates. These huge stone statues with big noses, beards, and top hats are caricatures of Europeans.

Bodhi Tree
It is said that this tree grew from a cutting of the one under which Buddha meditated in India.

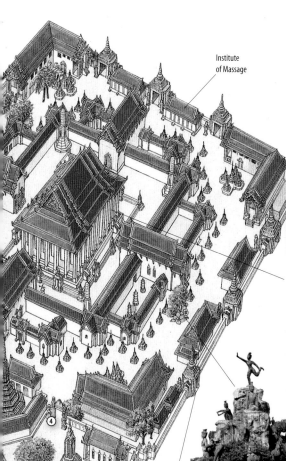

Institute
of Massage

Visitors'
entrance

④

Main Bot
The *bot* houses a bronze image
of a meditating Buddha salvaged
from Ayutthaya by Rama I's brother.
Scenes from the Ramakien *(see p63)*
are carved into the outer base and
inner doors.

Miniature Mountains
This stone mountain by the
southern *wihan* is one of
several within the complex.
It has statues of naked
hermits in different positions
of healing massage.

Traditional Massage

Since the 1960s, Wat Pho has run
the most respected massage
school in the city. *Nuat paen boran*,
or traditional Thai massage,
supposedly dates from the time
of the Buddha and is related to
Chinese acupuncture and Indian
yoga. The highly trained masseurs
at the *wat* specialize in pulling and
stretching the limbs and torso to
relieve various ailments ranging
from general tension to viruses.
Visitors can experience a massage
or learn the art through a 30- to
200-day course in Thai or English.

A traditional Thai massage at the
Institute of Massage

Ceramic Decoration
This porcelain design is on
the Phra Si Sanphet Chedi.

Staircase on the central *prang* at Wat Arun, Bangkok

❾ Wat Arun

วัดอรุณราชวราราม

Arun Amarin Rd. **City Map** 5 B1.
🚌 1, 25, 44. 🚤 Tien to Wat Arun.
Open 8:30am–5:30pm daily. 🎫 📷
🌐 watarun.net

Named after Aruna, the god of dawn, Wat Arun is a striking landmark in Bangkok, which looks best when viewed from across the river at sunset. Its name is derived from a legend which says that King Taksin (r.1779–82) arrived here at sunrise in October 1767, from the sacked capital of Ayutthaya. He soon enlarged the tiny temple that stood on the site into a Royal Chapel which housed the Emerald Buddha for a while.

Also known as the Olive Temple or Temple of Dawn, the structure was developed and decorated over the years by Rama I (r.1782–1809) and Rama II (r.1809–24), who are also responsible for the size of the current temple – the main *prang* is 260 ft (79 m) high and the circumference of its base is 768 ft (234 m). The colorful ceramics which cover the *prang* in enticing details of gods and demons are actually recycled pieces of porcelain that formed the ballast of merchant ships

from China. Unfortunately, these ran out and the king had to ask his people to donate broken pieces of crockery to complete the edifice; Rama III (r.1824–51) introduced this form of ornamentation. The monument's style, deriving mainly from Khmer architecture, is unique in Thailand.

The central *prang*, reached by a series of steep steps, is seen by Buddhists as a symbol of the path to enlightenment. Atop the *prang* is a thunderbolt which symbolizes the attainment of enlightenment. Four smaller *prangs* are located one on each side of the *wat*; they contain

Thailand's biggest bronze bell, in the tower of Wat Kalayanimit

statues of Phra Phai or Nayu, the wind god. Between the smaller *prangs* are painstakingly detailed *mondop* (altars), each containing a statue of the Buddha at various important stages of his life – birth, meditation, preaching his first sermon, and *nirvana*. The *bot* (ordination hall), located next to the *prangs*, houses an imposing image of the Buddha, which is supposed to have been molded by Rama II himself. Two guardians, figures from the Ramakien, guard the *wat* from the front, while the entire complex is guarded by eight *yakshas* (nature spirits).

❿ Wat Kalayanimit

วัดกัลยาณิมิตร

Soi Wat Kanlaya. **City Map** 5 B2.
🚌 5, 19, 73 to Pak Khlong Talad, then cross the river by ferry at the pier.
Open 8:30am–4:30pm daily.

This temple complex is among the five built in Bangkok by Rama III, who liked Chinese designs, as can be seen from the Chinese-style polygonal *chedi* and the detailed statuary around the courtyard. The statues were brought to Thailand as ballast on empty rice barges returning from China.

The complex's immense *wihan* contains a large image of the Sitting Buddha. In the temple grounds is the biggest bronze bell in Thailand.

Near the *wat*, on the other side of Khlong Bangkok Yai, is **Wichai Prasit Fortress**, built to guard the river approach to Thonburi when Ayutthaya (*see pp44–5*) was the dominant city in Thailand.

⓫ Wat Ratchabophit

วัดราชบพิตร

Fuang Nakhon Rd. **City Map** 2 D5.
Tel 0-2222-3930. 🚌 12, 15, 53.
🚤 Tien. **Open** 5am–8pm daily.

The circular structure of Wat Ratchabophit is a successful blend of Eastern and Western styles. The construction of this

Detail of porcelain tiles in the temple complex at Wat Ratchabophit

temple began under Rama V (r.1868–1910) in 1869 and continued for over 20 years. The whole complex is splendidly decorated with porcelain tiles, which were made to order in China. The focal point of the *wat* is the central, Sri Lankan-style gilded *chedi*, whose full height from the terrace is a good 140 ft (43 m).

Inside the *wat* are four Buddha images, each facing one of the cardinal points. Leading off from the circular gallery are the *bot* to the north, the *wihan* to the south, and two lesser *wihans* to the east and west – an unusual layout for a Thai *wat*.

East-West flourishes permeate the entire complex. The 10 door panels and 28 window panels of the *bot* are decorated with typically Thai mother-of-pearl inlay that illustrates the insignia of five royal orders, while the moldings over the door depict Rama V's seal. The carved, painted guards on the doors are distinctively *farang* (European), and the interior is decorated in an incongruous Italian-Renaissance style.

Accessible through the temple grounds (parallel to Khlong Lot) is a fascinating royal cemetery rarely explored by visitors. The monuments to members of Rama V's family are an eccentric yet admirable mix of Khmer, Thai, and European styles.

⑫ Wat Suthat and the Giant Swing

วัดสุทัศน์และเสาชิงช้า

Bamrung Muang Rd. **City Map** 2 E5. **Tel** 0-2222-6935. 🚌 12, 15, 42, 56, 96. **Open** 8:30am–4pm daily.

There are several unrivaled features in the famous Wat Suthat, a temple that was begun by Rama I in 1807 and completed by Rama III. Its *wihan* is the largest in Bangkok and its art and architecture beautifully exemplify the Rattanakosin style. Its central Buddha, at 26 ft (8 m) tall, is one of the largest surviving Sukhothai bronzes. The murals in the immense *wihan* are some of the most celebrated in Thailand. Amazingly intricate, they depict the Traiphum or Buddhist cosmology and were restored in the 1980s. The beautiful teak doors to the *wihan* are carved in five delicate layers and stand 18 ft (6 m) high. (The ones carved by Rama II are in the National Museum). The cloister around the outside of the *wihan* is lined with 156 golden Buddhas.

Golden Buddha statue, Wat Suthat

The Giant Swing, in the square in front of the *wat*, stood in that same spot for 224 years. It was finally moved in 2007 to the Devasathan Brahmin temple and replaced by a new swing which was made from six 100-year-old teak trees.

⑬ Wat Bowonniwet

วัดบวรนิเวศ

248 Phra Sumen Rd. **City Map** 2 D4. **Tel** 0-2281-2831. 🚌 12, 56. **Open** 8am–8pm daily.

Hidden in quiet, tree-filled grounds, this mid-19th-century temple was constructed by Rama III. The style bears his trademark Chinese influence. A central gilded *chedi* within the *wat* is flanked by two symmetrical chapels. The interior murals in the *wat* are attributed to monk-painter Khrua In Khong, who is famous for the introduction of Western perspective into Thai temple murals. As court painter to Rama IV (r.1851–68), he was exposed to Western ideas and adapted these to a Thai setting. The result was a series of murals that on first glance look wholly European, but which portray the same Buddhist allegories found in traditional Thai murals. For instance, a mural of a physician healing a blind man can be interpreted as symbolic of the illuminating power of Buddhism. The images are all the more remarkable for the fact that Khrua In Khong never traveled to the West. The main Buddha image, Phra Buddha Chinasara, is one of the best examples from the Sukhothai (*see p44*) period.

Rama IV served as abbot here during his 27 years in monk-hood and founded the strict Tammayut sect of Buddhism, for which the temple is now the headquarters. Several successors of Rama IV, including the current monarch Rama IX, also served their monkhood here. The temple also houses Thailand's second Buddhist university. Across the road from the temple is a Buddhist bookstore that also sells English-language publications.

Grounds of Wat Bowonniwet, away from the main city

Singhas guarding the entrance to Wat Benchamabophit

lived as a monk features murals depicting events that occurred during his reign.

Wat Benchamabophit is a popular place for witnessing monastic rituals, including Buddhist holiday processions and the daily alms round, in which merit-makers donate food to the monks lined up outside the *wat* along Nakhon Pathom Road. This is a reversal of the usual practice where the monks go out in search of alms.

⓯ Dusit Park
สวนดุสิต

See pp74–5.

⓰ Dusit Zoo
สวนสัตว์ดุสิต (เขาดิน)

Rama V & Ratchawithi Rds.
City Map 3 A2. **Tel** 0-2282-6125.
🚌 AC: 510, 515. **Open** 8am–6pm daily. 🅿 🆆 zoothailand.org

The Dusit Zoo forms a green wedge in between Dusit Park and Chitrlada Palace. One of Asia's better zoos, it has reasonable space for birds and mammals such as tigers, bears, elephants, and hippos, although some of the other enclosures are more confined. The grounds were originally the private gardens of Rama V, and some varieties of tropical flora are still grown here. It is a pleasant walk through the lawns, lakes, and wooded glades of this zoo. There are also elephant rides and several animal-feeding shows which make it an entertaining day out for locals as well as visitors.

⓮ Wat Benchamabophit
วัดเบญจมบพิตร

69 Rama V Rd. **City Map** 3 A3.
Tel 0-2281-2501. 🚌 72; AC: 503.
Open 8:30am–5:30pm daily. 🅿

The European influence on Thai architecture is exemplified by Wat Benchamabophit, the last major temple to be built in central Bangkok. In 1899, Rama V commissioned his brother Prince Naris and Italian architect Hercules Manfredi to design a new *bot* and cloister for the original Ayutthaya-period temple which stood on the site. The nickname for the new *wat* – Marble Temple – is derived from the gray Carrara marble used to clad the walls.

Laid out in cruciform with cascading roof levels, the *bot* is elegantly proportioned. Victorian-style stained-glass windows depict scenes from Thai mythology and represent a fusion of traditions. The *bot* stores the ashes of Rama V.

It also houses a copy of the revered Phitsanulok Phra Phuttha Chinnarat, a 14th-century Buddha image. This venerated bronze statue is a prime example of late Sukhothai art. The cloister has 53 different images of the Buddha from Thailand and other Buddhist countries, assembled by Rama V.

Inside the *wat* is one of the three sets of doors inlaid with mother-of-pearl that were salvaged from Wat Borom Buddharam in Ayutthaya. The building in which Rama V

Visitors enjoying a ride around Dusit Zoo

The Golden Mount, a distinctive Bangkok landmark

⓱ Wat Saket and the Golden Mount

วัดสระเกศและภูเขาทอง

Chakkaphatdi Phong Rd. **City Map** 2 F5. 🚌 15, 37, 47, 49. **Open** 7:30am– 5:30pm daily. 🅿️ 🏛️ Golden Mount Fair (Nov).

Built by Rama I in the late 18th century, Wat Saket is one of the oldest temples in Bangkok. During the 19th century, it served a rather macabre function as a crematorium where the bodies of the poor were often left as carrion for vultures and dogs.

Rama III built the first Golden Mount, but the soft soil around the structure led to its collapse. It was Rama V who provided the necessary technology to create the 250-ft (76-m) high representation of the mythical Mount Meru – an artificial hill with a golden tower on its crest. It is believed to house relics of the Buddha presented to Rama V by the Viceroy of India. A circular staircase lined with monuments and tombs leads to the top, where there is a small sanctuary. The view from the gallery takes in the Grand Palace (see pp60–65), Wat Pho (see pp68–9), Wat Arun (see p70), and the octagonal Mahakan Fort – among the 14 pivotal watchtowers of the old city.

Until the 1960s, the Golden Mount was one of the highest points in Bangkok. Although it has since been dwarfed by modern skyscrapers, the golden spire is a prominent landmark even today.

Visitors come to Wat Saket to climb the Golden Mount and to attend the fair and candle-lit procession that is held here every November.

⓲ Monk's Bowl Village (Ban Bat)

บ้านบาตร

Bamrung Muang Rd, Soi Ban Bat. **City Map** 2 F5. 🚌 AC: 508.

Monks' bowls were first seen 2,500 years ago and are still widely used in many Buddhist countries. Such bowls have been made at Monk's Bowl Village in Bangkok since the late 18th century as part of an age-old tradition. The bowls are mostly used for early-morning alms gathering.

It is quite difficult to find the village amid the maze of sois, especially since it once stretched as far as Wat Saket, and is now reduced to just three homes and a few small work-shops. These monks' bowls are available at Wat Suthat (see p71) as well. The process of making bowls is quite time-consuming and requires eight pieces of metal, representing the eight spokes of the wheel of Dharma. The first strip is beaten into a circular form to make the rim. Three pieces are then beaten to create a cross-shaped frame. Four triangular pieces complete the sides. After being welded in a kiln, the bowl is shaped, filed smooth, and fired again to produce an enamel-like surface. Just about 20 bowls are produced daily in the village.

At the center of this maze of alleys is also an unusual shrine, constructed from old Chinese cylinder bellows.

An artisan shaping pottery at Monk's Bowl Village

Royal White Elephants

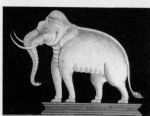

Manuscript depicting a white elephant

The importance of the chang samkhan (white elephant) in Thailand derives from a 2,500-year-old tale. Queen Maya, once barren, became pregnant with the future Buddha after dreaming of a white elephant entering her womb. Ever since the 13th century, when King Ramkhamhaeng (r.1279–98) gave the animal great prestige, the reigning monarch's importance has been judged in part according to the number of white elephants he owns. Indeed, the white elephant's status as a national icon was symbolized by its presence on the Siamese flag until 1917. The origin of the phrase "white elephant", meaning a large and useless investment, lies in the Thai tradition according to which all white elephants must belong to the king. They cannot be used for work and, therefore, have to be cared for at huge expense. Often, the white elephants are not fully albino. But tradition states that seven parts of their body – the eyes, palate, nails, tail hair, skin, hairs, and testicles – must be near-white.

⓯ Dusit Park

สวนดุสิต

This magnificent park is the major attraction of the Dusit area. Rama V, the first Thai sovereign to visit Europe, was determined to develop Bangkok after the style of the West, and the manicured gardens, elegant architecture, and teak mansions in Dusit Park all bear testimony to his efforts. The highlights include Vimanmek Mansion – the world's largest golden teak building – and the graceful Abhisek Dusit Throne Hall, which houses the SUPPORT Museum of traditional arts and crafts. A visit to the park and the neighboring zoo *(see p72)* can take a whole day.

Pagoda in Dusit Park

Royal Elephant Museum
Originally a stable for the royal elephants, this museum contains all kinds of paraphernalia, including mahouts' amulets, tusks, photos, and a model of the present king's favorite elephant.

King Bhumibol's Photographic Museum
Most of the photographs on display feature moments from the life of the royal family and many were taken by the current King Rama IX, an avid photographer.

KEY

① Perimeter wall

② Royal Paraphernalia Museum

③ Canal

④ Bridge

⑤ Ticket office

⑥ **Old Clock Museum** houses the collection of clocks acquired by kings Rama V and Rama IX on their trips to Europe. It includes timepieces of European, American, and Japanese origin.

Entrance

Antique Textile Exhibition Hall
This collection includes the luxurious robes of the kings Rama IV and Rama V. There are also displays of different types of Thai silk from all over the country.

★ Abhisek Dusit Throne Hall
This hall is a beautifully ornamented white edifice. The major attraction inside is the SUPPORT Museum, with its large collection of traditional artifacts, such as works using the exquisitely colored wings of jewel beetles.

VISITORS' CHECKLIST

Practical Information
City Map 2 F2. **Tel** 0-2628-6300-9. **Open** 9am–4pm daily. **Closed** for royal ceremonies. 🏛 Royal Mansion ticket (valid for 30 days) includes admission to Dusit Park and all buildings. 📷 Vimanmek Mansion: **Open** 9:30am–3:15pm Tue–Sun (last entry 3pm). 📷 SUPPORT Museum: **Open** 9:30am–3:15pm daily. 🌐 **palaces.thai.net**; **vimanmek.com**

Transport
🚌 18, 28, 70; AC: 70, 515.

Lakeside Pavilion
An elegant pavilion behind Vimanmek Mansion offers a great view across the lake to some particularly fine traditional Thai houses. The further bank is, however, closed to visitors.

| 0 meters | 50 |
| 0 yards | 50 |

★ Vimanmek Mansion
Built more in the style of a Colonial mansion than a Thai palace, this three-storied, golden teak structure was built using wooden pegs instead of nails. The palace is full of intriguing artifacts.

⓳ Phahurat Market
ตลาดพาหุรัด

Phahurat-Chak Phet Rd. **City Map** 6 D1.
🚌 7, 25, 40, 53, 56; AC: 507.

This predominantly Indian market offers all the sights and smells of India. The main bazaar, around Phahurat and Chak Phet roads, specializes in fabrics. Along these roads, cloth merchants sell everything from tablecloths to wedding saris. This is an ideal place to look out for traditional Indian accessories such as sandals, jewelry, and an eclectic selection of spices and incense. In the surrounding streets are delicious hole-in-the-wall Indian restaurants and samosa stalls. Off Chak Phet road is Shri Guru Singh Sabha, a Sikh temple.

⓴ Pak Khlong Market
ปากคลองตลาด

Maharaj Rd. **City Map** 5 C2.
🚌 2, 5; AC: 512. 🚤 Rachinee, Pak Khlong. **Open** daily.

Open 24 hours a day, Pak Khlong Market provides the city with fresh flowers and vegetables.

Known for offering the best array of flowers in Thailand, it is a florist's one-stop shop. Blooms arrive from 1am onward and by dawn, roses, orchids, lotus, jasmine, and Dutch tulips are on display. The widest variety can be seen at 9am. Visitors can buy bouquets or floral basket arrangements from here.

㉑ Chinatown
ตลาดเยาวราช

Yaowarat Rd. **City Map** 6 E1.
🚌 AC: 501, 507. 🚤 Ratchawong, Pak Khlong. **Open** daily.

Generally called Yaowarat by the Thais, this historic area is centered on and around Yaowarat Road, Ratchawong Road, and Sampeng Lane. The area is evocative of Bangkok's past and the dominant commercial role played by the city's ethnic Chinese population over the last 200 years. A plethora of gold stores, traditional Chinese medicine shops, bustling street markets, and beautiful temples dedicated to any or all of the *san jiao* (three religions) of Mahayana Buddhism, Taoism, and Confucianism, make the area well worth a visit.

The bustling Yaowarat Road with Chinese signage, Chinatown

㉒ Wat Traimit
วัดไตรมิตร

Tri Mit Rd. **City Map** 6 F2.
🚌 4, 7, 21, 25; AC: 501, 507.
Open 9am–5pm daily.

Also called the Temple of the Golden Buddha, Wat Traimit houses the world's largest solid gold Buddha. This 13-ft (4-m) high, 13th-century Sukhothai image is made of 18-carat gold and weighs five tons. It was discovered by accident, in 1955, by workers of the East Asiatic Company.
   Local Chinese residents come here to worship the Golden Buddha and to make merit by rubbing gold leaf on the temple's smaller Buddha images.

㉓ Hua Lampong Station
สถานีหัวลำโพง

Rama IV Rd. **City Map** 7 A2.
Tel 0-2220-4334. 🚌 4, 21, 29, 34, 40, 109; AC: 501, 529. Ⓜ Hua Lampong.

Rama V, a great champion of modernization, was the propagator of rail travel in Thailand. The first railroad line, begun in 1891, was a private line from Pak Nam to Hua Lampong. Today, this historic station is Bangkok's main rail junction. From here, trains leave for the north, northeast, the central plains, and the south. The city's other station, Bangkok Noi, was rebuilt in 2003.

Vendor selling a wide range of chilies, Pak Khlong Market

The Chinese in Bangkok

The first of the Chinese immigrants arrived in Thailand as merchants in the 12th century. During the late 18th and early 19th centuries, following years of war in Thailand *(see p45)*, Chinese immigration was encouraged in order to help rebuild the economy. The subsequent integration of the Chinese into Thai society was so successful that by the mid-19th century, half of Bangkok's population was of pure or mixed Chinese blood. There have been periods of anti-Chinese feeling and immigration restrictions, but the Chinese still dominate Thailand's commercial sector. At the same time, Chinese traditions and beliefs remain strong in their communities.

Chinese Shophouses

Shophouses are a common feature in Chinatown. The family lives on the first floor, which usually has a large living room and a ceramic-tiled floor. The ground floor is devoted to the family business, whether it is a small workshop or a store selling food or other household goods.

The front veranda joins to form a sheltered walkway called the five-foot way.

Sign painting is not just a decorative art form. These good luck messages, written in gold, are said to ward off evil and sickness. They are displayed in great numbers during the Chinese New Year.

Dim sum, which means "touch the heart", can be sampled in many of the area's Chinese restaurants. These bite-size snacks include shrimp toast and pork dumplings.

Leng Noi Yee Temple in Bangkok is an important Mahayana Buddhist shrine that also incorporates elements of Taoism and Confucianism. The temple, with its glazed ceramic gables topped by Chinese dragons, is a focal point of the Vegetarian Festival *(see p40)*.

Chinese opera, performed by traveling troupes, features martial arts, acrobatics, singing, and dance.

"Hell's banknotes" are a form of *kong tek* – paper replicas of real objects, burned to provide for the dead during their next life.

Neo-Classical façade of the Authors' Wing of the Mandarin Oriental

㉔ Mandarin Oriental

โรงแรมโอเรียนเต็ล

48 Oriental Ave, off Charoen Krung Rd. **City Map** 6 F4. **Tel** 0-2659-9000. 🚌 35, 75. 🚢 Oriental. 🅦 mandarinoriental.com

Repeatedly voted the world's best hotel for its service and attention to detail, Mandarin Oriental was Thailand's first large hotel. It was established in 1876 and completely rebuilt in 1887. More wings have since been added. The hotel owes much of its charm to the Armenian Sarkies brothers, creators of the luxurious Raffles Hotel in Singapore. Mandarin Oriental's status, lavish decor, and spectacular setting on the banks of the Chao Phraya River account for its elevated prices.

The hotel's original white-shuttered wing contains the renowned Authors' Suites. Somerset Maugham, the acclaimed author, stayed here in the 1920s. Recovering from a bout of malaria, he wrote of the "dust and heat and noise and whiteness and more dust" of Bangkok, although his perception of the city changed once he was able to explore the *wats* and *khlongs*. Classic, English-style high tea is served in the Authors' Lounge, a riot of potted plants and fan-backed wicker chairs. A teak barge shuttles back and forth to the Sala Rim

Naam on the opposite bank, one of the hotel's highly acclaimed restaurants. Here, guests can enjoy performances of traditional dance as they dine. The hotel also runs a respected school of Thai cookery.

㉕ Patpong

พัฒน์พงษ์

Silom Rd, Patpong 1 and 2. **City Map** 7 C3. 🚌 AC: 76, 177, 504, 514. 🚈 Sala Daeng (skytrain). Ⓜ Silom.

The streets of Patpong 1 and 2, named after Chinese millionaire Khun Patpongpanit, owner of the properties in the area, comprise what is probably the world's most notorious red-light district. In the 1960s, the area was the home of Bangkok's entertainment scene – the go-go bars sprang up to satisfy airline crews and US GIs on leave during the Vietnam War. Since the 1970s, the sex shows have been sustained mainly through tourist patronage. A less visible homosexual scene exists in adjacent Silom Soi 4, while Soi Taniya's hostess bars are frequented mainly by Japanese clients.

Poster inside a go-go bar

The Department of Tourist Police monitors Patpong, and the area is surprisingly safe. A night market, with stalls selling souvenirs, and original and fake fashions, gives the area a thin veneer of respectability. Besides the go-go bars, there are several restaurants and bars featuring live music. Many visitors come to Patpong out of curiosity rather than to indulge in the flesh trade.

㉖ Lumphini Park

สวนลุมพินี

City Map 8 D3. 🚌 14; AC: 50, 507. 🚈 Sala Daeng (skytrain). Ⓜ Silom, Lumphini. **Open** 5:30am–9pm daily.

Named after the Buddha's birthplace, Bangkok's main greenbelt sprawls around two boating lakes. The best time to visit the park is usually early morning, when it is used by Thais for jogging and by Chinese for practicing *tai chi chuan*. The superstitious can be seen consuming fresh snake blood and bile, purchased from stalls placed along the park's northern edge, to keep ill health at bay.

Lumphini Park is a relaxing place to take a stroll, observe elderly Chinese people play chess, and impromptu games of *takraw*, a type of volleyball that does not allow the use of hands. Dominating the Silom Road side of the park is an imposing statue of Rama VI (r.1910–25), who ordered the creation of the park.

Early morning visitors relaxing by a lake, Lumphini Park

Dancers in traditional Thai costume performing at Erawan Shrine

❷ Erawan Shrine
ศาลพระพรหมเอราวัณ

Ratchadamri Rd. **City Map** 8 D1.
🚌 AC: 501, 504, 505. 🚇 Ratchadamri or Siam (skytrain).

Local drivers usually take their hands off the steering wheel to *wai* (a gesture of respect) as they pass the Erawan Shrine; such is the widespread faith in the luck that this landmark is said to bring. The construction of the original Erawan Hotel in the 1950s, on the site now occupied by the Grand Hyatt Erawan Hotel, was plagued by a series of mishaps, including injuries to the laborers. In order to counteract the bad spirits believed to be causing the problems, this shrine dedicated to Indra, the god of rain and thunder, and his elephant mount, Erawan, was erected right in front of the hotel. Ever since, the somewhat gaudy monument has been decked with garlands, carved wooden elephants, and other offerings in the hope of, or thanks for, good fortune. Women dancers in beautiful traditional costumes can occasionally be paid by devotees to dance for the deity. This is a way of expressing gratitude for some recent good fortune or even a fulfilled wish.

On August 17, 2015, 20 people lost their lives and more than 100 others were injured in a devastating bomb attack at the shrine. As yet, it is not clear who the perpetrators were or what the motive behind the attack was.

❷ The Jim Thompson House
บ้านจิมทอมป์สัน

See pp80–81.

❷ Suan Pakkad Palace
วังสวนผักกาด

352 Si Ayutthaya Rd. **City Map** 4 D4.
Tel 0-2245-4934. 🚇 Phaya Thai (skytrain). 🚌 AC: 201, 513.
Open 9am–4pm daily. 🖼 📷
🌐 **suanpakkad.com**

This palace, a group of eight traditional teak houses, was originally the home of Prince and Princess Chumbhot. The houses were assembled in the 1950s, within a lush garden landscaped out of a *suan pakkad*, or cabbage patch, that gives the palace its name. Each building has been converted into a museum, and together they house an impressive collection of art and artifacts belonging to the royal couple.

The eclectic assortment ranges from Khmer sculpture, betel nut sets, and pieces of antique lacquered furniture, to Thai musical instruments and exquisite shells and crystals. Most important, perhaps, is the first-class collection of whorl-patterned red and white Bronze Age pottery, excavated from tombs at Ban Chiang in northeast Thailand. The highlight is the Lacquer Pavilion, which was built from two exquisite temple buildings retrieved by Prince Chumbhot from the Ayutthaya province.

Immaculately crafted, black and gold lacquered murals inside each edifice depict scenes from the Buddha's life and the Ramakien (*see p63*). They also portray ordinary Thai life from just before the fall of Ayutthaya, in 1767. These are some of the only murals to survive that period. Scenes include foreign traders exchanging goods, battles, and gruesome depictions of hell.

The elegant façade of the Lacquer Pavilion, Suan Pakkad Palace

❷❽ The Jim Thompson House
บ้านจิมทอมป์สัน

One of the best preserved Thai houses in Bangkok and finest museums in the country is the former home of Jim Thompson (b.1906). An enterprising American, Thompson revived the art of Thai silk weaving, which had waned before World War II. His house is in a flower garden across from the ancient silk weavers' quarter of Ban Khrua. In 1959, Thompson dismantled six teak houses in Ban Khrua and Ayutthaya and reassembled them here in an unconventional layout. An avid collector of antiques and art from all over Southeast Asia, his extensive array, which spans 14 centuries, is well displayed, and left as it was when he mysteriously disappeared in 1967. Unlike many other home museums, this one feels lived in.

Master Bedroom
Fine 19th-century paintings of the *jataka* tales line the walls of the master bedroom.

Second floor

Guest bedrooms

First floor

★ Jataka Paintings
This panel, in the entrance hall, is one of eight early 19th-century paintings in the house showing scenes from the Vessantara *jataka* (see p28). These show Prince Vessantara as Buddha's incarnation.

★ Burmese Carvings
Wooden figures of animist *Nat* spirits are part of an extensive collection of Burmese images. Buddhism in Burma incorporates pre-existing worship of *Nat* spirits.

One of six traditional teak houses

Key to Floor Plan

- ▨ Bedrooms
- ▨ Study
- ▨ Entrance hall
- ▨ Drawing room
- ▨ Dining room
- ▨ Secure room
- ▨ Bencharong room
- ▨ Silk Pavilion
- ▨ Other exhibition space

View from the Terrace
The terrace offers pretty views of Khlong Saen Sap and the gardens surrounding the house.

The steep roofs of traditional teak houses are ideal for ventilation, and the inward leaning walls create a greater sense of height.

Drawing Room
Carved wooden figures of Burmese spirits from the 18th century adorn the alcoves in the drawing room. Soft silk cushions in various hues give the place a colorful appeal.

VISITORS' CHECKLIST

Practical Information
6 Soi Kasemsan 2, Rama I Rd. **City Map** 3 C5. **Tel** 0-2216-7368. **Open** 9am–5pm daily. 🐾 📷 💌 ✏️
🏠 W jimthompsonhouse.com

Transport
🚇 National Stadium (skytrain).
🚌 15, 48, 204; AC: 508.

The *khlong* (canal) was once used by silk weavers, who dried threads of silk on poles along the banks.

Dining Room
Precious blue and white porcelain fills the cabinets along the walls in the dining room.

★ Dvaravati Torso of the Buddha
A torso of the Buddha, made of limestone, stands in the garden. Dating from the early Dvaravati period (7th century), it is said to be one of the oldest surviving Buddha statues in Southeast Asia.

Spirit house with offerings

Entrance

Who was Jim Thompson?

An architect by profession, Thailand's most famous American came here in 1945 as the Bangkok head of the Office of Strategic Services (OSS), a forerunner of the CIA. In 1948, he founded the Thai Silk Company Ltd, turning the ailing industry into a thriving business once again. Thompson became a social celebrity in Bangkok and finally achieved mythical status following his disappearance on Easter Sunday in 1967 while walking in the Cameron Highlands in Malaysia. Explanations for his vanishing include falling from a path or having a heart attack, to more sinister suggestions of CIA involvement.

Jim Thompson inspecting Thai silk in 1964

Farther Afield

Many interesting sights lie outside central Bangkok. Extending eastward is Sukhumvit Road, with a plethora of shops, restaurants, small galleries, and museums. Shopaholics will certainly not want to miss the bustling Chatuchak Market, perhaps the largest open-air market in the world, selling everything from handicrafts to live animals. The Damnoen Saduak Floating Market, southwest of the center, is a market for fresh products, sold mostly by women, on small, flat boats. The Crocodile Farm displays various species of crocodiles from across the world, and reptile wrestling is a major attraction.

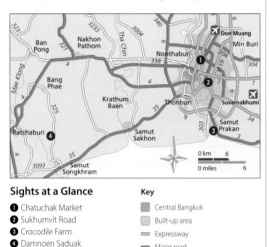

Sights at a Glance

1. Chatuchak Market
2. Sukhumvit Road
3. Crocodile Farm
4. Damnoen Saduak Floating Market

Key

- Central Bangkok
- Built-up area
- Expressway
- Major road
- Minor road

❶ Chatuchak Market

ตลาดจตุจักร

Road Map D1. Chatuchak district. Mo Chit (Skytrain). AC: 38, 510, 512, 513. M Kampangphet. TAT, Bangkok (1672). **Open** 6am–6pm Wed–Sun. chatuchak.org

Thailand's biggest market is held each weekend in.a northern suburb of Bangkok, between the Northern Bus Terminal and Bang Sue Railroad Station. The market is also open on Wednesdays and Thursdays for plants, and Friday nights (10pm–7am) for general goods. It is a chaotic collection of over 15,000 stalls divided into 27 sections; pick up a map on entering. It is always filled with eager shoppers, many of whom spend a whole day browsing among the large variety of products on display. Goods range from seafood to antiques, and from Siamese fighting fish to secondhand jeans. The plant section provides a good intro-

Buddha images for sale at the Chatuchak Market, Bangkok

duction to Thai flora, while the food stalls display every conceivable ingredient of Thai food. The antiques and hill-tribe handicrafts sections sell a good selection of artifacts and textiles, both fake and genuine, from all over Thailand as well as neighboring countries.

The market is also referred to as the "wildlife supermarket of the world," because endangered species, such as leaf monkeys, are illegally sold here. Sadly, frequent crackdowns have failed to halt this trade.

❷ Sukhumvit Road

ถนนสุขุมวิท

Road Map D1. Phra Khanong district. AC: 38, 501, 508, 511, 513.

This road begins at the eastern end of Bangkok's downtown and continues all the way to the Cambodian border in Trat province (*see p121*). In Bangkok, it is the main thoroughfare of an expanding business quarter popular with foreigners.

Although a long way from Bangkok's best-known sights, the area has numerous good-quality, moderately priced hotels and restaurants, and a few attractions of its own.

Foremost of these is the **Siam Society**, which was founded in the early 1900s by a group of Thais and foreign residents under the patronage of Rama VI, to research, rediscover, and preserve Thai culture. Within the grounds are two traditional teakwood northern Thai houses that comprise the country's only genuine ethnological museum. The Kamthieng House, a farm dwelling, was transported piece by piece in the 1960s to Bangkok from the bank of the Ping River, near Chiang Mai, in northern Thailand. The Sangaroon House is a later addition donated by the architect Sangaroon Ratagasikorn, who – inspired by the utilitarian beauty of rural utensils – amassed a sizable collection. Also on the grounds is a reference library on Thai culture, open to visitors. The *Journal of the Siam Society*, available in the library, is one of Asia's most respected publications on art history, culture, and society.

Located next to the Eastern Bus Terminal, the **Bangkok Planetarium** traces the history of space travel. It also includes an aquarium as well as a computer world.

The sprawling **King Rama IX Park**, inaugurated on the 60th birthday of Rama IX, the reigning monarch, is farther out toward Samut Prakan province. With its botanical gardens and area for watersports, this park is one of Bangkok's most pleasant oases. The park also has an exhibition on the king's life.

🏛 **Siam Society**
131 Soi Asoke, Sukhumvit Rd, Soi 21.
Tel 0-2661-6470. **Open** Tue–Sat.
🖳 siam-society.org

🏛 **Bangkok Planetarium**
928 Sukhumvit Rd. **Tel** 0-2391-0544.
Open Tue–Sun. **Closed** public hols. 📷

🐦 **King Rama IX Park**
Soi Udomsuk, Sukhumvit Rd, Soi 103.
Tel 0-2328-1385. **Open** daily. 📷 ✏

❸ Crocodile Farm
ฟาร์มจระเข้

Road Map D1. Old Sukhumvit Highway, Samut Prakan province. **Tel** 0-2703-4891. 🚌 AC: 511 to Samut Prakan, then *songthaew*, or join tour from Bangkok. **Open** 8am–6pm daily.
📷 📷 🖳 worldcrocodile.com

The largest among Thailand's (and, supposedly, the world's) crocodile farms, this breeding park, or zoo, is home to some 30,000 reptiles. Fresh and salt-water species, from South American caimans to fierce crocodiles from the Nile, can all be seen here. The farm also has the biggest crocodile ever kept in captivity – a 20-ft (6-m) long reptile weighing over 2,200 lb (1,000 kg).

The highlight of the farm is the hourly show during which visitors can see handlers wrestle with crocodiles, even putting their heads in the creatures' mouths. A souvenir shop nearby sells a variety of crocodile skin products such bags and key rings.

Reconstructed traditional living area in Kamthieng House, Sukhumvit Road

❹ Damnoen Saduak Floating Market
ตลาดน้ำดำเนินสะดวก

Road Map C1. 1 mile (2 km) W of Damnoen Saduak, Ratchaburi province. 🚗 🚌 🚐 or join tour from Bangkok. **Open** 4–11am daily.
ℹ TAT, Phetchaburi (0-3247-1005).

Like most of the floating markets in Bangkok, this is organized mainly for the benefit of tourists, but it is nevertheless a truly colorful spectacle.

Located 62 miles (100 km) southwest of Bangkok, the market is a labyrinth of narrow *khlongs* (canals) and actually comprises three separate markets. The largest, **Ton Khem**, is on Khlong Damnoen Saduak. On the parallel *khlong*, a short way south, is **Hia Kui**, where structures anchored to the banks function as warehouses selling souvenirs to large tour groups. Further south, on a smaller *khlong*, is **Khun Phitak**, the least crowded of the three markets.

Most vendors, mainly women, paddle around in *sampans* (rowing boats) wearing *mo homs* (traditional farmers' shirts) and a *ngop* (traditional hat). They sell farm-fresh produce, including fruit, vegetables, and spices. Some vendors also sell souvenir straw hats as well as refreshments.

The best way of getting around the three markets is by boat – trips can be taken along the *khlongs* and to the nearby coconut plantations. The best time to arrive is between 7am and 9am, when the market is in full swing.

Crocodile wrestling show at the Crocodile Farm

For hotels and restaurants in this area see pp294–301 and pp308–17

SHOPPING IN BANGKOK

Bangkok is regarded as a shoppers' paradise with its many retail outlets, high-quality products, and surprisingly good bargains. Staff in department stores are attentive, and whether it is designer clothes, traditional crafts, or electronic equipment, there are

some great deals to be had. Visitors enjoy bargaining in the open-air markets, where vendors often drop their prices by 50 percent or more. However, it is better to avoid the heat and humidity of mid-afternoon, and limit the buying spree to one or two locations per day.

Shoppers visiting the huge Siam Paragon mall

Practical Information

Opening hours are usually early morning to mid-afternoon in fresh markets, 10am–10pm in shopping malls, and 24 hours in convenience stores. Credit cards are accepted in shopping malls and modern boutiques, but market vendors expect cash payment. VAT refunds are possible, but the shop where the item is bought must fill out a form for customs, which can be time-consuming, so it is only worthwhile for significant savings. Bargaining is expected at street stalls and markets, but prices are fixed in department stores and boutiques. For more information, see pages 318–21.

Shopping Districts

Boutiques and markets are scattered all over the city, but there is a high concentration of shopping outlets around Siam Square, Silom, Phloen Chit, and Sukhumvit roads.

Shopping Malls

Leading the way in the race to be Bangkok's best and biggest mall, **CentralWorld Plaza** is Southeast Asia's largest shopping complex. Another favorite shopping destination is

Siam Paragon, where anything from a sports car to a bowl of noodles is available for a price. **Mahboonkrong** (or MBK) is more like a street market spread over eight floors. Other centrally located malls are **Siam Center and Siam Discovery**, **Emporium**, **Silom Complex**, **Amarin Plaza**, **Gaysorn Plaza**, and **Erawan**.

Markets

No self-respecting shopaholic can claim to know Bangkok without going to the city's vast **Chatuchak Market**, said to be the world's largest open-air market. Impossible to cover in a day, prudent visitors are selective about the places they see.

Bangkok's night markets in the Khao San, Patpong, and Sukhumvit Sois 3–15 regions

Brightly lit stalls selling various goods, night market at Patpong

consist of stalls set up each evening on the sidewalk. They make it possible to combine souvenir shopping with dining and clubbing, for visitors who are short on time.

Colorful display of authentic silk products at the Jim Thompson

Silk and Cotton

Thai silk is renowned for its high quality, unique designs, and reasonable price. In the night markets, some items that claim to be silk are, in fact, made of synthetic fabric.

It pays to visit a reputable shop, such as **Jim Thompson**, which has outlets in many top hotels, to ensure the authenticity of products. Those who have an eye for the real thing can head for the crowded **Phahurat Market**, where prices are much lower.

Thai cotton is also a good deal. The eye-catching designs on items such as bedspreads and cushion covers make distinctive souvenirs.

Clothes

With prices only a fraction of what they are in the West, it makes sense to stock up on clothes, either off-the-peg in shopping malls or tailor-made.

Tailors abound in all tourist areas, but workmanship varies, so it is better to visit a reputable tailor such as **Raja's Fashions** or **Marzotto**, and allow several days for preparation and fittings.

Antiques

So-called ancient craft items are available in many shops, but few of these are genuine antiques, for which a permit from the Fine Arts Department is required for export. A couple of reliable outlets are the **River City Complex**, which has four floors of antique furniture, carvings, and old maps, and **Oriental Plaza**, with rare collectibles such as beautiful sculptures and prints.

Thai Crafts

From silverware to celadon, lacquerware to woodcarvings, and basketry to hand-woven

Lacquerware items and wooden carvings at Chatuchak Market

textiles, Thailand has a rich variety of crafts. Good places to see a wide range of crafts include Chatuchak Market, **Narai Phand**, **Silom Village**, and **Nandakwang**.

Gems and Jewelry

As with antiques, extreme caution should be exercised when buying gems or jewelry, since potential customers are often exposed to sophisticated

scams. Serious shoppers may want to browse through the glittering displays of jewelry at **Peninsula Plaza** or the gem boutiques at reliable hotels.

Electronic Goods

Computer equipment, video games, cameras, and mobile phones are on sale in shopping malls throughout the city, but one place that specializes in such goods is **Pantip Plaza**. Customers should be aware that some items on sale, such as software, are pirated and offer no money-back guarantee.

Books

Book addicts should explore the massive selection at any one of the outlets of **Asia Books** and **Kinokuniya Books**. Other bookstore chains with outlets in central Bangkok are **B2S** and **Bookazine**.

DIRECTORY

Shopping Malls

Amarin Plaza
Phloen Chit Rd.
City Map 8 E1.
Tel 0-2650-4704.
amarinplaza.com

CentralWorld Plaza
Ratchadamri Rd. City Map 8 D1. Tel 0-2640-7000.
centralworld.co.th

Emporium
Sukhumvit Sois 24–26.
Tel 0-2269-1000.
emporium.co.th

Erawan
Phloen Chit Rd. City Map 8 E1. Tel 0-2250-7777.
erawanbangkok.com

Gaysorn Plaza
Phloen Chit Rd. City Map 8 D1. Tel 0-2656-1149.
gaysorn.com

Mahboonkrong
Phaya Thai Rd. City Map 7 B1. Tel 0-2620-7000.

Siam Center and Siam Discovery
Rama I Rd. City Map 7 C1.
Tel 0-2658-1000.
siamcenter.co.th

Siam Paragon
Rama I Rd.
City Map 7 C1.
Tel 0-2610-8000.
siamparagon.co.th

Silom Complex
Silom Rd.
City Map 8 D4.
Tel 0-2632-1199.
silomcomplex.net

Markets

Chatuchak Market
Kamphaeng Phet 2 Rd.

Silk and Cotton

Jim Thompson
9 Surawong Rd.
City Map 7 C3.
Tel 0-2632-8100.

Phahurat Market
Phahurat. City Map 6 D1.

Clothes

Marzotto
3 Soi Shangri-La Hotel,
Charoen Krung Rd.
City Map 6 F5.
Tel 0-2233-2880.
marzottotailors.com

Raja's Fashions
160/1 Sukhumvit Rd
(between Sois 6 & 8).
Tel 0-2253-8379.
rajasfashions.com

Antiques

Oriental Plaza
Charoen Krung Rd.
City Map 6 F4.

River City Complex
23 Trok Rongnamkaeng
Yotha Rd. City Map 6 F3.
Tel 0-2237-0077.
rivercity.co.th

Thai Crafts

Nandakwang
Sukhumvit Soi 23.
Tel 0-2259-9607.
nandakwang.com

Narai Phand
973 Ploenchit.
City Map 8 D1.
Tel 0-2656-0398.
naraiphand.com

Silom Village
Silom Rd.
City Map 7 A4.
Tel 0-2234-4448.
silomvillage.co.th

Gems and Jewelry

Peninsula Plaza
Ratchadamri Rd.
City Map 8 D1.
Tel 0-2253-9791.

Electronic Goods

Pantip Plaza
Phetchaburi Rd. City Map 4 D5. Tel 0-2250-1555.

Books

Asia Books
221 Sukhumvit.
Tel 0-2252-7277.
One of several branches.

B2S
CentralWorld Plaza,
Ratchadamri Rd.
City Map 8 D1.
One of several branches.

Bookazine
Silom Complex, Silom Rd.
City Map 8 D4.
One of several branches.

Kinokuniya Books
Siam Paragon.
City Map 7 C1.
One of several branches.

ENTERTAINMENT IN BANGKOK

Bangkok provides a fantastic range of entertainment, from classical puppet theater to nightclubs. One of the most popular choices for short-stay visitors is a cultural show accompanied by a Thai meal, but there are plenty of alternatives, such as transvestite cabaret shows or an unusual drink at one of the city's trendy cocktail bars. Many of the pubs and restaurants offer live music, ranging from traditional Thai ballads to rock classics, while the city's clubs are a musical melting pot where locals and foreigners find common ground. It is best to plan out journeys in order to beat Bangkok's notorious traffic snarls.

A traditional Thai puppet show

General Information

For information about daily events, visitors can consult English-language newspapers such as the *Bangkok Post* and *The Nation*, or pick up one of the free magazines, such as *BK Magazine*, that are distributed at tourist spots. Tickets for events are usually easy to come by. Visitors can ask at their hotel desk or a travel agent, or go online and take a look at the websites designed to help travelers. For more information, *see pp322–5*.

Cultural Shows and Theater

The nightly show at **Siam Niramit** is quite a cultural extravaganza, which features spectacular sets and more than 500 elaborately dressed dancers. Classical dance shows with buffet or à la carte dinners can be enjoyed at **Sala Rim Nam** and **Silom Village**, while the city's top cabaret location is **Calypso Cabaret** at Asiatique – a riverfront entertainment venue south of the city center. For performances of *khon*, or classical masked drama, the **Sala Chalermkrung Theater** and the **National Theater** are good options.

Puppet shows may seem like children's entertainment, but the puppeteers at the **Joe Louis Puppet Theatre**, also at Asiatique, and the **Aksra Theatre** are so accomplished that most adults will be as enthralled as their kids.

Muay Thai

To enjoy a more visceral kind of entertainment, visitors can head to the local Thai boxing ring. *Muay thai* (Thai kickboxing) is the national sport, which draws in a large crowd. Spectators usually bet on the outcome of *muay thai* matches, and cheer excitedly for their chosen fighter.

At **Ratchadamnoen Stadium** and **Lumpinee Stadium**, spectators can watch the boxers prepare for their matches with slow, concentrated movements to the accompaniment of wailing instruments.

Cinemas

It may seem strange to travel all the way to Thailand and end up going to the cinema, but with their air-conditioned interiors, comfortable seats, and cheap prices, cinema halls can be the antidote to a tiring shopping spree or a day spent sightseeing. Most modern cinemas are located in shopping malls, such as the **Paragon Cineplex** in Siam Paragon and **Major Cineplex** in CentralWorld Plaza, although a few independent theaters still exist, such as the **Scala** and **Lido** in Siam Square, which occasionally show arthouse cinema or independent films. The Thai national anthem is played before the screening of every film, and everyone is expected to stand, including foreigners. Travelers can also log on to websites to get more information and film listings.

The brightly lit exterior of Major Cineplex at CentralWorld Plaza

Rooftop views over the city at twilight from the elegant Moon Bar

Bars and Nightclubs

Bangkok has an astonishing range of bars to cater to different tastes. There is the hole-in-the-wall **Ad Here the 13th**, with an in-house band that plays soulful blues music and despite being a cramped space, the crowds keep pouring in and even spill on to the sidewalk. The super-chic **Sky Bar** is where the city's glitterati sip cocktails and admire the view from the 63rd floor. Many bars feature live bands in an effort to draw in the crowds – for example, **Saxophone** offers a heady mix of jazz, blues, and reggae, while **Hard Rock Café** has bands playing covers of rock classics. Visitors can dance till late at a number of clubs such as **Sugar Club, Q Bar, DJ Station**, and **Café Democ**. Those looking for a more sophisticated and elegant environment should make their way to **Diplomat Bar, Moon Bar**, or **Syn Bar**.

Bangkok has long been known for its liberal attitude toward alternative sexual preferences, and Silom has a number of gay bars, such as the **Telephone Pub**. The main areas in Bangkok famous for their hostess and go-go bars are the infamous Patpong, Nana Plaza, and Soi Cowboy. This is the other side of nightlife in Bangkok and many people visit these spots out of curiosity. However, it is best to avoid the seamier bars in Patpong, where scams have often left many foreign visitors with empty wallets.

Posh environs for live rock music and cocktails, Hard Rock Café

DIRECTORY

Cultural Shows and Theater

Aksra Theatre
8/1 Rangnam Rd.
City Map 4 D3.
Tel 0-2677-8888.

Calypso Cabaret
Asiatique, 2194 Charoen Krung Rd.
Tel 0-2688-1415.

Joe Louis Puppet Theatre
Asiatique, 2194 Charoen Krung Rd.
Tel 0-2688-3322.

National Theater
Rachinee Rd.
City Map 2 D4.
Tel 0-2224-1342.

Sala Chalermkrung Theater
Charoen Krung Rd.
City Map 6 D1.
Tel 0-2222-0434.

Sala Rim Nam
The Mandarin Oriental, 48 Oriental Avenue.
City Map 6 F4.
Tel 0-2659-9000.

Siam Niramit
Ratchada Theater, 19 Tiam Ruammit Rd.
Tel 0-2649-9222.

Silom Village
Silom Rd.
City Map 7 A4.
Tel 0-2234-4448.

Muay Thai

Lumpinee Stadium
6 Ramintra Rd, Anusaaree, Bang Khen.
Tel 0-2252-6843.

Ratchadamnoen Stadium
Ratchadamnoen Nok Rd.
City Map 2 F4.
Tel 0-2281-4205.

Cinemas

Lido
Siam Square.
City Map 7 C1.
Tel 0-2252-6498.

Major Cineplex
1221/39 Sukhumvit.
Tel 0-2381-4855.

Paragon Cineplex
Siam Paragon, Rama I Rd.
City Map 7 C1.
Tel 0-2129-4635.

Scala
Siam Square.
City Map 7 C1.
Tel 0-2251-2861.

Bars and Nightclubs

Ad Here the 13th
13 Samsen Rd.
City Map 2 D3.
Tel 08-9769-4613

Café Democ
Ratchadamnoen Klang Rd. **City Map** 2 E4.
Tel 0-2622-2571.

Diplomat Bar
Conrad Hotel, Wireless Rd.
City Map 8 E2.
Tel 0-2690-9999.

DJ Station
Silom Soi 2. **City Map** 7 C4. **Tel** 0-2266-4029.

Hard Rock Café
Siam Square.
City Map 7 C1.
Tel 0-2658-4090.

Moon Bar
Banyan Tree Hotel, South Sathorn Rd.
City Map 8 D4.
Tel 0-2679-1200.

Q Bar
Sukhumvit Soi 11.
Tel 0-2252-3274.

Saxophone
3/8 Soi Ratchawithi, 11 Phayathai Rd.
City Map 4 E3.
Tel 0-2246-5472.

Sky Bar
63rd Floor, lebua at State Tower, Silom Rd.
City Map 7 B4.
Tel 0-2624-9999.

Sugar Club
37 Sukhumvit 11.
Tel 08-2308-3246.

Syn Bar
Swissotel Nai Lert Park, Wireless Rd.
City Map 8 E1.
Tel 0-2253-0123.

Telephone Pub
Silom Soi 4.
City Map 7 C4.
Tel 0-2266-4029.

BANGKOK STREET FINDER

Map references for *wats*, entertainment venues, and other attractions in Bangkok refer to the Street Finder maps on the following pages. Map references are also provided for hotels *(see pp294–301)* and restaurants *(see pp308–17)* in Bangkok. The first figure in the map reference indicates which Street Finder map to turn to, and the letter and number that follow

give the grid reference on that map. The lack of standard transliterations for Thai words means that street names listed here will not always match those seen on street signs. Most *thanons* (major roads) have many numbered (and sometimes named) *sois* and *troks* (minor roads and lanes) leading from them. Symbols used for sights and useful information are displayed in the key below.

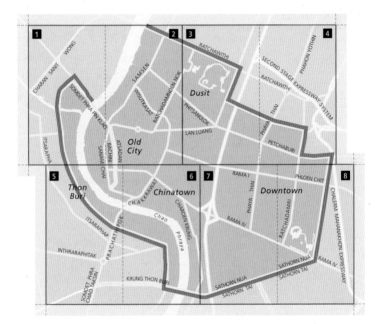

Key

Major sight	Chao Phraya Express pier	Railroad line
Place of interest	Tourist information	Skytrain route
Other building	Hospital with emergency room	Airport rail
M Subway station	Police station	Expressway
Railroad station	Wat	Pedestrian street
Skytrain station	Hindu temple	
Airport rail link	Church	
Riverboat pier	Mosque	

0 km 1
0 miles 1

Scale of Maps

0 meters 400
0 yards 400

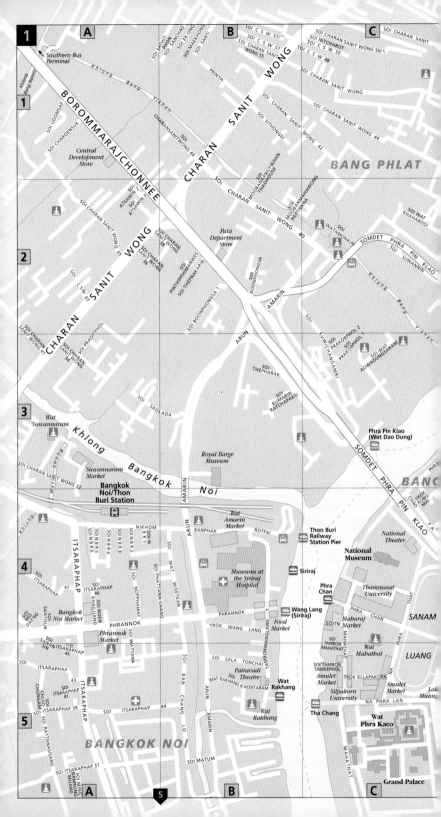

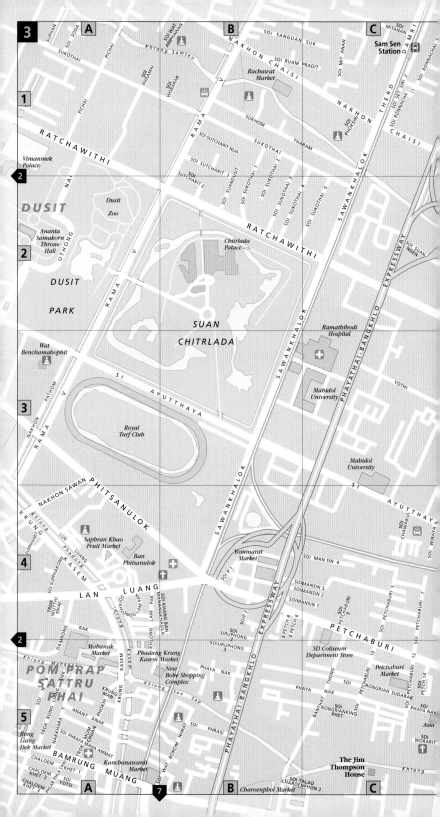

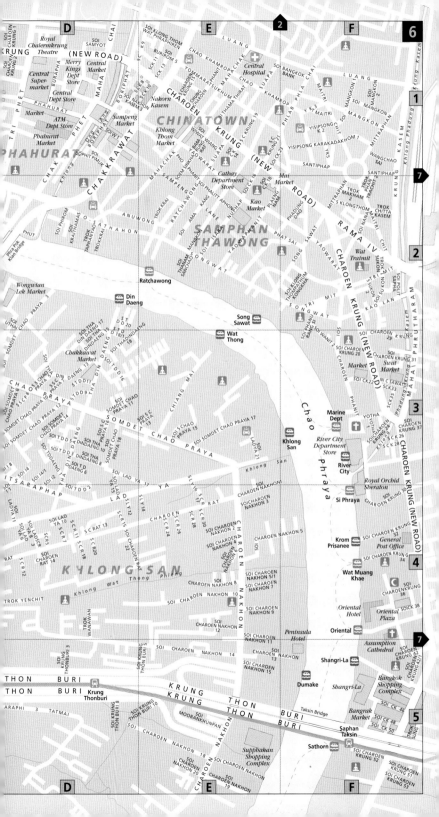

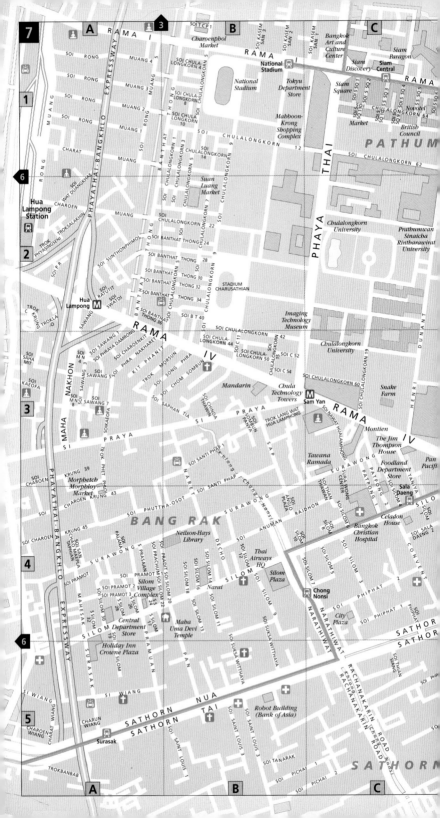

EASTERN SEABOARD

Thailand's Eastern Seaboard is a region of contrasts. While it is the nation's most developed region, with ports, oil refineries, and industrial complexes, it is also home to many picturesque and virtually untouched islands. Travelers can explore the varied dimensions of this region, which include commercial resorts, verdant archipelagos with pristine beaches of white sand, and little-visited national parks, all of which lie within easy reach of Bangkok.

Stretching from Bangkok to the Cambodian border, the Eastern Seaboard was originally a frontier between the Khmer and Sukhothai empires in the 15th century. As the Khmer Empire declined, ethnic Tais settled here attracted by the region's natural resources. They were joined by Vietnamese refugees fleeing persecution in Cambodia in the 19th century.

Industrial development in this area is aided by its proximity to Bangkok. The older occupations of gem-mining and fishing coexist with the newer oil and tourism industries. Good road links have helped in economic growth as well as tourism. However, this also has a downside, as many of the beaches have become too crowded. Visitors can head south farther away from Bangkok, to the less popular resorts such as Sri Racha, famous for its seafood, or to the stunning Nam Tok Phlio or Khao Kitchakut national parks, whose interiors shelter a wealth of flora and fauna. Pattaya continues to attract crowds of visitors to its go-go bars, restaurants, and raucous nightclubs. However, more intrepid travelers can go diving among Ko Chang's reefs or relax on its pristine beaches. Ko Samet is a popular weekend destination from Bangkok, while those interested in traditional Thai crafts can head to Chanthaburi's historical gem market to see the spectacular collection of gemstones.

With its vibrant nightlife, neon-lit streets, luxury resorts, virgin beaches, and traditional fishing villages, the Eastern Seaboard holds a wealth of attractions for a first-time visitor.

Gaudy neon signs hanging overhead along the famous Walking Street in South Pattaya

◀ Elaborate carvings on the teakwood Sanctuary of Truth temple, Pattaya

Exploring the Eastern Seaboard

Blessed with miles of idyllic beaches and warm temperatures, the Eastern Seaboard is a sun-lover's paradise. Visitors can choose to just unwind and enjoy the local food or try some of the many available watersports. Beach resorts range from busy Pattaya, with its lively nightlife, to lesser-known islands such as Ko Chang, part of a stunning national marine park. Other national parks such as Khao Kitchakut and Nam Tok Phlio are characterized by tropical forests, mountains, and waterfalls, and are home to a wealth of wildlife. The main town in the area is Chanthaburi, center of the thriving gem-mining industry.

Thai-style pavilion with landscaping at Nong Nooch Tropical Garden

Sights at a Glance

Towns and Villages

❶ Chonburi
❷ Bang Saen
❹ Sri Racha
❼ Pattaya pp108–12
❾ Chanthaburi pp118–19
⓬ Trat
⓭ Laem Ngop
⓴ Ban Hat Lek

National Parks and Zoos

❸ Khao Khieo Zoo
❺ Sri Racha Tiger Zoo
❿ Khao Kitchakut National Park
⓫ Nam Tok Phlio National Park

Beaches and Islands

❻ Ko Si Chang pp106–7
❽ Ko Samet pp114–17
⓮ Ko Chang pp122–30
⓯ Hat Sai Ngam
⓰ Hat Sai Kaew
⓱ Hat Thap Thim
⓲ Hat Samran
⓳ Hat Ban Chuen

Sunbathing on the beaches of South Pattaya

For keys to symbols *see back flap*

Getting Around

The Eastern Seaboard has a comprehensive transport system. Flights leave from U Tapao Airport, near Rayong, to Phuket and Ko Samui; Trat has a domestic airport, too. A twice-daily train service runs from Bangkok's Hua Lampong Station to Pattaya and Sri Racha. A VIP bus service links Suvarnabhumi Airport to Pattaya and Jomtien. Buses also run from Bangkok's Eastern Terminal (Ekamai) and Mo Chit Bus Terminal, near Don Muang Airport, to the main towns. For places not on bus routes, *songthaews* are available. On the mainland, transportation is provided by *songthaews* and tuk-tuks. Several ferries leave Ban Phe each day for Ko Samet. On the island, longtail boats can be hired to reach surrounding islands. Ko Chang and Ko Mak are reached by ferry from Laem Ngop, but the infrastructure on these islands is less developed.

Locals fishing on the pier at Sattahip

Key

- ═══ Expressway
- ── Major road
- ═══ Minor road
- ⋯⋯ Railway
- ▦▦▦ International border
- △ Peak

White flamingoes, one of the many bird species found at the Khao Khieo Zoo

❶ Chonburi
ชลบุรี

Road Map D1. 50 miles (80 km) SE of Bangkok. 250,000. Chonburi Water Buffalo Racing (Oct).

Capital of the Chonburi province and hub of the Eastern Seaboard's industrial zone, Chonburi has earned itself the epithet "Thailand's Detroit". The town's **Nacha Sa Thai Chue Shrine**, a four-story building located near the river pier, draws large crowds. This brightly colored Chinese temple houses several deities. The **Wat Yai Inthraram**, located near the old market, belongs to the Ayutthaya period (see pp44–5), as is evident from the architecture of its *bot* and *wihan*. The *wat's* highlight is a series of beautiful murals adorning the walls of the

bot. Another temple, **Wat Dhamma Nimitr**, which houses a 121-ft (37-m) high image of the Buddha covered with gold mosaic tiles, is also well worth a visit.

❷ Bang Saen
บางแสน

Road Map D1. 9 miles (14 km) SW of Chonburi. 25,000.

This pleasant beachfront town makes for an ideal day trip, and is a favorite destination for Thais seeking an escape from the big cities and their endless suburbs. It is not unusual to find entire families from Bangkok vacationing here; weekends are especially busy. Kids play fully clothed in the warm waters of Hat Bang Saen (Thais prize

pale skin and usually avoid sunbathing), while adults, especially women, can be found huddling under parasols on the sand, enjoying their picnics. The beach is an ideal place for a walk, particularly at dusk. This is the time when vendors start grilling seafood along the boardwalk. Deck chairs, inflatable tyres, and bicycles are available for hire.

Nong Mon market, near the center of the town, has stalls offering produce from every corner of Thailand. Highly recommended is the delectable *khao larm* – a traditional dessert made of sweet sticky rice, coconut milk, taro, bananas, and peanuts – served in a bamboo cylinder. Bang Saen does not have much of a nightlife and is quiet in the evenings – an ideal alternative to nearby Pattaya (see p108–12).

❸ Khao Khieo Zoo
สวนสัตว์เขาเขียว

Road Map D1. Off Route 344, 10 miles (16 km) SE of Chonburi. **Tel** 0-3831-8444. **Open** 8am–6pm daily; night safari till 9pm. kkopenzoo.com

This open zoo has over 50 species of birds and animals, including flamingoes, deer, gibbons, zebras, snakes, and tigers. The animals inhabit spacious enclosures, while birds are kept in a large aviary. There is a separate section from where

Vacationers relaxing under colorful umbrellas on Hat Bang Saen

visitors, including children, can buy food to feed the sheep, deer, turtles, and other animals. The night safari and zipline tours are added attractions.

Covering an area of 3 sq miles (8 sq km), a day at the zoo can mean a lot of walking. You can hire a bicycle or a golf cart to make your way around the park.

The wild marshland of **Bang Phra Reservoir**, 12 miles (19 km) south of Khao Khieo, is an ornithologist's haven, where the brown-spotted whimbrel, among other species, can be seen during the cool season (*see p40*).

Fierce competition during the Water Buffalo Racing, Chonburi

Chonburi Water Buffalo Racing

Thailand's version of the Kentucky Derby comes in the form of a three-day-long, bareback water buffalo racing competition, which takes place in October every year. Riding for trophies and prizes, the jockeys and cheering crowds take the event quite seriously, with a lot of illegal betting happening on the side. The buffaloes are whipped to get them to start sprinting, and the furious animals often throw the jockeys right off their backs. The event takes place in front of the Chonburi Town Hall and features buffalo strength competitions, a Miss Farmer beauty contest, and an outrageous, yet unique, buffalo "fashion show".

Local delicacies on display at a seafood stall, Sri Racha

➍ Sri Racha
ศรีราชา

Road Map D1. 12 miles (19 km) S of Chonburi. 🚗 20,000. 🚉 🚌 🚢
🎉 Songkran Si Maha Racha Festival (Apr 19–21). (Rice offerings to spirits).

Famous for its seafood and the spicy *nam prik si racha* (Sri Racha pepper sauce) – Thailand's answer to Tabasco sauce – this sleepy seaside town is the jumping-off point for trips to Ko Si Chang (*see pp106–7*). Several piers run off Jermjompol Road, Sri Racha's main waterfront street. At the end of each pier are breezy open-air restaurants, ideal for sampling delicious local delicacies such as *hoi nang rom* (oysters) and *hoi thot* (fried mussels) dipped in the famous fiery sauce.

➎ Sri Racha Tiger Zoo
สวนเสือศรีราชา

Road Map D1. 6 miles (10 km) SE of Sri Racha. **Tel** 0-3829-6556-8. **Open** 8am–6pm daily. 🅼 📷 ♿
📷 🆆 tigerzoo.com

With probably the largest collection of 400 Royal Bengal tigers in the world, the Sri Racha Tiger Zoo, situated around halfway between Chonburi and Pattaya, could be worth a visit, especially for families with children. However, the cramped conditions in which the animals are kept can make some visitors feel uneasy or even angry, especially as the admission price is nearly $20.

Apart from the tigers, the zoo also houses Indian elephants, birds and animals such as ostriches and wallabies, and over 10,000 crocodiles. Its accompanying circus features the record-breaking Scorpion Queen, who poses for photographs covered in deadly scorpions; and some hilarious dancing hogs.

There is also a shop selling memorabilia such as T-shirts, mugs, and wall-hangings. The zoo can be reached by tuk-tuk from Sri Racha.

A fully grown Royal Bengal tiger at the Sri Racha Tiger Zoo

❻ Ko Si Chang

เกาะสีชัง

A small and lovely island getaway, Ko Si Chang's rugged coastline has few coves or beaches, but is surrounded by clear waters that appeal to divers. The island has royal associations as it was the summer retreat of several kings of the Chakri Dynasty as well as an erstwhile French colony for a brief period in 1893 and still retains traces of this heritage. Several ruins stand testament to the history of the island, which was once a customs checkpoint for Bangkok-bound ships. Ko Si Chang today is a quiet holiday spot resplendent in its natural beauty, home to a variety of nesting seabirds and the yellow squirrel, which is endemic here.

Visitors sunbathing at Ko Si Chang's bustling beach, Hat Tham Pang

🅰 Saan Chao Paw Khao Yai

ศาลเจ้าพ่อเขาใหญ่

Open dawn to dusk daily.

An aura of mystery surrounds this colorful, multitiered Chinese temple, which dates back to the Chinese Ming Dynasty (1368–1644). It is commonly believed that a shrine was built at this site by Chinese seafarers after they spotted a light shining from a cave, which they used as a makeshift lighthouse for navigation and which kept them safe. The temple was built some time later, mainly for Chinese pilgrims. A steep flight of stairs leads up to the temple and offers picturesque views of the sea and the harbor. Visitors can also explore other caves in the area, many of which have been turned into shrines. The Chinese New Year (see p41) is the biggest festival here, drawing large crowds.

A trail from the temple leads to a small shrine housing what locals claim is the footprint of the Buddha.

🅱 Wat Tham Yai Prik

วัดถ้ำยายปริก

Tel 0-3821-6104. **Open** 8am–6pm daily. 📷

Also known as the Tham Yai Prik Vipassana Meditation Center, this monastery is built into a series of limestone caves. The monastery was discovered by the highly revered Buddhist monk, Prasit Thavaro, in 1970. He added to its existing spartan form, nearly rebuilding the entire structure along with his monks. His teachings revolved around a self-sufficient existence and inner peace that are still practiced at the monastery. The monks tend a vegetable garden set up by Thavaro that provides for the whole monastery. He died in 2007 and his body was embalmed and kept for a year before it was cremated. A relic has been preserved for devotees to pay their respects.

🅲 Hat Tham Pang

หาดถ้ำพัง

A backpackers' hangout, Hat Tham Pang is a thin and long crescent of white sand on the west coast of the island. This is Ko Si Chang's only real beach, with a few guesthouses and beachfront restaurants serving local delicacies as well as Western food. Visitors can also make use of camping facilities. This beach can be reached by motorized samlors (bicycle rickshaws) from the pier. The trip takes 30 minutes and costs around 80 baht.

Deck chairs, umbrellas, kayaks, and snorkeling gear can be easily hired on this beach. The clear waters are good for snorkeling, but enthusiasts usually head south for a more dazzling array of corals.

Devotee offering prayers at the temple of Saan Chao Paw Khao Yai

🏛 Palace of Rama V

วังรัชกาลที่ห้า

Open 9am–5pm daily.

This 19th-century palace, also known as Phra Chutathut Ratchasathan, has undergone extensive renovations. It was designed by Rama V (1868–1910), who used it as a sanctuary for members of the royal family in summer. The site is of particular interest to visitors who have seen the grand Vimanmek Mansion *(see p75)* in Bangkok. The structure was originally located at this site until it was moved, in 1901, to Dusit Park.

Surrounded by lotus ponds and frangipani trees, a visit to the palace grounds can take up to half a day. Four of the restored villas are used for a display themed around the king's association with Ko Si Chang, and one of them also houses a convenient coffee shop. Rama V's birthday is celebrated here in a grand manner with a *son et lumière* show and a beauty pageant showcasing period fashions.

🏯 Wat Atsadang

วัดอัษฎางค์

Open dawn to dusk daily.

Located on top of a hill, close to the ruins of the Palace of Rama V, is Wat Atsadang with its distinctive white *chedi*. The temple is best explored on foot while exploring the palace ruins. The *wat*, once favored by Rama V for meditation practice, is quite unusual in its architecture. It has a Sri Lankan-style round *chedi*, while the *bot* and the pagoda are constructed in European style with stained-glass windows.

The ornate gateway of the Palace of Rama V at Ko Si Chang

Tourist speedboat anchored in the waters off Hat Sai Kaew

🚻 Hat Sai Kaew

หาดทรายแก้ว

Also known as Crystal Beach, Hat Sai Kaew is a remote beach on the island's east coast. Best reached by *samlors* from the pier, the beach is an ideal picnic spot.

VISITORS' CHECKLIST

Practical Information
Road Map D1. 8 miles (13 km) W of Sri Racha. 🚌 6,000. 🛈 TAT, Pattaya (0-3842-7667). 🎉 Chinese New Year (Jan–Feb); Rama V Festival (Sep).

Transport
🚤 from Sri Racha.

A handful of restaurants and shops have sprung up in recent times along with a few other facilities. These include Thai massages as well as fresh seafood barbecued right on the beach. Hat Sai Kaew is an ideal snorkeling base for the tiny islands near the southern tip of the island. On a calm day, snorkelers can follow the rocky coastline southward to view the rich coral reefs teeming with a variety of marine animals.

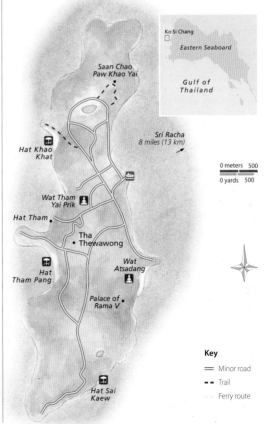

Ko Si Chang
Eastern Seaboard

Gulf of Thailand

Saan Chao Paw Khao Yai

Hat Khao Khat

Sri Racha
8 miles (13 km)

0 meters 500
0 yards 500

Wat Tham Yai Prik

Hat Tham

Tha Thewawong

Hat Tham Pang

Wat Atsadang

Palace of Rama V

Hat Sai Kaew

Key

═══ Minor road

▬ ▬ Trail

- - - Ferry route

For keys to symbols see back flap

⑦ Pattaya

พัทยา

Originally a quiet fishing village, Pattaya was transformed in the 1960s and 1970s by the arrival of US servicemen on R&R (Rest and Recreation) during the Vietnam War. Its subsequent reputation was built on the sex trade, and the industry continues to thrive; but today Pattaya has much more to offer. With more than 5 million visitors a year, it has emerged as Thailand's premier resort. Upscale hotels, restaurants, theme parks, adventure sports, numerous golf courses, and cabaret shows are just a few of its many attractions. A watersport enthusiast's haven, windsurfing and kiteboarding are especially popular in Pattaya.

Jet skis parked along Hat Pattaya as their riders take a break

🚌 Hat Pattaya

หาดพัทยา

A perfect tropical paradise at one time, Hat Pattaya is barely recognizable today. This 2-mile (3-km) long beach is usually packed with sunbathers, especially on the weekends. Having earned a seedy reputation and the nickname "Patpong by the Sea," it is more frequented by youngsters, who spend time in go-go clubs, bars, and massage parlors, than vacationing families. Among Hat Pattaya's most prominent features, the ever-popular transvestite shows have venues mainly at the northern end of the beach.

The Beach Road, which runs along the length of Hat Pattaya, overflows with food joints, bars, and shopping malls.

Visitors can try a variety of watersports such as parasailing, kayaking, and scuba diving, besides other activities such as golf and tennis.

🗿 Sanctuary of Truth

ปราสาทสัจธรรม

206/2 Moo 5, Naklua Soi 12, Pattaya-Naklua Rd. **Tel** 0-3836-7229. **Open** 8am–6pm daily.

🌐 sanctuaryoftruth.com

This magnificent teakwood temple stands 345 ft (105 m) high on the shoreline between Hat Pattaya and Ao Naklua. Every square inch of its architecture is carved with intricate figures reminiscent of Cambodian, Hindu, Buddhist, Chinese, and Thai religion and

Carved figure, Sanctuary of Truth

mythology. The temple complex hosts a variety of other activities such as dolphin training, horseback riding, and speedboat excursions. Visitors can also watch classical Thai dance performances while dining.

Ao Naklua

อ่าวนาเกลือ

2 miles (3 km) N of Hat Pattaya. 🏊 📷

With fishermen setting out from the pier every morning and returning at sundown with the day's catch, Ao Naklua, or Naklua Bay, has still managed to preserve the erstwhile charm of

For keys to symbols *see back flap*

Pattaya. Many of the town's local workers live by Ao Naklua, and their accommodations lend the area an authentic rural atmosphere, although several hotels and condominiums are beginning to crowd the beach. Fishing tackle is available on Soi Photisan for those who want to spend a day on the pier. Fresh seafood can also be bought daily at the Naklua market, next to Lan Pho Park. Devoid of the raunchiness of Hat Pattaya, it is a better option for families, with little traffic on the sea, and less noise and pollution.

Miniature replica of Bangkok's famous Wat Arun at Mini Siam

🔲 Mini Siam

มินิสยาม

387 Moo 6, Sukhumvit Rd. **Tel** 0-3872-7333. **Open** 7am–10pm daily. 🔲 🔲
🔲 **W** minisiam.com

First opened in 1986 as a research project and continually growing, this interesting theme park is divided into Mini Siam and Mini Europe. The park displays miniature models of renowned monuments and structures such as Bangkok's Grand Palace, the Sydney Opera House, Paris's Eiffel Tower, the Colosseum, and Cambodia's Angkor Wat. Each of these models has been built on a scale of 1:25 with the Democracy Monument in Bangkok being the first edifice to be replicated. Along with the other activities, including weddings, that take place in Mini Siam, there are daily traditional Thai dance shows. Quite popular with visitors to Pattaya, this theme park also has several souvenir shops nearby.

VISITORS' CHECKLIST

Practical Information
Road Map D1. 37 miles (60 km) S of Chonburi. 150,000. 🛈 TAT, 609 Moo 10, Pratamnak Rd, Pattaya (0-3842-7667). 🎵 Pattaya Music Festival (Mar 20–22); Pattaya Festival (mid-Apr, during Songkran). **W** pattayacity.com

Transport
🚌 🚍 🚐 🚤

Million Years Stone Park and Crocodile Farm

อุทยานหินล้านปีและฟาร์มจระเข้

22/1 Moo 1, Nongplalai, Banglamung. **Tel** 0-3824-9347–9. **Open** 8am–6:30pm daily. 🔲 🔲 🔲
W thaistonepark.org

Also known as Uttayan Hin Laan Pee, the Million Years Stone Park and Crocodile Farm features an eclectic mix of curiosities. Among the major attractions are petrified trees over a million years old, bonsai, rocks shaped like animals, gigantic catfish, and hundreds of crocodiles. It also boasts of having the largest artificial waterfall in Thailand.

🔲 Pattaya Elephant Village

หมู่บ้านช้างพัทยา

48/120 Moo 7, Tambon Nong Prue. **Tel** 0-3824-9818. **Open** 9am–5pm daily. 🔲 🔲 🔲 🔲
W elephant-village-pattaya.com

Locally known as Mooban Chang, Pattaya Elephant Village is more of a theme park than a zoo. Visitors get a chance to see elephants paint, play sports, and bathe. The admission fee includes lunch and rafting on the river.

Pattaya Town Center

① Hat Pattaya
② Sanctuary of Truth
③ Ao Naklua
④ Mini Siam
⑤ Million Years Stone Park and Crocodile Farm
⑥ Pattaya Elephant Village
⑦ Hat Jomtien
⑧ Pattaya Park Beach Resort
⑨ Underwater World
⑩ South Pattaya
⑪ Ripley's Believe It or Not

Curiously shaped stones at the Million Years Stone Park

Keen anglers taking a speedboat to catch game fish, Hat Jomtien

🚤 Hat Jomtien
หาดจอมเทียน

1 mile (2 km) S of Hat Pattaya.

Thailand's premier spot for windsurfing and kiteboarding, this 9-mile (14-km) long beach is generally abuzz with visitors. At its northern end lies Hat Dongtan, dominated by high-rise apartments and popular with gay and lesbian travelers. An ideal place for watersport enthusiasts, waterskiing and paragliding are among the leading activities on the beach.

Scuba diving and snorkeling trips set out from the shore, as do jet skis and kayaks. Speedboats are available for game-fishing trips too. Other activities include target shooting, horseback riding, tennis, and golf. Hat Jomtien also has several banana boats that can be hired to take children to and from the shore.

The southern end of the beach, however, is devoid of a lot of this activity and is a preferred spot for those who want to keep away from the crowds, noise, and excitement at the northern end.

Hat Jomtien is vibrant at night and a number of beer and go-go bars attract crowds in large numbers. A host of international restaurants, seafood shacks, Irish pubs, and German beer bars also vie for visitors' attention.

🏨 Pattaya Park Beach Resort
พัทยาปาร์คบีชรีสอร์ท

345, Hat Jomtien. **Tel** 0-3825-1201–8.
🚤 🚲 **W** pattayapark.com
Pattaya Park Funny Land:
Open 11am–10pm daily.

Located at the northern end of Hat Jomtien, Pattaya Park Beach Resort is the perfect destination for children. While it has a private shopping arcade and various dining facilities, its main appeal is the host of varied indoor activities. Kids delight in the whirlpools and waterslides, while adults busy themselves in swimming pools, a fitness center, sauna, jogging track, or

cable-pulled water ski. A center within the resort has scuba diving classes for beginners. Those less interested in strenuous physical activities can head for the snooker club.

Pattaya Tower, the highest point not only of the resort but in the whole of Pattaya, offers splendid views – across Pattaya to the north and Ao Jomtien to the south – from the Apex Observation Point on the 55th floor. Visitors can also use the tower for bungee jumping or taking a ride in the sky shuttle or speed shuttle. It has three different revolving restaurants on the 52nd, 53rd, and 54th floors.

Pattaya Park Funny Land, also designed to entertain children, boasts a fantastic range of rollercoaster rides, monorail, a musical carousel, and a bumper car ride.

🐠 Underwater World
อันเดอร์วอเตอร์เวิลด์

22/22 Moo 11, Sukhumvit Rd, Banglamung. **Tel** 0-3875-6879.
Open 9am–6pm daily. 🚤 🚲 📷
W underwaterworldpattaya.com

An excellent showcase for the rich and varied marine life in the region with over 200 species of marine animals, Underwater World is an impressive aquarium. Adults and children alike will love this place. Visitors begin their tour from the beach on the edge of the sea and are gradually taken underground, passing a variety of corals and other marine life on the way. Farther below is a 328-ft (100-m) long tunnel made of fiberglass

Visitors admiring the marine life visible from the large fiberglass tunnels, Underwater World

For hotels and restaurants in this region see pp295–7 and pp310–12

Neon signs drawing crowds to seafood restaurants and go-go bars, Walking Street, South Pattaya

through which various kinds of colorful fish, sea horses, turtles, sharks, corals, rays, and crustaceans can be viewed. Visitors can also go scuba diving in the coral reef tank or with the rays and sharks, for an additional fee.

Gold-painted Big Buddha, 300 ft (91 m) above Pattaya's coastline

South Pattaya
พัทยาใต้
W pattaya-bars.net

The area between Pattaya Beach Road and South Pattaya Road is crowded with hundreds of bars, nightclubs, and massage parlors. It is located about half a mile (1 km) from Hat Pattaya, in the *sois* (lanes) south of Soi 13 – between Soi 13/1 and Soi 13/5 – an area better known as Pattayaland. This zone is all about the sex trade. Hundreds of men, women, and *kathoey* or transvestites can be found crowding the bars and night-clubs, making the atmosphere in this part of Pattaya like the

world's largest bachelor party. Soi 3 is also known as Boyztown and is the center of the Pattaya gay scene, with several nightclubs and beer bars.

A half-mile (1 km) stretch of road to the south of Pattaya Beach Road is known as **Walking Street**. Vehicles are prohibited from entering this stretch from 7pm onward. Thronged by sex workers, it has open-air bars, fast food joints, private massage parlors, go-go bars, nightclubs, and cabaret shows in abundance.

For those looking for a more spiritual experience, to the south, on Buddha Hill, lies Pattaya Fitness Park with a large golden statue of the Buddha, called the **Big Buddha**. Visitors come to the park to admire this magnificent image as well as several other smaller images of the Buddha dotting the park.

🎯 Ripley's Believe It or Not
พิพิธภัณฑ์ริปลีส์
3rd floor, Royal Garden Plaza, 218 Moo 10, Beach Rd. **Tel** 0-3871-0294. **Open** 11am–11pm daily. 🎬 📷 in Cinema and Haunted House. 📷
W ripleysthailand.com

One of Pattaya's most popular attractions, Ripley's Believe It or Not features 10 theme galleries and over 300 extraordinary exhibits. These include a real shrunken head, a mask made from human skin, and an astonishing model of the *Titanic* made from 1 million matchsticks. The exterior of the building appears to be the site of a plane crash, with a giant plane nose-diving into its roof. Apart from the weird and wacky collection of trivia in the museum, there is a haunted house, a 4-D simulator cinema, an infinity maze, and various other activities for children.

Building exterior with "crashed" fighter plane, Ripley's Believe It or Not

Around Pattaya

There is a lot to see and do around Pattaya, especially on the coastal road south toward Sattahip and among the numerous offshore islands. Getting around independently is very easy as jeeps, motorcycles, and bicycles are readily available for hire. Most activities are aimed squarely at vacationers on package tours and families, with novelties and attractions imported from across Thailand. There are also plenty of sporting opportunities ranging from watersports to golfing.

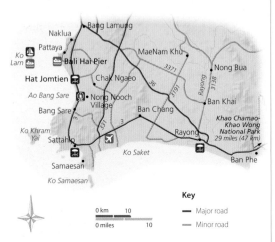

Key

0 km   10
0 miles   10

━━ Major road
━━ Minor road

of orchids. A great place for an educational trip, there are also several options for entertainment such as Thai boxing bouts and a Thai cultural show featuring traditional dance and music. Visitors can also make use of the swimming pool and picnic area. Pickups, directly from visitors' hotels in Pattaya, are available.

Sattahip

สัตหีบ
21 miles (33 km) S of Pattaya.
Once a Thai naval base which housed US servicemen during the Vietnam War, Sattahip today is best known for a small sea turtle conservation center located here. Visitors usually pass through Sattahip en route to Ko Samet, Rayong, or Ko Chang from Pattaya. A stopover at the sprawling floating market on Highway 3 is worthwhile. With around 80 boats selling various kinds of goods, it is a great place to pick up souvenirs.

Rayong

ระยอง
108 miles (174 km) SE of Pattaya.
Popular for weekend trips from Bangkok, Rayong is well-known for its cool breezes and great seafood. The beaches along the coast – Ban Phe, Suan Son, and Suan Wang Kaew – have plenty of hotels overlooking the sea. There are good camping and diving facilities at Ko Talu, located across from Suan Wang Kaew. Located 29 miles (47 km) east of Rayong, **Khao Chamao-Khao Wong National Park** is a scenic spot with waterfalls, caves, cliffs, and ponds.

Ko Larn

เกาะล้าน
5 miles (8 km) W of Pattaya. 🚤 📷
🚢 from Bali Hai Pier, Pattaya.
🌐 kohlarn.com

A tiny island about 2 miles (3 km) long and 1 mile (2 km) wide, Ko Larn is ringed by six picturesque little coves and offers fantastic offshore coral reefs. For its size, the island offers an amazing variety of activities; from tours in a semi-submerged glass-bottomed boat from which passengers can view coral and fish, to jet-skiing, parasailing, banana boat rides, scuba diving, snorkeling, fishing, and target shooting.

Visitors can get around Ko Larn on pickup truck taxis, motorcycle taxis, or rented motorcycles. Each beach has guesthouses, restaurants, shops, and tourist facilities. If traveling in a small group, visitors can also hire a speedboat for a few hundred baht from Pattaya.

🌿 Nong Nooch Village

สวนนงนุช
9 miles (15 km) S of Pattaya.
Tel 0-3842-9321.
Open 8am–6pm daily. 🚤 📷
🌐 nongnoochtropicalgarden.com

Essentially a theme park, Nong Nooch Village (pronounced "Nong Noot" in Thai) offers examples of Thai agriculture, Thai-style houses, a small zoo, a butterfly farm, and a beautiful botanical garden with a variety

French-style garden with beautiful landscaping at Nong Nooch Village

For keys to symbols see back flap

Elephants in Thailand

The largest land animal currently living in Asia, the elephant was first mentioned centuries ago in Hindu and Buddhist texts. They have long played a significant spiritual role in Thailand, enjoying a higher status than any other animal. Unfortunately, the elephant has become increasingly threatened by human encroachment on its habitat and, to a lesser extent, by poaching. The introduction of bulldozers and other heavy equipment has tended to make the legendary power of the elephant redundant, and a ban on most commercial logging in 1989 led to a sharp decline in the number of captive elephants. Today, their numbers in the wild are estimated to be just 1,000 to 2,000.

Popular as a means of transport, elephants were used to carry both heavy loads such as teak logs as well as people, with the *mahout* sitting astride the elephant's neck.

Elephants in History

Elephants were used in the construction of wats, clearing of forests, and logging. Throughout Thai history, they were also a symbol of prestige for Thai kings – the more elephants a king had, the more powerful he was.

White elephants, in fact albinos, have traditionally been attributed semi-divine status and are considered to be the property of the king. From 1855 to 1916, the Thai national flag depicted a white elephant on a red background.

Elephants were used in war, with Thai and Burmese rulers in particular choosing to enter the battlefield on elephant back.

Elephants Today

Increasingly endangered in Thailand today, elephants are more likely to be seen in sanctuaries and camps.

Wild elephants today are under the protection of only a few national parks.

Washing the elephants, and even bathing with them at camps such as Ban Kwan on Ko Chang *(see p123)*, is popular with visitors.

Elephant motifs are often engraved by Thai silversmiths on decorative objects.

❶ Ko Samet

เกาะเสม็ด

Located off the Rayong Coast, Ko Samet is blessed with clear blue waters and crystalline sands and is popular with foreign visitors and Thais alike. The island derives its name from the evergreen, flower-bearing Cajeput trees – *Samet* is the Thai word for Cajeput – found throughout the island. Despite attaining National Park status in 1981, Ko Samet has faced quite a bit of development. Its 5-mile (8-km) long eastern shore is a string of beautiful, white sand beaches populated with restaurants and bars. The western side of the island is less crowded, while the narrow interior is wild, undeveloped, and riddled with trails, making it ideal for exploring the flora and fauna.

Eastern Seaboard

Ban Phe · □ Ko Samet

Gulf of Thailand

Locator map

☐ Area illustrated

Ban Phe
4 miles (6 km) ↑

Ferries from Ban Phe on the mainland can also bring visitors directly to the island's west coast.

★ **Ao Phrao**
Located away from the bustle of the east coast, Ao Phrao is one of the quietest bays on Ko Samet and appeals to visitors who wish to soak up the natural beauty and enjoy the sun, sand, and sea.

Ao Wong Deuan
Home to the second-longest beach on the island, Ao Wong Deuan is enduringly popular with both Thais and foreigners. It offers a wide range of facilities including exotic seafood restaurants, bars, and a lively nightlife.

Ao Thia

Ao Wai
This bay shelters a quiet and pretty beach located south of all the action at Hat Sai Kaew. Shaded by coconut palms, Ao Wai is dominated by the Samet Ville Resort, offering dining, entertainment, and Thai massages.

*Ao Kui
Na Nai*

Ao Kui Na Nok

Laem Khut

Ao Karang

Ao Toei

Ko Chan

For hotels and restaurants in this region see pp295–7 and pp310–12

Na Dan
The small fishing town of Na Dan is the island's main ferry port. As its largest settlement, the town also functions as the de facto capital.

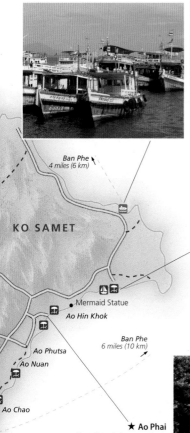

Ban Phe
4 miles (6 km)

KO SAMET

Mermaid Statue
Ao Hin Khok

Ban Phe
6 miles (10 km)

Ao Phutsa
Ao Nuan

Ao Chao

★ Hat Sai Kaew
A gorgeous stretch of white sand, Hat Sai Kaew is the longest and most developed beach on the island, offering watersports such as water-skiing, windsurfing, and parasailing.

★ Ao Phai
A small and lovely bay, Ao Phai's beach is rather busy with many restaurants and cafés. Popular with backpackers and sunbathers, the beach serves as a starting point for exploring trails across the island.

0 meters	750
0 yards	750

The Poetry of Sunthorn Phu

Sunthorn Phu (1786–1855) is Thailand's most respected poet. His long, lyrical verses made him a favorite of the Thai kings. The epic *Phra Aphaimani*, Sunthorn Phu's first poem, was inspired by beautiful Ko Samet, which he adopted as his home. The poem tells the story of a prince, Aphaimani, who is banished to an underwater kingdom ruled by a giantess. Helped by a mermaid, Phra Aphaimani escapes and then defeats the giantess by playing his magic flute which puts her to sleep. The prince is subsequently betrothed to a beautiful princess.

Statue on Ko Samet depicting characters from *Phra Aphaimani*

Key
==== Minor road
-- Trail
-- Ferry route

For keys to symbols *see back flap*

Exploring Ko Samet

A low-lying sliver of land, Ko Samet is easily accessible on a weekend trip from Bangkok. Its location has led to steady development over the years and, despite being a protected area, the island risks becoming overcrowded during peak season. Also known as Ko Kaew Phitsadan, or Magic Crystal Island, this place was immortalized in Sunthorn Phu's romantic epic *Phra Aphaimani*. Ko Samet offers visitors an idyllic tropical setting along with a lively nightlife as well as secluded beaches. Prices at restaurants and hotels, however, increase on busy weekends. Foreign visitors are required to pay an admission fee at the ferry port of Na Dan before venturing farther into the island.

Sailing, kayaking, and other watersports at Hat Sai Kaew

Shrine with offerings dedicated to Sage Pu Dam, Na Dan

🚢 Na Dan

หน้าด่าน

4 miles (6 km) S of Ban Phe. 🚤 📷

A small but fairly busy pier in the northeastern part of the island, Na Dan is the entry point into Ko Samet and is used by commercial as well as privately owned speedboats and ferries.

Na Dan is a nondescript fishing settlement with a clinic, a few Internet cafés, ATMs, and a market. It offers basic accommodations, but very few travelers actually stay here. Close to the pier is a shrine dedicated to Pu Dam, a venerated holy man – also known as Grandfather Black – who lived on this idyllic island. Communal taxis leave from Na Dan's pier to Ko Samet's many beaches.

🏖 Ao Phrao

อ่าวพร้าว

1 mile (2 km) SW of Na Dan.

The narrow white beach at Ao Phrao, or Paradise Bay, is interspersed with trees and a lush mountainous background. It was badly affected by an oil spill in July 2013, though it has now recovered.

This is the only developed beach on the rocky west coast of Ko Samet. Apart from a few guesthouses, Ao Phrao also has two luxury resorts with swimming pools and spas. There is a PADI center for those interested in diving.

However, this is the extent of facilities on this rather peaceful beach. Visitors can hire taxis at Na Dan or take a boat from the mainland.

🏖 Hat Sai Kaew

หาดทรายแก้ว

📷📷

One of the most popular beaches in Thailand, especially busy with weekend visitors from Bangkok, Hat Sai Kaew is a beautiful crescent of crisp, white sand located just half a mile (1 km) southeast of Na Dan.

The 2-mile (3-km) stretch is lined with bungalows, guesthouses, bars, restaurants, and shops. Although the sea still looks pristine, the beach has lost some of its charm due to overcrowding. The large number of beach activities often make it difficult to find a quiet spot.

Hat Sai Kaew is a revelers' beach with many nightclubs and bars that stay open till dawn. Visitors can sign up for

Quiet beach at Ao Phrao backed by a thickly forested hillside

PADI authorised diving courses as well as indulge in a plethora of watersports such as jet-skiing, banana boat rides, water-skiing, snorkeling, and scuba trips.

Ao Hin Khok

อ่าวหินกก

A short distance from Hat Sai Kaew and separated by a rocky hill, the beach at Ao Hin Khok is dominated by the statue of a prince and a mermaid – the central characters in *Phra Aphaimani* written by Sunthorn Phu. A backpackers' haven, the beach is lined with rows of small huts, basic restaurants, and loud neon-lit bars. There is also a gymnasium, and a Thai boxing ring. Typical evening entertainment includes fire juggling.

Ao Phai

อ่าวไผ่

Located just half a mile (1 km) southwest of Hat Sai Kaew, Ao Phai is a famous party zone attracting partygoers from all over the island. The beach hosts parties for just about any reason, but full moon celebrations tend to go over the top. It is a popular rendezvous for young backpackers. Visitors can also mingle with the local Thais during these celebrations.

Ao Phai has some small shops and mid-range hotels, but it is the nightly revelry that draws crowds.

Ao Nuan

อ่าวนวล

2 miles (3 km) SW of Hat Sai Kaew.

Just south of the commercial beaches of Hat Sai Kaew and Ao Phai are a couple of small secluded coves for those who want to get away from the madding crowds.

Ao Nuan is a little rocky for swimming, but the stretch of sand is set amid unspoiled nature. The beach hut accommodations are very basic, but visitors can enjoy the excellent restaurant or spend evenings under a beautiful canopy of stars unhindered by other lights. Just north of Ao Nuan is the

Visitors enjoying beers at an open-air beach restaurant, Ao Hin Khok

even quieter **Ao Phutsa**, also known as Ao Tubtim. Devoid of vendors and loud music, it is very peaceful.

Five minutes south of Ao Nuan is **Ao Cho**, which draws weekend crowds. It has basic and upscale accommodations as well as a small pier ideal for fishing and snorkeling.

Ao Wong Deuan

อ่าววงเดือน

2 miles (3 km) SW of Hat Sai Kaew.

A horseshoe-shaped cove in the middle of the east coast, Ao Wong Deuan is serviced by ferries from the mainland. It is popular with holiday-makers on package tours and Thai families, and is more upscale than Hat Sai Kaew.

A designated lunch stop for day-trippers, the beach at Ao Wong Deuan is lined with restaurants and bars and has a lively nightlife. It also offers a

wide range of watersports. The central part of the beach is often covered at high tide and visitors should be careful.

Ao Wai

อ่าวหวาย

3 miles (5 km) SW of Hat Sai Kaew.

Heading farther south along the east coast, the beaches become quieter and less commercial. Ao Wai is a good option for mid-range accommodations, intimate dining, and a less raucous nightlife. The soft sandy beach is partially shaded and has a couple of shops with Internet access.

The beach is also close to the southern coves of Ao Kui Na Nai, and Ao Khut. Located offshore, the secluded mini island of Ko Chan has an interesting underwater landscape, ideal for snorkeling.

Colorful kayaks for hire at Ao Phai

❾ Chanthaburi

จันทบุรี

Surrounded by acres of chili and rubber plantations, Chanthaburi, which means City of the Moon, is one of Thailand's most charming towns and the capital of the Chanthaburi province. King Taksin (r.1768–82) is the most revered monarch here with several shrines and monuments that commemorate his famous victory over the Burmese. The town has a diverse ethnic population and strong historical and cultural links with both France and Vietnam due to its proximity to the former French Indochina. A gem-trading center since the 15th century, Chanthaburi is a prosperous city and a significant part of the present-day economy.

Ornate golden shrine inside the Chanthaburi Cathedral

Vietnamese-style houses on stilts along Chanthaburi River

Thailand's largest Christian edifice. Also known as the Church of the Immaculate Conception, this structure is designed in the French Provincial style and was built by Christian missionaries in the 18th century. Since then it has been renovated a number of times, especially due to the influx of many Vietnamese Christians. Some of the stained-glass windows in the church date from before its 19th-century restoration.

Gem Market

ตลาดพลอย

Thanon Sri Chan-Trok Kachang.
Famous as a gem center for more than five centuries, Chanthaburi has drawn prospectors, dealers, traders, and adventurers to its gem markets throughout history. The gem market, locally known as *talat phloi*, is located on the banks of the Chanthaburi River. Known for its natural wealth of sapphires and rubies, Chanthaburi continues to be an important center of this trade despite the exhaustion of its natural resources. Today, most stones are brought from areas along the Cambodian frontier, yet the market continues to be famous for the workmanship of its gem cutters. All kinds of precious and semi-precious stones are bought and sold for jewelry production. There is a range of rare gems and beads from all over Southeast Asia and

even as far as Madagascar. Visitors can go to the market to see dealers and prospectors doing business. The best gem stores are along Trok Kachang and Thanon Sri Chan. This market is at its busiest on weekends.

🏛 Chanthaburi Cathedral

โบสถ์จันทบุรี

Chanthanimit Rd.
Located just across the river, east of the Gem Market, is Chanthaburi Cathedral,

Gem dealer examining some precious stones at the Gem Market

Vietnamese Quarter

ตลาดเวียดนาม

Thanon Rim Nam.
Extending along the west bank of Chanthaburi River, and a short distance from the Gem Market, the Vietnamese Quarter is the most interesting part of Chanthaburi. The Vietnamese have migrated to Thailand for over a century, initially to avoid persecution and later as political refugees.

This quarter has a distinct flavor, which is evident in its architecture and cuisine. The houses along Thanon Rim Nam are lovely old structures made out of bamboo or wood and standing on stilts. They follow the style of Vietnamese tube architecture and are usually narrow in width, with the living quarters extending along the building's depth.

The nearby market offers a whole array of delicious Vietnamese snacks. Great stacks of Vietnamese spring roll

Thailand's Vietnamese

The Vietnamese came to Thailand in a three-part exodus – refugees escaping French colonial rule in the 19th century, Vietnamese Catholics fleeing the communist regime in the 1950s, and migrants who left after the collapse of the Southern regime in 1975. The Thais mistrusted them because of an age-old rivalry and the Vietnamese were constantly displaced because of wars. However, over time, this community has been assimilated into the country's diverse ethnic fabric, bringing with them distinct elements of their own culture.

Vietnamese farmer in rice fields

wrappers and local desserts offer appetizing alternatives to traditional Thai fare. Today, there are few immigrants who speak the Vietnamese language, and the process of integration into Thai society is well advanced.

🔲 King Taksin Park
สวนพระเจ้าตากสิน
Thanon Leap Noen.
A lush, open space located half a mile (1 km) west of the Gem Market, King Taksin Park is a popular spot with the citizens of Chanthaburi for walks or early morning exercises. The main park area is divided by two lakes filled with a variety of fish. The park is dominated by a great bronze statue of King Taksin in a heroic pose on the battlefield.

This iconic image also figures on the 20-baht note. Tall trees providing shade make this an excellent place for a picnic or a stroll. Visitors can also sample some of the tropical fruits for which Chanthaburi is famous.

VISITORS' CHECKLIST

Practical Information
Road Map E2. 113 miles (182 km) SE of Pattaya. 🏠 50,000. 🚉 TAT Rayong (0-3865-5420). 🛒 daily. 🎪 Fruit Festival (May/Jun).

Transport
🚌

King Taksin Shrine
ศาลพระเจ้าตากสิน
Tha Luang Road.
A nonagonal structure with a helmet-shaped roof, King Taksin Shrine is a curious structure. Constructed in 1920, the shrine houses a statue of the king that is revered by locals. Every year on December 28, a ceremony is held commemorating Taksin's accession to the throne.

Helmets and weaponry placed as offerings at King Taksin's Shrine

Chanthaburi Town Center

① Gem Market
② Chanthaburi Cathedral
③ Vietnamese Quarter
④ King Taksin Park

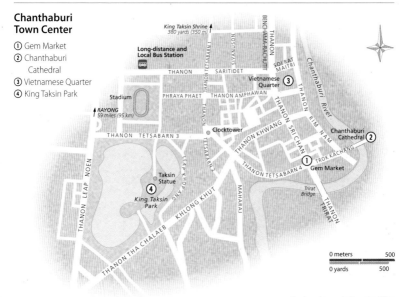

For keys to symbols *see back flap*

⑩ Khao Kitchakut National Park
อุทยานแห่งชาติเขาคิชฌกูฏ

Road Map E1. Park HQ off Hwy 3249, 15 miles (24 km) NE of Chanthaburi. 🚐 Chanthaburi, then *songthaew*. ℹ️ Park HQ (0-3945-2074). 🚻

Covering an area of about 23 sq miles (60 sq km), Khao Kitchakut National Park is one of Thailand's smallest national parks and encompasses Khao Kitchakut, a granite mountain just over 3,300 ft (1,006 m) high. The park's best-known site, the 13-tier **Krathing Waterfall**, lies near the park headquarters. From here, visitors can follow an easy trail to the mountain's peak.

More ambitious hikers and a large number of pilgrims make the arduous 4-hour climb to the summit of the impressive Phrabat mountain, 10 miles (16 km) from the park headquarters. This mountain is famous not only for an impression of the Buddha's footprint etched in granite, but also for its strange collection of natural rock formations shaped like an elephant, a large turtle, a pagoda, and a monk's bowl.

Khao Kitchakut is located near the much larger, but less visited, **Khao Soi Dao Wildlife Sanctuary**, which covers about 290 sq miles (751 sq km). Both protected areas enclose some of the last surviving tracts of a once-great lowland forest. They are vital to the economy of the region as important

water reservoirs and provide protection to many endangered species. These include sun bears, spot-bellied eagle owls, spiny-breasted giant frogs, and binturongs. The upland forests of Khao Soi Dao provide a habitat for the tree-dwelling pileated gibbon.

🦎 Khao Soi Dao Wildlife Sanctuary
Park HQ off Hwy 317, 16 miles (26 km) N of Chanthaburi. 🚐 Chanthaburi, then *songthaew*. 🚻

Phlio Waterfall, sourced from an underground stream

⑪ Nam Tok Phlio National Park
อุทยานแห่งชาติน้ำตกพลิ้ว

Road Map E2. Park HQ off Hwy 3, 9 miles (14 km) SE of Chanthaburi. 🚐 Chanthaburi, then *songthaew*. ℹ️ Park HQ (0-3943-4528); Forestry Dept (0-2562-0760) for bungalow bookings. 🚻 🌐 **dnp.go.th**

Immensely popular with Thais, this 52-sq mile (135-sq km) park contains some of Thailand's richest rain forest. It is also a haven for wildlife, with over 156 species of birds and 32 species of mammals including the Asiatic black bear, tiger, leopard, barking deer, and macaque. The park's other attractions are its pretty waterfalls – the most impressive being **Phlio Waterfall**. Nearby are two *chedis* – the Alongkon *chedi* and the 10-ft (3-m) high pyramid-shaped *chedi* Phra Nang Reua Lom, built by Rama V (r.1868–1910) in honor of Queen Sunantha, who died by drowning in the Chao Phraya river at Bang Pa-in in 1876.

A tough hike leads to the 66 ft (20 m) roaring Trok Nong Falls and the forest-encircled Klang Waterfall.

One of the 13 tiers of the Krathing Waterfall, crossed by a bridge

⓬ Trat

ตราด

Road Map E2. 36 miles (58 km) SE of Chanthaburi. 🚹 72,000. 🚌 🚍 𝑖 TAT, Trat (0-3959-7259-60). 🛥 daily. 🛎 Rakham Fruit Fair (May–Jun).

This provincial capital is a small but busy commercial town. Currently, most travelers pass through Trat en route to Ko Chang (see pp122–30). However, it is likely that the town will draw larger crowds as more and more travelers visit the archipelago. Trat has several attractions, including its markets, most of which are centered around Tat Mai and Sukhumvit roads. The busy market on Sukhumvit Road has a fine selection of food and drink stalls.

Also of interest are the gem-mining villages, such as Bo Rai, around Trat, where rubies are mined. Local guesthouses can arrange trips for visitors. Located about 1 mile (2 km) southwest of Trat, **Wat Bupharam**, or Flower Temple, is set in pleasant grounds with large, shady trees. Some of the original buildings within the temple complex, including the *wihan*, the bell tower, and the *kutis* (monks' quarters), are quite old and date from the late Ayutthaya period (see pp44–5).

Wat Bupharam, the oldest temple in Trat

⓭ Laem Ngop

แหลมงอบ

Road Map E2. 12 miles (19 km) SW of Trat. 🚹 18,000. 🚌 🚍 𝑖 TAT, Trat (0-3959-7259-60). 🛥 Ko Chang Naval Battle Commemoration (Jan 17–21).

A small, sleepy, fishing port, Laem Ngop serves as the ferry point for nearby Ko Chang and the islands that lie beyond. In January 1941, the Thai Navy engaged French forces at this point, losing three vessels but claiming a moral victory that is still celebrated today. Traditional merit-making ceremonies are performed for the deceased, and there is an exhibition by the Royal Thai Navy. The town also has a monument and museum dedicated to the martyrs of the battle.

Laem Ngop has little to offer the visitor beyond a wooden pier where rows of boats and ferries are tied. Although very much a one-horse town, it has a number of privately operated tourism information centers and several hotels for those who miss the ferry to Ko Chang and decide to stay overnight, as well as some excellent restaurants.

The Cambodian Connection

Visitors waiting to cross the border to Cambodia, Hat Lek

Thailand's long, narrow, easternmost tip stretches far down the coast of the Gulf of Thailand, all but severing Cambodia's Cardamom region from the sea. In times past, this has led to tensions between the two countries, but today, both Bangkok and Phnom Penh seem happy to cooperate in profiting from the region's development as a tourist destination. The small but picturesque port of Khlong Yai is the last settlement in Thailand before the riverine border crossing to Cambodia at Hat Lek. Thai visitors generally cross to the somewhat notorious town of Koh Kong to indulge in gambling at local casinos. A vibrant trekking industry around the Cardamom Mountains is also beginning to develop in the region.

Visitors traveling by ferry from Laem Ngop to Ko Chang

⑭ Ko Chang

เกาะช้าง

Named after the largest island in an archipelago of 52, Ko Chang is one of the best-known national marine parks in Thailand. Its appeal lies in its ruggedness – stunning beaches, a thick, jungled interior teeming with a wide variety of flora and fauna, and beautiful coral reefs. The prominent beaches on the island are scattered along its western and southern coasts, while the eastern coast is more suited for trekking and bird-watching. Marine life enthusiasts will find the waters south and west of Ko Chang endowed with fascinating coral formations. The northwest coast of Ko Chang is the most developed part of the island, with several upscale restaurants and a variety of accommodation options.

Locator map

☐ Area illustrated

Hat Sai Khao

The largest and most developed beach on Ko Chang, Hat Sai Khao is also the most crowded, with plenty of bars and restaurants, and the liveliest nightlife.

Hat Khlong Phrao

A great spot for a family vacation, Hat Khlong Phrao is lined with restaurants that offer some of the freshest and most delicious seafood on the island.

KEY

① **Hat Kai Bae** is an ideal spot for sea-kayaking, with kayaks easily available for hire.

② **Ban Khlong Son** is the main settlement on the island.

③ **Hat Sai Yao**, a favorite with backpackers, is an ideal diving and snorkeling spot.

★ **Bang Bao Fishing Village**

A pretty village along the southern coast, Bang Bao is easily identified by its simple wooden houses on stilts built near or over the water.

★ Khlong Phlu Waterfall
Flowing along Khlong Phrao on the west coast, this waterfall has a freshwater pool on its uppermost level, which is accessible by a gentle 2-mile (3-km) hike.

0 km   4
0 miles   4

Laem Ngop
3 miles (5 km) ↑

)an Mai

Than Mayom

< HQ *i*

★ Than Mayom Waterfall
The most popular waterfall on the island, Than Mayom was visited by Rama V, VI, and VII. Evidence of their visits can be seen on the rocks near the falls which bear the kings' insignia.

Hat Wai Chek
Among the quieter and more serene beaches on Ko Chang, Hat Wai Chek is popular with campers. The beach is inaccessible by road and can only be reached by trekking across the island's forested interior.

Salak
Phet

Ao Salak
Phet

③

Ko Laoya   Ko Ngam   Ko Mai
Si Yai

> Khlum

Ko Kham 13 miles (21 km),
Ko Rang 11 miles (18 km),
Ko Mak 14 miles (22 km),
Ko Kradat 16 miles (26 km),
Ko Kut 21 miles (34 km)

Ko Wai

Ko Pai Dong

Key
═══ Minor road
═ ═ Dirt track
– – Ferry route

For keys to symbols *see back flap*

Idyllic palm-fringed beach on Ko Chang ▶

Exploring Ko Chang

The serenity and outstanding beauty of Ko Chang, the second-largest island in Thailand, have combined to place it prominently on the visitors' map. Easy accessibility from Bangkok combined with the island's scenic beauty, which includes mangrove forests, cliffs, and clear waters, make this an ideal place for a varied holiday experience. While the best beaches on Ko Chang are on its west coast, the coastal road, which was begun in the early 1990s, has helped to increase accessibility to other remote beaches on the island as well. Increased development also means that Ko Chang now has no shortage of upscale hotels, resorts, and spas catering to an ever-increasing influx of visitors.

🚉 Hat Sai Khao

หาดทรายขาว

7 miles (11 km) W of Tha Dan Kao.

The longest, most popular beach on the island, Hat Sai Khao, or White Sands Beach, is easily accessible from Tha Dan Kao, one of the many piers where ferries heading to Ko Chang arrive.

The narrow 1-mile (2-km) stretch of beach is crowded with hotels, resorts, and beach bars, all competing for a glimpse of the sea. An information center on the beach arranges boat trips, fishing and snorkeling. Most guesthouses also offer fishing, snorkeling, and motorcycle rental.

The road running parallel to the beach is lined with shops, travel agents, seafood shacks, bars, and a few small shopping malls. While the available accommodations are

Visitors enjoying refreshments outdoors at Hat Khlong Phrao

inadequate as well as overpriced, there are some less expensive places for the budget traveler at the northern end of the beach, which is also quieter. Swimming in the waters is not recommended here, as the current can get very strong and dangerous.

🚉 Hat Khlong Phrao

หาดคลองพร้าว

3 miles (5 km) S of Hat Sai Khao.

A small fishing port with one of the most popular family beaches on Ko Chang, Hat Khlong Phrao is best suited for visitors seeking mid-range accommodations. The beach is divided into two, the northern and southern parts, each with its own peaceful stretch of sand. The southern end has the added advantage of being screened off from the main road by a thick cluster of coconut trees.

🏞 Khlong Phlu Waterfall

น้ำตกคลองพลู

1 mile (2 km) NE of Hat Khlong Phrao.

Ko Chang's highest waterfall, the three-tiered Khlong Phlu, locally known as Nam Tok Khlong Phlu, cascades down 65 ft (20 m) into a small pool of clear water surrounded by smooth rocks. Located almost in the middle of the island, the fall flows down to Hat Khlong Phrao on the west coast, forming an estuary. Visitors usually follow the 2-mile (3-km) walk upstream by taking the road inland between Ko Chang Plaza in Laem Chaichet and Chang Chutiman Tours to reach this beautiful site.

The waterfall is very popular with visitors and quite crowded at all times, except in the early morning. A great spot for picnics,

The picturesque Khlong Phlu Waterfall, best viewed in the rainy season

For hotels and restaurants in this region see pp295–7 and pp310–12

visitors can jump off the rocks into the cool waters below, swim, and trek in the dense rain forest surrounding the waterfall. Sharp-eyed visitors may be lucky enough to spot a civet cat, macaque, or mongoose – all part of the fauna at the national park.

Foreign visitors have to pay an entry fee (which varies for children and adults) at the ranger station, located at the car park a short distance from the waterfall, as the cascade is part of the Ko Chang Marine National Park.

Basic beach accommodations, Ao Bai Lan

Kayaks available to residents to explore nearby islands, Hat Kai Bae

🚏 Hat Kai Bae
หาดไก่แบ้
7 miles (11 km) S of Hat Sai Khao. *Songthaew* from Tha Dan Kao or Hat Sai Khao. 🗺️ 📷

A narrow beach overgrown with shrubs, Hat Kai Bae all but disappears at high tide. Despite its size, the beach has been undergoing considerable development, and Hat Kai Bae has a few upscale resorts with private swimming pools and a handful of modest restaurants and bars, as well as supermarkets. Visitors can hire kayaks to explore the tiny islands just off the west coast. Motorcycles and boats are also available for hire at the dive shops.

🚏 Hat Tha Nam
หาดท่าน้ำ
6 miles (10 km) S of Hat Sai Khao. *Songthaew* from Tha Dan Kao. 🗺️ 📷

Better known as Lonely Beach, Hat Tha Nam was discovered by backpackers years ago as an ideal location for swimming and scuba diving. Despite the name, visitors continue to flock here in droves. Several resorts with concrete, air-conditioned bungalows have opened shop in recent times, but cheap wooden huts also dot the landscape.

Hat Tha Nam is probably the best area for swimming on the island, with a shallow seabed, although the northern end of the beach has a steep shelf and swimmers need to be careful. Scuba-diving equipment is easily available for hire from a dive shop on the beach, as are kayaks and motorcycles at most of the bungalow accommodations.

Youngsters frequent Hat Tha Nam playing frisbee, juggling balls, and drinking beer. The nights are often busy with noisy parties.

🌊 Ao Bai Lan
อ่าวใบลาน
8 miles (13 km) S of Hat Sai Khao.

Quieter and more private than Lonely Beach, Ao Bai Lan is the perfect destination for backpackers. Built around a pier, where a few fishing vessels moor and locals cast lines, Ao Bai Lan has no beach, just rocks, clear pristine water, and a chance to snorkel around the reef.

A few resorts have been springing up, including the luxurious Mercure Koh Chang Hideaway, which nestles among the more traditional picturesque huts set on stilts.

Vacationers partying late into the night at the many lively bars on Ao Bai Lan can also head for a relaxing sauna treatment at the popular Herbal Sauna Bailan.

Sunbathing along the poolside, Sea View Resort and Spa *(see p296)*, Hat Kai Bae

Water gushing down tiers of the spectacular Than Mayom Waterfall

completely off the tourist map. There are currently no road signs leading to it. Those keen to visit the picturesque and isolated beach can take the Salak Phet-Bang Bao route, which passes first through a rubber plantation, then to the coconut plantation and the beach, a short distance away. There is little development on the beach, and there are no guesthouses, restaurants, or shops. However, it is gradually becoming more accessible because of the construction of a road between Bang Bao and Ban Salak Phet which completes the long, winding loop around the island.

Visitors are allowed to camp overnight on the beach, but must remember to carry their own supplies. Those keen to undertake some physical activity can go hiking along the narrow wooded trails or hire a motorcycle or 4WD jeep from Ban Bang Bao.

Bang Bao
บางเบ้า

12 miles (19 km) S of Hat Sai Khao.

A unique experience awaits visitors to Bang Bao – it is a village built entirely on stilts, overlooking the bay. The wooden houses as well as shops, guesthouses, and restaurants are connected by narrow bridges, creating a miniature colony over the sea. Several shacks have been converted into seafood restaurants, famed locally for their giant crabs and prawns.

Keen anglers can go fishing, perhaps directly from their balcony; snorkeling, diving, and swimming are other options. Dolphins and sea turtles often swim off the southern coast, and tracking them can prove to be a rewarding experience, as long as visitors hire the services of an experienced tour guide. Boats and other equipment are also easily available.

Bang Bao usually witnesses a steady flow of camera-happy visitors, but the evenings are blissfully peaceful, especially after the crowds have dispersed and the souvenir shops have closed.

A hilly trail, which is marked out between Bang Bao and Ao Bai Lan, 3 miles (5 km) to the north, is excellent for hiking. A short distance south from the village is the small, albeit picturesque, beach called Hat Sai Noi. Some 330-ft (101-m) long, the beach has a small restaurant, a few fresh fruit bars, and some scattered chairs, with women offering traditional Thai massages.

Hat Wai Chek
หาดไว่เชฺก

3 miles (5 km) E of Bang Bao.
from Bang Bao.

One of Thailand's last untouched slices of paradise, the isolated cove of Hat Wai Chek is almost

Than Mayom Port and Waterfall
น้ำตกธารมะยม

4 miles (6 km) S of Tha Dan Kao.
The east coast of Ko Chang is lined with mangroves and has few facilities for visitors or beaches and scant accommodations. The Than Mayom Port has a pier where various varieties of fruit are loaded for the mainland, but there is little other activity. A 1-mile (2-km) walk south of the port leads to the Than Mayom Waterfall on a steep hill toward the interior. This natural cascade is surrounded by lush vegetation and offers spectacular views

Wooded hills and trails ideal for trekking, Hat Wai Chek

Panoramic view of calm waters and outlying islands off Ko Chang

over the coastline. Camping around the waterfall is usually permitted, but visitors need to bring their own supplies. Successive kings of Thailand have visited the falls as the inscriptions on the rocks indicate. Foreign visitors have to pay an entry fee, which covers all of the sites within the marine national park.

Squid drying at the fishing village of Ban Salak Phet

Ban Salak Phet

บ้านสลักเพชร
10 miles (16 km) S of Tha Dan Kao.

A traditional fishing village with houses on stilts, Ban Salak Phet has found a place for itself on the tourist map, especially after the construction of the long, winding road around the island.

Visitors can take diving or snorkeling tours from the bay to the wreckage of two Thai naval ships which were sunk by the French Navy during World War II. For a more leisurely activity, a visit to the fish and shrimp farms and the lighthouse is

recommended. There are a couple of beautiful waterfalls within 2–3 miles (3–5 km) of Salak Phet called Ke Rephet and Khlong Nung. Two Buddhist temples – Wat Salak Phet, built during the reign of Rama V (r.1868–1910), and another about 6 miles (10 km) from it – are also worth a visit.

🚩 Hat Sai Yao

หาดทรายยาว
14 miles (22 km) S of Tha Dan Kao.
Located on the southeastern tip of Ko Chang, Hat Sai Yao, or Long Beach, had so far been one of the least developed areas on the island. Endowed with breathtaking views, it is an ideal sanctuary for backpackers searching for solitude. However, Hat Sai Yao is now changing slowly – the winding bumpy road to the beach has improved,

and taxis are more willing to negotiate a pretty reasonable fare from either Salak Phet or Salak Kok.

Hat Sai Yao is the closest point for swimming, snorkeling, and fishing trips to a handful of tiny, yet picturesque islands nearby, including Ko Wai *(see p130)*, Ko Mai Si Yai, Ko Mai Si Lek, and Ko Mai Daeng, some of which still remain uninhabited. Hat Sai Yao is not without its bit of intriguing history; close to the coastline is a memorial dedicated to Thai soldiers who lost their lives in a battle against the French in 1941. Visitors can trek to this site.

Keen photographers might want to climb the 1,500-ft (457-m) high mountain behind the Treehouse Lodge to capture the panoramic views of the islands and coastline below.

Thatched accommodations at the beachfront, Hat Sai Yao

Exploring Ko Chang's Outlying Islands

The stunning islands of Ko Kham, Ko Wai, Ko Mak, and Ko Kut, with their beautiful, deserted beaches, are perfect for swimming and sunbathing. Located south of Ko Chang, these islands are accessible by ferry or speedboat and offer some of the best snorkeling and diving experiences in the Gulf of Thailand. Underwater explorers can see a wealth of marine life among the reefs as well as the wrecks of two naval warships – the *Songkhla* and the *Chonburi* – which sank in these waters. These have since become notable dive sites.

Traditional fishing village backed by mangroves at Ko Kut

Diver exploring the rich and unspoiled coral reefs off Ko Chang

Ko Kham
เกาะขาม
13 miles (21 km) SE of Ko Chang. 🚤 from Bang Bao. 🛈

Isolated Ko Kham, also known as Emerald Island, is so small that visitors can swim or snorkel around it in just 40 minutes. This is one of the few islands where black volcanic rocks are found on the beaches. The west coast has a profusion of mangroves and wild orchids, while the east coast has two small beaches.

The island was bought by a developer in 2008 who began construction of a luxury resort but the project is currently at a standstill.

Ko Wai
เกาะหวาย
6 miles (10 km) SE of Ko Chang. 🚤 from Bang Bao or Laem Ngop. 🛈 🏨

Bounded by white sands, palm trees, and coral reefs, Ko Wai provides the perfect tropical setting with gorgeous views of the neighboring islands. The surrounding waters are so clear that the ocean floor can be viewed even without snorkeling gear. This L-shaped island is hilly and connected in the middle by shallow lagoons, which are safe even for young children. The locals are very friendly and there are a handful of resorts offering simple accommodations. These can be accessed on foot via a jungle path along the northern coast. Ko Wai does not have many facilities, but its pristine beauty makes it ideal for a family holiday.

Ko Mak
เกาะหมาก
14 miles (22 km) S of Ko Chang. 🚤 from Bang Bao or Laem Ngop. 🛈 🏨

Covered with coconut and rubber plantations, Ko Mak is named after the areca nut – *Mak* is the Thai word for areca nut – found all over the island. Most of Ko Mak is privately owned by the powerful Prompakdii family – civil servants who later turned landowners. Almost deserted until the late 1990s, Ko Mak is now home to about 30 resorts. There is electricity, Internet, boats for hire, and a good choice of restaurants and shops.

Most of the action is on Ao Suan Yai and Ao Kao. Scuba diving is a popular activity on Ko Mak and the surrounding cluster of tiny islands – Ko Rayang, Ko Kra, Ko Rang, and Ko Kradat.

Ko Kut
เกาะกูด
21 miles (34 km) S of Ko Chang. 🚤 from Bang Bao. 🛈 🏨

The second-largest island of the Ko Chang archipelago, Ko Kut is also the farthest from the mainland. The original inhabitants of this island were both Cambodians and Thais who fled to this remote spot during the French occupation of Trat (*see p121*) in 1904.

Agriculture is the mainstay of the locals – coconut and rubber are the most important crops. Most beaches are on the west coast and Khlong Chao and Hat Tapao are the most popular spots. The pristine, untouched interior of this island is home to the beautiful Khlong Chao Waterfall. Visitors can also stop by the fishing village of Ao Salad and sample the fresh seafood on offer.

Thick coconut plantations along the coast of Ko Mak

Beach Life

The sunny, tropical beaches of the Eastern Seaboard are a hedonistic escape from the daily grind. Popular with both foreign visitors and locals due to their proximity to Bangkok, they are both a hub of activity and a place to lie back and relax, with all the concomitant pleasures of the sun, sand, and watersports. Visitors can choose between basic backpacker haunts and luxurious, romantic getaways; deserted beaches or bustling commercial spots with a vibrant nightlife. The clear aquamarine waters provide good diving and snorkeling opportunities offering a wealth of marine life. Other attractions such as seafood, beach parties, traditional massages, and souvenir shops complete the perfect holiday.

Sunbathing is a favorite occupation with travelers and most of the popular beaches have deck chairs and umbrellas to lounge under. However, it is easy to get serious sunburn, and a good sunscreen is a must.

Beach games such as soccer, netball, and volleyball are extremely popular. Nets strung up on the beach with youngsters playing impromptu matches are a common sight.

Thai foot massages use traditional techniques to relieve tension. Many beaches have expert masseurs who charge very reasonable rates.

Thai beach vendors tend to be friendly rather than pushy or impolite and sell everything from fresh seafood snacks to trinkets.

The beach nightlife includes cabarets, full moon parties, fire shows, and live bands. Apart from this, groups of revelers are often seen singing around a bonfire.

Beach shacks are simple thatched structures serving iced drinks and delicious local snacks. They provide shade from the sun as well as the perfect vantage point to enjoy the sea.

Watersports of all kinds are available at Pattaya and other developed beaches. These range from kayaking – available on even the smaller beaches – to more extreme sports such as parasailing, windsurfing, and kiteboarding.

Poolside bungalows at a beach resort, Hat Thap Thim

⓯ Hat Sai Ngam
หาดทรายงาม

Road Map E2. 24 miles (39 km) SE of Trat. 🚌 ⚡ 📷

On the mainland east of Ko Chang is a sliver of land along the shore that connects the provincial town of Trat *(see p121)* with the border crossing to Cambodia at Ban Hat Lek. This stretch is home to a string of small fishing villages, as well as some of the loveliest and as yet undeveloped beaches in Thailand. Hat Sai Ngam, or Beautiful Sands Beach, is a small and lovely stretch of pure white sand running parallel to a grove of pine trees. Facilities are fairly simple – although it should always be possible to get something to eat and drink. This is an ideal place to try out shrimp paste and dried fish, which are famous local products. This beach is visited by relatively few people – Thai or foreign travelers – and it is still possible to unwind by the sea without being assailed by commercial development. To get to the beach visitors need to cross a 144-ft (44-m) long wooden bridge.

⓰ Hat Sai Kaew
หาดทรายแก้ว

Road Map E2. 25 miles (40 km) SE of Trat. 🚌 ⚡ 📷

A quiet beach, Hat Sai Kaew, or Crystal Sands Beach, is yet to be discovered by travelers. Crisp white sands shaded by a narrow fringe of casuarinas and coconut palms along the shore makes this beach attractive to those who are looking for peace and tranquility. The area is best explored on motorcycles or longtail boats. It is possible to reach Hat Sai Kaew by minibus from Trat.

⓱ Hat Thap Thim
หาดทับทิม

Road Map E2. 30 miles (48 km) SE of Trat. 🚌 ⚡ 📷

Located near the village of Ban Mai Rut, Hat Thap Thim, or Ruby Beach, is close to the narrowest strip of Thai territory dividing the Cambodian mountains from the Gulf of Thailand. This 1,500-ft (450-m) narrow sliver of sand is a pretty spot ideal for picnics or a day trip en route to Cambodia.

Basic accommodations are available here and the beach with its seafood shacks is often filled with Thai locals from Trat who come to Hat Thap Thim on weekends. The ambience here is laid-back and decidedly different from the international vibe of nearby Ko Chang.

⓲ Hat Samran
หาดสำราญ

Road Map E2. 36 miles (58 km) SE of Trat. 🚌 ⚡ 📷

Located between Trat and the Thai-Cambodian frontier at Hat Lek, Hat Samran, better known as Hat Mai Rut, is an almost deserted beach. Despite limited facilities, its relative quiet and stunning beauty adds to its

Colorful boats anchored at the fishing village, Hat Samran

charm and appeal. While some of the regular watersports such as windsurfing or diving might not be available due to lack of infrastructure, this beach is an excellent spot for swimming. Visitors can also enjoy the authentic experience of a fishing village at Ban Mai Rut with plenty of seafood and an insight into the lives of the local fishermen.

⑲ Hat Ban Chuen
หาดบานชื่น

Road Map E2. 39 miles (63 km) SE of Trat. 🚌 ✏️ 📷

Located between Ban Mai Rut and Khlong Yai, Hat Ban Chuen is the longest beach in Trat. This stretch of powdery sand crosses the foundation structure of a non-functional Cambodian refugee camp. Simple bungalow accommodations offer lodging to overnight visitors and a small restaurant sells fresh seafood dishes. This beach attracts a lively local crowd from Trat.

⑳ Ban Hat Lek
บ้านหาดเล็ก

Road Map E2. 57 miles (92 km) SE of Trat. 🚌 4,500. 🚌 🚌 🚌 🛖 daily.

The tiny settlement of Ban Hat Lek marks the actual border crossing between Thailand and Cambodia. It is an outpost from

Thatched beachside seafood shacks at Hat Ban Chuen

where travelers can take a boat out of the country to Cambodia. Visas and other immigration formalities can be completed at Khlong Yai – the last town before the border crossing.

However, this region has had a troubled past due to incessant political instability and geographical proximity to Cambodia. During the time of Pol Pot and the Khmer Rouge, and the subsequent disputes over control of the country from 1975 to 1986, this area was referred to as "bandit country" and was quite unsafe. Things

have changed now, but there is still a palpable "Wild East" feel to the place, with touts and scam artists charging up to $100 for a Cambodian visa (the official price is about £30). On the other side is a similar, if slightly more debauched, remote frontier post. Although officials are beginning to crack down, it is better to be careful here, especially after dark.

The border is currently open from 7am to 8pm daily. Travelers crossing over to Cambodia can stay overnight at Koh Kong, the first town on the other side.

Cambodian houses along the border at Ban Hat Lek

UPPER WESTERN GULF COAST

The alluring Upper Western Gulf Coast extends from Phetchaburi to Chumphon, covering a distance of almost 292 miles (470 km). Close to Bangkok, notably around the old, historic town of Phetchaburi and the royal getaway Hua Hin, the beach resorts are well developed and extremely popular. Further south, however, there are fewer people, and miles of long, white, sandy beaches stretch gloriously into the distance.

Steeped in history and culture, Thailand's Upper Western Gulf Coast is characterized by historically relevant towns such as Phetchaburi, with its crumbling architectural remnants of the Khmer, Mon, Ayutthaya, and Rattanakosin epochs.

The Tenasserim Mountains, rising to 4,350 ft (1,326 m), form a long spine down the peninsula, dividing Thai territory from that of neighboring Myanmar. This range absorbs much of the rain that falls during the southwest monsoon, keeping the region relatively dry, even when there is heavy rain on the nearby Andaman Coast to the west. However, this coastal region is still fertile, famed for its juicy, tropical fruits such as pineapples, coconuts, sugarcane, "lady finger" bananas, sugar palms, and mangosteens. The Upper Western Gulf

Coast's heavily forested interior and spectacular beaches, which are sheltered by mountains, attract vacationers more than its historic buildings and museums. The beautiful, casuarina-lined fronts of Cha-am and Hua Hin are enduringly popular, particularly with weekenders from Bangkok, as are gorgeous and unspoiled strands such as Hat Ao Noi and Ao Manao at Prachuap Khiri Khan. The many golf courses within easy reach of Cha-am and Hua Hin make this area arguably the country's premier golf destination. Trekkers and bird-watchers will also be drawn to the natural beauty of Khao Sam Roi Yot and Kaeng Krachan national parks, where migratory birds rest and feed in the salt marshes between the months of August and April.

Fishing boat sailing in calm waters off Bang Saphan Yai at sunset

◀ Buddhist shrine on Khao Takiab, a hill overlooking the beach at Hua Hin

Exploring the Upper Western Gulf Coast

This long, narrow coastal strip, backed by a range of mountains along the Burmese border, stretches from the cultural center of Phetchaburi to the quiet fishing port of Chumphon and the beaches as far beyond as isolated Hat Arunothai. In the north lie one of Thailand's oldest beach resorts, Hua Hin, and the more modern resort of Cha-am. This area is also home to several wildlife sanctuaries such as the green and hilly Kaeng Krachan National Park, as well as the characteristic limestone outcrops of the coastal Khao Sam Roi Yot National Park. Chumphon, in the south, traditionally marks the point where central Thai culture gives way and Thailand's Muslim presence gradually grows stronger.

Fleet of fishing boats near the harbor,
Hat Thung Wua Laen

Sights at a Glance

Towns, Cities, and Villages

1 Phetchaburi pp138–41
2 Cha-am
5 Hua Hin pp144–5
6 Pranburi
12 Prachuap Khiri Khan
17 Dan Singkhon
21 Bang Saphan
25 Chumphon

National Parks

3 Kaeng Krachan National Park
8 Khao Sam Roi Yot National Park pp148–9

Theme Parks

19 King Mongkut Memorial Park of Science & Technology

Historic Buildings and Religious Sites

4 Marukhathaiyawan Palace
13 Wat Khao Tham Khan Kradai

Beaches, Islands, and Bays

7 Hat Naresuan
9 Hat Sam Roi Yot
10 Hat Laem Sala
11 Hat Sam Phraya
14 Hat Ao Noi
15 Ao Bang Nang Rom
16 Ao Manao
18 Hat Wa Kaw
20 Hat Ban Krut
22 Hat Thung Wua Laen
23 Ko Ngam Yai and Ko Ngam Noi
24 Hin Lak Ngam
26 Hat Sai Ri
27 Ao Thung Makham
28 Hat Arunothai

Farmers harvesting rice in a field, Prachuap Khiri Khan

Getting Around

Most attractions in the region are easily accessible from Highway 4, the main route between Bangkok and the south. The major towns are linked to each other and to the capital by bus and train services. The train from Bangkok takes around 6 hours; the bus is quicker – the direct VIP bus service from Bangkok's Suvarnabhumi Airport to Hua Hin can complete the journey in about 4 hours. Flights to and from Chumphon are operated by Nok Air, which uses Bangkok's Don Muang Airport. Songthaews, motorcycles, or trishaws can be hired for trips to local sights. However, the easiest and most convenient way to explore the area is with a rental car.

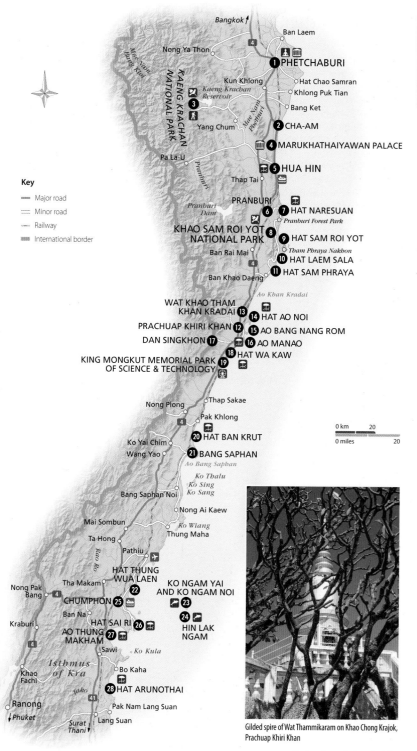

Bangkok

Ban Laem

Nong Ya Thon

4

🏕🏛 **1** PHETCHABURI

Kun Khlong

Hat Chao Samran

Kaeng Krachan Reservoir

Khlong Puk Tian

Bang Ket

KAENG KRACHAN NATIONAL PARK

3

Yang Chum

2 CHA-AM

🏛 **4** MARUKHATHAIYAWAN PALACE

Pa La-U

🏖 **5** HUA HIN

Mae Nam Pranburi

Mae Nam Bang Koi

Mae Nam Phetburi

Thap Tai

PRANBURI

6 **7** HAT NARESUAN

Pranburi Forest Park

Pranburi Dam

KHAO SAM ROI YOT NATIONAL PARK

8

9 HAT SAM ROI YOT

Ban Rai Mai

Tham Phraya Nakhon

10 HAT LAEM SALA

4

11 HAT SAM PHRAYA

Ban Khao Daeng

Ao Khan Kradai

WAT KHAO THAM KHAN KRADAI **13**

14 HAT AO NOI

PRACHUAP KHIRI KHAN **12**

15 AO BANG NANG ROM

DAN SINGKHON **17**

16 AO MANAO

18 HAT WA KAW

KING MONGKUT MEMORIAL PARK OF SCIENCE & TECHNOLOGY **19**

Nong Plong

Thap Sakae

4

Pak Khlong

20 HAT BAN KRUT

Ko Yai Chim

Wang Yao

21 BANG SAPHAN

Ao Bang Saphan

Ko Thalu

Ko Sing

Ko Sang

Bang Saphan Noi

Nong Ai Kaew

Mai Sombun

Ko Wiang

Thung Maha

Ta Hong

Pathiu

Rao Ro

HAT THUNG WUA LAEN

Tha Makam

22

KO NGAM YAI AND KO NGAM NOI

Nong Pak Bang

4

CHUMPHON **25**

23

Ban Na

24 HIN LAK NGAM

Kraburi

HAT SAI RI **26**

AO THUNG MAKHAM **27**

Sawi

Ko Kula

Khao Fachi

Isthmus of Kra

Bo Kaha

Tako

28 HAT ARUNOTHAI

Ranong

41

Phuket

Pak Nam Lang Suan

Surat Thani

Lang Suan

Key

— Major road

═ Minor road

⋯ Railway

▬ International border

0 km — 20

0 miles — 20

Gilded spire of Wat Thammikaram on Khao Chong Krajok, Prachuap Khiri Khan

For keys to symbols *see back flap*

❶ Street-by-Street: Phetchaburi

เพชรบุรี

Settled since at least the 11th century, Phetchaburi (often spelled Phetburi) is one of Thailand's oldest towns. Capital of the Phetchaburi province, it has long been an important trading and cultural center, and Mon, Khmer, and Ayutthayan influences can be seen in its 30 temples. During the 19th century it became a favorite royal retreat, and Rama IV *(see p155)* built a summerhouse here on a hill, Khao Wang, west of the center. This is now part of the Phra Nakhon Khiri Historical Park *(see p140)*. Other major sights are the 17th-century Wat Yai Suwannaram, the five Khmer *prangs* of Wat Kamphaeng Laeng, and an old quarter that has retained much of its original charm. However, accommodations are scant and most visitors come only on day trips from Bangkok.

Fountain, Phra Nakhon Khiri

To Phra Nakhon Khiri Historical Park

BANDAI-IT

Wat Mahathat Worawihan
The five white Khmer-style *prangs* of this much-restored 14th-century temple dominate the town's central skyline. Figures of angels and gods decorate the roofs of the main *wihan* and *bot*.

0 meters 75
0 yards 75

To Wat Tho

Wooden Shophouses
Concrete may have replaced wood in most Thai towns, but attractive wooden buildings, many lining the riverbank, are still a feature in Phetchaburi.

Key

— Suggested route

★ Phra Nakhon Khiri Historical Park
As an avid astronomer, Rama IV had this observatory conveniently built next to his hilltop summer palace; this is now a museum. The surrounding park is magnificently landscaped and forested, offering extensive views of Phetchaburi.

VISITORS' CHECKLIST

Practical Information
Road Map C1. 75 miles (120 km) SW of Bangkok. 80,000. *i* TAT, Cha-am (0-3247-1005). daily. Phra Nakhon Khiri Fair (8 days in early Feb).

Transport

★ Wat Yai Suwannaram
Built during the Ayutthaya period (see pp44–5), the temple is notable for the lovely original murals of Hindu gods in the *bot*. A scripture library stands on stilts in the middle of a large pond on the grounds.

To Wat Chisa-in

AMNOEN KASEM

CHISA-IN

PHET

PHANIT JEROEN

PONGSURIYA ROAD

PHRA SONG

MATAYAWONG

To Wat Yai
Suwannaram

Market

To Wat
Kamphaeng Laeng

★ Wat Kamphaeng Laeng
This is one of the few surviving Khmer shrines in Thailand outside the northeast. The five laterite *prangs* of the temple, in varying states of disrepair, are typically Khmer in design and may date from the 12th century. Originally a Hindu temple, it was later adapted for Buddhist use.

Exploring Phetchaburi

An old city replete with historical buildings and temples, Phetchaburi, which means "Diamond Town", is a royal city of frangipani flowers and exotic sweets. It is divided by the Phet River, which winds its way through this provincial capital. Many of Phetchaburi's *wats* and temples, especially from the Ayutthaya period, are well preserved and others have been expertly restored. The city skyline is dominated by the pinnacles of the *wats* and three large hills over its western side. Phetchaburi's architecture is influenced by Buddhist iconography and is a combination of Oriental, Indian, European, and Khmer styles.

Three-tiered gilded Buddha images at Wat Mahathat Worawihan

Sunlight illuminating the main chamber at Khao Luang Cave

Khao Luang Cave

ถ้ำเขาหลวง

3 miles (5 km) NW of town center. **Open** 8am–6pm daily. voluntary donation.

The large and spectacular Khao Luang Cave has three linked chambers filled with stalactites and a number of Buddha images, including a *phra non* (Reclining Buddha). The main bronze image was cast on the orders of Rama V (r.1868–1910) and dedicated to his illustrious predecessors, Rama III (r.1824–51) and Rama IV (r.1851–68). There is a natural opening in the roof of the second chamber and sunlight streams through, especially on clear days, illuminating the images inside. To the right of the cave entrance at the foot of the hill is **Wat Tham Klaep**. Also known as Wat Bun Thawi, the monastery's distinctive *wihan* and *bot* have beautifully carved wooden doors.

Khao Wang and Phra Nakhon Khiri Historical Park

เขาวังและอุทยานประวัติศาสตร์พระนครคีรี

Off Phet Kasem Road. **Tel** 0-3242-5600. **Open** 8:30am–4:30pm daily (last entry 3:30pm).

Perched on the summit of the 302-ft (92-m) high Khao Khiri hill, Phra Nakhon Khiri, literally "Celestial City of the Mountain", is now a historical park dominating the northwestern skyline of Phetchaburi. This palace complex was built as the summer residence of Rama IV in the 1850s and the hill is now locally known as Khao Wang or Palace Hill. The king ordered the building of this complex as a getaway from Bangkok. Chinese, European, and Japanese architectural flourishes are blended with local Thai designs. Set among forests, rocks, and caverns, it offers a fine view of the town as well as a panoramic vista of the province. The entire complex extends over three peaks and includes royal halls, temples, palaces, and other buildings. The Royal Palace and

Ho Chatchawan Wiangchai, an observatory tower built for Rama IV who was an accomplished astronomer, are both perched on the western rise. The Phra That Chomphet, a white *chedi* erected by Rama V, stands on the central rise while Wat Maha Samanaram, containing some fine murals, dominates the eastern rise.

In 1988, the complex was converted into a historical park. Access to the summit is either by way of winding cobblestone paths, or by funicular railway to the west of the hill, for visitors who do not want an energetic uphill trek. This park merits at least a half-day excursion.

Wat Mahathat Worawihan

วัดมหาธาตุวรวิหาร

Thanon Damnoen Kasem. **Open** 8:30am–4pm daily.

Located in the center of town, the five unmissable white *prangs* of the Wat Mahathat Worawihan rise against the skyline forming the spiritual heart of Phetchaburi.

Phra Nakhon Khiri Historical Park, surrounded by lush greenery

It is thought to have been built in the 14th century, but attained *mahathat* status – the rank of a monastery with a *chedi* containing a relic of the Buddha – only in 1954. The relic at Worawihan was donated by the present king, Rama IX. The temple, distinguished by its *prangs* – the central one 180-ft (55-m) high – and its Khmer-style *chedi*, is influenced by the Mahayana school of Buddhism. The sacred *sema* stones that mark the temple precincts may be relics of an even older version of the *wat*. Some of these stones date back to the late Dvaravati period *(see p43)*. There is a large *wihan* in front of the temple, housing a splendid multitiered Buddha statue. The walls of the *wihan* are decorated with more than 100 murals. Many of these depict Thai people dressed in European-style clothing from the Victorian era.

Buddha statue among Khmer ruins, Wat Kamphaeng Laeng

Ancient murals depicting Buddhist mythology, Wat Yai Suwannaram

🛕 Wat Yai Suwannaram

วัดใหญ่สุวรรณาราม

Thanon Phongsuriya.
Open 8:30am–4pm daily.

Perhaps the most appealing of Phetchaburi's many temples, Wat Yai Suwannaram is a 17th-century temple noted for its series of 300-year-old murals of *thevada* (Buddhist angels) on the interior walls of the main *wihan*. Nearby lies a teak *sala* with finely carved doors, one of them bearing a cut reportedly made by an invading Burmese soldier's sword during the war of 1767 *(see p45)*. The main *bot*, constructed in the Ayutthaya style, is without any windows.

The complex also has an unusual *hor trai* (scripture repository) in the middle of a lotus-filled pond. It is raised on stilts above the water to protect the palm leaf manuscripts from white ants and other destructive insects.

🛕 Wat Kamphaeng Laeng

วัดกำแพงแลง

Thanon Phongsuriya.
Open 8:30am–4pm daily.

Located in the eastern part of Phetchaburi, Wat Kamphaeng Laeng is undoubtedly the town's oldest surviving structure. This semi-ruined Khmer building indicates that the city was probably the southernmost part of the Khmer Empire (9th–13th century) that stretched east as far as the Mekong delta and the South China Sea, and north to central Laos. Originally believed to be a Hindu place of worship, it was converted into a Buddhist temple. Five rather ramshackle Khmer *prangs* survive, each of which was probably dedicated to a particular Hindu deity. They are set in a cruciform arrangement facing east. Made of sandstone and laterite, with Dvaravati stucco work on the walls, the complex dates back to the 11th or 12th century.

🏛 Phra Ratchawang Ban Puen

พระราชวังบ้านปืน

1 mile (2 km) S of town center.
Tel 0-3242-8506–9. **Open** 8am–4pm daily.

Located in the middle of the Phetchaburi military barracks, Phra Ratchawang Ban Puen is an early 20th-century palace. Constructed by Rama V, the building is more a grand European-style villa than a palace. The work began shortly before his death in 1910, but was not completed until 1916. The palace designed by German architects is in the modernist European style patronized by Thai monarchs and has beautiful glazed tiles adorning its interiors.

Glazed tiles and marble figurines inside Phra Ratchawang Ban Puen

Thailand's Sweet and Dessert Capital

Phetchaburi is well-known throughout Thailand for the variety and excellence of its sweets, which are based on natural local products such as palm sugar, palm seeds, coconut, banana, rose apple, pineapple, and many other fresh seasonal fruits. Phetchaburi *tanot* (palm sugar) is believed to be particularly sweet and refreshing, and is combined with other ingredients such as flour, eggs, and rice. These *Thai khanom* (Thai sweets) differ in textures and cooking styles from their Western counterparts and are often served with ice, wrapped in banana leaves, or as small cakes. Two of Phetchaburi province's most important festivals – the Phra Nakhon Khiri Fair and Thai Song Dam Festival – showcase these local sweets. Villagers dressed in traditional costumes demonstrate traditional sweet-making and also sell them at the festival fairs.

Thai khanom, unlike Western sweets, are rarely stored or wrapped. They are usually made for swift consumption and taste better fresh.

Sweet and Desserts Market

Almost all markets in Thailand have a sweet and dessert section offering everything from national favorites to local specialties. Most vendors are happy to let visitors sample the merchandise before purchase.

Mangoes and pineapples flourish in this region, as does the sugar palm, the crystallized sap of which is used in many Thai sweets.

Khao tom mat sai kluay is made using another typical Thai base – sweetened sticky rice. Flavored with coconut milk and steamed in a banana leaf, this dessert is eaten with fresh fruits such as ripe bananas and durians.

The golden three – *thong yip, thong yawt,* and *foy thong* – are famous Phetchaburi desserts made by boiling duck egg yolks in a palm sugar syrup. Different textures emerge due to the cooking process.

Wun maphrao is a colorful jelly made with coconut, agar-agar, and sugar. It is often found in open-air markets.

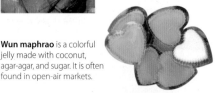

Tako is a delicious custard made out of green pea flour, water chestnuts, sugar, and coconut cream. It is cooked in pandanus leaves and served chilled.

Kalamae is a local toffee made out of coconut cream, sugar, and flour that is thickened into a sticky solid and then cut into bite-sized pieces.

Long verandas connecting different halls and chambers in Marukhathaiyawan Palace

❷ Cha-am

ชะอำ

Road Map C1. 21 miles (34 km) S of Phetchaburi. 🚌 20,000. 🚗 🚌 🛈 TAT, 500/51 Phet Kasem Rd, Cha-am (0-3247-1005). 🚌 daily.

Famous for its 3-mile (5-km) long sandy beach, Cha-am has experienced a dramatic surge in popularity since the mid-1980s. From a quiet fishing village and market town, it has developed into a lively weekend getaway for visitors from Bangkok.

Other attractions in the town include the large market for fresh produce, the fishing pier lined with seafood restaurants, and Wat Cha-am, a small cave temple dating back to the Ayutthaya period (see pp44–5). The town caters chiefly to Thais who are fond of their food and drink and there are plenty of options in and around the beach. Stalls and vendors sell delicious grilled fish and other

fresh seafood alongside local specialties of roast chicken and roast pork. Large resorts have sprung up alongside the beach. Apart from this, there are also some formal dining options along the northern end of the beach.

❸ Kaeng Krachan National Park

อุทยานแห่งชาติแก่งกระจาน

Road Map C1. Park HQ off Hwy 3175, 30 miles (48 km) W of Cha-am. 🛈 Park HQ (0-3246-7326); Forestry Dept (0-2562-0760) for bungalow bookings. 🚗 🚌 📷 🌐 dnp.go.th

Containing pristine tracts of tropical evergreen forest, Kaeng Krachan National Park attracts few visitors despite being the largest national park in Thailand. Established in 1981, it spans an area of 1,150 sq miles (2,920 sq km), covering nearly half of the Phetchaburi province. It is home to at least 40 species of

mammals, including tigers, leopards, elephants, gibbons, and Asiatic bears. Thousands of migratory birds come here from as far as China and Siberia to breed and feed in the salt marshes.

Kaeng Krachan offers visitors some excellent hiking, as well as boat rides through the 45-sq km (17-sq mile) **Kaeng Krachan Reservoir**, fed by forest streams and rivers.

❹ Marukhath-aiyawan Palace

พระราชวังมฤคทายวัน

Road Map C2. Off Hwy 4, 5 miles (9 km) S of Cha-am. 🛈 TAT, Cha-am (0-3247-1005). 🚌 from Cha-am. **Open** 8:30am–4:30pm daily. 📷 donation. 📷 in bedroom.

The erstwhile summer home of Rama VI (r.1910–25), Marukhathaiyawan Palace, meaning "Palace of Love and Hope", is a grand teak building. Designed by an Italian architect, this palace was constructed in just 16 days in 1923. However, it was abandoned when Rama VI died two years later and stood neglected for decades. It has since been restored to its original glory. Yet, despite its accessibility, the palace is rarely visited.

The airy building, with its simply decorated halls, veran-das, and royal chambers, is painted in pastel shades. The walkways have lovely views of the beach and the sea.

Horses for hire along the long stretch of beach at Cha-am

For hotels and restaurants in this region see pp297–8 and pp312–13

❺ Hua Hin

หัวหิน

Hua Hin was Thailand's first beach resort. The key to its success was its rail connection to Bangkok, completed in 1911. Following the international trend for recuperative spa resorts at the time, Hua Hin became a popular retreat for minor Thai royalty, Bangkok high society, and affluent foreign visitors. A nine-hole golf course was built in 1922 and Prince Chulachakrabongse (1908–63) built a summer palace here in 1926, which he called Klai Klangwon – literally, "Far from Worries". Despite a decline in fortunes post World War II, this seaside town has grown into an international vacation spot, with several upscale resorts along the seafront.

Red- and white-tiled platform at Hua Hin Railway Station

Hua Hin Railway Station

สถานีรถไฟหัวหิน

Thanon Liap Thang Rot Fai. 🖉 📷

Billed as Thailand's "most beautiful train station", this is also one of the oldest, dating back to the late 19th century. The most striking feature is the main wooden building, which today serves as the passenger reception and waiting room. It was originally a royal pavilion at the Sanam Chan Palace in Nakhon Pathom. Constructed in the late Rattanakosin style of Rama VI (r.1910–25), it features temple-like multitiered roofs with typically Thai uptilted eaves, as well as elongated, lozenge-shaped vertical windows painted in rust red and creamy yellow. A gleaming retired steam locomotive is on display opposite the platform. The building exudes a seductive, period charm and is a favorite with most camera-happy visitors to Hua Hin.

Railway Hotel

โรงแรมรถไฟ

1, Thanon Damnoen Kasem.
Tel 0-3251-2021. 🖉 📷
🌐 centarahotelsresorts.com

Built in 1923, the Colonial-style former Railway Hotel provides an insight into the Hua Hin of the 1920s. A luxurious upscale spa and resort in its modern guise, the hotel, now known as the Centara Grand Resort and Villas, retains its period charm with winding teak staircases and high-ceilinged rooms. It is almost obligatory to stop by for a drink, just to soak in the atmosphere. The hotel fell into disrepair in the 1960s, but sensitive restoration won it the Outstanding Conservation Award in 1993. It was used in the film *The Killing Fields*, as a stand-in for the Renakse Hotel in Phnom Penh, Cambodia.

🚇 Hat Hua Hin

หาดหัวหิน

Thanon Damnoen Kasem. 🖉 📷

Named for the large, smooth, boulders that litter its northern end, Hat Hua Hin, or Hua Hin Beach, is a surprisingly good beach with clean, soft, white sand. Extending for about 3 miles (5 km), it is lined with small souvenir shops, bars, and restaurants. The best stretch, however, is in front of the Railway Hotel. Set back from Hat Hua Hin for much of its length is a long line of condominiums and luxury homes. Relatively quiet on weekdays, the beach is usually bustling with activity on weekends. Good for swimming, Hat Hua Hin also offers pony rides for children and a variety of thrilling watersports such as water-skiing and kiteboarding.

🎪 Night Market

ตลาดโต้รุ่ง

Thanon Dechanuchit West.
Open 5pm to midnight daily. 🖉 📷

Bustling with people and activity, the Hua Hin night market extends for a short

Beachside restaurant with great sea views, Railway Hotel

For hotels and restaurants in this region see pp297–8 and pp312–13

Picturesque park with walking track atop Khao Hin Lek Fai

distance along both sides of Thanon Dechanuchit, and especially at the Thanon Sasong crossroad. The market is open from 5pm to midnight. The area is usually teeming with locals intent on commerce and visitors who flock to the various reasonably priced stalls, bargaining for souvenirs and other purchases. The roadside eateries, usually quite clean and hygienic, are wonderful for a delicious fresh seafood dinner, made to order. This is also the place to buy souvenir T-shirts and other cheap clothing, DVDs, as well as secondhand books in English and other Western languages.

🌀 Khao Hin Lek Fai

เขาหินเล็กไฟ

2 miles (3 km) W of town center. 🖉 📷
A 518-ft (158-m) high hill, Khao Hin Lek Fai, or Flintstone Hill, has a quiet park at the top offering scenic vistas from six separate viewpoints. The park's entrance is by Suksamran Temple.

Khao Takiab

เขาตะเกียบ

4 miles (6 km) S of town center. 📷
Rising just 250 ft (76 m) above sea level, Khao Takiab, or Chopstick Hill, is covered with several small shrines and images of Guan Yin, Goddess of Mercy. Near the foot of the hill is a 66-ft (20-m) tall statue of a Standing Buddha.

Nearby stands Wat Khao Lad, an impressive Buddhist temple with a distinctive pagoda.

Black Mountain Water Park

สวนน้ำ แบล็ค เมาน์เทน หัวหิน

10 miles (16 km) NW of town center.
Tel 0-3261-8444. **Open** 10am–5pm daily. 🏊 🖉

About 30 minutes by shuttle bus from Hua Hin Clock Tower, this small water park makes a fun family outing, with water slides, rapids, and a wave pool.

Vananava Jungle Water Park

3 miles (5 km) S of town center.
Tel 0-3290-9606. **Open** 10am–6pm (some areas to 9pm) daily. 🖉 📷
This fun family attraction, the first park of this type in Asia, has water slides, waterfalls, and jungle areas. It can be reached by free shuttle from several pickup points in Hua Hin.

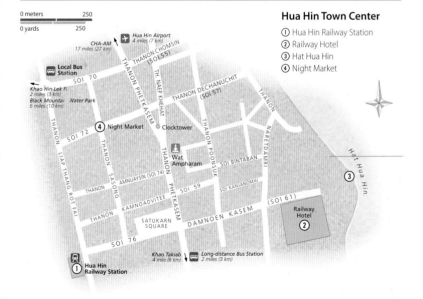

Hua Hin Town Center

① Hua Hin Railway Station
② Railway Hotel
③ Hat Hua Hin
④ Night Market

Walkway through the treetops, Pranburi Forest Park

❻ Pranburi

ปราณบุรี

Road Map C2. 22 miles (35 km) S of Hua Hin. 🚗 70,000. 🚌 🚐 🛳 daily.

A small town which is now becoming a preferred destination for visitors to Thailand, Pranburi is blessed with pristine beaches and a handful of good resorts. A popular attraction here is the **Pranburi Forest Park**, an area of mangrove forests located by the Pranburi River. Declared a forest park in 1982, it covers an area of 2 sq miles (5 sq km). The reserve lies close to the sea and boasts a 1-mile (2-km) long beach, lined with palm trees. An elevated wooden platform runs above part of the mangrove swamp

making it easy to trek through the forest. River trips by boat can be arranged from the park office open throughout the day. Pranburi is also well located for visitors to Hat Naresuan and Khao Sam Roi Yot National Park nearby.

🌳 **Pranburi Forest Park**
Open dawn to dusk daily. 🏞

❼ Hat Naresuan

หาดนเรศวร – ปากน้ำปราณ

Road Map C2. 6 miles (10 km) E of Pranburi. 🚌 🚐 ℹ️ TAT, Cha-am (0-3247-1005). 🌐 📷

Perhaps the first quiet beach south of Bangkok, Hat Naresuan is a long stretch of almost

deserted golden sand, lined with tall palm and casuarina trees. The beach is known by several names. A small hill at its southern end which resembles a *kalok* (skull) gives it the popular name of Hat Khao Kalok, or Skull Hill Beach. Another name for the beach is Pak Nam Pran after the town located 5 miles (8 km) to its north, at the mouth of the Pranburi River. Its official name, Hat Naresuan, however, honors King Naresuan *(see p45)* who re-established Siamese independence and drove out the Burmese in the late 16th century. Originally frequented by rich Thai families, it is now developing into a busy resort with several upscale as well as inexpensive boutique hotels and restaurants, a few small markets, and a variety of utility stores. Although not a spectacular beach, Hat Naresuan is popular for its attractive and reasonably priced accommodations. Dolphins playing in the sea are a common sight here and can usually be seen directly from the shore. There are several seafood restaurants in Pak Nam Pran town, as well as along the beachfront, which serve fresh food.

❽ Khao Sam Roi Yot National Park

อุทยานแห่งชาติเขาสามร้อยยอด

See pp148–9.

Popular beachfront restaurant on Hat Naresuan

❾ Hat Sam Roi Yot
หาดสามร้อยยอด

Road Map C2. Khao Sam Roi Yot National Park. 🚌 ℹ️ TAT, Cha-am (0-3247-1005). 🗓️ 📷

A clean beach with crisp, golden sand and shaded by palm trees, Hat Sam Roi Yot, also called Hat Nom Sao, runs through the eastern part of the Khao Sam Roi Yot National Park. This beautiful beach is considered safe and good for swimming. Basic, yet comfortable beachside accommodations are available and there are also a number of small and friendly restaurants and bars. Hat Sam Roi Yot also serves as the jumping-off point for several small, offshore islands, including Ko Nom Sao, Ko Kho Ram, Ko Rawing, and Ko Rawang, all excellent for snorkeling and private sunbathing. These islands are easily accessible by speedboat.

Beautiful Hat Sam Phraya, an ideal beach for campers

❿ Hat Laem Sala
หาดแหลมศาลา

Road Map C2. Khao Sam Roi Yot National Park. 🚌 ℹ️ TAT, Cha-am (0-3247-1005). 🗓️ 📷

An attractive beach surrounded by steep limestone hills and fringed by casuarina trees, Hat Laem Sala is an isolated stretch of sand. Located at the eastern edge of the Khao Sam Roi Yot National Park, the beach is equipped with a visitor center, restaurants, and basic bungalow accommodations. Beachfront restaurants serve a variety of fried seafood. The water here is safe for swimming; other outdoor activities include camping, trekking, and cave diving. Hat Laem Sala also marks the approach to **Tham Phraya Nakhon**. Built for Rama V (r.1868–1910), it is among the most popular caves in Thailand.

⓫ Hat Sam Phraya
หาดสามพระยา

Road Map C2. Khao Sam Roi Yot National Park. 🚌 ℹ️ TAT, Cha-am (0-3247-1005). 🗓️ 📷

A relatively untouristed white-sand beach, Hat Sam Phraya is well-equipped for campers visiting the Khao Sam Roi Yot National Park, with washing facilities as well as toilets on either end of the beach. There are also adequate, if not luxurious, bungalow accommodations, and small seafood restaurants and shops. Fine views across Hat Sam Phraya can be had from the summit of nearby Khao Daeng, or Red Hill, especially at sunset. Visitors can also embark on a cruise to explore **Khlong Khao Daeng**, or Khao Daeng canal. Located only about 1 mile (2 km) from the park, the canal is fringed by mangroves. This relaxing trip, lasting over an hour, covers a distance of 3 miles (5 km), and is best taken at sundown.

Rocky outcrop with thick vegetation, Hat Sam Roi Yot

❶ Khao Sam Roi Yot National Park

อุทยานแห่งชาติเขาสามร้อยยอด

A small coastal park, Khao Sam Roi Yot, which means "Mountain of Three Hundred Peaks", covers an area of 38 sq miles (98 sq km). It is a region of contrasts – sea, sand, and marsh, backed by mountains and caves. The park is best known for its distinctive limestone pinnacles, the highest of which, Khao Krachom, rises to a height of 1,985 ft (605 m). The park's fine beaches, freshwater marshes, and mangrove forests provide sanctuary to millions of migratory birds flying from Siberia to Sumatra and Australia; these birds rest, feed, and breed here. It is also home to the dusky langur, the slow loris, and crab-eating macaques.

Villagers fishing in the rich waters off Khao Sam Roi Yot National Park

★ **Spectacular Birdlife**
Located on the East Asian-Australian Flyway, the marshland areas of the park are home to some 300 species of birds – migratory species account for almost half of these. They can be seen between the months of September and November and from March to May.

Mangroves
Mangrove swamps and forests form an important coastal defence against high waves and storms; they also provide an impenetrable sanctuary for all kinds of wildlife, notably macaques and crabs.

KEY

① **The southern marshlands** have been little affected by encroaching shrimp farms. These pristine areas remain the best bird-watching spots.

② **Khao Krachom** dominates the limestone crags of the park. At 1,985 ft (605 m), it is not an easy climb.

③ **Ban Rong Jai** is the location of one of the three park headquarters at Khao Sam Roi Yot. It has an attached nature study center.

④ **Tham Sai**, a small cavern, provides sanctuary for numerous bats and swiftlets.

Pranb
27 miles (43 k

Thung Sam
Roi Yot

③ ⓘ **Bang Rong Jai**

Hua Hin
25 miles (40 km)

Khao Krachom
1,985 ft (605 m) ▲
②

①

Ban Don
Yai Nu

Kh
Dae
Viewpo

Prachuap
Khiri Khap
30 miles (48 km)

1026

1020

0 km 2
0 miles 2

★ View of the Three Hundred Peaks
The park's many limestone peaks are clad in evergreen and deciduous bushes and trees. These peaks do not make easy walking or climbing, but offer a wonderful spectacle, particularly at sunrise and sunset.

VISITORS' CHECKLIST

Practical Information
Road Map C2. Park HQ off Hwy 4, 27 miles (43 km) S of Pranburi.
ℹ️ Park HQ (0-3282-1568); Forestry Dept (0-2562-0760).
🏠🏠 Ⓦ dnp.go.th (for bungalow bookings).

Transport
🚌 Pranburi, then songthaew.

Hat Sam Roi Yot
Well served with facilities such as public washrooms, picnic areas, and restaurants, Hat Sam Roi Yot lies just outside the park. It also has good mid-range accommodations.

an Khao Niaw

Dolphin Bay

Ko Lam

an hu Noi

Ko Nom Sao

Gulf of Thailand

Hat Phu Noi

Bang Pu

Tham Kaew

Ko Sattakut

Hat Laem Sala

an Hup a Khot

Ban Khung Tanot

④

Hat Sam Phraya

an hao aeng

Key

  ═══ Minor road

  – – Trail

  - - Park boundary

For keys to symbols *see back flap*

★ Tham Phraya Nakhon
This mesmerizing cave was made famous after Rama V ordered the building of an attractive *sala* (pavilion) for himself here. Its attractions include the curiously shaped "crocodile rock" and "pagoda rock."

Hiking trails
Marked hiking trails are scattered throughout the park. The Khao Daeng Viewpoint Trail, however, remains the most popular. The panoramic views from its summit, of the park and surrounding sea, are breathtaking.

Light pouring in through the collapsed roof of the Tham Phraya Nakhon cave ▶

Wat Thammikaram atop Khao Chong Krajok at Prachuap Khiri Khan

across the town and bay. Hundreds of macaques live in the area and visitors often come here to watch them. Every evening, the monkeys climb to the top to feed on the many beautiful frangipani trees.

The town makes up for its lack of entertainment with its fantastic cuisine. Freshly caught seafood is available at quality restaurants and stalls along the promenade near the pier. Prachuap Khiri Khan is also a good base to explore the surrounding areas. The common mode of transport here is the *saaleng* (an improvised motorcycle with a sidecar).

⓬ Prachuap Khiri Khan
ประจวบคีรีขันธ์

Road Map C2. 47 miles (75 km) S of Pranburi. 🚌 🚐 🚤 ⓘ TAT, 39/9 Phetkasem Rd (0-3251-3885). 🛥 daily.

Located along the narrowest stretch of Thailand, between Myanmar on the west and the Gulf of Thailand on the east, Prachuap Khiri Khan is a fairly significant fishing port. A prominent provincial capital in southern Thailand, the town was prosperous during the Ayutthaya period *(see pp44–5)*, but is excluded from most tourist itineraries nowadays.

Historically, Prachuap is significant as one of the seven landing points where Imperial Japanese troops stormed ashore in 1941, on their way to

occupy Malaysia and Singapore. Today, the town is rather pleasant and laid-back. Fishing is the primary occupation, and colorful painted fishing vessels are usually anchored in the local harbor. Pineapple farms and coconut plantations occupy many acres of land and contribute to the economy of the area. The inland edge of the town is ringed with limestone mountains. A famous landmark – **Khao Chong Krajok**, or Mirror Tunnel Mountain – derives its name from a natural opening that resembles a giant mirror. **Wat Thammikaram** perched on its peak is Prachuap's most revered site, and offers visitors fine panoramic views right

Monk's residence, Wat Khao Tham Khan Kradai

⓭ Wat Khao Tham Khan Kradai
วัดถ้ำเขาทันกระได

Road Map C2. 5 miles (8 km) N of Prachuap Khiri Khan. 🚐
Open 8:30am–4pm daily. 🚫 📷

A Buddhist cave temple set above the beautiful Ao Khan Kradai, also known as Ao Khan Bandai, Wat Khao Tham Khan Kradai is slightly off the beaten track. The road to the temple winds its way up a limestone hill overlooking the bay. There is a trail paved with shells and signposts marking the route. From the cave entrance, there are stunning views across the broad sweep of Ao Khan Kradai. The *wat*

Buddha images lining the inner chamber at Wat Khao Tham Khan Kradai

Handcrafted fishing boats anchored along the shore at Ao Bang Nang Rom

Fishermen go out in these vessels to catch the *ching chang* – a prized local fish and an important source of livelihood. These small saltwater fish, part of the anchovy family, are cleaned, dried, and then preserved with condiments. These fish are popular among South Asian buyers. Although there is not much to do here, the friendly locals and the beautiful, well-located beach make it worth a stopover.

⓰ Ao Manao
อ่าวมะนาว

Road Map C2. 4 miles (6 km) S of Prachuap Khiri Khan.

Prachuap's loveliest bay, Ao Manao, or Lemon Bay, is lined by a fine beach. Originally an R&R (Rest and Recreation) site for officers from the nearby Royal Thai Air Force base, the beach is well maintained thanks to the military presence. A fair is held every December in the Air Force compound commem-orating the soldiers who died during the Japanese landing in 1941. Facilities at the beach include loungers, umbrellas, cold drink stands, and a few restaurants. The locals are friendly, but visitors may be asked to show their passports.

complex comprises two caves; entrance is through the smaller cave. This opens into a larger cave with a *phra non* (Reclining Buddha). A chamber near the entrance is filled with Buddha images brought by devotees as part of merit-making acts. Carrying a flashlight is useful, as the interior is quite dark.

Visitors from Prachuap Khiri Khan will need to arrange a *songthaew* or *saaleng* from town. Those with vehicles can combine a visit to the *wat* with a picnic at Hat Ao Noi.

⓮ Hat Ao Noi
หาดอ่าวน้อย

Road Map C2. 3 miles (5 km) N of Prachuap Khiri Khan.

A quiet, laid-back bathing spot, Hat Ao Noi, or Little Bay Beach, is a casuarina-lined beach popular with joggers and day-trippers from nearby Prachuap Khiri Khan. To the northern end of the bay lies the small fishing village of Ao Ban Noi. The southern end is connected to the busier Ao Prachuap by a bridge. The beach is quite deserted but offers good accommodations along with a few restaurants that serve appetizing seafood. The northern end of the bay is protected by a limestone massif.

⓯ Ao Bang Nang Rom
อ่าวบางนางรม

Road Map C2. 3 miles (5 km) E of Prachuap Khiri Khan.

Located close to Prachuap Khiri Khan and its satellite beach, Hat Ao Noi, Ao Bang Nang Rom is home to a prosperous fishing village reputed for its excellent handmade wooden fishing vessels. These colorful boats are used either by the local fishermen themselves or sold to neighboring communities.

Scenic view of the wide-sweeping bay at Ao Manao

Burmese products from across the border on sale in shops at Dan Singkhon

⓱ Dan Singkhon

ด่านสิงขร

Road Map C2. 12 miles (19 km) S of Prachuap Khiri Khan.

A small border post of considerable historical interest, Dan Singkhon is perched high on a watershed in the Tenasserim Mountains that divide Thailand from neighboring Myanmar. This crossing used to mark the Mawdaung Pass, which was the most important road link between the Tenasserim province and old Thailand, with a regular movement of people and commodities between the two countries until the British conquest of Burmese Tenasserim in 1826. Since then, this trade route has been closed and is now only used by local Burmese and Thai merchants. Dan Singkhon is at Thailand's narrowest point – the distance from the village to the Gulf of Thailand is a mere 8 miles (13 km). The mountain road allows visitors to look across the hills into southern Myanmar. This outpost is positioned to become a gateway for the Tenasserim archipelago.

The real attraction of Dan Singkhon, however, is the weekend flower market with a variety of rare flora, in particular orchids, imported from neighboring Myanmar. Unfortunately, many of the species are endangered, but the illegal trade continues to flourish. One of the unusual specimens on sale at Dan Singkhon is the rafflesia, the world's largest flower, whose buds are sold here. However, as the plant is parasitic and cannot be cultivated artificially, its life span is limited.

The drive to Dan Singkhon makes an interesting day trip from nearby Prachuap Khiri Khan, and unusual migratory birds can be seen en route. It is best to avoid purchasing plants protected under the Convention on International Trade in Endangered Species of Wild Flora and Fauna (CITES).

Rafflesia in full bloom

⓲ Hat Wa Kaw

หาดหว้ากอ

Road Map C2. 10 miles (16 km) S of Prachuap Khiri Khan.

A beautiful casuarina-lined beach encircling a small bay, Hat Wa Kaw is a quiet and clean beach. It is an ideal place for a day trip especially for visitors based in Prachuap Khiri Khan nearby. Facilities here include simple bungalow accommodations as well as a number of small restaurants serving local food. Although there are relatively few overseas travelers to be found at Hat Wa Kaw, the beach is a popular picnic spot for Thai families, especially school children visiting the King Mongkut Memorial Park.

⓳ King Mongkut Memorial Park of Science and Technology

พิพิธภัณฑ์วิทยาศาสตร์รัชกาลที่สี่

Road Map C2. 10 miles (16 km) S of Prachuap Khiri Khan. **Tel** 0-3266-1098. **Open** 9am–4pm daily.

The largest open-air park in Thailand, King Mongkut Memorial Park of Science and Technology is both a memorial and an educational facility. Established in 1989, this park is dedicated to the memory of King Mongkut, or Rama IV (r.1851–68), one of Thailand's most revered monarchs. This park commemorates his contribution to modern Thai science. More specifically, it celebrates his visit to the area in 1868 to view an eclipse that he had predicted. Attractions include an exhibition on outer space and astronomy, a butterfly garden, and a good aquarium with a walk-through glass tunnel with many local species of fish and other marine life. Other exhibits include a statue of King Mongkut and an American steam locomotive dating back to 1925. Located close to Prachuap, the park is ideal for a day trip and is frequented by Thai families and students, who usually combine a trip to the park with a picnic at Hat Wa Kaw.

Feeding fish in the aquarium at King Mongkut Memorial Park

Mongkut, Thailand's Scholar King

King Mongkut, or Rama IV, was the fourth in the line of the present ruling Chakri Dynasty, and father of the illustrious Rama V (r.1868–1910). He ruled the country from 1851 until his death in 1868. A serious, scholarly man and an able ruler, Mongkut was interested in matters of religion and brought important changes in Buddhism. His government also formed new alliances with the Western world and began a series of far-sighted reforms which contributed to Thailand's uninterrupted independence right through the period of Colonial rule elsewhere. A liberal and educated man, he traveled extensively, learning about different aspects of his country and its people. Mongkut continues to be venerated as one of Thailand's most important monarchs and bears the posthumous title of *maharat* (Great King).

Mongkut's envoys at the court of Queen Victoria were part of his policy to gain the backing of European powers. He turned away from his traditional allies and corresponded with foreign rulers to develop new ties with the West.

Mongkut took on the title of Rex Siamensis (King of Siam) after the style of Western kings. His ideas on monarchy were very progressive, influenced by international governments. Mongkut's foresight contributed much to the development of the nation.

Wat Bowonniwet is where Mongkut served as a monk and later became abbot, devoting the first half of his life to religion. It still continues to be patronized by the royal family.

A mural at Wat Ratchapradit, Bangkok, depicts Mongkut observing a solar eclipse. He took a great interest in astronomy and was regarded as the father of modern Thai science.

Mongkut's son Chulalongkorn, or Rama V, was given a liberal education by his father and exposed to Western ideas. He grew up to become Thailand's greatest king, taking Mongkut's legacy forward in modernizing the country.

A popular resort and spa at beautiful Hat Ban Krut

⑳ Hat Ban Krut
หาดบ้านกรูด

Road Map C2. 44 miles (71 km) S of Prachuap Khiri Khan. 🚌 🚐 🅸 TAT, Prachuap Khiri Khan (0-3251-3885). 🖊 📷

With the beautiful Thong Chai Mountains forming a backdrop, Hat Ban Krut is a lovely, 4-mile (6-km) stretch of beach facing the clear, aquamarine waters of the Gulf of Thailand. The beach is used mainly as a weekend destination by Thais and remains deserted during the week. This quiet stretch of coast between Prachuap Khiri Khan and Chumphon *(see p158)* is still developing. Hat Ban Krut, however, is easily accessible, with its own bus station, 8 miles (13 km) from the long shoreline, and train station, 3 miles (5 km)

from the beach. There are comfortable, mid-range bungalow accommodations available here, as well as numerous restaurants, cafés, and bars set back from the shore along the palm-fringed coastal road. The area is also well-known for batik production. These products are available at local shops and make excellent souvenirs.

The northern end of the beach is dominated by a Buddhist temple, Wat Phra Mahathat Phraphat, easily identified by its nine golden stupas and a 49-ft (15-m) high golden statue of the Buddha, locally known as the Big Buddha.

The picturesque offshore island of Ko Lamla is a great spot for snorkeling and easily accessible by boat. The clear waters surrounding the island are a haven for exotic marine life.

Buddha at Wat Phra Mahathat Phraphat

㉑ Bang Saphan
บางสะพาน

Road Map C3. 56 miles (90 km) S of Prachuap Khiri Khan. 🚌 🚐 🅸 TAT, Hua Hin (0-3251-3885). 🖊 📷

A quiet fishing harbor with good rail and road links to the cities of Bangkok and Chumphon, Bang Saphan dominates an attractive bay,

Ao Bang Saphan, that faces south and east across the Gulf of Thailand. Bang Saphan's two beaches, **Bang Saphan Yai** and **Bang Saphan Noi**, 10 miles (16 km) to the south, are usually frequented by Thais from Bangkok and locals from the nearby areas, who visit these spots on weekends and vacations. The town also offers plenty of other attractions in the form of several stunning waterfalls, caves, and a driving range for golfers.

Three small islands in the vicinity of Bang Saphan Yai, **Ko Thalu**, Ko Sang, and Ko Sing, are located about 20 minutes away by boat, and are ideal for swimming and sunbathing. Ko Thalu, in particular, is an excellent snorkeling destination with schools of moon wrasse and parrot fish as well as corals inhabiting the clear, warm waters. Snorkeling tours can be arranged for visitors between the months of January and May.

Bang Saphan Yai provides plenty of mid-range accommodations, reasonably priced seafood restaurants, beachside bars, and motorcycle rentals. The beaches are particularly crowded around holidays such as Songkran *(see p38)* and it is advisable to make hotel bookings in advance.

Houses on stilts and anchored boats belonging to the fishing community at Bang Saphan

For hotels and restaurants in this region see pp297–8 and pp312–13

Kiteboarding along the beach at Hat Thung Wua Laen

㉒ Hat Thung Wua Laen
หาดทุ่งวัวแล่น

Road Map C3. 10 miles (16 km) N of Chumphon. 🚗 🚌 𝒊 TAT, Surat Thani (0-7728-8818). 🚤 🏊 🏕

An extremely popular beach, Hat Thung Wua Laen's name, which means "Running Bull Field", derives from a local legend about a magical bull that came alive while being skinned by hunters and ran into the forest. The beach is a long, lovely stretch of white sand that slopes gently into the warm waters of the Gulf of Thailand. Popular with local Thais, Hat Thung Wua Laen now draws growing numbers of vacationers who come here for the relative solitude, reasonable prices, and excellent authentic Thai seafood. The picturesque beachfront is lined with a few resorts offering bungalow accommodations. A number of good seafood restaurants have also opened shop.

Hat Thung Wua Laen is a perfect spot for swimming and also offers great snorkeling opportunities. The surrounding waters are home to some fine coral reefs supporting sea fans, marine sponges, sea flowers, and shoals of tropical fish. Visitors can hire canoes, bicycles, and motorcycles from shops along the beach to explore the area or take a ferry to the popular dive sites nearby.

㉓ Ko Ngam Yai and Ko Ngam Noi
เกาะงามใหญ่และเกาะงามน้อย

Road Map C3. 11 miles (18 km) E of Hat Thung Wua Laen. 🚤 from Hat Thung Wua Laen. 𝒊 TAT, Surat Thani (0-7728-8818).

Located within easy reach of Hat Thung Wua Laen, the twin islands of Ko Ngam Yai, or Big Beautiful Island, and Ko Ngam Noi, or Small Beautiful Island, are especially popular among vacationers and day-trippers for their excellent dive sites. The islands are best known locally, however, for their tens of thousands of swiftlets, tiny inhabitants that ensure a rich harvest of nests for Thailand's famous bird's-nest soup. The surrounding clear waters are home to coral reefs, unusual underwater rock formations, and caves. Snorkelers will find a rich variety of marine creatures including humpback snappers, clams, oysters, and sea anemones. These islands make for an ideal day trip by chartered boat from Hat Thung Wua Laen.

㉔ Hin Lak Ngam
หินหลักงาม

Road Map C3. 5 miles (8 km) S of Ko Ngam Yai. 🚤 from Hat Thung Wua Laen. 𝒊 TAT, Surat Thani (0-7728-8818).

A rocky outcrop lying offshore from Hat Thung Wua Laen, Hin Lak Ngam, along with nearby Hin Pae, is one of the most rewarding dive spots off Chumphon's coast. The outcrop, just a few feet wide, is devoid of any vegetation or even a landing spot. The appeal of Hin Lak Ngam, however, lies not above water, but beneath it. The surrounding waters offer fantastic undersea views of coral reefs, gardens, and narrow swim-through caves, as well as an amazing variety of brightly colored shoals of fish and other marine life. On a good day, visibility is around 64 ft (20 m), although at low tide or in choppy weather it is much less. The rock is sometimes visited by sea turtles, as well as flights of migratory seabirds. Although an excellent dive spot, divers must be aware that there are poisonous fish which frequent the underwater reefs including lionfish, devilfish, and trigger fish.

A colony of white-bellied swiftlets on a cliffside in Ko Ngam

The slow boat that travels between Chumphon and the island of Ko Tao

㉕ Chumphon

ชุมพร

Road Map C3. 105 miles (169 km) S of Prachuap Khiri Khan. 🚐 35,000. 🚌 🚐 🚌 🚢 daily.

An important provincial capital and transport hub, Chumphon, sometimes called "the gateway to the south", has its own airport and is also a transit point for boats to Ko Samui (see pp166–75), Ko Phangan (see pp176–81), and Ko Tao (see pp186–9). The town is located on the Isthmus of Kra with the mountain range of Ranong province to the west and the Gulf of Thailand to the east, and forms a cultural border

between the Thai-Buddhist north and the Thai-Muslim south. In ancient times, Chumphon used to be a military post of strategic importance. It was used by the army and navy as a place to rally their forces before any major war engagements. The town supposedly derives its name from the Thai word chumnumphon, which means accumulation of forces.

One of its main attractions is the **National Museum** showcasing the province's history. The **Military Youth Monument**, located a few miles from the town, commemorates the bravery of the Thai soldiers

who fought against the Japanese during World War II. The town was also the residence of Admiral Phra Borommawong Thoe Kromluang Chumphon, one of the sons of Rama V (r.1868–1910). Also known as Prince Chumphon, the admiral was regarded as the father of the Royal Thai Navy.

There are several attractive beaches at Hat Thung Wua Laen (see p157) to the north, and at Hat Sai Ri and Ao Thung Makham to the south. There are about 47 offshore islands and the town is a good base to explore the surrounding reefs. Visitors can also head to the nearby beach of Hat Paradonpap, which is famous for its seafood.

Thatched seafood shacks lining the beach at Hat Sai Ri

㉖ Hat Sai Ri

หาดทรายรี

Road Map C3. 8 miles (13 km) S of Chumphon. 🚌 🏍 🏠

The main beach in this area, Hat Sai Ri (not to be confused with Hat Sai Ri Sawi further south), and the small village of Ban Hat Sai Ri, are easily accessible by bus or motorcycle from Chumphon. The beach is a long curving stretch of white sands backed by coconut palms. It doubles as an idyllic spot for holiday-makers as well as a ground for local fishermen.

This beach hosts the annual **Chumphon Sea World Fair** in March to promote tourism, preserve the natural beauty of the region, and raise awareness

The Kra Canal

For almost 400 years an idea has been mooted for building a canal across the Thai-Malaysian peninsula, approximately between Ranong on the Andaman Coast and Lang Suan on the Gulf of Thailand. The Kra Canal was proposed to cut across the peninsula at its narrowest point, the Isthmus of Kra, where the distance is just 28 miles (45 km). This would shorten shipping routes by creating a direct passage between the Andaman Sea and the Gulf of Thailand. Actual plans were first floated under Narai the Great (r.1656–88) as early as 1677, when he asked French engineers at his court to evaluate the possibility of a trans-peninsular canal.

A century later, Ferdinand de Lesseps, the designer of the Suez Canal, visited the area but his plans were foiled by the British, who wished to maintain the prominence of the port of Singapore. Proposals have resurfaced regularly without any effect, as the consequent politico-economic advantages would tilt the axis of power in Southeast Asia. Thus, although the Kra Canal exists only on paper, its projected strategic benefits refuse to let the concept disappear altogether.

King Narai the Great

about the local ecology. The nearby **Prince Chumphon Monument** includes a much revered shrine as well as the 225-ft (68-m) long decommissioned torpedo boat HMS *Chumphon*.

Most people prefer to visit Hat Sai Ri as a day trip from Chumphon. However, the beach has several resorts, restaurants, and bars to cater to visitors who might decide to stay the night.

㉗ Ao Thung Makham
อ่าวทุ่งมะขาม

Road Map C3. 15 miles (24 km) S of Chumphon.

The next stop down the coast from Hat Sai Ri is neighboring Ao Thung Makham, a twin bay with two shallow semi-circles fringed by a long white-sand beach backed by pretty casuarinas and coconut palms. Right in the middle of the twin bay is a small rocky peninsula, which acts as a dividing spit of land between Ao Thung Makham Nai to the north, and Ao Thung Makham Nok to the south. Toward the southern end of the latter is **Wat Suwan Khuha Wari Wong**. Known locally as Wat Pong Pang, this venerated temple set in front of a 256-ft (78-m) high cliff and shaded by coconut trees. The beach is visited by locals

Ao Thung Makham pier, a jumping-off point to nearby islands

from Chumphon, and the seafood restaurants and bars primarily cater to them. However, Ao Thung Makham is becoming increasingly popular with foreign visitors en route to more popular destinations such as Ko Samui *(see pp166–75)*. It is a good place to stay and recuperate from traveling as well as escape the crowds on the commercial beaches for a few days.

㉘ Hat Arunothai
หาดอรุโณทัย

Road Map C3. 38 miles (60 km) S of Chumphon.

A lovely beach close to the Tako River estuary south of Chumphon, Hat Arunothai is at the very edge of the Chumphon province. Located 6 miles

(10 km) off Highway 41, the long palm-lined stretch of white sand curves gently away to the south. The beach has a memorial shrine to Admiral Chumphon, revered by sailors and fishermen alike throughout the province. This beach also has a series of small seafood restaurants, food stalls, bars, and mid-range accommodations. Longtail boats are available for hire to visit the many offshore islands.

Hat Arunothai is, in fact, a good place to experience the local flavor of the Chumphon province. The picturesque fishing village of Ban Ao Mamuang is just about 9 miles (14 km) north of the beach. Visitors can also stop at the nearby estuary of **Pak Nam Thung Tako** to take in the colorful sight of fishermen departing for their daily catch.

Panoramic view of the Gulf of Thailand at sunset from Hat Arunothai

LOWER WESTERN GULF COAST

The Lower Western Gulf Coast extends south from the Isthmus of Kra to Nakhon Si Thammarat, the ancient cultural center of southern Thailand. This region is home to the beautiful palm-clad islands of Ko Samui and Ko Phangan, the diving hub of Ko Tao, and the unmatched splendor of the Ang Thong Marine National Park, collectively offering visitors a choice of destinations including gorgeous tropical beaches, lush forests, and historical temples.

For over 2,000 years, the Lower Western Gulf Coast has been a major cultural crossroads with Hindu, Buddhist, and Islamic influences. It has also been an important part of the ancient trade routes through the Straits of Malacca. Finds from historic trading centers around the Isthmus of Kra testify to strong links with China, India, the Middle East, and the Roman Empire before AD 1000. From the 16th century onward, development of trade ties with the Spanish and Portuguese, followed a century later by trade with the Dutch and British, introduced greater diversity to this region. The Srivijaya Empire held sway over these parts between the 7th and 13th centuries, and upon its decline both Myanmar and Thailand fought to control this territory.

This coastal area also acts as a bridge between the Buddhist-north and the Malay-Muslim influenced Deep South.

The forested Tenasserim Mountains continue south into the Lower Western Gulf Coast tapering away after Ranong. The mountains give way to rich and wide agricultural lands. Palm trees stud the coast while sharp limestone peaks characterize the interiors. Both the mainland and the offshore islands offer a wide choice of beaches, from the bustling Hat Lamai and Hat Chaweng at Ko Samui to the more isolated stretches at Ko Phangan. The rich waters of the Gulf of Thailand can best be explored at Ang Thong Marine National Park and Ko Tao, while historic Nakhon Si Thammarat and the ancient port of Chaiya offer an insight into the area's past.

Holiday-makers enjoying a sundowner at a beachfront café, Ko Tao

◄ The view from Ko Wua Talab, one of the islands in the Ang Thong Marine National Park

Exploring the Lower Western Gulf Coast

This part of the coast overlooking the Gulf of Thailand has miles of beautiful white-sand beaches. It is home to the gorgeous Samui archipelago with its luxurious hotels, as well as the lesser developed Ko Phangan favored by young backpackers. Ko Tao, to the north, is a diver's paradise, while Ang Thong Marine National Park is a tiny archipelago whose natural beauty is unmatched in all of Thailand. Apart from the surrounding islands, the Lower Western Gulf Coast has attractive beaches, some of which are quieter than their busy offshore counterparts. Historic towns such as Chaiya, an ancient Srivijaya settlement, and Nakhon Si Thammarat, the cultural capital of southern Thailand, are also located here. Farther inland, the Khao Luang National Park shelters some of this area's extraordinary wildlife.

Palm trees on beautiful cliffs overlooking Hat Tong Yi

Sights at a Glance

Snorkeling in the clear waters around Ang Thong

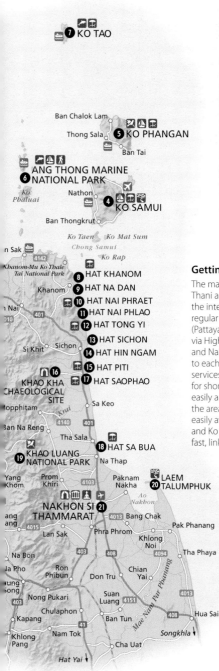

KO TAO **7**

Ban Chalok Lam

Thong Sala **5** KO PHANGAN

Ban Tai

ANG THONG MARINE
6 NATIONAL PARK

Ko
Phaluai

Nathon

4 KO SAMUI

Ban Thongkrut

Ko Taen   Ko Mat Sum

Chong Samui

Ko Rap

n Sak

Khanom-Mu Ko Thale
Tai National Park

8 HAT KHANOM

Khanom

9 HAT NA DAN

n Nai

10 HAT NAI PHRAET

11 HAT NAI PHLAO

12 HAT TONG YI

Si Khit   Sichon

13 HAT SICHON

14 HAT HIN NGAM

16

15 HAT PITI

KHAO KHA
CHAEOLOGICAL
SITE

17 HAT SAOPHAO

Sa Keo

Iopphitam

Krai

Ban Na Reng

Tha Sala

18 HAT SA BUA

19 KHAO LUANG
NATIONAL PARK

Na Thap

Yang
Khom

Prom
Khiri

Paknam
Nakha

20 LAEM
TALUMPHUK

Ao
Nakhon

NAKHON SI
THAMMARAT **21**

ang
ang

Bang Chak

Lan Sak

Phra Phrom

Pak Phanang

Na Bon

Ron
Phibun

Don Tru

Chian
Yai

Khlong
Noi

Tha Phaya

ung
ong

Nong Pukari

Suan
Luang

Chulaphon

Ban Tun

Hua Sai

Kapang

Nam Tok

Songkhla

Khlong
Pang

Cha Uat

Hat Yai

Getting Around

The main domestic airports in the region are at Surat
Thani and Nakhon Si Thammarat on the mainland, and
the international airport is at Ko Samui. There are also
regular flights between Ko Samui, Phuket, and U Tapao
(Pattaya). Most of the mainland attractions are linked
via Highway 41 and Highway 401 leading to Surat Thani
and Nakhon Si Thammarat. The major towns are linked
to each other and to Bangkok by regular bus and train
services. Taxis, *songthaews,* and tuk-tuks can be hired
for short trips, and motorbike and bicycle rentals are
easily arranged. The most convenient way to explore
the area is by self-driven car. Car rental facilities are
easily available at Surat Thani, Nakhon Si Thammarat,
and Ko Samui. Ferry services are frequent and fairly
fast, linking Ko Tao, Ko Phangan, and Ko Samui.

Key

▬ Major road

═ Minor road

⌁ Railway

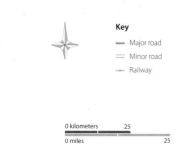

0 kilometers   25

0 miles   25

For keys to symbols *see back flap*

❶ Chaiya
ไชยา

Road Map C4. 367 miles (591 km) S of Bangkok. 🚗 48,000. 🚉 🚌 ℹ TAT, Surat Thani (0-7728-8818). 🚌 daily. 🎎 Chak Phra Festival (Oct–Nov).

Once an important center of Srivijaya culture in southern Thailand, modern Chaiya still contains a number of significant archaeological sites that have survived from the Srivijaya period *(see p43)*. Situated on the main railway line between the well-known towns of Chumphon *(see p158)* and Surat Thani, Chaiya was the regional capital of the mighty Srivijaya kingdom in the 5th–13th centuries. Its name is probably a derivative of *Srivijaya*, which means "radiant victory". Chaiya boasts such intriguing sights as rare statues of Bengali-style Buddha images and deities such as Vishnu, part of the Hindu holy trinity. These fascinating statues, proud survivors of a bygone era, are evidence of the Mon-Dvaravati and Indic-Srivijaya influences on the art of the time. These, together with a variety of votive tablets, are preserved and displayed at the **Chaiya National Museum**, located a 10-minute walk from the railway station. Also on display at the museum are several other examples of art from the later Ayutthaya period *(see pp44–5)*. The most important surviving

Stone relief on the side of the meditation hall, Wat Suan Mokkhaphalaram

relic is **Wat Phra Boromathat Chaiya**, an important Srivijaya temple. Within the compound of the *wat* stands a central *chedi* that has been painstakingly restored. This square-shaped structure has four porches which ascend in tiers and are topped with small towers. Dating from the 8th century, the *chedi* is built of brick covered with stucco. Other less well preserved, but still beautiful, relics of Chaiya's luminous past include three ancient and crumbling *chedis* at Wat Hua Wiang, Wat Lhong, and Wat Kaew, all of which are located on a north-south axis within the precincts of the town.

🏛 **Chaiya National Museum**
Phra Boromathat Chaiya, 1 mile (2 km) W of town center. **Tel** 0-7743-1066. **Open** 9am–4pm Wed–Sun. **Closed** public holidays. 🎟
ⓦ **thailandmuseum.com**

❷ Wat Suan Mokkhaphalaram
วัดสวนโมกข์

Road Map C4. Off Hwy 41, 4 miles (6 km) S of Chaiya. **Tel** 0-7743-1552. 🚉 🚌 from Chaiya. ℹ TAT, Surat Thani (0-7728-8818). **Open** daily. ⓦ **suanmokkh.org**

Perhaps the best known and most popular meditation temple in Thailand, Wat Suan Mokkhaphalaram (often shortened to Wat Suan Mokkh), meaning "Temple of the Garden of Liberation", is associated with the well-known International Dhamma Heritage movement. Run by the World Fellowship of Buddhists, it is an organization that seeks to promote *dhamma* (teachings of the Buddha) through meditation.

The inspiration behind the *wat*'s meditation techniques is the back-to-basics Buddhist

Buddha images at Wat Phra Boromathat Chaiya, one of the few remaining temples from the Srivijaya period

For hotels and restaurants in this region see pp298–9 and pp313–14

philosophy of the temple's founder, Buddhadhasa Bhikku, who died in 1993. Within the temple a strict regimen of physical labor, cleaning, and gardening underpins a simple monastic life devoid of the elaborate religious ceremonies, superstition, and spirit worship usually associated with Buddhism in Thailand.

The *wat* complex includes the monks' quarters, a spiritual theater, a meditation hall, and a sculpture workshop, as well as a library. A clearing on the top of a hill, which is reached by walking past the monks' quarters and the cremation site of Buddhadasa Bhikku, marks the most holy spot in the complex. It is decorated with statues of the Buddha and the Buddhist Wheel of Law. Ten-day meditation retreats are held here, beginning from the first of each month.

❸ Surat Thani
สุราษฎร์ธานี

Road Map C4. 38 miles (60 km) S of Chaiya. 🚉 126,000. ✈ 19 miles (31 km) SW of Surat Thani. 🚍 🚐 🚌 ℹ TAT, 5 Talat Mai Rd, Surat Thani (0-7728-8818). 🎊 Rambutan Fair (Aug); Chak Phra Festival (Oct–Nov).

Strategically located at the mouth of the Tapi and Phum Duang rivers, Surat Thani was a prominent commercial center as far back as the Srivijaya period. Today, it is significant as the capital of the Surat Thani province, the largest province in southern Thailand. The town, whose name literally means "City of the Good People", is an important center with an economy that is heavily dependent on its fishing harbor, commercial seaport, and

Boat anchored on the Phum Duang riverfront, Surat Thani

cultivation of rambutan, rubber, rice, and coconut. It features on visitors' itineraries, however, as an airport and ferry port as well as an important stop on the railway line between Bangkok and Hat Yai *(see p284)*. Despite having little to offer, except its links to the past, Surat Thani's prominence as a jumping-off point to the islands in its vicinity is well established. Visitors usually stop overnight on their way to Ko Samui *(see pp166–75)*, Ko Phangan *(see pp176–81)*, or even Ko Tao *(see pp186–9)*.

The riverside is also an appealing area with small boats ferrying people back and forth to the busy markets on the waterfront. These bustling markets sell fresh produce such as coconut and flowers.

Monks' living quarters in the midst of the jungle, Wat Suan Mokkhaphalaram

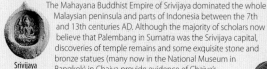

Chaiya's Role in the Srivijaya Empire

The Mahayana Buddhist Empire of Srivijaya dominated the whole Malaysian peninsula and parts of Indonesia between the 7th and 13th centuries AD. Although the majority of scholars now believe that Palembang in Sumatra was the Srivijaya capital, discoveries of temple remains and some exquisite stone and bronze statues (many now in the National Museum in Bangkok) in Chaiya provide evidence of Chaiya's importance. Its strategic geographical position as a coastal port meant that the town played an important role in the trade between India, the Thai peninsula, and China. In fact, Chaiya was mentioned in the writings of the Chinese monk I Ching, who, while visiting the area in the late 7th century, testified to its religious and cultural sophistication. It is known that some of Chaiya's rulers were connected by marriage to those of central Java. Furthermore, it is possible that the name "Chaiya" originated as a contraction of "Siwichaiya" (a different transliteration of *Srivijaya*), which follows the local tendency to emphasize the final syllable of a word.

Srivijaya votive tablet

An 8th-century bronze statue, Chaiya

❹ Ko Samui

เกาะสมุย

Located in the Gulf of Thailand south of Bangkok, Ko Samui is Thailand's third-largest island after Phuket and Ko Chang. It was originally settled by mariners from China who began cultivating coconut on the island. Even today, its inhabitants refer to themselves as *chao samui*, or people of Samui. A backpackers' haven in the 1970s, tourism has now become its main income generator. Rapid development, the arrival of major hotel and spa chains, persistent promotion by tourism authorities, and its beautiful beaches have led to a huge influx of visitors. Despite this, Ko Samui retains its position as a tropical paradise.

Getting ready for a dip at the cooling Na Muang Waterfalls

Bophut
The bustling village of Bophut includes bungalows, hotels, banks, bars, restaurants, and a range of water sports. The 1-mile (2-km) long beach is popular with families and backpackers.

Secret Buddha Garden
Also known as Uncle Nim's Garden after its founder Nim Thongsuk, the Secret Buddha Garden features statues of various figures from Buddhist mythology. The garden is surrounded by lush tropical forests.

KEY

① **Ko Taen** is a gorgeous offshore island with isolated beaches of white sand and some beautiful coral reefs.

For hotels and restaurants in this region see pp298–9 and pp313–14

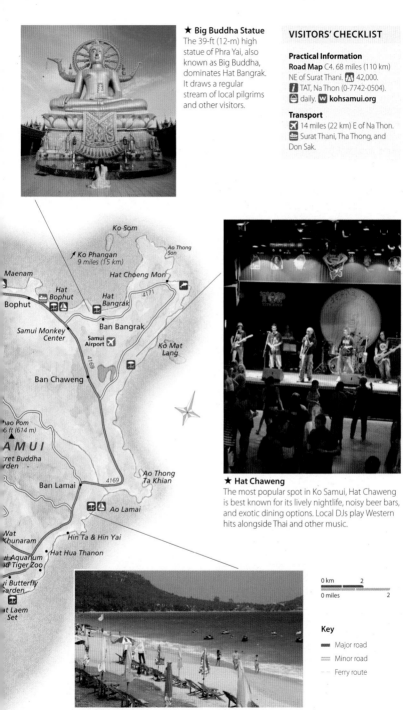

★ **Big Buddha Statue**
The 39-ft (12-m) high statue of Phra Yai, also known as Big Buddha, dominates Hat Bangrak. It draws a regular stream of local pilgrims and other visitors.

VISITORS' CHECKLIST

Practical Information
Road Map C4. 68 miles (110 km) NE of Surat Thani. 🚍 42,000. 🛈 TAT, Na Thon (0-7742-0504). 🚢 daily. **W** kohsamui.org

Transport
✈ 14 miles (22 km) E of Na Thon. 🚍 Surat Thani, Tha Thong, and Don Sak.

★ **Hat Chaweng**
The most popular spot in Ko Samui, Hat Chaweng is best known for its lively nightlife, noisy beer bars, and exotic dining options. Local DJs play Western hits alongside Thai and other music.

★ **Hat Lamai**
Ko Samui's second-longest beach, Hat Lamai is great for watersports. Swimming is possible year-round; visitors can also go water-skiing or windsurfing.

Key
- ▬ Major road
- ▭ Minor road
- -- Ferry route

0 km 2
0 miles 2

For keys to symbols *see back flap*

Exploring Ko Samui

Exploring Samui is both easy and enjoyable. The mountainous interior is ringed by a narrow two-lane, well-maintained road. Public transport is by *songthaew*, tuk-tuk, or taxi. Those who prefer driving can hire a vehicle – there are car rental outlets at the airport and in large towns, and plenty of shops renting motorbikes and bicycles. But drivers must be careful while venturing out on their own at night, particularly around Hat Lamai and Hat Chaweng, where drunk driving is common; flash floods in the rainy season are another hazard. It is also possible to hire longtail boats as taxis along the coast.

Surf breaking on the gorgeous beach at Hat Maenam

Delicious tropical fruits for sale at the local market in Na Thon

🚏 Na Thon

หนแแมแนาทอน

🖊️ 📷

Founded in 1905 as the administrative center of Ko Samui, Na Thon is the island's capital and main ferry port. A sleepy town with a distinct charm of its own, Na Thon is home to a majority of the local populace and also well equipped, with a supermarket, post office, police station, and immigration office, as well as foreign exchange facilities. Although the beach here is not spectacular, the local market, which sells fresh produce such as fruits, vegetables, and seafood, is certainly worth a visit, also for a taste of the delicious local cuisine. A haven for shoppers, visitors can strike some great deals at the various batik and souvenir shops in the area.

Few visitors stay here, using the town only as a transit point from which to catch the early morning boat to Surat Thani *(see p165)*. The town is also well connected to other places on the island through the main 31-mile (50-km) long circular road. Local *songthaews* departing from Na Thon's ferry port travel either toward Hat Chaweng and the airport in the north, or popular Hat Lamai in the south.

🚏 Ao Bang Pho

อ่าวบางปอ

4 miles (6 km) NE of Na Thon. 🖊️

Located close to the northwestern tip of Ko Samui, Ao Bang Pho receives relatively few visitors. The bay is backed by a beautiful stretch of beach, fringed with palm trees and offering stunning views across the Gulf of Thailand as far as Ko Phangan *(see pp176–81)*. The clear waters off the beach present good snorkeling opportunities. During the northeast monsoon from November to March, when the winds are particularly strong, visitors can also go windsurfing and kiteboarding.

🚏 Hat Maenam

หาดแม่น้ำ

7 miles (11 km) NE of Na Thon. 🖊️ 📷

A 2-mile (3-km) long beach with gorgeous views across the waters to Ko Phangan, Hat Maenam is a

Fishermen setting out to sea in longtail fishing boats from the pier at Na Thon

fairly quiet beach and a great place to unwind. The main road behind the beach is lined with several go-go and beer bars, cafés, and Thai restaurants, as well as shops selling local handicrafts such as handbags, coconut bowls, Buddha statues, and beautiful ceramics.

Visitors flock to Hat Maenam for the excellent windsurfing opportunities, aided by the strong breeze that blows onshore during the northeast monsoon. Swimming is another relaxing option. Hat Maenam is easily accessible by *songthaew* or a hired motorcycle from the nearby town of Na Thon.

Staircase leading to the towering Big Buddha, Ko Faan, Hat Bangrak

Quiet road in Fisherman's Village, Hat Bophut

🏊 Hat Bophut

หาดบ่อผุด
11 miles (18 km) NE of Na Thon.
🏊 📷

Popular with families and backpackers alike, Hat Bophut is a 1-mile (2-km) long beach with better facilities than those at Hat Maenam. Fisherman's Village, located to the east of the beach, is the center of Bophut. Bungalow accommodations, a bank, bars, and restaurants, are some of the utilities available in the village, Ban Bophut. There is also a range of watersports and several dive shops.

Hat Bangrak

หาดบางรัก
13 miles (21 km) NE of Na Thon.
🏊 📷

An ideal getaway for a family vacation, Hat Bangrak, also known as Big Buddha Beach,

stretches for nearly 3 miles (5 km) and its eastern end is a great spot for snorkeling. A narrow causeway links this end of the beach to **Ko Faan**, a tiny islet also on the eastern end, dominated by a 39-ft (12-m) high Buddha statue, which lends the beach its name. This statue is popular with locals as well as foreign visitors. A bazaar of souvenir stalls and cafés has sprung up at the foot of the staircase, decorated with *nagas* (serpents), leading to the statue. There are plenty of accommodation options ranging from bungalows to upscale resorts. Visitors can enjoy watersports, swimming, and Thai massages.

Ao Thong Son and Hat Choeng Mon

ท้องสนและเชิงมน
15 miles (24 km) NE of Na Thon.
🏊 📷

A peaceful inlet with great views across Hat Choeng Mon, Ao Thong Son is dominated by a rocky cove on one side and a beach on the other. The bay is ideal for swimming, diving, and snorkeling, while the beach is lined with restaurants and bars – great for spending a quiet evening. This area is dominated by several upscale resorts and spas offering state-of-the-art facilities, but inexpensive accommodations are hard to come by.

Sandy headland jutting into the sea at Hat Choeng Mon

Busy Hat Chaweng, the longest and most attractive beach on Ko Samui

🚇 Hat Chaweng

หาดเฉวง

14 miles (22 km) E of Na Thon. 🚗 📷

The longest, busiest, and most beautiful beach on Ko Samui, Hat Chaweng stretches for 3 miles (5 km) down the east coast of the island. Its warm waters, white sands, and back-to-nature beach bungalows have attracted budget travelers for many years.

At the northern end of Hat Chaweng is a tranquil 3-ft (1-m) deep lagoon, ideal for children and novice windsurfers. The southernmost end, Chaweng Noi, is bordered by coconut palms and separated from the main beach by a small headland and a narrow stream. This part of the beach is not only quieter than the long northern strand, but also more beautiful – large boulders alternating with discreet sandy coves. The beach offers a wide range of sporting activities including windsurfing, canoeing, paragliding, scuba diving, tennis, and beach volleyball. The fine coral reefs offshore make the beach an ideal spot for some easy diving and snorkeling.

Hat Chaweng also boasts the most developed tourist infrastructure on Ko Samui. Upscale resorts, luxury hotels, and spas dominate the area, while travel agencies, banks, supermarkets, and car and bike rentals can be easily located. Although a great place for a family vacation, Hat Chaweng is predominantly visited by young travelers, who come

here particularly for the exciting nightlife centered in the area known as Soi Green Mango. This part of the beach is cluttered with an increasing number of bars, restaurants, and clubs. Visitors spend the nights partying, drinking, and dancing till the early hours.

🚇 Hat Lamai

หาดละไม

12 miles (19 km) SE of Na Thon.
🚗 📷

The second-largest and second most popular beach on Ko Samui, Hat Lamai caters primarily to European budget travelers. Initially a quiet fishing village, tourism has slowly taken over, becoming the mainstay of tiny Ban Lamai, at the northern end of the beach. The main focus is at the center of the 2-mile (3-km) long beach. The long road behind the beach here is lined with all kinds of bars,

Picturesque Hat Lamai with drooping palms skirting the sea

nightclubs, and restaurants serving delicious Thai and Western food. This is also the spot where most of the beach's nightlife is centered.

Although Ban Lamai still has many old teak houses, most buildings have tiled roofs – a sign of the growing prosperity of the area. The village's main cultural sight is **Wat Lamai Cultural Hall**, built in 1826, with a small folk museum dedicated to local arts and crafts. Just south of Hat Lamai, almost as an extension, is another long stretch of sandy beach known as **Hat Hua Thanon**. This pretty beach has a predominantly Muslim fishing village at its center. A fresh market sells a large variety of fruits, vegetables, and seafood.

🔵 Secret Buddha Garden

สวนพระ

7 miles (11 km) SE of Na Thon.

Tucked away in the heavily forested interior of Ko Samui, the Secret Buddha Garden, also known as Magic Garden, was founded by a 76-year-old fruit farmer, Nim Thongsuk, in 1977. Surrounded by lush tropical forest and rocky hillsides, the garden is studded with beautiful statuary. Made of concrete, the stunning statues represent various deities, mythical beasts, and human beings in different postures, including a statue of a seated Nim Thongsuk. A beautiful waterfall continues as a stream through the length of the garden. Set in the highest part of the island, the garden also offers spectacular views across the tall coconut palm-covered lowlands and the Gulf of Thailand. Getting to the garden, however, can prove to be quite challenging, as it is only sometimes accessible via a dirt track using a 4WD from Hat Lamai. The easiest way to do this is to take a jungle tour from Hat Lamai.

Na Muang Waterfalls

น้ำตกหน้าเมือง

7 miles (11 km) SE of Na Thon.

Along Route 4169, near Ban Thurian, a steep side track beside a rushing stream leads off into the central mountains of Ko Samui. About 1 mile (2 km) along this track is a stunning cascade known as Nam Tok Na Muang, or Na Muang Waterfall. A 2-mile (3-km) trek farther into the interior leads to another waterfall, also called Na Muang by the locals. Tour operators generally refer to the two as Na Muang 1 and Na Muang 2. The larger of the two falls, Na Muang 2, is a popular local picnic spot. About 98 ft (30 m) in height, the falls form a deep basin at the foot, creating a cool and pleasant pool which is great for swimming and bathing. Both the falls are at their spectacular best in the months of December and January, when the monsoon has ended and they swell with fresh rainwater from Ko Samui's hilly interior. An elephant trekking company operates in the area and will take visitors to the foot of Na Muang 2 by arrangement.

Popular picnic spot for locals, the spectacular Na Muang Waterfalls

Hin Ta and Hin Yai

หินตาหินยาย

11 miles (18 km) SE of Na Thon.

Located on a tiny headland immediately between Hat Lamai and Hat Hua Thanon, Hin Ta and Hin Yai, or Grandfather Stone and Grandmother Stone, are natural rock formations bearing an uncanny resemblance to the human male and female sexual organs. According to local lore, in times past a fisherman and woman fell in love, but were caught in a storm off this small headland and drowned. Through supernatural forces, the rocks on the headland took on their present shape, celebrating and commemorating the love of the two fisherfolk for eternity. These rock formations are perhaps the most visited site on Ko Samui after the Big Buddha statue. Small souvenir stalls selling T-shirts, snacks such as *galamae* (a Thai sweet dish), and other knick-knacks have sprung up in the area.

View of the curiously shaped Hin Ta, or Grandfather Stone

Wat Khunaram

วัดคุณาราม

8 miles (13 km) SE of Na Thon.

Located near Ban Thurian just south of Route 4169, Wat Khunaram is one of Ko Samui's more unusual spiritual attractions. While the *wat* is architecturally appealing, it has no historical significance. What draws visitors to it are the mummified remains of a famous Buddhist monk, Phra Khru Sammathakittikhun, who died here in 1973. The preserved mummy of the monk, sitting in an upright position in a glass casing, is on display in a separate building within the complex. The place is highly venerated by the locals who come here to place flowers and incense on the remains of this former abbot of the *wat*. In surprisingly good condition and still quite undecomposed, the remains are said to be here in accordance with the wishes of Phra Khru himself.

One of the many varieties of butterflies at the Samui Butterfly Garden

🦋 Hat Laem Set
หาดแหลมเส็ด

10 miles (16 km) S of Na Thon. 🚗 📷

A tiny but lovely beach at the southern end of Hat Hua Thanon, Hat Laem Set's soft sand is strewn with huge smooth boulders. The main attraction on this beach is the Ko Samui Kiteboarding Center at the well-known Samui Orchid Resort. Kiteboarding is a relatively new but exhilarating addition to the busy water-sports scene on the island and is at its best off Hat Laem Set during the cool season from November to February. The Kiteboarding Center offers courses for all abilities and hires out kiteboards for rental. In addition to kiteboarding, visitors can snorkel out to a beautiful offshore coral reef nearby. The sea is shallow at this point, and the sandy bottom clearly visible. Beyond the reef, however, the waters are deep and can get treacherous, especially during choppy seas and high winds. Snorkelers and swimmers must be careful before venturing any further. There are a few upscale resorts and spas on the beach, as well as a handful of good restaurants serving local food.

🐟 Samui Aquarium and Tiger Zoo
สมุยอควาเรียม และสวนเสือ

33/2 Moo 2, Maret, 10 miles (16 km) SE of Na Thon. **Tel** 0-7742-4017-8. **Open** 9am–5pm daily. 🚗 📷 📷
W samuiaquariumand tigerzoo.com

An ideal stop for marine and wildlife enthusiasts, the Samui Aquarium and Tiger Zoo is a fascinating place to experience the fauna of the region. Perfect for a day trip, especially with children, the aquarium has a variety of marine creatures, such as tropical fish, sharks, sea turtles, corals, mollusks, starfish, and sea horses, housed in large, clear, acrylic aquariums. Visitors can also take a look at an amazing variety of birds kept here while enjoying a fascinating bird show. Being photographed with the birds is permitted.

The affiliated **Tiger Zoo** nearby houses large numbers of big cats, including Royal Bengal tigers, leopards, clouded leopards, and lions, enabling visitors to get a closer look at these predators and their way of life. Those willing can have themselves photographed with these splendid creatures for a few hundred baht. The souvenir shop in the complex sells T-shirts and stuffed toys.

🦋 Samui Butterfly Garden
สวนผีเสื้อสมุย

10 miles (16 km) SE of Na Thon. **Tel** 0-7742-4020. **Open** 8:30am–5pm daily; observatory opens 10am–4pm. 📷 🚗 📷

Situated on the side of a small hill at Laem Na Tien, the Samui Butterfly Garden is set in lush tropical gardens. It features hundreds of species of protected butterflies and moths, which are kept from escaping by a series of high nets. The butterflies, of which there are more than 100 Thai and Malaysian varieties, are truly beautiful. Honeybee hives and a selection of less appealing insects such as scorpions, tarantulas, and spiders are kept safely behind glass casings to avoid unpleasant encounters.

Large smooth boulders strewn across the sand and water at pretty Hat Laem Set

Enthusiastic divers among coral reefs in the clear waters off Ko Taen

The fee to the Butterfly Garden includes a welcome drink as well as a visit to a hillside observatory with a number of observation platforms. These platforms offer sweeping views across the coast and the Gulf of Thailand. Marine life enthusiasts can take a trip in a glass-bottomed boat to observe corals in the surrounding sea.

🦋 Ko Taen

เกาะเทียน

10 miles (16 km) S of Na Thon.
🚤 from Ban Thongkrut. 🏊 📷

A picturesque island located just off Samui's southwest shore, tiny Ko Taen is easily reached by boat from the small settlement of Ban Thongkrut. Formerly home to an isolated fishing community, it has now been transformed into a marine nature reserve. The island is an ideal spot for diving, snorkeling, or land-based activities such as trekking. There are just three resorts on the island, which has a population of less than 30 permanent residents. The two most popular attractions here are **Ao Ok**, a bay with fine coral reefs which are great for diving or snorkeling, and **Ao Tok**, a small bay with perfect white sands backed by a mangrove forest, home to a variety of birds and animals. A wooden walkway runs through this forest, making it easy for visitors to explore the area. Several dark caves in the interior are the bastion of thousands of bats. The waters offshore are deep, clear, and perfect for diving and snorkeling.

🚉 Laem Hin Khom

แหลมหินคม

9 miles (14 km) S of Na Thon. 🏊 📷

Located at the southern end of Samui's undeveloped west coast, Laem Hin Khom is a rocky headland that cuts off Ban Thongkrut from Ao Phangkha. Thong Tanote, a long, narrow, and sandy beach, backed by tall, slender coconut palms and tropical jungle, runs along the southern shore of the cape and is the setting for one of Ko Samui's most isolated getaways, the beautiful Coconut Villa Resort and Spa. This intimate and luxurious development has both beachfront and seaview villas. The quiet beach at Laem Hin Khom is ideally suited for long walks and swimming, although the latter should be avoided at high tide.

🚉 Ao Phangkha

อ่าวพังกา

8 miles (13 km) S of Na Thon. 🏊 📷

Located just north of Laem Hin Khom is the perfectly gorgeous bay Ao Phangkha, also known as Emerald Cove. Isolated from the rest of Ko Samui by the 1,312-ft (400-m) Khao Kwang, a jungle-covered massif to the northeast, this is certainly one of the most remote escapes on the island. Once the almost exclusive preserve of the backpacker

Swimming pool at Coconut Villa Resort and Spa, Laem Hin Khom

crowd, Ao Phangkha is now becoming increasingly upscale. Phangkha Paradise Resort, among the popular resorts in the area, is prominently set back from the center of the crescent beach, along with a couple of smaller bungalow-type accommodations. There is not much to do here, but visitors can take a boat to some of the offshore islands, such as Ko Thalu, Ko Din, Ko Maleng Po, and Ko Mae Ko, for snorkeling over the colorful coral reefs. Alternatively, the soft white sands of the beach at Ao Phangkha provide an ideal basking place for die-hard sunbathers.

Longtail fishing boats anchored at the small pier at Ao Phangkha

Long, curving stretch of coast at Ao Taling Ngam

🏖 Ao Taling Ngam

อ่าวตลิ่งงาม

5 miles (8 km) S of Na Thon. 🖊 📷

The main west coast bay to the south of Na Thon, Ao Taling Ngam stretches for almost 2 miles (3 km). The beach along the bay is a long, narrow curve of sand, with the small settlement of Ban Thong Yang – the port for ferries from Don Sak – to its south. Relatively undeveloped, Ao Taling Ngam is divided into Five Islands Beach to the south and Dhevatara Cove to the north by a tiny stream and low headland, now home to the Am Samui Resort. Visitors will find clean, inexpensive accommodations here. Looming above the bay and with its own section of private beach lies what many consider to be one of Samui's classiest hotels – Baan Taling Ngam Resort and Spa.

🏖 Ao Thong Yang

อ่าวท้องยาง

4 miles (6 km) S of Na Thon. 🖊 📷

A quiet spot, much like the other places on the west coast of Ko Samui, Ao Thong Yang is conveniently located a 20-minute stroll from the Ko Samui Immigration Office, which lies to its north. The headland to the south of the bay belongs to the Royal Thai Navy and is a prohibited area. The area offers a variety of options for fine dining including restaurants that serve delectable local Thai food.

🏔 Samui Highlands

สมุยไฮแลนด์ส

3 miles (5 km) E of Na Thon. Wat Hin Lat **Tel** 0-7742-3146. 🖊 📷

A short drive inland from Na Thon along Route 4172 due east leads to the forested highlands of Ko Samui. An easy getaway far from the sun and sand, the Highlands are an excellent point to start jungle treks and visit Samui's famous waterfalls. Visitors who want to trek the hard way will need sturdy boots. These mountains are accessed using a network of steep, rough tracks. Other sights worth visiting include **Wat Hin Lat**, a meditation temple offering daily courses in Vipassana meditation. It features a walking path, a charming garden, religious sculptures, and several images of the Buddha. One such image is housed in a natural niche formed in a large boulder and surrounded by lush vegetation. The beautiful **Hin Lat Waterfall** is a steep 2-mile (3-km) hike from Wat Hin Lat, but the journey follows a beautiful jungle path and can be rounded off with a swim in the clear pool at the foot of the falls. Unlike most other waterfalls on Ko Samui, Hin Lat is quite off the beaten track, and rarely visited by island tour package groups. It is a great place for swimming and picnics, but hikers must remember to keep their legs covered and wear good walking shoes, especially during the rains, when leeches can be a problem. Those looking for some more adventure can press on further for 2 miles (3 km) to the Wang Sao Tong Falls. Experienced bikers can also explore the area on a dirt bike, but should avoid doing so during the rainy season.

Statue of Seated Buddha at Wat Hin Lat, Samui Highlands

For hotels and restaurants in this region see pp298–9 and pp313–14

Coconut Monkeys

Coconut harvesting was once the main source of income for the people of Ko Samui. Much of the island's interior is covered with coconut palms and, even today, coconuts remain a significant economic crop. Palm trees can grow up to 130–160 ft (40–50 m) high and harvesting coconuts is a difficult, dangerous, and time-consuming process. To make it easier, locals train macaques to pluck the rich harvest for them. These monkeys are usually trained at the Monkey Training School on the island. Another place to see monkeys being trained is the Samui Monkey Center, which also holds demonstrations three times a day. Visitors can see these monkeys at work on coconut plantations all over Ko Samui, especially along the northwest coast around Ban Maenam, Ban Tai, and Ban Bang Pho.

Coconut Harvesting by Monkeys

A male macaque is capable of picking between 1,000 and 1,500 coconuts a day, while a female macaque can pick 600 to 700. This makes excellent economic sense, especially when compared to a human male, who can pick only about 80 coconuts a day.

Trainers in Ko Samui treat their monkeys almost like members of the family.

Somporn Saekow, who died in 2002, began his monkey training school in 1957. He applied the Buddhist principles of tolerance and insisted on humane treatment of his "students".

Ropes tied to the monkey are used to guide its movements and are not meant to restrain it.

Coconut palms are extremely difficult to climb because their tall, thin trunks have no branches. Besides, strong winds add to the risk.

Monkey training schools are fairly common on Ko Samui. Here monkeys learn to harvest the coconuts – turn the coconut with their paws and legs, place the plucked nut in a bag, and bring the bag back to the owner. The entire learning process takes about six months.

Coconut harvesting, together with fishing, were the mainstays of Ko Samui's economy before the onset of tourism. Even today, they remain a vital part of its economy.

⑤ Ko Phangan

เกาะพะงัน

About two-thirds the size of Ko Samui, Ko Phangan is the original backpacker's destination. The cheap accommodations, full moon parties, and bohemian atmosphere make the island attractive to young people and budget travelers, while its powdery beaches, calm bays, accessible corals, excellent dive sites, and a rugged forested interior make it a perfect destination for nature enthusiasts. Large parts of the island are undeveloped due to its difficult terrain. Much of it is accessible only by sea or along rutted roads by pickup trucks. Yet, it is Ko Phangan's virgin beauty that makes it more attractive than commercial tourist spots.

Thong Sala

ท้องศาลา

The largest settlement and de facto capital of Ko Phangan, Thong Sala is the most important town on the island. Although it is not very big, Thong Sala is the main port from where boats and ferries depart to other parts of the island as well as to nearby Ko Samui and Ko Tao. The town provides useful facilities for visitors including banks, a post office, supermarkets, and travel agencies. This is also the only place on Ko Phangan with an international hospital, pharmacies, and a police station. There are a fair number of restaurants, budget hotels, and bars. It is also famous for its Thai massage, which locals claim is the best on the island. Visitors to the island can explore it by renting motorcycles or jeeps. Alternatively they can get around by hiring a *songthaew* from next to the pier.

Longtail fishing boats anchored at the pier, Ao Wok Tum

🚩 Ao Wok Tum

อ่าววกทุม

3 miles (5 km) N of Thong Sala.

Immediately around a small headland from Thong Sala is the long, undeveloped beach at Ao Wok Tum. Although its sandy stretches are good for sunbathing or strolls, the main attraction here are the coral reefs. Located 320 ft (300 m) offshore, these reefs are perfect for novices as the shallow bay offers safe and easy snorkeling. Small cafés, bars, and restaurants, a fishing village, and a local temple – Wat Amphawan – are located nearby. There are bungalow accommodations as well as a 24-hour convenience store.

🚩 Ao Hin Kong

อ่าวหินกอง

4 miles (6 km) N of Thong Sala.

Ao Wok Tum blends almost imperceptibly into Ao Hin Kong. A narrow coastal road runs along the bay all the way to Hat Yao, an undeveloped beach that offers a 2-mile (3-km) stretch of clean, white sand running down to the water's edge. The coral reefs skirting Ao Wok Tum continue here and the palm-fringed beach is backed by mangroves. Serviced by a few low-scale bungalow operations and reasonably priced cafés and restaurants, Ao Hin Kong appeals to backpackers intending a long stay on Ko Phangan. Although it offers little by way of entertainment, it is within cycling distance of Thong Sala, from where visitors can make their way to the more bustling nightspots. Swimming in this shallow bay is only possible during high tide.

🚩 Ao Si Thanu

อ่าวศีธนุ

5 miles (8 km) N of Thong Sala.

Located just a short distance beyond the Laem Si Thanu headland, Ao Si Thanu has a small beach considered to be among the most beautiful in Ko Phangan. There are adequate bungalow accommodations here as well as two small and attractive hotels, Loy Fa and Chai Country, near the top of the cape, which offer excellent views of the nearby offshore islands and beyond. A small fishing village located at the western end of Ao Si Thanu offers basic facilities, including Internet access, noodle stalls, fruit and vegetable shops, and a few bars. The main appeal of this bay, apart from the gorgeous sunset views, is the accessible offshore coral reef.

Mangroves growing along the water's edge at Ao Hin Kong

Beach bungalows along the water's edge at Ao Chaophao

🏖 Ao Chaophao
อ่าวเจ้าพ่อ
6 miles (10 km) N of Thong Sala.
📝 📷

The coastal route north from Ao Si Thanu cuts inland for a short distance before coming out into the palm-fringed bay of Ao Chaophao. Its long beach used to be quite undeveloped and only visited by those seeking to get away from the crowded beaches of the south coast. However, in recent times, Ao Chaophao has become busier and facilities have sprung up to keep pace with the increased footfall. These include a few bungalow operations, restaurants, and bars. The Pirate Bar, set in a hidden cove at the end of the beach, is definitely worth a visit.

🏖 Hat Yao
หาดยาว
7 miles (11 km) N of Thong Sala.
📝 📷

The main beach resort on Ko Phangan, Hat Yao is a lovely curved stretch of white sand. Although it is getting busier by the year, the beach is wide enough to accommodate the upcoming resorts, restaurants, and bars, along with other facilities, without seeming crowded. Visitors can explore the surrounding waters on sea kayaks or travel inland on motorcycles and jeeps, which are available for hire. The surrounding waters are good for diving and snorkeling.

🏖 Hat Salad
หาดสลัด
8 miles (13 km) N of Thong Sala.
📝 📷

The beautiful, small and deeply recessed bay around Hat Salad is fairly off the beaten track even by Ko Phangan standards. Despite this, it has a few guest-houses, small shops, and bike rental, as well as Internet access. According to local legend, this beach used to be a loading point for pirate ships of yore and this adds to the appeal of the beach. Visitors can read, laze, or enjoy a nap in the hammocks strung up between palm trees.

Key
▬ Major road
═ Minor road
= = Dirt track
- - Ferry route

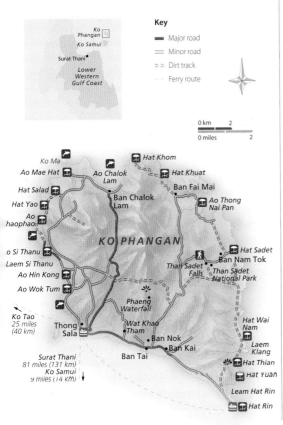

0 km   2
0 miles   2

Long swings suspended from coconut palms at Hat Salad

For keys to symbols *see back flap*

🔧 Ao Mae Hat
อ่าวแม่หาด
9 miles (14 km) N of Thong Sala.
🔧🏚

An isolated and beautiful cove with crisp white sand, Ao Mae Hat is located on the coast just beyond Mae Hat village in the northwestern part of the island. The eastern end of the beach is mostly used by the fishermen who go out looking for the crabs that populate this area and their longtail boats often lie anchored here. The western end is far more beautiful and has long been a favorite with travelers; however, Mae Hat's stunning natural beauty has led to the development of upscale resort-style accommodations to keep pace with the tourist influx. Apart from being a good spot for swimming and snorkeling, the beach is also linked to the tiny island of Ko Ma by a beautiful sandy causeway that gets exposed at low tide and is shallow enough to cross by wading through the water. The reefs off Ko Ma are among the best snorkeling spots in all of Ko Phangan. A short walk from Mae Hat is the Wang Sai Waterfall with a clear rocky pool that is perfect for swimming.

🔧 Ao Chalok Lam
อ่าวโฉลกหลำ
6 miles (10 km) NE of Thong Sala.
🔧🏚

The pretty bay of Ao Chalok Lam is home to Ko Phangan's most authentic, and consequently

Fisherwomen drying squid in the sun at Ban Chalok Lam

also the smelliest fishing village. Ban Chalok Lam offers an insight into the typical rural life on the island. Piles of squid drying on the beach are a common sight, and the smell of the freshly caught fish is part of the overall experience. Fishing-related activities such as mending nets and gutting fish coexist with shophouses selling pizzas and other snacks. Visitors often stop here to buy fish after a trip to the revered Chinese shrine dedicated to the goddess Chao Mae Koan Im just outside the village. There is also a Buddhist temple near Ban Chalok Lam.

Located offshore from Ao Chalok Lam, **Hin Bai**, or Sail Rock, is one of Thailand's premier dive sites. Diving and snorkeling are popular activities here and the bay has a number of well-equipped bungalows

and resorts to cater to the diving crowd. Yet Ao Chalok Lam is usually treated as a stop-over between Thong Sala and **Hat Khom**, a small and attractive beach near the northernmost point of Ko Phangan.

🔧 Hat Khuat
หาดขวด
10 miles (16 km) NE of Thong Sala.
🛥 from Ban Chalok Lam. 🔧🏚

An idyllic spot, Hat Khuat, or Bottle Beach, is one of those glorious unspoiled beaches that draw millions of visitors to Thailand's coast. It is accessible by a dirt track from Hat Khom, but this entails a tough trek through heavy undergrowth. More easily reached by longtail boats, this beach has now become a mid-range destination that is popular with the younger crowd. A delightful expanse of sand, looking out over pristine waters in different shades of aquamarine, Hat Khuat is sheltered inland by the wooded flanks of the 1,408-ft (429-m) high Khao Kin Non. Those seeking affordable bungalow accommodations in a beautiful setting away from the noisy parties will find this beach appealing. However, visitors must avoid this beach during bad weather, as they can be stranded without a way back. A short stroll along a dirt track leads to Ban Fai Mai village with a few small grocery stores and snack bars.

Holiday-makers relaxing on the picturesque beach at Ao Mae Hat

Cafés and bungalows along a rocky outcrop, Ao Thong Nai Pan

🔲 Ao Thong Nai Pan

อ่าวธงนายพรานน้อยใหญ่

11 miles (18 km) NE of Thong Sala.
🚌 from Thong Sala. 🔲 🔲

Beyond Hat Khuat, Ko Phangan's coastline curves to the southeast and opens into Ao Thong Nai Pan, a lovely and deeply indented bay backed by forested hills and facing east across the Gulf of Thailand. A tall rocky outcrop divides the bay into two coves – **Ao Thong Nai Pan Noi** to the north and **Ao Thong Nai Pan Yai** to the south. This is perhaps the least accessible bay on the island, and as a result Ao Thong Nai Pan is relatively less crowded. However, the bay offers some of the most attractive scenery on Ko Phangan. Only one rough dirt road links it to Ban Tai on the southern coast, which is 9 miles (14 km) to the south and is a bumpy and bone-jarring ride. Alternatively, it can be reached by boat from Ko Samui between September and January, which is a more comfortable option.

Despite being isolated, Ao Thong Nai Pan has developed a fair bit, offering restaurants, bars, Internet cafés, travel agents, and banking facilities. Both sides of the beach are equally appealing, with shallow, warm waters which are ideal for swimming or snorkeling. The eastern end of Ao Thong Nai Pan Yai has some rock formations which are good for climbing. Visitors should note that the road to Ban Tai can become impassable during heavy rains, posing a serious hazard to motorcyclists and drivers.

🔲 Hat Sadet

หาดเสด็จ

10 miles (16 km) NE of Thong Sala.
🚌 from Thong Sala. 🔲 🔲

An untouched and fairly inaccessible spot, Hat Sadet is a replica of the romantic and deserted beaches shown in films. Access by land is along the difficult dirt track that runs north from Ban Tai. It is far easier to reach this cove by boat from Thong Sala. Neighboring the island's only national park, the beach has basic seaside bungalows. Despite lacking restaurants, bars, or entertainment options, Hat Sadet is a delightful spot. The beach is narrow, as it is flanked by steep rocky outcrops which come straight down to the sea and this further contributes to its isolated charm.

🔲 Than Sadet National Park

อุทยานแห่งชาติธารเสด็จ

10 miles (16 km) NE of Thong Sala.
🚌 from Thong Sala. 🔲 🔲

Established in 1983, Than Sadet National Park was originally much smaller before being enlarged to its present size of 25 sq miles (65 sq km) in 1999. The park is named after the Sadet River. The word *sadet* in Thai means a "stream visited by royalty"; the name was given after Rama V's (r.1868–1910) visit to the spot in 1889. The largest waterfall on the island – **Than Sadet Falls** – is at the end of a popular hiking trail and has become a favored destination among visitors interested in an alternative to beach activities. The highest point in the park is Khao Ra, which rises to a height of 1,984 ft (605 m). Much of Than Sadet is covered with dense forest, although there are a few trails. The most accessible point is at Hat Sadet, where the Sadet River meets the sea. In the past, this area was popular with Thai monarchs, and Rama V even left his royal monogram inscribed on a large boulder, as did his successors Rama VII (r.1925–35) and the present king, Rama IX. In fact, it is said that Rama V liked this place so much that he visited it on as many as 10 occasions between 1888 and 1909.

Sadet river cascading down in rocky pools, Than Sadet National Park

Secluded palm-lined cove with aquamarine waters, Hat Thian

Hat Thian

หาดเทียน

8 miles (13 km) E of Thong Sala.
from Hat Rin.

South of Hat Sadet, the east coast of Ko Phangan is almost inaccessible and well off the beaten path. There are hardly any roads along the coast that are better than dirt tracks and one of them extends southward right through the small settlement of Ban Nam Tok to join up with the main southern coastal road near Hat Rin. It is probably wiser and easier to visit the island's east coast by boat from Hat Rin, especially during the rainy season, from June to September. There is a small ferry that makes the daily run between Hat Rin and Ao Thong Nai Pan and stops at Hat Thian on the way, but it is easier to take a water taxi.

Hat Thian is the best among the cluster of three beaches around the headland at Laem Klang. The main reason for staying in this out-of-the-way place is its isolated beauty, although it has undergone some development. There is a decent selection of restaurants serving Thai and Western food, and a few bars with live music and parties on weekends. There are about four resorts around this cove with bungalow-style accommodations and a spa and even a wellness center offering alternative treatments. There are some good dive sites nearby that are famous for sightings of whale sharks.

Hat Yuan

หาดญวน

8 miles (13 km) E of Thong Sala.

Just south of Hat Thian, and within easy walking or even swimming distance, is the even smaller beach at Hat Yuan. This beach, strewn with rocks at either end, has a family atmosphere and there are cafés offering oven-fresh food and fruity yogurts alongside more traditional Thai dishes. This is a good and safe spot for swimming and snorkeling, although visitors should be careful during stormy weather. Although Hat Yuan is just a short distance away from noisy Hat Rin, it is laid-back, quiet, and far removed from the party scene. Visitors to this beach can indulge in regular beach activities such as swimming, sunbathing, and snorkeling.

Hat Rin

หาดริน

7 miles (11 km) SE of Thong Sala.

Located on the southeastern tip of Ko Phangan, the bustling beach of Hat Rin and the

Bungalows along the palm-fringed beach at Hat Yuan

adjoining village of Ban Hat Rin are the most developed places on the island as well as its party paradise. Set astride a narrow, sandy peninsula, Hat Rin is divided into two beaches – the lively **Hat Rin Nok**, or Sunrise Beach, to the east and the quieter **Hat Rin Nai**, or Sunset Beach, to the west. Hat Rin is popular with young people who enjoy loud music and definitely for those travelers who come to Ko Phangan for its full moon parties. These famous parties, held on the beach each month, start after dark and go on beyond sunrise the next day. Although the parties are concentrated around the southern end of Hat Rin, especially at Hat Rin Nok, the crowds often overflow to other parts of the beach. A festive ambience is created with lamps, makeshift bars, fire shows, and food and drink stalls. During these parties, visitors should take care of their belongings and be wary of strangers.

Hat Rin has a constantly expanding group of hotels, guesthouses, restaurants, bars, and Internet cafés. Accommodations are often fully booked for a week on either side of the full moon parties.

In the past, most visitors to Hat Rin were drawn to the clean, wide expanse of sand. Unfortunately, the tourist influx has reduced some of this charm. Today, the beach is often noisy and littered with flotsam, and should certainly be avoided by those seeking isolation.

Wat Khao Tham
วัดเขาถ้ำ
3 miles (5 km) E of Thong Sala.
w nunamornpun-kohphangan.com
Ko Phangan is known for its lovely beaches and unspoiled vistas. Old temples or Buddhist architecture are not what a visitor would expect to see here. However, Wat Khao Tham, located to the northwest of Ban Tai on the island's southern coast, draws both Asian and Western visitors keen to participate in its meditation retreats. More a meditation center than a monastery,

Serene backdrop for meditation retreats at Wat Khao Tham

Wat Khao Tham is an interesting place for the spiritually inclined. Sessions on healing the body and mind are held on a monthly basis over several days. The entry costs are quite reasonable and include food and accommodations. Billed as a Theravadin Buddhist Monastery and Retreat Center, the monastery is run by two resident foreigners, Rosemary and Steve Weissman, who are also the teachers. The objective of the retreat is to gain insight into human nature through a mental development practice. The monastery is a perfect contrast to the crowds and the wild, over-the-top full moon parties at Hat Rin just around the corner.

Full Moon Party

These famous parties are held at Hat Rin every month during full moon. From small origins some 25 years ago, they now encourage partygoers to flock here from all over the world. As enthusiasts gather at the beach, the numbers can reach anything between 10,000 and 20,000 a month. The event features a mix of international and Thai DJs playing every kind of music from techno to commercial pop. Visitors paint themselves with ultraviolet colors and also carry lights and other props that glow. Alcohol – which is legal – flows freely and is usually sold as cocktail buckets. Unfortunately, a variety of illegal psychotropic drugs are also easily available. These are best avoided, as they can cause severe illness or even death by overdosing. Possession of these drugs can result in fines or even imprisonment.

Revelers crowding the beach at a full moon party, Hat Rin

Traditional daybeds on a west coast beach, Ko Phangan ▶

❻ Ang Thong Marine National Park

อุทยานแห่งชาติทางทะเลอ่างทอง

The Ang Thong, or Golden Basin, archipelago includes nearly 42 stunning and virtually uninhabited islands covering an area of 39 sq miles (101 sq km). A former naval base, it became accessible to the public only in 1980, when it was declared a marine national park. The islands are the submerged peaks of a flooded range of limestone mountains, some of which soar above sea level to 1,400 ft (427 m). Ang Thong's beauty attracts visitors who come to relax on the mica white sands, explore the lush forests and caves, and snorkel among excellent corals. Another attraction is the abundant wildlife, both on land and in the sea.

Locator map

☐ Area illustrated

Key

- ▪▪ Trail
- ‑‑ Ferry route

0 km   1
0 mile   1

★ **Thale Nai Crater Lake**
A stunning green seawater lake in the middle of Ko Mae Ko, Thale Nai Crater Lake is the golden basin that gives Ang Thong its name. Encircled by limestone cliffs, and linked to the open sea by an underground passage, the lake offers spectacular views which more than compensate for the strenuous hike.

Kayaking
Professionally guided sea-kayaking tours in and around Ang Thong can be easily arranged from Hat Chaweng or Hat Lamai on nearby Ko Samui (see pp166–75).

KEY

① **Ko Phaluai**, the largest island in the archipelago, is inhabited by a community of fishermen.

② **Thale Nai Crater Lake**

③ **The Stone Bridge** at Ko Sam Sao is a natural formation popular with sea-kayakers.

Hiking
Distances are short in Ang Thong, but some climbs are steep, and it can get very hot in the day. Visitors are advised to carry hats, sunscreen, and lots of water.

Ko Naayphud

Ko Wa Yai

Ko Hindab

Ko Pae Yat

Ko Wuakantang

Ko Sam Sao

Ko Mae Ko

Ko Phi

Park HQ

Ko Wua Talab

Ko Samui 16 miles (26 km)

Mod ang

Phaluai

Ko Kluai

Ko Sam Sao
This tiny island is a favorite with divers and snorkelers, offering the best coral reefs in the whole park.

VISITORS' CHECKLIST

Practical Information
Road Map C4. Park HQ on Ko Wua Talab, 16 miles (26 km) NW of Ko Samui. **Tel** 0-2562-0760 (bookings). ℹ Park HQ (0-7728-6025). **Closed** Nov–mid-Dec.

Transport
🚤 from Ko Samui.

★ Tham Bua Bok Cave
A strenuous hike leads to this cave near the summit of Ko Wua Talab. Its interior is filled with stalactites and stalagmites that resemble lotus flowers, giving the cave its name – Bua Bok, meaning Waving Lotus.

★ Ko Wua Talab Viewpoint
Located at the summit of this island, this viewpoint is at the end of a fairly difficult trek. However, it offers stunning views of the green islands rising out of the waters of the Ang Thong archipelago. Ko Wua Talab also has basic bungalow accommodations for visitors to the park.

Boat trips
These operate in good weather between Ko Samui, Ko Phangan (see pp176–81), and Ang Thong. Some tours are specifically for divers and snorkelers while other more expensive options offer overnight accommodations.

For keys to symbols *see back flap*

❼ Ko Tao

เกาะเต่า

Picturesquely located in the midst of the Gulf of Thailand, north of Ko Phangan *(see pp176–81)*, Ko Tao is the smallest of the three main islands in the Samui archipelago. While the island itself is rugged, with dense forest inland, quiet coves along the east coast, and a fine sweep of sandy beach on the western side, the surrounding sea offers excellent underwater visibility, a wide range of dive sites, and a variety of coral and marine life. The Chumphon Pinnacle, 7 miles (11 km) northwest of Ko Tao, is among the best dive sites in the area, with known sightings of the gray reef shark. Ko Tao is also a significant breeding ground for hawksbill and green turtles.

Longtail boats and speedboats anchored along Hat Ao Mae

Ban Mae Hat

บ้านแม่หาด

The unofficial capital of Ko Tao, Ban Mae Hat is one of the few large settlements on the island. A small, pleasant fishing village that is now being rapidly transformed into a small tourist town, Ban Mae Hat houses various facilities and services – banks, clinics, and pharmacies, Internet cafés, a post office, police station, and super-markets. It becomes all the more important because of the main ferry pier from which a surfaced road leads inland to Ao Chalok Ban Kao on the southern coast. The town is large enough to offer a reasonable selection of accommodations, the best dining facilities on the island, as well as a few Irish pubs, pool tables, and video and sports bars with wide-screen televisions. Motorcycles are available for

hire for those who wish to explore the island for a day or two before making a choice of resort or beach bungalow.

🏖 Hat Ao Mae

หาดอ่าวแม

Located in a shallow bay, a short distance north of the Ban Mae Hat ferry pier, and perhaps too close to the village for visitors seeking a tranquil holiday, Hat Ao Mae is a small beach. Nevertheless, it is well equipped with a comfortable resort, the Montra, offering convenient access to Ban Mae Hat to the south and the beautiful Hat Sai Ri to the north – both within easy walking distance of the beach. The area is also famous locally for Laem Jor Por Ror, or the Rama V Cape, a historically relevant site – on June 18, 1899, Rama V (r.1868–1910) visited Ko Tao and left his monogram

carved on a large rock here, called the Rama V boulder. This site has since been venerated, especially by locals.

🏖 Hat Sai Ri

หาดทรายรี

1 mile (2 km) N of Ban Mae Hat.

An idyllic beach, perfect for admiring spectacular sunsets over the Gulf of Thailand, Hat Sai Ri is the longest stretch of sandy beach on Ko Tao. It is framed to the east by swaying coconut palms, with an increasing number of small restaurants, bars, and simple bungalow accommo-dations. The beach is paralleled by a narrow surfaced path and, slightly further inland, by a small paved road leading to the settlement of Ban Hat Sai Ri. Once a tiny fishing village, it now serves as a service center for the fast-growing local tourism industry with dive centers, travel agents, and small supermarkets; there are even ATMs and Internet cafés. Beyond the beach, the surfaced road continues to the upscale Dusit Buncha Resort and Nangyuan Terrace. Beyond this point, the road ends in steep cliffs and jungle.

🏝 Ko Nang Yuan

เกาะนางยวน

2 miles (3 km) N of Ban Mae Hat. ☒ from Ban Mae Hat.

Perhaps the most beautiful natural formation off Ko Tao, Ko Nang Yuan is a group of three islets linked by a narrow causeway of white sand. The smallest among them is also known as **Japanese Garden**. This spectacular location is easily reached by ferry and makes a popular sunbathing

Utility market offering ATMs and other facilities, Hat Sai Ri

Sparkling azure waters surrounding the islets of Ko Nang Yuan

and swimming day trip. Strict regulations are in force to protect the environment and no cans, plastic bags, or bottles are permitted. Visitors have to pay a nominal fee to land, although full-day all-inclusive tours, with a picnic lunch and snorkeling or diving, can be arranged at one of the many travel agencies in Ban Mae Hat. The islands are administered by the Nangyuan Island Dive Resort *(see p299)*, and visitors staying here receive free transfers to and from the mainland.

Ao Mamuang

อ่าวมะม่วง

3 miles (5 km) NE of Ban Mae Hat.

Located on the northernmost shore of Ko Tao, Ao Mamuang, or Mango Bay, is a long, lovely, cove backed with lush greenery. It has a shallow offshore reef which usually draws snorkelers on day trips from Ban Mae Hat and elsewhere on the island. There is a small beach here, as well as comfortable bungalow accommodations, restaurants, and bars. Getting here, however, is not so easy, although visitors can either take a boat or follow the narrow, unpaved track that leads east across the hump of the island from Ban Hat Sai Ri, forking to the north toward the beach. The bay is framed by two beautiful capes – Nam Dok to the west and Grachom Fai (with a lighthouse) to the east. Although quite isolated, it is comfortably appointed, and a great place to relax.

Ao Hinwong

อ่าวหินวง

4 miles (6 km) NE of Ban Mae Hat.

Located on the northeastern shore of Ko Tao, well away from the bustle of Ban Mae Hat, Ao Hinwong is a delightful isolated cove surrounded by charming coconut groves and large boulders. Best reached by boat, Ao Hinwong can also be approached by a narrow track across the island from Ban Hat Sai Ri. The track, however, is only suitable for motorcycles, rugged pickups, or vehicles with 4WD. Despite its isolation, it is becoming popular with visitors to Ko Tao, as it offers two comfortable resorts and a bungalow complex. Its appeal lies in its overwhelming peace, and the clear, and sheltered waters of the beautiful bay, with dark shoals of sardines clearly visible from above. A hill to the north offers great ocean views. Ao Hinwong is an ideal spot for snorkeling and diving enthusiasts.

VISITORS' CHECKLIST

Practical Information

Road Map C3. 25 miles (40 km) N of Ko Phangan. 5,000. TAT, Chumphon (0-7750-1831/2).

Transport

from Ko Phangan and Chumphon.

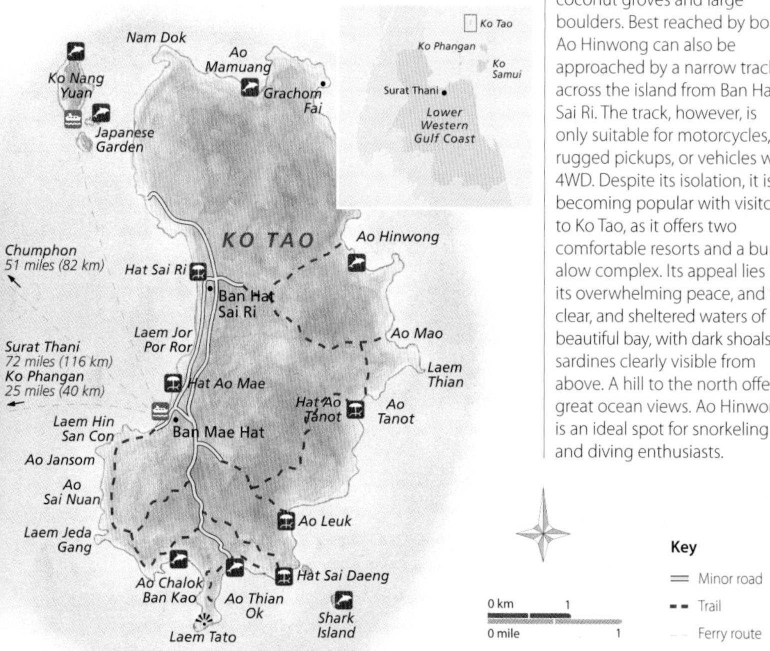
Ko Tao
Ko Phangan
Ko Samui
Surat Thani
Lower Western Gulf Coast
Nam Dok
Ao Mamuang
Grachom Fai
Ko Nang Yuan
Japanese Garden
KO TAO
Ao Hinwong
Chumphon 51 miles (82 km)
Hat Sai Ri
Ban Hat Sai Ri
Laem Jor Por Ror
Ao Mao
Surat Thani 72 miles (116 km)
Ko Phangan 25 miles (40 km)
Laem Thian
Hat Ao Mae
Hat Ao Tanot
Ao Tanot
Laem Hin San Con
Ban Mae Hat
Ao Jansom
Ao Sai Nuan
Ao Leuk
Laem Jeda Gang
Ao Chalok Ban Kao
Ao Thian Ok
Hat Sai Daeng
Shark Island
Laem Tato
0 km 1
0 mile 1
Key
Minor road
Trail
Ferry route

For keys to symbols *see back flap*

Sandy cove at Ao Tanot dotted with roofs of resort buildings

🛥 Laem Thian
แหลมเทียน

4 miles (6 km) E of Ban Mae Hat.
🛏 ✎ 🏖

An isolated cape located almost midway down the deserted east coast of Ko Tao, Laem Thian is a tiny waterbody with a white, sandy beach. Sheltered in the southern lee of a rocky headland, it is best reached by boat, although there is a treacherous dirt track that crosses the center of the island. The northern branch of this track leads to Ao Mamuang and Ao Hinwong, and the southern branch to Laem Thian. Among the more popular sites for snorkeling enthusiasts on Ko Tao, Laem Thian is well-known for its underwater tunnels and swim-through passages. Made of limestone, they are easy to navigate. The area is also known for frequent sightings of the exotic unicorn fish. Comfortable bungalows and other basic facilities are available on the beach here.

🛥 Ao Tanot
อ่าวโตนด

4 miles (6 km) E of Ban Mae Hat.
🛏 ✎ 🏖

A small, horseshoe-shaped bay facing east across the Gulf of Thailand, Ao Tanot is a beautiful setting, well-known for its vistas of fine sunrises. Just south of Laem Thian, and clearly visible across Ao Tanot is the isolated and beautiful beach, Hat Ao Tanot. As with the other beaches on the east coast of Ko Tao, its appeal lies in its

relative inaccessibility. Large boulders lie scattered across Hat Ao Tanot, as do a wide variety of seashells. The primary activity here is snorkeling, and enthusiasts can hire equipment from the dive shops nearby. There are several good resorts and some simple bungalow accommodations, as well as a dive school, and small, attractive terrace bars set against colorful groves of bougainvillea. Ao Tanot can also be reached by a southern track leading inland and over the mountainous spine of Ko Tao from the Ban Mae Hat-Ao Chalok surfaced road.

🛥 Ao Leuk
อ่าวลึก

3 miles (5 km) SE of Ban Mae Hat.
✎ 🏖

Located close to Ko Tao's south-easternmost point, Ao Luek has among the most beautiful beaches on Ko Tao and offers a variety of outdoor activities. Visitors can go sea-kayaking, water-skiing, and windsurfing,

all of which can be easily arranged through any one of the several resorts on the beach. Sunbathing and swimming are other options. There are beautiful coral reefs offshore, and snorkeling in the clear waters is another delightful pastime. Despite its reputation, the waters off the bay are quite safe, with the only shark sighted being the inoffensive blacktip. Both accommodation options and dining facilities are good, as are the few inviting bars.

🛥 Hat Sai Daeng
หาดทรายแดง

3 miles (5 km) SE of Ban Mae Hat.
🛏 ✎ 🏖

An attractive and unspoiled white-sand beach, backed by a narrow peninsula jutting into the warm waters of the Gulf of Thailand, Hat Sai Daeng is located along the busier and more accessible southern coast of Ko Tao. The beach, also known as Red Sands Beach, points directly at the popular

Kayakers rowing across the waters off Shark Island, Hat Sai Daeng

diving and snorkeling site around tiny, unpopulated Shark Island, which is also known as Ko Chalam. Hat Sai Daeng offers good views across the sea, lying in the shelter of a mangrove-covered headland. The beach has adequate bungalow accommodations, restaurants, and bars. It is easily approached by a narrow, seldom-used track running east from the main Mae Hat-Ao Chalok road, which is usable the year round. However, visitors should be careful to avoid using the smaller tracks, which are quite dangerous, and even impassable, during heavy rains.

Beautiful, rocky beachfront backed by thick foliage, Hat Sai Daeng

Ao Thian Ok

อ่าวเทียนออก

2 miles (3 km) SE of Ban Mae Hat.

The southernmost bay on the island, Ao Thian Ok has one of the prettiest beaches in Ko Tao. It is sheltered on the east by the Hat Sai Daeng headland and Shark Island, and to the west by the much larger headland of Laem Tato. Despite being frequented by reef sharks, the waters off Ao Thian Ok are very popular with divers. The beach offers luxurious spa accommodations as well as a few reasonably priced bungalows, a series of bars with spectacular ocean views, and some of the best restaurants on the island. Visitors can also take courses in Thai massage, yoga, and *chi gong* (a component of Chinese martial arts) as well as enjoying the usual maritime activities – swimming, snorkeling, and diving in the surrounding waters.

Enjoying a relaxed evening at a beachside shack, Ao Chalok Ban Kao

Ao Chalok Ban Kao

อ่าวโฉลกบ้านเก่า

1 miles (2 km) S of Ban Mae Hat.

The largest, most developed, and best-appointed beach resort on Ko Tao, Ao Chalok Ban Kao is sheltered by Laem Tato on the east and Laem Jeda Gang on the west. Easily accessible by a good, if narrow, road from Ban Mae Hat, this beautiful bay is protected by forest-clad hills during both the northeast and southwest monsoons. The bay is home to three separate, but closely linked beaches – Freedom Beach to the southeast, Hat Chalok in the center, and smaller Hat San Jao to the west. Ao Chalok Ban Kao is among the biggest dive centers on Ko Tao, with a large number of divers, snorkelers, and keen anglers frequenting the beach. As a result, the beach is equipped with several dive shops, travel agents, guesthouses, decent restaurants, and bars. In the center of Laem Tato, **Jon Suwan Mountain Viewpoint** offers fine views across the deeply indented bay and the surrounding wooded hills.

Sunbathing on the white sandy beach, Ao Thian Ok

Ao Sai Nuan

อ่าวสายนวล

A group of sandy coves fringed by tall palms and warm, azure waters come together to form this attractive spot. Ao Sai Nuan, a short distance southwest of Ban Mae Hat, is really a southern extension of the village and is characterized by a string of bungalows and several upscale resorts. Backed and sheltered by a densely wooded 620-ft (189-m) high mountain, the bay offers mesmerizing vistas of picture-perfect sunsets across the Gulf of Thailand. Good for diving and snorkeling, there are several spots from which enthusiasts can plunge into the waters around Laem Jeda Gang and Laem Hin San Con. The ease of accessibility makes Ao Sai Nuan a popular spot with visitors to Ko Tao. It can be approached on foot or motorcycle from Ban Mae Hat, although it is advisable to avoid four-wheeled vehicles. Various facilities including dive shops, restaurants, and bars combine to make any visit to Ao Sai Nuan a pleasant experience.

Open-air restaurant at a beach resort, Hat Na Dan

❽ Hat Khanom

หาดขนอม

Road Map C4. 56 miles (90 km) E of Surat Thani. 🚌 ℹ️ TAT, Nakhon Si Thammarat (0-7534-6515). 🚤 📷

A long and attractive beach, Hat Khanom is a part of the largest bay in the region. However, despite being easily accessible by road, it does not feature on most itineraries. The beach is also the center for the **Hat Khanom-Mu Ko Thale Tai National Park**, which covers mainland areas in the districts of Khanom and Sichon as well as the offshore islands of Ko Noi, Ko Wang Nai, Ko Wang Nok, Ko Tan, Ko Rap, Ko Tha Rai, and

Ko Phi. Hat Khanom is to the north of Khanom town, a small coastal settlement dating back to the Ayutthaya period (see pp44–5). Originally a major trading and cultural center, Khanom is today a tranquil and sleepy fishing town. Coconut and rubber plantations provide the main source of livelihood apart from fishing. It has a few restaurants, cottages, and a single hotel. However, most visitors prefer the beaches, especially as they also offer a wider range of accommodations right by the sea, ranging from luxurious resorts to homely bungalows. The area is rich in natural beauty as it is located near a string of lovely beaches

sheltered by limestone mountains. These outcrops are riddled with several caves; **Khao Wang Thong Cave** is the most significant among them. Located about 9 miles (14 km) from Khanom town, it has unusual stalagmite and stalactite formations. With the Samui archipelago (see pp166–75) becoming more congested, Ao Khanom is being developed as the next big holiday destination.

There is also a growing diving and snorkeling industry in this area, and tour operators can organize overnight stays or day trips to the nearby islands. They also arrange fishing trips to the Gulf of Thailand. This bay is a popular spot for sea golf, which takes place between April and July. During this time locals organize golf tournaments on the exposed flat sands of the seabed as the water drains out almost completely during low tide.

Limestone mountains forming a scenic backdrop to Khanom town

❾ Hat Na Dan

หาดหน้าด่าน

Road Map C4. 6 miles (10 km) S of Hat Khanom. 🚌 ℹ️ TAT, Nakhon Si Thammarat (0-7534-6515). 🚤 📷

Moving southward along the coastline from Hat Khanom is the pristine Hat Na Dan. This is a long, curving, white sand beach fringed by coconut palms and washed by the warm aquamarine waters of the Gulf of Thailand. Although this beach is only half an hour away by boat from Ko Samui, it is not very popular with foreign visitors. There is little by way of facilities,

Pink Dolphins of Sichon and Khanom

One of the unusual attractions of the Sichon-Khanom coast is the pod of rare pink dolphins that lives in the shallow waters of the Gulf of Thailand just offshore. It is usually possible to see these friendly and intelligent creatures by boat. The best time to view these mammals is between October and April. Formally known as Chinese White Dolphins, the adults of the species are usually gray or white in color. The much rarer pink variety is found here and on the South China coast. Unfortunately, this dolphin is threatened by overfishing in both areas and is now officially protected by the government.

A pink dolphin and its calf swimming along the water's surface

although there are a few beach vendors who sell local specialties such as dried squid. However, the pristine nature of the beach is changing with the arrival of sprawling resorts. The calm bay is good for swimming but there are no coral reefs. It is as yet undisturbed by the noise or pollution of jet skis and watersports. However, it is only a matter of time before it becomes a commercial spot.

❿ Hat Nai Phraet
หาดในแพรด

Road Map C4. 2 miles (3 km) S of Hat Na Dan. 🚌 ℹ️ TAT Nakhon Si Thammarat (0-7534-6515). 📶 📷

Lying immediately to the south of Hat Na Dan, Hat Nai Phraet is a gorgeous, long, and curving beach that is almost deserted, especially on weekdays. This peaceful spot has been drawing locals for years, but remains relatively unknown to foreign visitors. The beach is composed of crisp, golden sand backed by coconut palms and casuarina trees. There are some large boulders strewn about the beach that add to the ambience and natural beauty, as well as providing some shade from the midday sun. Facilities are minimal, although there are a few simple beachside restaurants serving local food and cold drinks. There are also

Rustic beach bungalows with tiled roofs at Hat Nai Phraet

some basic bungalows right by the beach for an overnight stay. However, most travelers make their way to the busier town of Khanom, for more options.

⓫ Hat Nai Phlao
หาดในเพรา

Road Map C4. 3 miles (5 km) S of Hat Na Dan. 🚌 ℹ️ TAT Nakhon Si Thammarat (0-7534-6515). 📶 📷

Located south of Hat Nai Phraet, Hat Nai Phlao is the longest beach in the Khanom district and its most popular attraction – although most visitors are local Thais on a weekend break. The beach is bordered by the Gulf of Thailand to the east,

and the forest-clad hills of the Khao Luang range to the west, creating an idyllic setting. This beach offers basic and affordable bungalow accommodations and campsites. There are also a couple of simple restaurants and bars offering local seafood delicacies along with beer or iced drinks. A few upscale resorts have also come up in recent years. Travel agencies are also developing watersports facilities such as snorkeling and fishing. Visitors can take longtail boats to the nearby islands, or hike to pretty Nam Tok Hin Lat along a 2-mile (3-km) long trail that winds its way through a scene of rural tranquility, surrounded by lush vegetation.

Waves washing over the expansive sandy shore, Hat Nai Phlao

Breathtaking Hat Tong Yi in an idyllic tropical setting

⑫ Hat Tong Yi
หาดท้องหยี

Road Map C4. 25 miles (40 km) S of Hat Nai Phlao. 🚌 ℹ TAT, Nakhon Si Thammarat (0-7534-6515). ⊘ 📷

A slender stretch of sand, beautiful Hat Tong Yi is a little-known beach, completely cut off from other beaches to its north and south by thickly wooded headlands. This picture-perfect beach is accessed by following a rough laterite road from Hat Nai Phlao's *(see p191)* Rachakiri Resort for about 2 miles (3 km). However, the journey is worth the trouble, especially when welcomed by the sheer isolation of the beach. Simple accommodations are available at Hat Tong Yi, but most visitors choose to stay at better-appointed Hat Nai Phlao to the north, visiting the beach only as a day trip. There are very few facilities available at the beach, so bringing along a picnic basket is advisable. Those keen to experiment with local flavors can find simple yet exotic seafood specialties, such as fried rice or grilled squid, nearby.

⑬ Hat Sichon
หาดสิชล

Road Map C4. 1 miles (2 km) S of Hat Tong Yi. 🚌 ℹ TAT, Nakhon Si Thammarat (0-7534-6515). ⊘ 📷

Sichon is still a small settlement and port, little more than a fishing village. However, it has seen some development and basic accommodations and restaurants have set up shop here. Beautiful Hat Sichon, also known as Hat Hua Hin Sichon, is distinguished by large numbers of rocky boulders strewn along the white sand, and is popular with locals, just like its namesake Hat Hua Hin *(see p144)*. Tall palms fringe the beach, while the small pier is lined with colorful longtail fishing boats. Hat Sichon is also a regular swimming spot, but those looking for somewhere even quieter could move southward to pretty Hat Piti.

Visitors wishing to get away from regular beach activities can also head to the scenic Nam Tok Si Khit, or Si Khit Falls, some 10 miles (16 km) inland from Hat Sichon, along Highway 4105. The Si Khit River originates in the Khao Luang Mountains to the west and flows through gorgeous natural surroundings before reaching these falls. Securing the area as a protected national park site is currently under consideration.

⑭ Hat Hin Ngam
หาดหินงาม

Road Map C4. 2 miles (3 km) S of Hat Sichon. 🚌 ℹ TAT, Nakhon Si Thammarat (0-7534-6515).

Covered with small rocks and boulders of various colors which give this beach its name, Hat Hin Ngam, or Beach of Beautiful Stones, is best visited as a day trip from nearby

Busy pier at Hat Sichon, lined with fishing boats

Unspoiled sweeping bay of Hat Hin Ngam

Hat Sichon. While it is a good place for diving and snorkeling, Hat Hin Ngam is pretty quiet, and there are no accommodation options or restaurants, so bringing along food and water is advisable.

Thatched shelter providing shade from the tropical sun at Hat Piti

⓰ Hat Piti
หาดปิติ

Road Map C4. 1 mile (2 km) S of Hat Hin Ngam. 🚌 ℹ️ TAT, Nakhon Si Thammarat (0-7534-6515). 🌊 📷

A favorite with locals who frequent the beach for its beauty and relative anonymity, Hat Piti is now witnessing a rise in the number of foreign visitors to its shores. Blessed with a white sandy beach and rows of coconut palms that provide adequate shade, the beach is a great place to sunbathe. Swimming and watersports such as windsurfing, albeit limited, are other options. However, there are no facilities available and visitors should head to nearby Sichon in the north for accommodations and restaurants serving local Thai as well as other cuisine.

⓰ Khao Kha Archaeological Site
แหล่งโบราณคดีเขาคา

Road Map C4. Tambon Sao Phao, 6 miles (10 km) S of Hat Piti. 🚌 ℹ️ TAT, Nakhon Si Thammarat (0-7534-6515). **Open** 8am–5pm daily.

Located on a mountain in the Tambon Sao Phao district, the Khao Kha Archaeological Site dates back almost 1,500 years. An ancient city with a laterite shrine, the site was restored in 1997 by the Thai Fine Arts Department before it was opened for public viewing. Khao Kha appears to be a predominantly Hindu site, formerly sacred to the Saiwinikai sect, which was known to worship Shiva as the supreme deity of the Hindu pantheon. The site has revealed several monuments, with the most important of them being located at its northern end. Many interesting artifacts from Saivite rituals including *lingas* (symbolic phalluses), a sacred tank, holy water pipes, and other related ruins, have also been excavated. These relics have now been preserved in a bungalow-like building located near the site, and are also maintained by the Fine Arts Department. Even today, archaeologists continue to study the numerous artifacts unearthed here in relation to the once-popular Hindu Saivite sect.

Building housing relics from the Khao Kha Archaeological Site

Local fisherwoman drying shrimp near the waterfront, Hat Saophao

⑰ Hat Saophao
หาดเสาเภา

Road Map C4. Tha Sala, Hwy 401, 36 miles (60 km) N of Nakhon Si Thammarat. 🚌 ℹ️ TAT, Nakhon Si Thammarat (0-7534-6515). 🚲 📷

Perfect for a pleasant day trip from nearby Nakhon Si Thammarat *(see pp196–9)*, Hat Saophao is a long, often deserted strip of sand. Devoid of the regular tourist influx, this beautiful beach continues to be a safe haven for holiday-makers looking for some peace and quiet. The beach is equipped with small restaurants and cafés aimed chiefly at the locals. Further inland are vast shrimp farms and tiny, predominantly Thai Muslim villages. Visitors will find Muslim kitemakers selling their wares – beautiful colored kites – on the road between Nakhon and Hat Saophao. The beach is best reached by local bus from Nakhon Si Thammarat or by motorcycle taxi, and draws mainly young backpackers.

⑱ Hat Sa Bua
หาดสระบัว

Road Map C4. 24 miles (39 km) N of Nakhon Si Thammarat. 🚌 ℹ️ TAT, Nakhon Si Thammarat (0-7534-6515). 🚲 📷

A picturesque beach about 3 miles (5 km) long and dotted with lovely coconut groves, Hat Sa Bua is a favorite weekend resort for locals. Just north of Nakhon, the road to the beach winds through pleasant rural scenery, past small fishing villages and rustic kilns used for firing bricks and pottery. Tamarisks and palm trees shade stretches of sandy shoreline, while thatched umbrellas provide cool, shaded sanctuaries. There are simple bungalow accommodations available, along with numerous small bars and seafood restaurants, which are quite reasonably priced.

⑲ Khao Luang National Park
อุทยานแห่งชาติเขาหลวง

Road Map C4. Park HQ off Hwy 4015, 28 miles (45 km) NW of Nakhon Si Thammarat. 🚌 ℹ️ Park HQ (0-7530-0494). 🚲 🚲

One of the largest and least developed national parks in southern Thailand, Khao Luang covers an area of 230 sq miles (596 sq km). Declared a national park in 1974, Khao Luang surrounds the region's main peak, Khao Luang, which is 6,020 ft (1,835 m) high. The park is home

to a wide variety of tropical flora and fauna, and provides sanctuary to several endangered species.

Animals inhabiting the park include musk deer, Malaysian tapir, binturong, and serow. Park authorities have also identified more than 200 species of birds, including both permanent residents and migratory species. The flora in the park is tropical, dense, and magnificent with colorful orchids and rhododendrons.

The most popular attraction of the park is the nine-tiered **Krung Ching Waterfall**, accessible by a steep 3-mile (5-km) trek from the park entrance. Overnight accommodations are available in the park, as are camping facilities.

Cascading waters of the nine-tier Krung Ching Waterfall

⑳ Laem Talumphuk
แหลมตะลุมพุก

Road Map C4. 14 miles (22 km) NE of Nakhon Si Thammarat. 🚌 ℹ️ TAT, Nakhon Si Thammarat (0-7534-6515). 🚲 📷

A long and narrow cape facing Nakhon Si Thammarat to the east, Laem Talumphuk is a popular haven for local fishing vessels. The coast at this point is divided into two sections where the Phanang River runs down to Ao Nakhon from the mountains nearby. The eastern shore is inhabited in places with small fishing villages and shrimp farms, as well as a long, beautiful beach fringed with towering palm trees. Although an area of great natural beauty, the beach here has limited facilities beyond a few small shops and restaurants, and is best visited as a day trip from Nakhon Si Thammarat.

A typical fishing settlement close to Hat Sa Bua

Shadow Puppets

An art form said to have been practiced as early as 400 BC in Southeast Asia, *nang talung* is a popular southern Thai version of puppetry that originated in Phatthalung. Light is shone behind the puppets, creating shadows on a cloth screen, giving it the name "shadow puppets." Often compared with *wayang kulit*, shadow puppetry in neighboring Malaysia, *nang talung* performances generally begin after dark and last well into the night. They remain an essential, although diminishing, part of village life in southern Thailand. It is the task of a single skilled person, the *nai nag* (puppet master) to conceptualize the whole show. While the more formal *nang yai* is based on traditional stories from the Ramakien (*see p63*), *nang talung* often takes its inspiration from daily life. Each story is created by the *nai nag* and includes easily recognizable characters.

Illuminated cloth screens are used to create the shadow of the puppets

The *nai nag* maneuvers up to six puppets per screen

Musicians accompany the *nai nag* in *nang talung* performances

Nang Talung Theater

Theater performances of nang talung *are held in large open spaces. The changing tone of voice of the puppet master, who manipulates the puppets through complex movements from behind the screen, differentiates between the characters. A traditional orchestra adds tension to the plot.*

Nang (water buffalo leather) is cut, colored, and rendered movable by joints to make the 20-inch (50-cm) high shadow puppets. This is highly skilled work done only by master craftsmen.

Nang talung, smaller shadow puppets, portray comic figures with exaggerated features. From demons and heroes to farmers, these characters play a central role in performances.

Ramakien stories, depicted through *nang yai* or large shadow puppets, are adapted from the original epic. Here, Hanuman, the monkey god, is usually given a prominent role.

㉑ Nakhon Si Thammarat

นครศรีธรรมราช

Although the historic town of Nakhon Si Thammarat features on few tourist itineraries, the cultural capital of southern Thailand is a lively center with several attractions. Under the name of Ligor, it is said to have been the capital of Tambralinga prior to the 7th century. From the 7th to the 13th centuries it was an important city of the Srivijaya Empire (see p43), when it became a religious center with the Sanskrit name Nagara Sri Dhammaraja, meaning "City of the Sacred Dharma King". Many Indian traders settled here and Hindu shrines are common, as are nang talung (see p195) plays and intricately etched nielloware (see p34).

Relaxing way of taking in the sights, Nakhon Si Thammarat

Delicately carved southern Thai wooden house, Wat Sao Thong Tong

🏛 Wat Sao Thong Tong

วัดเสาธงทอง

Ratchadamnoen Rd. **Open** daily.
The main attraction of Wat Sao Thong Tong is the southern Thai wooden house, started in 1888 and finished in 1901. The wat now occupies the area which had earlier housed the first primary school in the district. It is actually three houses joined together by a common pointed roof and features delicately carved wooden door panels, gables, and window surrounds. The Architects' Association of Thailand gave a conservation award to the building in 1993.

🏛 Ancient City Wall and North Gate

กำแพงเมืองเก่า

E of Ratchadamnoen Rd.
The ancient city wall, built as a fortification, originally contained an area which was 1,320 ft by 7,350 ft (402 m by 2,240 m). It was restored in the 14th and again in the 17th century. The red brick North Gate is a reconstruction of the original gate.

🏛 Ho Phra I-suan

หอพระอิศวร

Ratchadamnoen Rd. **Open** daily.
In the hall of this shrine is a 3-ft (1-m) linga, a phallic image of the Hindu god Shiva, which may date back to the 6th century AD. The worship of Shiva was a potent force in the early peninsular city-states of the first millennium AD.

🏛 Ho Phra Narai

หอพระนารายณ์

Ratchadamnoen Rd. **Open** daily.
Five lingas (phallic symbols) discovered on the site of this shrine may date from before AD 1000. They are now in the Wihan Kien Museum (see p199).

🏛 Ho Phra Buddha Sihing

หอพระพุทธสิหิงค์

Ratchadamnoen Rd. **Open** Wed–Sun.
The Phra Buddha Sihing is one of Thailand's most revered images. The replica kept in this shrine is of an original cast in Sri Lanka in AD 157 and brought to Nakhon at the end of the 13th century. Local artisans put their characteristic stamp on the Buddha by giving it a half-smile, a rounder face, and a full chest. This style has a special name – khanom tom, or banana and rice

Reconstructed Ancient City Wall and North Gate

pudding. It is similar to Buddha images in Wat Phra Sing in Chiang Mai in northern Thailand.

Shadow Puppet Theater

บ้านหนังตะลุงสุชาติ

10/18 Si Thammasok Soi 3. **Tel** 0-7534-6394. **Open** daily.

The *nang talung* workshop of puppeteer Suchart Subsin keeps alive a uniquely Southeast Asian form of entertainment in danger of dying out. Visitors can watch the puppets being cut from leather and buy the finished product. Sometimes impromptu shows are also staged.

 Wat Phra Mahathat Woramahawihan

วัดพระมหาธาตุ

See pp198–9.

National Museum Nakhon Si Thammarat

พิพิธภัณฑสถานแห่งชาตินครศรีธรรมราช

Ratchadamnoen Rd, 1 mile (2 km) S of town center. **Tel** 0-7534-1075. **Open** Wed–Sun.

The centerpiece of this branch of the National Museum *(see p66–7)* is the 9th-century statue of Vishnu, part of the Hindu holy trinity, in the Pala style of South India. It was found in the base of a tree in Kapong district near Takua Pa in Phang Nga province,

Buddha image in characteristic local style, Ho Phra Buddha Sihing

then a major transit point for Indians colonizing the south. Two rare bronze drums made by the Dong Son people of northern Vietnam are another highlight. The Thai gallery displays religious art from the

Dvaravati and Srivijaya periods to the Rattanakosin era. The Buddha images in the distinctive local Sing style, characterized by stumpy features and animated faces, are also worth a visit.

Imposing façade and grounds, National Museum, Nakhon Si Thammarat

Nakhon Si Thammarat Town Center

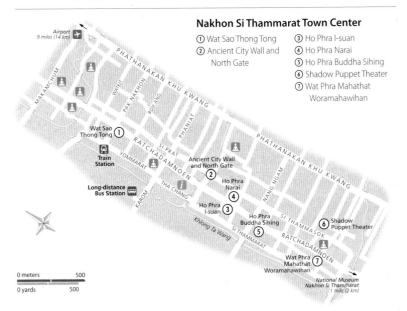

① Wat Sao Thong Tong
② Ancient City Wall and North Gate
③ Ho Phra I-suan
④ Ho Phra Narai
⑤ Ho Phra Buddha Sihing
⑥ Shadow Puppet Theater
⑦ Wat Phra Mahathat Woramahawihan

Airport 9 miles (14 km)

Wat Sao Thong Tong ①

Train Station

Long-distance Bus Station

Ancient City Wall and North Gate ②

Ho Phra Narai ④

Ho Phra I-suan ③

Ho Phra Buddha Sihing ⑤

Shadow Puppet Theater ⑥

Wat Phra Mahathat Woramahawihan ⑦

National Museum Nakhon Si Thammarat 1 mile (2 km)

0 meters 500
0 yards 500

For keys to symbols *see back flap*

Nakhon Si Thammarat:
Wat Phra Mahathat Woramahawihan
วัดพระมหาธาตุ

Wat Phra Mahathat Woramahawihan, or Temple of the Great Chedi, is one of the most revered temples in southern Thailand. It is believed to contain a sacred tooth relic of the Buddha. Legend says that Prince Thanakuman and Queen Hemchala brought this relic to Hat Sai Kaew and built a pagoda to mark its location. Later, in the 13th century, when King Si Thammasokarat founded Nakhon Si Thammarat, he constructed a new temple and shifted the relic there. The buildings inside the *wat* are an amalgam of different Thai styles. The present *wat* has a Sri Lankan design and its *chedi* is an important Thai symbol, featuring on the provincial seal as well as the current 25 satang coin.

Offerings in front of King Taksin's statue outside the *wat* complex

Royal Wihan

★ **Phra Chedi Boromathat**
The 247-ft (77-m) high Sri Lankan-style *chedi* houses the tooth relic. This structure is supposedly built over an older Srivijaya *chedi*, and its spire is covered in pure gold.

KEY

① **173 smaller chedis** surround the Phra Chedi Boromathat and are replicas of the central spire.

② **Dharma Sala Wihan**; in the temple's east wall, is dedicated to the study of dhamma, or teachings of the Buddha.

③ **The Phra Rabieng Wihan** is an elongated, cloistered gallery that surrounds the temple on all sides. It shelters many gilt Buddha images.

④ **A roof** of glazed red and emerald green tiles protects the gallery.

⑤ **Pho Lanka Wihan** houses donated artifacts and reflects the *wat's* ancient ties with Sri Lanka.

Visitors' entrance

Wihan Tap Kaset
Surrounding the main *chedi* is the Wihan Tap Kaset, a gallery with lines of golden Buddha images in varied styles. The *wihan* is also decorated with statues of elephant heads.

★ Royal Wihan
South of the main *chedi* and outside the cloister walls is a large *ubosot*, or ordination hall, called the Royal Wihan. It houses several Buddha images as well as a beautiful elephant figurine.

VISITORS' CHECKLIST

Practical Information
Ratchadamnoen Rd, Nakhon Si Thammarat. **Open** dawn to dusk daily. 🗲 🕓 Hae Pha Khuen That (Feb/May); Chak Phra Pak Tai (Oct). Wihan Kien Museum: **Open** 8am–5pm daily. 🗲

★ Wihan Phra Song Ma
An ornamental stairway located inside the Wihan Phra Song Ma leads to the most important part of the complex – the walkway around the *chedi*. It is decorated with figures from both Hindu and Buddhist mythology.

Wihan Kien Museum
This is a small temple-museum housing images, amulets, and other artifacts. It is located next to Wihan Phra Song Ma.

Statue of Rama and Sita
A three-tier gilt umbrella shelters this statue of Rama and Sita and represents Nakhon's ancient links with Hinduism.

UPPER ANDAMAN COAST

The abiding image of Thailand's Upper Andaman Coast is of sandy beaches backed by swaying palms, a lush forested interior, and hundreds of limestone outcrops rising dramatically out of azure waters. This region provides a multitude of options for travelers, from the pristine coral reefs of the Surin and Similan archipelagos to the luxurious comforts of Phuket, Thailand's largest island and premier beach resort.

From the earliest times, both Thais and foreigners have been attracted to the Andaman Coast. Merchants and traders were drawn by its strategic position on the spice route, prospectors came for the rich tin deposits, and visitors were attracted by the outstanding natural beauty of the region. The ancient Srivijaya port at Takua Pa, and the distinctive architecture of the Chinese shophouses and the Sino-Portuguese mansions of Phuket town reflect these historical connections.

The Upper Andaman Coast is a prosperous and fertile region with rubber, cashew, banana, durian, and coffee plantations making it a prime agricultural zone. Yet it also offers urban facilities including designer resorts, chic bars, and gourmet restaurants on the island of Phuket. The entire coastline is lined by lovely beaches while the hinterland is covered with virgin rain forests preserved in national parks such as Khao Sok. The limestone stacks of Phang Nga Bay are home to a variety of wildlife while the waters of the Andaman Sea teem with rich marine life. This underwater landscape is best visible at the Surin and Similan Islands which offer unparalleled diving opportunities.

This region is a melting pot of towns populated by Thais of Tai and ethnic Chinese descent, fishing villages inhabited by Thai Muslims and a few communities of sea gypsies, all of whom have enriched the cultural traditions of this region. Although the Upper Andaman Coast was badly affected by the tsunami in 2004, it has recovered well.

Towering karst formations dominating the landscape at Khao Sok National Park

◄ Scuba diver exploring marine life over a coral reef, Similan Islands

Exploring the Upper Andaman Coast

Extending along the Andaman Sea, the Upper Andaman Coast is home to some of the most inviting beaches in Southeast Asia. The internationally renowned resort of Phuket serves as a good base for visitors to explore this region with its wide range of shopping, dining, entertainment, and watersports options. The stunning limestone stacks of Phang Nga are definitely worth a day trip, while the thickly forested hills of Khao Sok National Park and the mangroves of Laem Son National Park shelter a variety of birds and animals and are perfectly suited for nature lovers. The extensive sandy stretches along the Khao Lak coast form an idyllic retreat, and the Similan and Surin archipelagos are famous for their spectacular underwater landscape and rich marine life, making them a haven for divers and snorkelers.

Devotees thronging outside San Chao Chui Tui temple in Phuket

Sights at a Glance

Towns, Cities, and Villages
- **1** Ranong
- **10** Khuraburi
- **14** Takua Pa

National Parks
- **4** Laem Son National Park
- **5** Khlong Nakha Wildlife Sanctuary
- **11** Mu Ko Ra-Ko Phra Thong National Park
- **12** *Surin Islands Marine National Park pp208–9*
- **13** *Khao Sok National Park pp210–11*
- **16** Khao Lak-Lam Ru National Park
- **18** *Similan Islands Marine National Park pp214–15*

Beaches, Islands, Bays, and Estuaries
- **2** Ko Chang
- **3** Ko Phayam
- **6** Ko Khang Khao
- **7** Ko Kam Noi
- **8** Ko Kam Yai
- **9** Hat Praphat
- **15** Hat Khao Lak
- **17** Khlong Thap Liang
- **19** *Phang Nga Bay pp216–21*
- **20** *Phuket pp224–43*

0 kilometers   25

0 miles   25

Visitors relaxing on one of the six beaches along Khao Lak coast

Getting Around

Most visitors make use of Phuket's airport, and this island is the best base from which to explore the Upper Andaman Coast. Reliable air-conditioned bus services link Phuket, Phang Nga, and Ranong, although renting a car in Phuket or Ranong is more convenient. There is no railroad in the region. The Similan Islands are accessible from Phuket, while the Surin archipelago can be reached by boat from Ranong, Khao Lak, and Khuraburi. Longtail boats are the easiest mode of transportation for exploring the smaller bays and islands such as Phang Nga Bay and Ko Chang.

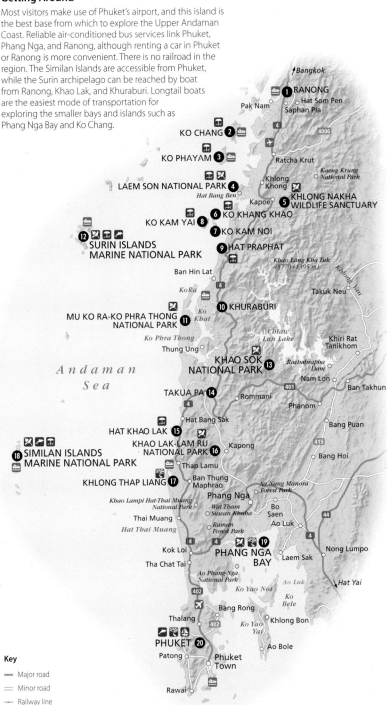

Bangkok

1 RANONG
Hat Som Pen
Pak Nam
Saphan Pla

KO CHANG 2

KO PHAYAM 3
Ratcha Krut

Kaeng Krung National Park

LAEM SON NATIONAL PARK 4
Khlong Khong
Hat Bang Ben
Kapoe

5 KHLONG NAKHA WILDLIFE SANCTUARY

6 KO KHANG KHAO
KO KAM YAI 8
7 KO KAM NOI

9 HAT PRAPHAT
Khao Lang Kha Tuk 4577ft (1395 m)

Ban Hin Lat
Ko Ra
Takuk Neu

12 SURIN ISLANDS MARINE NATIONAL PARK

Ko Khai
10 KHURABURI

MU KO RA-KO PHRA THONG NATIONAL PARK 11
Ko Phra Thong
Chiaw Lan Lake
Thung Ung
Khiri Rat Tanikhom

Andaman Sea

KHAO SOK NATIONAL PARK 13
Raebarabpra Dam
Nam Lon
Ban Takhun

TAKUA PA 14
Rommani
Phanom
Bang Puan

HAT KHAO LAK 15
Hat Bang Sak

KHAO LAK-LAM RU NATIONAL PARK 16
Kapong
Bang Hoi

18 SIMILAN ISLANDS MARINE NATIONAL PARK
Thap Lamu

KHLONG THAP LIANG 17
Ban Thung Maphrao
Sa Nang Manora Forest Park

Khao Lampi Hat-Thai Muang National Park
Phang Nga
Wat Tham Suwan Khuha
Bo Saen
Ao Luk

Thai Muang
Hat Thai Muang
Raman Forest Park

Kok Loi
Tha Chat Tai
PHANG NGA BAY 19
Laem Sak
Nong Lumpo

Ao Phang-Nga National Park
Ko Yao Noi
Ao Luk
Ko Bele

Thalang
Bang Rong
Khlong Bon
Ko Yao Yai

PHUKET 20
Patong
Ao Bole
Phuket Town
Rawai

Key

— Major road
═ Minor road
⋯ Railway line
△ Peak

For keys to symbols *see back flap*

❶ Ranong

ระนอง

Road Map B3. 351 miles (565 km) SW of Bangkok. 🚗 175,000. 🚌 🚐 🚢 ℹ️ TAT, Chumphon (0-7750-1831/2). 🚲 🏠

This town was originally settled in the late 18th century by Hokkien Chinese, who were hired to work as laborers in the region's tin mines. The area grew rich, and Ranong became a major border town. From here Thai nationals can travel to **Victoria Point** in Myanmar on half- or full-day boat trips. Foreign nationals, however, are not allowed to go to Victoria Point without a visa. Referred to as Kawthaung by the Burmese, Ranong is well-known for duty-free goods and handicrafts available at bargain prices.

Ranong's main attractions are the Bo Nam Ron (Ranong Mineral Hot Springs) that rise by the Khlong Hat Sompen river at **Wat Tapotaram**, just east of the town center. These are channeled into three concrete tubs called Mother, Father, and Child. At an average temperature of 65°C (150°F), the water is too hot for bathing. However, a short walk down the river, the Jansom Thara Spa Resort Hotel has tapped and cooled the water; visitors not staying at the hotel can also take a spa bath for a nominal fee.

Fishing boats, ideal for rowing around rustic Ko Chang

❷ Ko Chang

เกาะช้าง

Road Map B3. 15 miles (24 km) SW of Ranong. 🚢 from Saphan Pla, Ranong. 🚢 🚲 🏠

Located in the warm waters of the Andaman Sea, this idyllic little island is much less developed than its more famous namesake on the Eastern Seaboard (see pp122–3). There is little to do on Ko Chang but lie back and relax in a beach bungalow, the basic accommodations available, or make trips to the island's tiny fishing village capital for supplies. Visitors could, however, head for **Hat Ao Yai**, a white, sandy beach on the west coast of the island, which is a great place to watch sunsets. Among the prettiest beaches in the area, it offers guesthouses for those who prefer to stay the night.

❸ Ko Phayam

เกาะพยาม

Road Map B4. 21 miles (34 km) S of Ko Chang. 🚌 from Saphan Pla. 🚢 from Ko Chang. 🚢 🚲 🏠

A picturesque island with a population of only 500 inhabitants, Ko Phayam offers reasonably priced bungalow accommodations, charming beachside restaurants, and the occasional sleepy bar. Locals earn their livelihood through shrimp, crab, and squid fishing, or farming sator beans and cashew nuts. However, there is an abundance of flora and fauna, with a wide variety of snakes, monkeys, and hornbills. Motorcycle taxis provide service on the island's popular routes. The island offers few facilities – even electricity is switched off by 11pm.

Visitors washing around a hot spring tub, Wat Tapotaram

For hotels and restaurants in this region see pp299–300 and pp314–16

❹ Laem Son National Park

อุทยานแห่งชาติแหลมสน

Road Map B4. Park HQ off Hwy 4, 37 miles (60 km) S of Ranong. 🚌 🚹 Park HQ (0-7786-1431 or 0-2562-0760). 🚻 ⚕ 🏕 **W** dnp.go.th

Extending south from Kapoe district in Ranong province to Khuraburi district in Phang Nga province, Laem Son National Park, the sixth-largest national park in Thailand, covers 122 sq miles (316 sq km) of mangrove swamps and forests, and around 63 miles (101 km) of the Andaman shoreline – the longest protected shoreline in Thailand. Established in 1983, much of the park is undeveloped and does not feature on most tourist itineraries.

Laem Son, which is home to 138 different species of birds, has its headquarters at **Hat Bang Ben**, the most attractive and accessible beach in the park. This casuarina-lined beach has a few unpretentious bungalows, but visitors can also hire tents and camp beneath the shady trees. Swimming is good and safe all year round – although it is a good idea to approach the Andaman Coast with caution, especially during the height of the wet and stormy southwest monsoon from June to September. Several other islands in the area, including Ko Kam Yai, Ko Kam Noi and Ko Khang Khao *(see p206)*, are accessible by longtail boat, which can easily be arranged through the park office.

It is also possible to explore the fascinating mangrove forests, home to crab-eating macaques, sea turtles, fishing eagles, wild boars, white-bellied sea eagles, hawk eagles, hornbills, and sandpipers.

❺ Khlong Nakha Wildlife Sanctuary

เขตรักษาพันธุ์สัตว์ป่าคลองนาคา

Road Map B4. Park HQ off Hwy 4, 48 miles (77 km) S of Ranong. 🚌 ⚕ ⚕ 🏕

Established in 1972 and covering an area of 205 sq miles (531 sq km), Khlong Nakha Wildlife Sanctuary is one of Thailand's older and larger national reserves. However, it is relatively less frequented. Wildlife here includes some large mammals such as the Asiatic elephant, serow, Malaysian tapir, gaur, ox, Malayan sun bear, sambar deer, and the common

Malayan sun bear

Statues at the entrance to Khlong Nakha

barking deer. Wild tigers and leopards are reported to roam the jungle interiors, but most visitors will be lucky to hear more than a nighttime roar.

As with most national parks in southern Thailand, it is best visited during the cool season from November to February and avoided during the steamy southwest monsoon, when leeches can become unwelcome companions for trekkers. A popular trekking destination within the sanctuary is the **Nam Tok Phan Met**, or One-Thousand-Meter Waterfall, set amid verdant rain forest. However, it is advisable to make reservations at least a month in advance before visiting the park.

Longtail boat waiting to carry passengers to the nearby islands, Laem Son National Park

Navigating a motorized longtail boat off Ko Khang Khao

❻ Ko Khang Khao
เกาะค้างคาว

Road Map B4. 6 miles (10 km) S of Hat Bang Ben. 🚤 from Hat Bang Ben. 🏖️ 🏕️

This remote island off the Andaman Coast, south of Hat Bang Ben *(see p205)*, was earlier uninhabited and home to bats, resulting in its name – Ko Khang Khao, meaning "Bat Island". Located on its northern coast is the beautiful Hat Hin Ngam, a white-sand beach strewn with colorful circular pebbles.

Ko Khang Khao is a verdant, untouched tropical island where visitors can relax on the warm sands or go snorkeling in the shallow waters surrounding the island. Although there are some colorful corals just offshore, the underwater visibility is not very good due to proximity to inland rivers flowing into the sea. Ko Khang Khao is a perfect day trip from Hat Bang Ben. The island is accessible through the year, except during the rainy season from June to September.

❼ Ko Kam Noi
เกาะก้ามนุ้ย

Road Map B4. 11 miles (18 km) SW of Hat Bang Ben. 🚤 from Hat Bang Ben.

Located offshore from Hat Bang Ben, Ko Kam Noi is a popular spot among campers. Uncluttered by commercial infrastructure, this island is undisturbed in its serenity. The western coast is rocky, while the northeastern side has the sandy stretches. Grassy patches on the island can be used to pitch tents and fresh water is available. Visitors can also go snorkeling in the surrounding waters.

❽ Ko Kam Yai
เกาะก้ามใหญ่

Road Map B4. 10 miles (16 km) SW of Hat Bang Ben. 🚤 from Hat Bang Ben. 🏖️ 🏕️

Despite being fairly large and busy, Ko Kam Yai is quite laid-back. The island is almost completely encircled by white-sand beaches. Lush, forested hills provide plenty of bird-watching opportunities as a variety of migrating birds make their way here, especially during the cool season from November to February. There are also camping facilities and bungalow accommodations. Just 660 ft (201 m) away lies the tiny island of **Ko Tam Tok**, which is connected to Ko Kam Yai by a sandy strip that gets exposed at low tide. It can be easily reached by swimming or taking a boat.

❾ Hat Praphat
หาดประพาส

Road Map B4. 31 miles (50 km) S of Hat Bang Ben. 🚌 🏖️ 🏕️

Located on the Andaman Coast, Hat Praphat has a long sandy frontage backed by graceful

Scrub-covered rocks on the shores of Ko Kam Yai

Fishing boat against the backdrop of the setting sun, Hat Praphat

casuarinas and pines, and is a nesting ground for sea turtles. There are simple bungalow accommodations as well as a few beach shacks serving fresh seafood. This area suffered some damage during the 2004 tsunami, but has recovered well. Laem Son National Park *(see p205)* has a second park office on Hat Praphat.

⓫ Khuraburi
คุระบุรี

Road Map B4. 88 miles (142 km) S of Ranong. 🚌 🚌 🚌 ⬛ ⬛

The small town of Khuraburi is a jumping-off point for the Surin archipelago *(see pp208–9)*, 38 miles (60 km) offshore. It is also the main ferry port for the nearby Mu Ko Ra-Ko Phra Thong National Park.

Set amid rubber, palm oil, and coconut plantations, this one-horse town is kept busy by coaches traveling along Highway 4 between Phuket, Ranong, and all points north of Bangkok. The town has adequate accommodations, a good selection of restaurants, and a few shops and businesses.

Khuraburi also has some community-based tourism programs run by NGOs that allow visitors to experience and understand the culture and ecosystem of the area. The funds raised from these initiatives are pumped back into the local economy.

⓫ Mu Ko Ra-Ko Phra Thong National Park
อุทยานแห่งชาติหมู่เกาะระ เกาะพระทอง

Road Map B4. 6 miles (10 km) W of Khuraburi. 🚤 from Khuraburi pier. 🛈 Park HQ (0-7649-1378). 🌐 dnp.go.th

Covering an area of 248 sq miles (642 sq km) on both land and water, the Mu Ko Ra-Ko Phra Thong National Park was declared a protected area in September 2000 amid much controversy and protest from the locals, especially fishermen who would lose their rights to fish in the surrounding rich waters. The main islands within the park are **Ko Phra Thong** and **Ko Ra**. Of the two, tiny Ko Ra is a lovely and uninhabited island running about 6 miles (10 km) from north to south, and about 2 miles (3 km) from east to west. It is covered in dense rainforest which shelters many birds including several species of hornbill. There are some fine beaches along its western coast facing the Andaman Sea. This end of the island is usually deserted and can be reached either by longtail boats or sea kayaks.

Visitors coming to Ko Ra on a rented boat should ensure that it is available for the return journey as well. Sea-kayaking is another alternative, but novices should beware of potentially strong currents, particularly along the west coast. There are no permanent facilities here, so visitors are advised to carry food and water. The hilly terrain is ideal for trekking and the whole island can be covered on foot.

Unlike Ko Ra, Ko Phra Thong has a handful of inhabitants. The eastern part of the island is covered with mangrove forests, while beaches line the western part. Ko Phra Thong is being developed as an eco-resort with several resorts offering accommodations. This island is also home to the luxurious Golden Buddha Beach Resort *(see p300)*. A temporary park office is also located on this island and its beaches are a nesting site for the giant leatherback turtle. Other wildlife includes flying foxes and the occasional dugong.

Visitors waiting for boats to the offshore islands, Khuraburi pier

Snorkeling in the clear waters off Ko Surin Nua

⑫ Surin Islands Marine National Park

อุทยานแห่งชาติหมู่เกาะสุรินทร์

Road Map B4. 38 miles (60 km) NW of Khuraburi. 🚌 🚤 from Ranong, Khao Lak, and Khuraburi. 🚤 ℹ️ Park HQ (0-7647-2145) or Forestry Dept (0-2562-0760). **Open** mid-Nov–mid-May. 📷 🚻 🏊 ♿ 🏕️ ⓦ dnp.go.th

Comprising a group of five enchanting islands set in the heart of the Andaman Sea, the Surin Islands were declared a national park in 1981 and remain one of the most pristine and beautiful maritime destinations in Thailand. The archipelago offers unparalleled diving and snorkeling opportunities, especially around Richelieu Rock and Burma Banks, with under-water visibility of up to 80 ft (25 m). Ko Surin Nua and Ko Surin Tai, the two larger islands, are separated by a narrow strait about 650 ft (200 m) wide.

This strait contains some of the most spectacular coral reefs in the Andaman Sea. The three smaller islands – Ko Ri, Ko Kai, and Ko Klang – are mere rocky islets with sparse vegetation and remain uninhabited even today. The islands boast rich marine life, as well as sandy beaches, mangroves, and stretches of verdant rainforest, that provide ample opportunities for hiking and bird-watching. Vacationers should look out for crab-eating macaques, Bengal monitors, and over 57 species of birds. The Surin Islands are also home to the flying fox, a rare species of bat, which lives in trees.

Ko Surin Nua

เกาะสุรินทร์เหนือ

Ko Surin Nua, or Surin North Island, is the largest island of the Surin archipelago, and is heavily forested with tall hardwood trees. The island has several bays, the largest being Ao Mae Yai. The surrounding sea offers an outstanding array of soft corals and frequent sightings of shovel-nose rays, bow-mouthed guitar fish, and whale sharks.

Some of the best and most accessible dive sites are to be found off the park headquarters in the so-called HQ Channel between the two main islands. The clear water makes diving or snorkeling quite redundant as the corals can easily be observed from above. Although excessive fishing and the 2004 tsunami have caused some damage in the area, disturbing its natural ecological balance and leading to a slight depletion in marine life, the damage has been minimal.

There are excellent hiking trails on the island, especially around Ao Mae Yai, as well as some good campgrounds. The site of the park headquarters, Ko Surin Nua also has a restaurant that provides Thai food and simple but adequate overnight accommodations in bungalows.

Shoals of brightly colored fish on the reefs off Surin Islands

Moken children playing outside their huts, Ko Surin Tai

Sea Gypsies

Probably the earliest inhabitants of the region, the *chao lae*, or sea gypsies, are thought to be descendants of Malaysia's *orang laut*, or sea people. Numbering around 5,000, they continue to lead a nomadic life, living on the Andaman Coast in houseboats called *kabang*. Their largest group, the Urak Lawoi, numbering around 3,000, live in simple shacks making a living by fishing and are well integrated into Thai society. The smaller groups comprise the Moklen and Moken, the latter being the least sophisticated of the group. They make their living by harvesting the bounty of the seas – sea cucumbers, oysters, and shellfish – and selling handicrafts to visitors. They believe in propitiating tutelary spirits, especially those associated with nature and the sea. Their annual rites include a spiritual cleansing ceremony to rid themselves of evil spirits.

Ko Surin Tai
เกาะสุรินทร์ใต้

Ko Surin Tai, or Surin South Island, is the second-largest island in the Surin archipelago and similar to Ko Surin Nua as far as the flora and fauna is concerned, but without the park facilities. The simple village of Chao Thalae, populated by the Moken sea gypsies, is also located on this island. Ao Tao, a beautiful bay situated to the southeast of the island, is home to sea turtles. Snorkeling in the waters off the bay is the perfect way to admire not just the turtles, but also the gorgeous coral reefs in the area.

Richelieu Rock
ไรเชเวีย รอค

9 miles (14 km) SE of Surin Islands.

An isolated limestone seamount shaped like a horseshoe and almost completely submerged in the sea, Richelieu Rock is considered to be among the best dive sites in Thailand. The rocky summit of the seamount just about manages to break the surface at low tide and is a navigational hazard for

Huts on stilts and fishing boats at Chao Thalae, Ko Surin Tai

boats in the area, as it rises perpendicularly from the sea floor 100 ft (30 m) below.

Fortunately, Richelieu Rock did not suffer during the 2004 tsunami and the marine ecology of the area remains intact. It provides feeding grounds and shelter to a wide variety of fish including barracuda, jacks, batfish, manta rays, and whale sharks, although their numbers have declined over the years. The coral reefs are also home to a great variety of marine life including the tigertail sea horse, harlequin shrimps, frog fish, and lion fish, as well as the yellow and spiny pineapple fish. Visitors wishing to dive here should only do so if accompanied by an experienced dive operator who knows the area well.

Burma Banks
ชายแดนพม่า

38 miles (60 km) NW of Surin Islands.

More remote and probably more exotic than Richelieu Rock, Burma Banks is a succession of submerged seamounts. The three main seamounts – Silvertip, Rainbow, and Roe – offer an unparalleled diving experience over pristine coral reefs, home to an amazing variety of large fish and other exotic marine creatures such as the great barracuda and moray eels. Day trips for visitors can be organized from either Khuraburi (see p207) or from Khao Lak (see p212).

Diving here is recommended only for the experienced, since divers must go into the open ocean. The main attraction is the almost guaranteed sighting of sharks such as the nurse shark, which can grow up to 10 ft (3 m) in length; the silvertip; and the exotic leopard shark.

Key

— Ferry route

0 km 2
0 miles 2

Thick rainforest backed by dramatic limestone peaks at Khao Sok National Park

⓫ Khao Sok National Park
อุทยานแห่งชาติเขาสก

Road Map B4. Park HQ off Hwy 401, 53 miles (85 km) S of Khuraburi. 🚌 ℹ️ Park HQ (0-7739-5154). 🐘 🛶 🥾 📷 🌐 **dnp.go.th**

Together with the neighboring reserves of Mu Ko Ra-Ko Phra Thong National Park *(see p207)* and Khao Lak-Lam Ru National Park *(see p212)*, the Khao Sok National Park forms the largest tract of virgin rainforest in southern Thailand. Khao Sok is a part of the oldest forest system that has remained unchanged through the Ice Ages of the past and dates back 160 million years. The 285-sq mile (738-sq km) park rises to a height of 3,150 ft (960 m) and includes more than 100 spectacular islands formed as a result of the construction of the Rachabrapha Dam in 1982.

Elephants, tigers, bears, tapirs, gibbons, and monkeys are found in the park, along with over 300 species of birds, including hornbills and argus pheasants. Sightings of the larger animals are usually at night, and animal tracks are regularly seen along the marked trails. Sadly, poaching of the animals persists despite the efforts of park officers.

There is also a wide range of interesting flora, including the rare *Rafflesia kerrii*; Khao Sok is

one of the few places in the world where it grows. This foul-smelling plant is wholly parasitic and lies dormant inside the roots of the host tree. Once a year it breaks the surface of the bark and over a few months grows into the world's largest flower, measuring up to 31 inches (79 cm) in width. The flower's fetid smell attracts pollinating insects. However, it has a short life span and shrivels into a putrescent mass within a few days.

Khao Sok receives the brunt of both the southwest and northeast monsoons, which results in an extended rainy season from May to November. Thus the best time to visit the park is between January and April.

The park is famous for its beautiful karst limestone peaks, numerous waterfalls, and caves.

Great Asian hornbill

Longtail boats, a convenient mode of transportation at Khao Sok

Along with the limestone outcrops, the Chiaw Lan Lake forms the most distinctive geographical feature of Khao Sok.

This park is a popular spot and offers activities such as kayaking and the extreme sport of spelunking, where participants go diving into a series of subterranean caves. Khao Sok also has a number of hiking trails; most are suitable for all levels. A few demanding trails might suit experienced trekkers. Basic accommodations and food are available inside the park. There are also a few mini-markets just outside the entrance to Khao Sok and at the park headquarters.

Nam Tok Than Sawan
น้ำตกธารสวรรค์
4 miles (7 km) W of Park HQ.
A spectacular waterfall, the Nam Tok Than Sawan, or Heavenly Waterfall, is at the end of a picturesque trekking trail which can get quite inaccessible at the height of the rainy season. The waterfall bursts from the edge of a steep cliff, and creates a stunning rainbow effect due to the reflection of the sunlight in the water.

Nam Tok Sip-Et Chan
น้ำตกสิบเอ็ดชั้น
3 miles (5 km) N of Park HQ.
A large waterfall that descends over eleven tiers of rock stairs, Nam Tok Sip-Et Chan is not too far from the park headquarters, but takes up to three hours to reach because of the difficult

terrain and the number of river crossings. Trekkers should watch out for wildlife such as gibbons and hornbills along the way.

Chiaw Lan Lake
ทะเลสาบเชี่ยวหลาน
41 miles (66 km) NE of Park HQ.

A star attraction of the park, Chiaw Lan Lake is approximately an hour's drive from the park headquarters. This large freshwater reservoir, created by the construction of the Rachabrapha Dam in 1982, is also known as Rachabrapha Lake. Spectacular karst outcrops, isolated from the mainland by the flooding waters, rise from the lake to almost 3,000 ft (914 m) in height – about three times the height of similar karst outcrops at Phang Nga Bay (see pp216–21). Gibbons and eagles can be seen on these peaks, which are a haven for rare wildlife but are inaccessible to all but the most intrepid climbers. Accommodations are in the form of floating chalets or eco-friendly huts built on the lake which offer spectacular views of the surroundings.

Tham Nam Thalu
ถ้ำน้ำทะลุ
One of the most rewarding spots in the park, Tham Nam Thalu is a 2,625-ft (800-m) long horseshoe-shaped cave

Distant karst outcrops across Chiaw Lan Lake

which is located near the southwestern shore of Chiaw Lan Lake. A visit to the cave is an exciting trek through dark and slippery terrain and is not really recommended for those who are frightened of bats, or suffer from claustrophobia. A marked trail follows a small river into the cave system and visitors have to wade through water for a part of the journey. Anyone entering Nam Thalu must wear suitable footwear and carry a flashlight. It is not advisable to visit the cave during the the rainy season, despite whatever guides may say, as there have

been several casualties. Hazards aside, a visit to this cave is a highlight of the Khao Sok experience, offering visitors an unparalleled opportunity to see rare cave creatures.

Tham Si Ru
ถ้ำสี่รู
Another well-known cave system, Tham Si Ru, or Four Holes Cave, has four converging cave passages that were used as a secret base by communist insurgents in southern Thailand during the 1970s. The caves can be reached on foot from the southern shore of the lake.

Key

- ▬▬ Major road
- ═══ Minor road
- ▪ ▪ Trail
- ▪ ▪ Park boundary

Nam Tok Sip-Et Chan

Chiaw Lan Lake

Tham Nam Thalu

Tham Si Ru

KHAO SOK NATIONAL PARK

Endemic Species Trail

ℹ Park HQ

Tang Nam Gorge

Wing Hin Waterfall

Nam Tok Than Sawan

Sok River

401

Takua Pa
22 miles (35 km)

Khuraburi

Chiaw Lan Lake

Khao Sok National Park

Area Illustrated

401

0 km		3
0 miles		3

For keys to symbols see back flap

⓮ Takua Pa
ตะกั่วป่า

Road Map B4. 33 miles (53 km) S of Khuraburi. 🚌 35,000. 📟

Known to have been one of the finest harbors in peninsular Thailand, Takua Pa, also known as Takkolam or Takola, was once a busy port handling mercantile traffic between the ancient kingdoms of Srivijaya (*see p43*) and the Tamil kingdoms of South India. The town is divided into two distinct areas, better known as the old and the new quarters. While the former is reminiscent of Takua Pa's historic past with several charming Sino-Portuguese-style houses, the latter is situated along the Takua Pa River. Vacationers can roam the streets of this little-visited friendly town, dotted with Buddhist and Chinese temples, or head for the exotic **Hat Bang Sak**, or Teak Tree Beach, Takua Pa's best-known spot. A lovely stretch of white sand shaded by casuarinas, Hat Bang Sak is best reached by following Highway 4 between Thai Muang and Takua Pa. It currently offers simple accommodations, but plans for more upscale hotels and resorts are already on the table.

Sunbathers taking a stroll along pretty Hat Khao Lak

⓯ Hat Khao Lak
เขาหลัก

Road Map B4. 21 miles (34 km) SW of Takua Pa. 🚌 from Takua Pa or Phuket. 🛈 TAT, Phuket (0-7621-1036).

The coastline south of Takua Pa consists of long stretches of rocky and sandy beaches. Hat Khao Lak, halfway between Takua Pa and Thai Muang, is the southernmost of six beaches separated by rocky outcrops. It has so far been relatively quiet but is now beginning to attract more visitors. Commercial development is also on the rise and a variety of accommodations are now available.

Hat Khao Lak is a fine beach and makes a good base from which to explore the pristine Surin (*see pp208–9*) and Similan Islands (*see pp214–15*), which are located 4 hours away by boat. Many visitors come here to book their dive trips. Between November and April, the fishing ports of Thap Lamu and Hat Khao Lak operate as ferry points for trips to these islands.

Sights such as the 199-ft (61-m) high Nam Tok Sai Rung, or Sai Rung Waterfall, vie for visitors' attention. This lovely waterfall, situated close to the beach off Highway 4, is good for swimming, although caution is advised.

Observation deck at Khao Lak-Lam Ru National Park

⓰ Khao Lak-Lam Ru National Park
อุทยานแห่งชาติเขาหลมรู

Road Map B4. Park HQ off Hwy 4, Laem Hin Chang, 21 miles (34 km) SW of Takua Pa. 🚌 from Takua Pa or Phuket. 🛈 Park HQ (0-7648-5243). **Open** 8am–4:30pm daily. 📷 🚻 🏕 🕨 **dnp.go.th**

Established as a land-based park in 1991, Khao Lak-Lam Ru National Park was made into a marine national park in 1995 due to the inclusion of several offshore areas. The park covers an area of 49 sq miles (127 sq km) and is justly famous for its outstanding natural beauty, encompassing islands, sea cliffs, forested hills, and beaches, in addition to karst and granite outcrops dating from the Cretaceous period. The park is home to a variety of flora and

Open-air restaurant with thatched pavilions along the coast, Hat Bang Sak

Colorful flags adorning the entrance to Khao Lak-Lam Ru

⓱ Khlong Thap Liang

คลองทับเหลียง

Road Map B4. 6 miles (10 km) SW of Khao Lak-Lam Ru. 🚌 🚢 ⬛ ⬛

An interesting and exciting addition to any visit to Khao Lak is a longtail boat trip to the nearby Khlong Thap Liang estuary, and the contiguous Khlong Thung Maphrao and Khlong Hin Lad waterways. The mangrove forests here are worth a visit and are inhabited by troops of crab-eating macaques, who generally venture from the mangroves to the mudflats in search of food at low tide. These estuaries – styled *khlongs* (canals) – lie immediately to the south of Thap Lamu between the southern limits of the verdant Khao Lak-Lam Ru National Park and the northern limits of the nearby Hat Thai Muang National Park.

fauna. The tropical evergreen forests on the hills near Khao Lak have a three-tier canopy with some gigantic trees towering over them. The lower level is rich in epiphytes such as orchids and ferns, as well as the useful rattan vines.

Species of fauna in the park include macaques, langurs, black drongos, Asiatic black bears, gold-whiskered barbets, reticulated pythons, giant black squirrels, wild boar, and several types of hornbill. There are a number of treks leading to several waterfalls, the most popular of which is the spectacular **Nam Tok Lam Ru**, also known as the Lam Ru Waterfall, which is located about 19 miles (31 km) from the park headquarters at Laem Hin Chang. Others worth seeing include Nam Tok Saeng Thong and Nam Tok Chong Fa. Thai visitors also like to trek to a popular jungle shrine dedicated to Chao Po Khao Lak, said to be the tutelary guardian spirit of the national park.

Longtail boats stranded in an estuary at low tide, Khlong Thap Liang

Takua Pa, the Ancient Srivijaya Port of Takola

Originally named Takola, Takua Pa is one of the oldest human settlements in southern Thailand, dating as far back as the Srivijaya era *(see pp42–3)*, when it was an important port. The name Takola is thought to have been derived from the Tamil word *takkolam* (pepper), and is indicative of the area's strong historic links with South India. Takola was probably the main harbor on the Andaman Coast for trade between the Thai-Malay kingdom of Srivijaya and the southern Indian Tamil kingdoms of the Pallavas (4th–9th centuries) and the Cholas (9th–13th centuries). It is believed to have played an important role in the spread of South Asian, Hindu, and Buddhist culture and beliefs throughout southern Thailand and the Malay Peninsula. Little physical evidence survives from this period. However, the single most important artifact of this era is a tall statue, nearly 8 ft (2 m) high, of Lord Vishnu, god of the Hindu holy trinity, found at Takua Pa. It is now on display at Thalang National Museum *(see p238)* in Phuket.

Statue of Lord Vishnu displayed at Thalang National Museum, Phuket

Extraordinary rock shapes and pristine waters off Ko Similan

⓲ Similan Islands Marine National Park

อุทยานแห่งชาติหมู่เกาะสิมิลัน

Road Map A4. 38 miles (60 km) W of Thap Lamu. 🚌 from Thap Lamu, Kha Lak, and Phuket. 🚌 𝐢 Park HQ (0-7645-3272); bungalow bookings: 0-2562-0760. **Open** Nov–May. 🎿 🎣 🖊 📷 🖥 dnp.go.th

Established in 1982, the enchanting Similan Islands Marine National Park covers an area of 54 sq miles (140 sq km). The name Similan is derived from the Malay word *sembilan* (nine), for the number of islands in the archipelago. These granitic islands, rising from the Andaman Sea, are stunning – verdant rainforest surrounded by a ring of white-sand beaches, coral reefs, and azure sea. The seabed is decorated with staghorn, star, and branching corals. In these seemingly perfect waters there are also some potentially threatening species of fish, such as giant groupers, poisonous stone fish, and lion fish, as well as a variety of sharks including leopard sharks, hammerheads, bull sharks, and whale sharks, which can be found swimming off these islands.

Ko Similan, the largest island in the archipelago, covers an area of 2 sq miles (5 sq km) and is home to a variety of marine animals, land mammals, and reptiles such as crabs, snakes, and bats, as well as some 40 species of birds.

The main attraction, however, are the 20 or so recognized dive sites offering all levels of diving experience. The underwater grottoes and swim-through tunnels appeal to both divers and snorkelers.

However, it is necessary to book a dive tour at Thap Lamu or through an agency in Phuket, since there are no diving agencies in the park. Half-day park-run snorkeling tours depart for Ko Miang on a daily basis. It is also possible to arrange day trips from Ko Miang to the more remote islands such as Ko Bon further north.

Ko Bangu

เกาะบันตู

The northernmost island in the Similan archipelago, Ko Bangu, also known as Hua Kalok, or Skull Island, has a couple of excellent dive spots just off the shore. Christmas Point is particularly good, with some exciting fish such as jacks and bluefin trevally. Another great snorkeling site lies in the sheltered eastern lee of the island, which is also home to a park ranger station.

Ko Similan

เกาะสิมิลัน

The largest island, Ko Similan is located near the northern-most point of the archipelago. Although it has no accom-modations, there are two favored dive spots – Fantasy Reef to the west of the island, and a scuba spot to the south of Ao Nang Chan, the longest beach, on the island's eastern shore. Fantasy Reef has been closed indefinitely to allow recovery from the 2004 tsunami.

Snorkeling, one of the main outdoor activities on Ko Similan

Hin Pusa

หินปูษา

Set in the Andaman Sea, just south of Ko Similan and to the north of Ko Payu, Hin Pusa, or Elephant Head, is really just a rocky outcrop. The various

Ko Bangu, an idyllic swimming spot where the forest comes down to the beach

boulders that make up Elephant Head form a series of tunnels, arches, and swim-through channels which can be quite challenging, even for accomplished swimmers. A very popular dive spot, it has a host of spectacular marine creatures clearly visible even without snorkeling gear. These include a colony of spider crabs, a range of soft corals, cuttlefish, mantis shrimps, the twin-colored parrot fish, an occasional olive ridley turtle, and even the gentle whale sharks.

Vacationers disembarking from the boat at Ko Miang

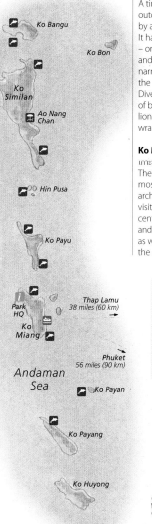

Ko Payu
เกาะพายุ

A tiny forest-capped marble outcrop, Ko Payu is surrounded by a reef of staghorn corals. It has two excellent dive sites – one to the east of the island, and the other just west of the narrow headland that marks the island's northern extremity. Divers can see large numbers of big and small fish such as lion fish, triggerfish, box fish, wrasse, and eels.

Ko Miang
เกาะเมียง

The most important and the most developed island in the archipelago, Ko Miang is where visitors will find the information center, restaurant, bungalows and dormitory accommodations, as well as a campground. Just to the east of the island, beyond a narrow headland, lie the tiny seamounts of Hin Muan Diao. There are recommended dive sites in the shallow waters to the north and south.

In addition to diving and swimming opportunities, Ko Miang offers a few short but sometimes steep inland trails, combined with the possibility of sighting the rare Nicobar pigeon, which thrives here. The two most popular trails are Viewpoint Trail, leading to the island summit, and Sunset Point, leading – as the name suggests – to an idyllic spot from where truly glorious sunsets over the Andaman Sea can be enjoyed.

Ko Payang
เกาะพยาง

Verdant, pristine, and quite uninhabited, tiny Ko Payang is yet another haven for enthusiastic divers. There are dive sites just off the northern shore, and farther to the east off Ko Payang, as well as at a nearby seamount called Hin Phae or Shark Fin Point.

Ko Huyong
เกาะหูยง

The southernmost island in the Similan archipelago, Ko Huyong has a long, white beach where sea turtles lay eggs. It also has a turtle breeding station. The island is not open to visitors, nor are there any offshore diving sites here. However, it is a beautiful place to sail around. The shallow waters allow plenty of sunlight to penetrate through, making the seabed around the island a real haven for its teeming diversity of marine creatures and numerous corals.

Key

– – Ferry route

0 km   2

0 miles   2

For keys to symbols *see back flap*

⑲ Phang Nga Bay
อ่าวพังงา

No one area epitomizes the splendor of southern Thailand's landscape as perfectly as the 155-sq mile (401-sq km) Phang Nga Bay. Its scenic grandeur derives from the towering limestone stacks rising out of azure waters. Boat tours are available for visitors to explore sights such as the Panyi fishing village and the famous James Bond Island, as well as a number of fascinating caves with prehistoric paintings and Buddhist shrines. However, due to erosion, tourist boats are banned from large areas of Phang Nga Bay, though viewing is possible from a distance.

Locator map

☐ Area illustrated

Wat Tham Suwan Khuha
Tiny shrines, a Reclining Buddha, and *chedis* are found among the stalactites and stalagmites in this cave temple.

Sa Nang Manora Forest Par

Takdat

Phang Nga

Wat Tham Suwan Khuha

Suan Somdet Phra Sinakharin Park

Bang Toe

Takua Thung

Tha Dan

Thai Muang
11 miles (18 km)
Phuket
56 miles (90 km)

Ao Phang Nga National Park

Ka Lai

★ Panyi Fishing Village
About 120 Muslim families live in this village built entirely on stilts above water. Islanders sell fish sauce, dried shrimp, and shrimp paste for a living.

Khlong Khian

①

KEY

① **Ko Phanak** has many *hongs* (sea chambers) with vegetation-clad walls and marooned snakes and monkeys.

② **Tham Lot** is a 165-ft (50-m) long sea tunnel through limestone caves with stalactites hanging from its roof.

③ **Tham Hua Gralok**, which means "Skull Cave", contains prehistoric paintings in colored pigments of humans and strange animals.

★ James Bond Island
Ko Khao Phing Kan, popularly known as James Bond Island, and nearby Ko Tapu featured prominently in the 1974 James Bond classic, *The Man With the Golden Gun*.

Areas of Mangrove
It is possible to explore many mangrove channels in a small boat at high tide, although skillful piloting is often required.

Rubber Plantations
Rubber is a major cash crop and plantations cover large areas of the bay. Latex tapped from the trees is left to harden in shallow trays.

Bo Saen

Khao Yai

Au Luk Nua

Ao Luk

Ban Klang

Khlong Hin

Laem Sak

Ao Luk Noi

Khao Khram

Krabi
13 miles (21 km)

Ko Yao Noi

Rock Paintings
Prehistoric rock art can be seen around the Ao Phang Nga National Park and is a popular spot with visitors on boat tours around the bay.

James Bond and the Island Hideout
In the movie *The Man With the Golden Gun* (1974), James Bond (Roger Moore) comes to Thailand in search of the villain Scaramanga (Christopher Lee). Bond eventually goes to Scaramanga's hideout, an island just off China. The island, in fact, that is visible in the background is Ko Khao Phing Kan and the sheer rock nearby containing the secret weapon is Ko Tapu.

Scaramanga and Bond In Phang Nga

Phang Nga Bay Limestone Stacks

Phang Nga Bay is, in fact, the most spectacular remnant of the once mighty Tenasserim Mountains, which still form a spine through Thailand to China. Its limestone stacks rise sheer from calm, shallow waters up to 1,150 ft (350 m). There are about 40 stacks and inside many of them are narrow tunnels and sea caves. The karst scenery with its majestic pinnacles continues inland to the east, where cliffs soar above the hidden valleys with cascading rivers. A protected site, the bay is home to diverse ecosystems and a variety of wildlife.

Mangroves at the bay's silted northern end are Thailand's largest and best preserved mangrove area.

Isolated stacks are a number of sheer, thin projections in the bay. These columns of rock are splinters of limestone that are shaped through heavy erosion by the sea.

Caves form quickly at sea level. Some are exposed only at low tide.

Calcite deposits result in speleothems, or cave formations, such as stalagmites and stalactites due to the combination of chemicals, air, water, and bacteria.

Forest scrub clings to cracks in the limestone.

Fissures allow water to rapidly penetrate and erode the limestone.

Cross Section of Typical Stacks in Phang Nga Bay

The limestone landscape at Phang Nga Bay is known by geologists as drowned karstland. Karst is characterized by its internal drainage system, whereby water finds its way into the interior of the limestone through fissures, then erodes the rock from within, riddling it with tunnels, chasms, and vast hongs.

Undercut cliffs form as wave action erodes the base of the stacks, at the rate of about 3 ft (1 m) every 5,000 years.

The aerial view of Phang Nga Bay is a striking sight, with vertical formations jutting straight out of the surrounding azure waters.

The weak roof of the cave will eventually collapse.

Ko Hong has a vast network of lagoons, chasms, and tunnels running underneath it. As a conservation measure, access to the area is forbidden at present.

How Phang Nga Bay was Formed

Hard and soft corals

Deposits of calcite from dead coral build up.

130 million years ago, the area was part of a vast underwater coral reef. Calcite deposits from dead coral built up in thick layers.

Calcite turns into limestone over millions of years.

Fissures form from rain action.

Gaps occur due to uneven calcite deposits.

75 million years ago, plate movements pushed these deposits, which had turned to limestone, out of the ocean. The rigid rock ruptured.

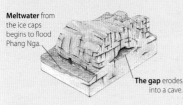

Meltwater from the ice caps begins to flood Phang Nga.

The gap erodes into a cave.

20,000 years ago, at the end of the last Ice Age, the sea level rose, flooding Phang Nga. Waves and tides accelerated the process of erosion.

Wave action sculpts the stacks.

The cave is much larger.

8,000 years ago, the sea reached its highest level, about 13 ft (4 m) above its present height, sculpting a shelf, visible on most of the stacks.

Exploring Phang Nga Bay

Phang Nga Bay can be easily reached either from Phuket *(see pp224–42)* or Krabi *(see p248)*. Distances are not great and most places on the mainland are accessible by bus, taxi, car, or motorcycle. Visitors should keep in mind that the natural beauty of the area attracts a large number of people, so those who want to avoid the crowds should hire a longtail boat as an alternative to packed tour boats. An even better option is to join a day-long sea-kayaking tour and explore the collapsed cave systems that make the offshore islands fascinating. Phang Nga is a good base for those who want to spend some time exploring the bay.

Limestone cliffs forming a backdrop to charming Phang Nga

Phang Nga

พังงา

56 miles (90 m) NE of Phuket town.

As the capital of Phang Nga province, Phang Nga is perhaps destined to be overshadowed by the livelier island of Phuket, but it more than makes up for this, owing to its spectacular location. There is a great deal to do and see in the vicinity, most notably in and around the beautiful Phang Nga Bay. Very few visitors choose to stay in the town given the variety of accommodations available at the luxurious beach resorts on neighboring Phuket. Yet Phang Nga is laid-back, friendly, and provides an authentic Thai experience for those who want to escape the bustle of a commercial tourist spot. It is an ideal place for an overnight stay.

Thai Muang

ไทยเมือง

32 miles (51 km) W of Phang Nga. Turtle Releasing Festival (Mar).

A small Sino-Thai market town on the Andaman Sea coast, Thai Muang is best known for

the **Thai Muang Beach Golf Course and Resort**. This 18-hole golf course is one of the most popular seaside golf clubs in Thailand. The town is a jumping-off point for the **Khao Lampi Hat Thai Muang National Park**. Hat Thai Muang is a nesting ground for sea turtles. Other animals in the park include the oriental honey-buzzard and Malayan pit viper. The town is also famous for its celebration of the Turtle Releasing Festival at the end of the nesting season in March. During this festival, participants release turtles bred by the fishery department into the sea.

⊠ Sa Nang Manora Forest Park

วนอุทยานสระนางมโนราห์

Off Hwy 4, 5 miles (8 km) NE of Phang Nga. Park HQ (0-7535-6134). dnp.go.th

This beautiful but little-visited park features simple dirt trails running through dense rain forest with many streams, waterfalls, and pools for swimming. The park is named after the mythical Princess Manora. According to legend, she supposedly bathes in the pools of this forest when no one is around – a tale which undoubtedly adds to the forest's charm. The various waterfalls are linked by a series of trails which are good for hiking. Picnic tables laid out at intervals can be used for rest or grabbing a bite. Visitors should carry enough drinking water as the park has very high humidity levels.

Waterfalls dotting the interior of the Sa Nang Manora Forest Park

Reclining Buddha statue within the larger cave at Wat Tham Suwan Khuha

🧘 Wat Tham Suwan Khuha

วัดถ้ำสุวรรณคูหา
6 miles (10 km) SW of Phang Nga.
Open dawn to dusk daily. 🚗 🅿️

Venerated by locals, Wat Tham Suwan Khuha is one of Phang Nga province's chief attractions, and is almost as popular as Phang Nga Bay.

This temple fascinates most visitors with its two conjoined caves filled with images of the Buddha in all shapes and sizes. The larger cave has a 50-ft (15-m) Reclining Buddha and is lined with tiles in the Laikhraam and Benjarong ceramic styles. Various spirit flags as well as the statue of a seated hermit adorn the caves. In the past, the cave-temple has attracted royal visitors, and the seals of several Chakri *(see pp46–7)* kings including Rama V (r.1868–1910), Rama VII (r.1925–35), and the current king, Rama IX, are etched in the wall of the smaller cave. Visitors should watch out for the large number of monkeys in the vicinity.

🌳 Suan Somdet Phra Sinakharin Park

อุทยานสวนสมเด็จพระศรีนครินทร์ -
สวนสมเด็จย่า
Off Nonthaburi Pathum Thani Rd,
2 miles (3 km) SW of Phang Nga.
Open dawn to dusk daily.

An attractive botanical park, the Suan Somdet Phra Sinakharin Park is surrounded by karst peaks, limestone pinnacles, and beautiful gardens. The park has two entrances and is replete with caves, tunnels, and limestone formations, as well as a large lake with a fountain and a sundial. Paddle boats are available for hire and can

be used to explore the lake. Wooden walkways have been built to link the main caverns both for ease of access and to keep visitors' feet dry, as many of the caves and tunnels are often flooded.

One of the caves, **Tham Reusi Sawan**, shelters the golden statue of a hermit wearing a tiger skin, who is regarded as a symbol of good fortune. Another well-known cave is the **Tham Luk Seua**, which means "Tiger Cub Cave", although the word *luk seua* also means "Boy Scout" in Thai. The park can be easily reached on motorcycles.

🏞️ Ao Phang Nga National Park

อุทยานแห่งชาติอ่าวพังงา
Off Hwy 402, 7 miles (11 km) S of Phang Nga. ℹ️ Park HQ (0-7648-1163); TAT, Phang Nga (0-7648-1900). 🚻 **Open** dawn to dusk daily. 🚗 🅿️
🚗 🅿️ 🌐 **dnp.go.th**

Inaugurated in 1981, Ao Phang Nga National Park covers an area of around 155 sq miles (401 sq km) and is made up of a number of small and large islands, karst outcrops, inaccessible and tall cliff faces – some as high as 980 ft (299 m) – overlooking the Andaman Sea. The coastal areas of the park are lined with mangrove forests, the largest remaining area of the original primary mangrove forest in Thailand. The park is home to a wide variety of land and marine creatures, including Malayan dolphins, hammerhead sharks, manta rays, finless porpoises, and the 7-ft (2-m) long water monitor. Most people, however, visit the park for the fantastic vistas of the surreal limestone towers rising from the surrounding waters, teeming with sea eagles and macaques – a complete haven for nature enthusiasts.

Dramatic cliffside entrance to Suan Somdet Phra Sinakharin Park

A boat approaches Ko Khao Phing Kan, known as James Bond Island, Phang Nga Bay ▶

⑳ Phuket

ภูเก็ต

Thailand's largest island, Phuket first became prosperous as a result of tin production, but now tourism is the major earner. This is one of Southeast Asia's most popular holiday destinations, with its stunning beaches, clear waters, and vibrant nightlife. In recent years, there has been a huge growth in chic resorts and spas on Phuket. Phuket town is the island's administrative capital and cultural center. The northern tip of Phuket is separated from the mainland just by a narrow channel, over which runs the 2,295-ft (700-m) long Sarasin Bridge.

Game fishing
The rich waters off Phuket attract keen anglers.

Half-Buried Buddha
Wat Phra Thong is built around an unusual Buddha image, half-buried in the ground. Legend says that whoever tries to remove it will die.

Key

- ▬ Main road
- ═ Minor road
- -- Ferry route
- ▪ ▪ Park boundary

KEY

① **Laem Promthep** is the southernmost accessible point on Phuket. The sunset views from this rugged headland are among the most stunning sights on the island.

② **The Gibbon Rehabilitation Center** in Khao Phra Taew Park teaches gibbons reared in captivity to fend for themselves in the wild.

③ **Phuket Butterfly Garden and Insect World** houses many species of tropical butterflies as well as other insects.

④ **Phuket Town** (see pp226–7).

★ West Coast Beaches
The clearest waters, best sands, and the most luxurious hotels are on the west coast. Patong is the most developed resort; Karon and Kata are quieter.

Map labels:

Sarasin Bridge
Thachatchai Nature Trail
Hat Sai Kaeo
Hat Mai Khao
Phuket International Airport
SIRINATH NATIONAL PARK
Hat Nai Yang
Ao Hin Kruai
Hat Nai Thon
Wat Phra Thong
Hat Bang Thao
Thalang
Ao Bang Thao
Phra Nar Sar
Ao Pansea
Hat Surin
Hat Laem Singh
Hat Kamala
Phuket FantaSea
Kathu Waterfa
Hat Kalim
Ao Patong
Hat Patong
Freedom Beach
Patong
Hat Karon Noi
Ao Karon
Wat Chalong
Hat Karon
Laem Sai
Ko Pu
Ao Kata Yai
Hat Kata Yai
Hat Kata Noi
Hat Rawai
Hat Nai Harn
Ko Bon
Ko Kaeo Pisadan
Ko Racha Yai 9 miles (14 km)

0 kilometers 5
0 miles 5

Sirinath National Park
Spreading over land and water, this park supports a variety of flora and fauna. It is especially famous as a nesting ground for endangered sea turtles.

Heroines' Monument
This monument is dedicated to two sisters who rallied the local women to successfully defend Phuket against Burmese invaders during the Battle of Thalang in 1785.

Ko Ngam

Laem Khut

Ko Raet

Ko Naga Yai

Ao Po

Bang Pae Waterfall

② KHAO PHRA TAEW NATIONAL PARK

Ton Sai Waterfall

Ko Naga Noi

Naga Pearl Farm

Ko Yao Yai, 6 miles (10 km)
Ko Yao Noi 12 miles (20 km)

Thalang National Museum

Heroines' Monument

Ao Sapam

Ko Rang Yai

Ko Maphrao Yai

③

★ Monkey Hill
In addition to the resident macaques, for which this place is named, Monkey Hill is a good spot to visit for views and a popular Taoist shrine.

④

Ko Sire Gypsy Village

Ao Chalong

Phuket Deep Sea Port

Laem Phanwa

Ko Phi Phi 25 miles (40 km)

Ko Lon

Ko Hai

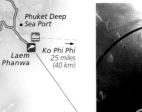

★ Phuket Aquarium
This well-designed aquarium is a part of the Phuket Marine Biological Center. It houses sea and freshwater fish, turtles, and mollusks.

For keys to symbols *see back flap*

Phuket Town

Around the beginning of the 19th century, Phuket town grew to prominence, with the island's tin resources attracting thousands of Chinese migrants. Many merchants made fortunes from tin, built splendid residences, and sent their children to British Penang in Malaysia for education. Hokkien-speaking tin-mining families soon intermarried with the indigenous Thai population. Today, the busy downtown area retains some of its earlier charm, although, unlike most of Phuket, it is geared toward residents rather than visitors. The Chinese influence remains intact in the Sino-Portuguese shophouses, temples, and the local cuisine.

Devotee placing incense sticks in a canister at San Chao Chui Tui

Rang Hill

เขารัง

Located to the northwest of the town center, Rang Hill is a beautiful spot, shaded by a thick canopy of tropical trees and covered with soft grass. Extremely popular with couples, students, and visitors, the hill provides breathtaking views of the town. There is also a fitness park and a jogging track here. On the top of the hill stands a

Bronze statue of Khaw Sim Bee Na-Ranong, Rang Hill

bronze statue of Khaw Sim Bee Na-Ranong (1857–1913), governor of Phuket for 12 years from 1901 onward. He enjoyed considerable autonomy from Bangkok, but is credited with bringing the island firmly under central rule. An enterprising visionary, he also imported the first rubber tree into Thailand. Vachira Road, which leads to the hill, has a Buddhist temple with a statue of a golden Seated Buddha. There are also some excellent restaurants in the area.

🅐 San Chao Chui Tui

ศาลเจ้าจุ้ยตุ่ย

Ranong Rd. **Open** dawn to dusk daily. Elaborately decorated and painted bright red and gold, this Chinese temple receives a steady flow of devotees. Visitors come here, in particular, to shuffle numbered sticks kept in a canister dedicated to the vegetarian god Kiu Wong In. Each number corresponds to a preprinted fate that, according to belief, the person will inherit. Most popular with Chinese

residents in the area, the temple is particularly crowded during the Vegetarian Festival (see p229).

🅐 San Chao Put Jaw

ศาลเจ้าปู่จ๋า

Ranong Rd. **Open** dawn to dusk daily. The cultural and economic influence of Phuket's urban Chinese business class is apparent at San Chao Put Jaw, the island's most celebrated shrine. A temple dedicated to the three teachings of northern Buddhism practiced in Vietnam and China, the temple has little to associate it with Theravada Buddhism. Founded by settlers from southern China, it was originally located on Soi Ang Ah Lai until it was severely damaged by fire and moved to its present location. Rebuilt in characteristic Chinese style with guardian lions at the gates and a traditional roof, it is a riot of color and clouds of incense smoke, especially during festivals.

Chinese Mansions

ตึกจีน

Thalang, Yaowarat, Dibuk, Krabi, and Phang Nga Rds.

The heart of Phuket town is the old Sino-Portuguese quarter with its spacious, if now rather run-down, Colonial-style residences set in large grounds. Most of them date from the reigns of Rama IV and Rama V. Among the best examples are those used today as offices by the Standard Chartered Bank and Thai Airways International on Ranong Road as well as the restored residential estates on Dibuk and Thalang roads. However, none of them have been converted into museums and are not open to visitors.

Exterior façade of typical Chinese mansion, set in lush grounds

Typical Rattanakosin-style architecture at Wat Mongkol Nimit

Wat Mongkol Nimit

วัดมงคลนิมิต
Yaowarat Rd.
Open dawn to dusk daily.

A large, Rattanakosin-style temple, Wat Mongkol Nimit exudes an air of austerity. The *wat*, a fitting example of classic Thai architecture, has a soaring multitiered roof, finely carved doors, glass tiling, and beautiful mosaic work, all of which combine to give it an extremely bright and colorful effect. Highly revered by the local Chinese population, the *wat's* compound acts as a community center where monks play sporting activities such as *takraw* (kick-volleyball) with the laity.

Phuket Philatelic Museum

พิพิธภัณฑ์ไปรษณียากร
Phuket Post and Telegraph Office, Montri Rd. **Tel** 0-7621-6951.
Open 9am–5:30pm Tue–Sat.

This charming little museum, set in the restored old Phuket Post Office, is a delight for visitors. The building, with typical Sino-Portuguese-style architecture, is a historical site in its own right, reminiscent of how the town looked almost 40 years ago, before the advent of commercial tourism in Thailand. Although more of a curiosity for its old-world charm than as a center for any major stamp collection, the Phuket Philatelic Museum nevertheless has a collection which includes many series of fascinating stamps from early Thai postal history; the service dates back to the early years of the 20th century.

Phuket Town Center

① Rang Hill
② San Chao Chui Tui
③ San Chao Put Jaw
④ Chinese Mansions
⑤ Phuket Philatelic Museum
⑥ Wat Mongkol Nimit
⑦ San Chao Sang Tham
⑧ San Chao Bang Niew

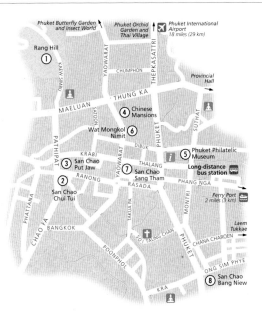

0 meters 500
0 yards 500

San Chao Sang Tham, a Chinese temple in Phuket's old town

San Chao Sang Tham

ศาลเจ้าแสงธรรม

Yaowarat Rd. **Open** dawn to dusk daily.
Another significant link in the
string of shrines that serve
Phuket's Vegetarian Festival, San
Chao Sang Tham is said to be
almost 200 years old. The shrine,
a beautiful symbol of Chinese
architecture, is decorated in a
dazzling array of colors. Inside is
a plethora of Buddhist and Taoist
divinities, ancestor tablets, and
clouds of incense smoke.
Although visitors do not need
to take off their shoes here, they
must be modestly dressed. They
should avoid standing on the
threshold when entering the holy
building, as this is traditionally
considered to bring bad luck.

San Chao Bang Niew

ศาลเจ้าบางเหนียว

Phuket Rd. **Open** dawn to dusk daily.
One of Phuket's oldest and most
revered Chinese temples, San
Chao Bang Niew is thought to
have been founded by migrants
from Fujian in the 19th century.
The temple is dedicated to Giu
Ong and Yok Ong, spirits who
must be invited from *bang niew*
(the sea) at the beginning of the
Vegetarian Festival to bless the
community and to banish evil
spirits said to disrupt proceedings.
   The inner compound of the
temple is devoted to several
Chinese mythological gods. The
most prominent are Siew, Hok,
and Lok, representing longevity,
power, and happiness. San Chao

Bang Niew is known for the
spectacle created by *naga*
devotees while climbing knife
ladders during the festival.

Provincial Hall

ศาลากลาง

Narison Rd.
This fine building, inaugurated
by Rama VI in 1917, still functions
as an administrative office for
the governor and his staff, but is
not open to visitors. Originally
built with 99 doors but no
windows, it may be recognized
as a setting from Roland Joffe's
movie *The Killing Fields* (1984).
The outer corridor is adorned
with a number of framed
photographs which pictorially
narrate the history of Phuket.
   The elaborately detailed
fretwork on the exterior is a
fine example of the original
architecture of the town. Each
piece is said to have taken
almost six years to complete.

Laem Tukkae

แหลมตุ๊กแก

2 miles (3 km) SE of town center.
Chao Le Boat Floating Festival, 6th and
11th lunar months.

With around 1,500 sea gypsies,
Laem Tukkae is home to Phuket's
second-largest community of
chao thalae after Hat Rawai. They
make a living from traditional
pursuits such as fishing.
   These *chao thalae* organize the
Chao Le Boat Floating Festival, a
ceremony similar to Loy Krathong
(*see p41*) in which small boats
are released into the sea during
evening hours to drive away evil
spirits and bring good luck.

Phuket Butterfly Garden and Insect World

สวนผีเสื้อและโลกแมลงภูเก็ต

2 miles (3 km) N of town. **Tel** 0-7621-
0861. **Open** 9am–5pm daily.
phuketbutterfly.com

A haven for tropical butterflies,
the Phuket Butterfly Garden
breeds 40 species of butterflies
from across Thailand each year.
The accompanying Insect World
is home to a variety of arachnids,
giant millipedes, and scorpions.

Phuket Orchid Garden and Thai Village

ภูเก็ตออร์คิดการ์เด้นแอนด์ไทยวัลเลจ

3 miles (5 km) N of town. **Tel** 0-7621-
4860. **Open** 9am–9pm daily.

A popular cultural center, the
Thai Village hosts cultural
performances and animal
shows from different regions of
Thailand. The village is a great
place to buy *yan lipao* (reed
grass bags) and ornaments. The
nearby Phuket Orchid Garden
grows and sells more than
40,000 orchids each year.

Façade of the grand Phuket Provincial Hall

Phuket's Vegetarian Festival

Phuket hosts a nine-day Vegetarian Festival each year, at the start of the ninth lunar month of the Chinese calendar. This tradition, accompanied by gruesome rites, began over 150 years ago when a troupe of Chinese entertainers in Phuket recovered from the plague by adhering to austere rituals practiced in China. Today, believers use the festival to purge the body and soul of impure thoughts and deeds. Devotees follow a 10-rule regimen during the festival which includes dressing in white, following a vegetarian diet, and abstaining from alcohol and sex. While events are held at various temples, the highlight of the festival is the parade of *nagas* (spirit mediums), whose flesh is pierced by metal rods. Other *nagas* climb ladders of knives, plunge their hands into hot oil, or walk on burning coals. The worse the suffering, the greater the reward is said to be for the *naga* and his temple.

Street Parades

The main shrines organize street parades on different days during the festival. Devotees burn firecrackers and beat drums in order to drive away evil spirits, making these parades quite noisy and even dangerous at times.

Carriage bearers are young men of ethnic Chinese origin, who compete for the honor of carrying the festival divinities around town on their shoulders.

Deity carriages are elaborately decorated in bright red and gold – symbolic of good luck in Chinese communities.

Chui Tui temple and neighboring San Chao Put Jaw (*see p226*) are two of Phuket's most celebrated shrines. Offering tables are set up in front of the temple gates and the inner shrines.

Commercial and privately owned shops are set up as stalls or altars outside houses or at nearby temples. They offer cups of tea and fresh fruits to passers-by and *nagas*.

Self-mutilation involves piercing various parts of the body with sharp instruments such as knives, yet bloodshed is minimal. This gruesome ritual is a highlight of the Vegetarian Festival.

Walking on hot coals is another form of self mortification in which devotees walk barefoot on a bed of red-hot glowing embers. Like other forms of self-torture, devotees endure it to invoke the gods.

Firework displays are popular during the Vegetarian Festival. Loud crackers are burst by devotees in the belief that the din will keep evil spirits at bay.

Mansions of Phuket

The traditional architecture of Phuket is an amalgam of Sino-Thai and Portuguese styles and is similar to the 19th-century architecture found in Singapore, and Penang and Malacca in Malaysia. Shophouses began to spring up to serve Phuket's affluent Chinese migrants and by the turn of the 20th century, these wealthy settlers started building elaborate mansions that can be seen to this day. The construction blended Chinese architecture with Western styles, ranging from Classical Greek to Art Deco, and was distinguished from the local houses by its sheer size and grandeur. Opulently decorated with imported furniture and marble, these mansions reflected the status of their owners. Many have been restored and they add a distinct character to present-day Phuket.

Brightly colored façades of Sino-Portuguese houses in Phuket

Mansion façades

Phuket's Sino-Portuguese mansions are called ang mor lau, *or red head buildings, based on a common epithet for Europeans. Constructed with large windows and plenty of shaded spaces, these buildings were designed to ensure that the interiors stayed well ventilated and cool.*

Chinese characters on buildings are often stylized, indicating the wealth and influence of Phuket's sizable migrant ethnic Chinese community.

Windows often feature louvered shutters to permit easy circulation of air.

Elaborate stucco designs decorate many eaves and arches adding ornate touches as well as grandeur to these mansions.

Chinese-style buildings are decorated with pilasters or false pillars. These elaborate mansions have a triple-arched façade common to other buildings of the time. The increasingly prosperous Chinese migrants who climbed the social ladder usually demonstrated their status through the grand houses they built.

Greco-Roman motifs were widely used. The upper classes blended Classical and Chinese designs, creating a hybrid style that is reflected in public buildings such as the Thai Hua Museum.

Large arches and pillars support shaded terraces and verandas, providing access to the inhabitants and visitors while also sheltering them from the piercing tropical sun and the frequent monsoon downpours.

Birds and animals feature in elaborate and fanciful stucco designs. Swooping cranes, dragons, phoenixes, bats, stylized peacocks, and various other mythological creatures are considered to be symbols of good luck.

Tiled roofs were regarded as a status symbol in Thai society where thatch or corrugated iron were the common roofing materials.

Elaborate doors and lintels characterize *ang mor lau* mansions, with Chinese characters prominently displayed over the door and intricate gingerbread fretwork suspended from the eaves.

Art Deco style became popular among Phuket's Chinese businessmen from about 1918 onward, and was incorporated into designs used for doors and windows. Largely adopted as an imitation of European sophistication, this was part of the style statement of the *nouveaux riches*.

Phra Pitak Chinpracha Mansion

Built in the late 1930s for the Tantawanitj family, this well-preserved mansion is set in sprawling gardens. It is among the grandest red-roofed mansion in the city, reflecting the luxurious lifestyle of the erstwhile tin barons and their families. It now houses a branch of the Blue Elephant Restaurant & Cooking School.

Chinpracha Mansion nestled in its wooded estate

Exploring Phuket's West Coast

Phuket owes its fame to the beauty, warmth, and safety of its beaches, nearly all of which are situated on the island's western, Andaman Coast, which runs from Hat Nai Harn in the south to Hat Sai Kaeo in the north. The beaches around Patong – around 40 minutes' drive from the airport – are among the best known; Hat Patong itself boasts a glitzy, sybaritic nightlife, unlike the more sedate Karon and Kata beaches farther south. Hat Mai Khao, in northwest Phuket, remains the island's quietest beach, with rare sea turtles – which are being encouraged by local ecologists to return to the beaches – nesting there from time to time. All of Phuket's west coast offers a fine choice of accommodations, dining, and watersports, as well as mesmerizing views, especially toward dusk, when the sun sets across the idyllic waters of the Andaman Sea.

Pristine waters with the Royal Phuket Yacht Club in the background, Hat Nai Harn

🚩 Hat Nai Harn

หาดในหาน

11 miles (18 km) SW of Phuket town.

🅿️ 🏠 🆆 tourismthailand.org

Crisp white sands and clear offshore waters make Hat Nai Harn one of Phuket's most attractive beaches. Its relative tranquillity, when compared to the bustle and development of nearby Hat Patong in particular, comes at a price – Hat Nai Harn is not aimed at the budget traveler. Restaurants and cafés at Hat Nai Harn are also exclusive and expensive, with uniformly high standards. The beach is dominated by the exclusive Royal Phuket Yacht Club. Much of Hat Nai Harn is owned by the Buddhist foundation Samnak Song Nai Harn, which has helped to keep all major commercial activity

away. Set back from the beach are two beautiful lagoons surrounded by coconut palms, rubber trees, and brightly colored bougainvillea. This spot is frequented by visitors looking for cheaper accommodations.

Hat Nai Harn is not suitable for offshore swimming during the southwest monsoon from June to September, when waves can be high and completely unpredictable. Bright red flags warn swimmers of dangerous swimming conditions. However, the beach is excellent for sunbathing and swimming in shallow waters.

The prestigious Phuket's King's Cup Regatta, an exciting yachting event with international participants, is held on the beach each year in December (see p41).

🚩 Hat Kata Noi

หาดกะตะน้อย

10 miles (16 km) SW of Phuket town.

🅿️ 🏠

The beach at Ao Kata, or Kata Bay, is divided into Kata Noi, or Little Kata, to the south and Kata Yai, or Big Kata, to the north. Hat Kata Noi is undoubtedly one of the livelier beaches on Phuket. A great place for young travelers, who will enjoy the vibrant atmosphere and delectable local food the beach has to offer, Hat Kata Noi also attracts the bohemian vacationer who prefers to stay away from the crowds. The beach at Kata Noi is more deserted than the one at Kata Yai, but is well equipped with comfortable accommodations, a fine selection of some of the best restaurants and cafés on the island, and facilities for watersports and other outdoor activities.

🚩 Hat Kata Yai

หาดกะตะใหญ่

10 miles (16 km) SW of Phuket town.

🅿️ 🏠

Like Hat Kata Noi, Hat Kata Yai is also popular for its snorkeling, diving, shopping, and exquisite food. Sheltered by rocky promontories, the sea here is quite shallow for nearly 100 ft (30 m) offshore, making access to coral reefs, and their colorful accompanying marine life, easier and safer than anywhere else on the island. Ko Pu, or Crab Island, lies a short distance off Laem Sai, which separates the two beaches. A tiny island, Ko Pu has its own coral reef which can be easily reached by boat or by swimming.

Visitors sunbathing on beach chairs, Hat Kata Yai

Vacationers sunbathing and jet-skiing on the pretty beach at Hat Karon

Hat Karon

หาดกะรน

12 miles (19 km) SW of Phuket town.

A long, gently curving beach with almost 3 miles (5 km) of pristine white sand, Hat Karon usually does not witness too much commercial activity, except during the peak season, when it gets slightly crowded.

Although the northern part of the beach is not worth a visit, the southern end, where most restaurants, cafés, and hotels line the beachfront, is quite pleasant. The beach is backed by a heady mix of small sand dunes, coconut palms, and casuarina trees. This is also the section where some of the most upscale accommodations on the beach are located, although reasonably priced bungalows are also available. Visitors can partake of some of the most deliciously fresh seafood on the beach and, while the prices are not the lowest on the west coast, there is usually something available to suit most budgets.

During the rainswept months of the southwest monsoon, swimming off the beach can be affected by sharp currents and dangerous undertows, sometimes necessitating the flying of warning flags. Most of the time, however, the high waves that sweep across the bay are good for surfing, particularly at the southern end where boards can be hired. Just to the north of Karon, sheltered between two headlands, is a shallow bay backed by the small and picturesque Hat Karon Noi. To the south of this beach lies a fine coral reef, excellent for snorkeling. Completely dominated by the exclusive upscale Le Meridien Phuket, an expensive place by any standards, Hat Karon Noi can be reached by road from either Hat Karon to the south or busy Hat Patong to the north.

Hat Patong

หาดป่าตอง

10 miles (16 km) W of Phuket town.

Heavily developed and with an active nightlife, Hat Patong is one of the most popular beach destinations on Phuket and is always bustling with visitors.

Breathtaking view of the beachfront and skyline, Hat Patong

A 2-mile (3-km) long, crescent-shaped expanse of white sand, Hat Patong is set magically between low, palm-covered hills and the clear blue waters of the Andaman Sea. Dotted with a confusingly large choice of guesthouses, hotels, restaurants, cafés, banks, shops, and bars – including go-go bars – it is more reminiscent of Pattaya and Patpong (see p78) than Phuket. The beach offers a wide range of watersports, including water-skiing, jet-skiing, parasailing, windsurfing, fishing, and sailing.

Here visitors will find plenty to keep themselves entertained. It also has its fair share of restaurants offering a variety of cuisines. Authentic Thai food, however, may be hard to come by, so those keen to experience the local flavors must head for Phuket town (see pp226–9). By night, Hat Patong is the busy nerve center of Phuket's increasingly risqué nightlife, especially in the central area around Soi Bangla.

Visitors who might want to escape from the overwhelming activities on Hat Patong for a while can head for the quieter Freedom Beach just round the southern tip of Hat Patong. This beach is only accessible by boat from Patong. A short distance to the north, Hat Kalim, an extension of Hat Patong, is another quiet retreat with clear waters and corals – home to a variety of marine life.

Entrance to Phuket FantaSea, amid lush mountains

visitors can pause at Khao Phanturat, a hill from which they can enjoy magnificent vistas of Hat Kamala's 2-mile (3-km) sweep of dazzling white sands, azure ocean, and tall casuarina trees. The sea, especially near the northern end of the beach, is well-known for its clear waters, with colorful coral reefs lying not far offshore. This makes Hat Kamala an excellent place for snorkeling and diving enthusiasts.

To the center of Hat Kamala lies an authentic Muslim fishing village, with a couple of mosques and a few restaurants serving excellent Thai, Muslim, and southern Thai cuisine. The locals are very warm and friendly, but visitors should remember to dress respectably in the village – no bikinis or thongs, and certainly no topless displays – particularly in the vicinity of the mosques.

Phuket FantaSea
ภูเก็ตแฟนตาซี
16 miles (26 km) W of Phuket town.
Tel 0-7638-5000. **Open** 5:30–11:30pm
Fri–Wed.
W phuket-fantasea.com

Phuket FantaSea is billed as a cultural theme park which, at a fairly steep price, offers displays of traditional Thai dances on an elaborate, Angkor-inspired stage with sophisticated sound systems and state-of-the-art lighting. There are plenty of souvenir shops and places to eat and drink, such as a 4,000-seater buffet restaurant, which serves royal Thai cuisine, in an enchanting forest setting.

Phuket FantaSea is all about showtime extravaganza – a good place for children.

Hat Kamala
หาดกมลา
16 miles (26 km) W of Phuket town.

A relaxed beach, in marked contrast to nearby Patong, Hat Kamala is a popular destination for those seeking a quiet time sunbathing on the white sands or swimming in the clear waters with little else for distraction. Ao Kamala, arguably Phuket's prettiest bay, can be easily reached by a 10-minute drive from the beach. On the way,

Hat Laem Singh
แหลมสิงห์
15 miles (24 km) W of Phuket town.

Just a stone's throw north of Hat Kamala, beyond a small, rocky headland, is tiny Hat Laem Singh, concealed from Hat Kamala and the coastal road by palm-covered hills. The approach is by way of a narrow footpath, leading to about 640 ft (195 m) of pristine white sand and some of the best snorkeling and scuba-diving sites off Phuket island. Facilities on this beach are limited, especially compared to Hat Patong, but so are the number of hawkers and masseurs.

Sweeping white sands ideal for sunbathing, Hat Kamala

For hotels and restaurants in this region see pp299–300 and pp314–16

Pontoon used for swimming and diving, Hat Surin

🚉 Hat Surin

หาดสุรินทร์

14 miles (22 km) W of Phuket town.

🖉 📷

Like Hat Kamala nearby, Hat Surin is much quieter and less developed than Hat Patong. With the beach running down to the warm waters of the Andaman Sea, it is a great place to sunbathe and relax. However, it is not recommended for swimming and diving because the beach slopes quite steeply, making for treacherous currents and a palpable undertow during the wet southwest monsoon from June to September.

Hat Surin is also a good place to drink and dine, especially in the evenings after the sun goes down. There are dozens of inexpensive food joints lining the beach which dish out some of the best seafood in Phuket. The beach is also home to the most attractive mosque on the west coast, the tiny but pleasing **Matsayit Mukaram**, which is open for visitors at all times except during prayers. Visitors, however, must remember to dress appropriately before visiting the mosque. A golf course overlooking the beach is located nearby.

🚉 Ao Pansea

อ่าวแพนเซ

14 miles (22 km) W of Phuket town.

🖉 📷

Separated from Hat Surin by a small headland, Ao Pansea and the accompanying beach of the same name are among the best locations on Phuket. The beach is also one of the most exclusive spots and the accommodations are similarly pricey. Ao Pansea is more or less the private preserve of two world-class establishments – the Chedi and the **Amanpuri** *(see p300)* – which jointly control access to the beach. Amanpuri Resort in particular draws a lot of celebrities who find it a glamorous retreat. Ao Pansea, blessed with a beautiful coral reef, provides quiet getaways in the form of upscale and relatively private

The vibrant
hibiscus flower

access to some of the best diving and snorkeling on the island.

🚉 Hat Bang Thao

หาดบางเทา

13 miles (21 km) W of Phuket town.

🖉 📷

Immediately to the north of Ao Pansea, Hat Bang Thao is as broad and wide a sweep of white coral sand as the former is small. Fringed with casuarina and palm trees, this crescent-shaped beach is breathtakingly beautiful and stretches for 5 miles (8 km), and is hugely popular with visitors. The central part of the bay is dominated by a luxurious resort, the Laguna Beach Resort, which is actually a group of several interdependent hotels set on the banks of a placid lagoon. It has several attractive gardens complete with artificial waterfalls, and every convenience and luxury conceivable.

Hat Bang Thao is the site of the Phuket Laguna Triathlon, held here every December. In addition to the usual watersports facilities, the bay is also home to the exclusive Phuket Laguna Riding Club, a good place for horseback riding. A constant sea breeze makes the bay ideal for windsurfing.

The exclusive Laguna Beach Resort, Hat Bang Thao

Beach restaurant overlooking the bay at Hat Nai Yang

🗺 Sirinath National Park

อุทยานแห่งชาติสิรินาถ

19 miles (31 km) NW of Phuket town.
ℹ Park HQ (0-7632-7152).
Open dawn to dusk daily. 🅿

Covering an area of 29 sq miles (75 sq km) on water, and 9 sq miles (23 sq km) on land, this small national park was inaugurated in 1981, with the primary objective of conserving the offshore coral reefs. The sandy beaches near the northern boundary of the park are protected territory as they are a nesting ground for various species of marine turtles. On land, the park is little more than a narrow strip of sand running between Hat Sai Kaeo in the north and Hat Nai Yang to the south. There are numerous species of trees lining the coast, including ironwood and screwpine. There are also large tracts of mangrove forest near the northern end of the park which support a diverse ecosystem. The area is known for birds such as mynahs and the Asian fairy bluebird.

🗺 Thachatchai Nature Trail

ทางเดินเท้าท่าฉัตรไชย

Sirinath National Park.
Open 8:30am–2:30pm daily. 🅿 🅿

Named after the tiny fishing village on the northwestern shores of Phuket, Thachatchai Nature Trail is part of the island's Sirinath National Park. The trail is located 2,250 ft (686 m) south of the Sarasin Bridge, which connects Phuket to the mainland. It winds through the mangroves giving visitors an insight into its complex ecosystem. There are a handful of simple guesthouses and restaurants in the village of Ban Thatchatchai. The trail itself is just 1,920 ft (600 m) long, and follows a raised wooden walkway through the mangrove swamp. Signs written in Thai and English explain the ecology of the region. The surroundings swarm with all kinds of wildlife that include fiddler crabs, shrimps, small fish, and the occasional crab-eating macaque monkey.

🗺 Hat Nai Yang

หาดในยาง

Sirinath National Park. 🅿 🅿

A gorgeous bay with a beach shaded by pine trees, Hat Nai Yang is pristine and quiet. The park headquarters for Sirinath National Park are also located on this beach. This is a great place for a picnic, with a long

Stream running through the mangrove forest at Sirinath National Park

For hotels and restaurants in this region see pp299–300 and pp314–16

coral reef located less than a mile offshore that is ideal for snorkeling. However, it is recommended for good swimmers only, as the currents can get quite strong. Enthusiastic visitors can hire a boat to experience the beauty of the surroundings in comfort and safety. This beach is still untouched by commercial development, although there are some chic beach cafés and bars, as well as a few upscale spas. Travelers can also camp here without a permit.

🚇 Hat Mai Khao
หาดไม้ขาว
Sirinath National Park. 🎫 📷

Situated within the precincts of Sirinath National Park, Hat Mai Khao stretches for over 6 miles (10 km), and is the longest sandy beach on Phuket. It is also known as Hat Sanambin, or Airport Beach, due to its proximity to the Phuket airport. Hat Mai Khao is still off the tourist map, and is quite tranquil and untouched, especially when compared to the more developed and commercial southern beaches. Although construction is controlled in this protected area, camping is permitted at several locations and is a popular option for many travelers, especially backpackers.

This is a famous nesting site for sea turtles, who come onshore in hordes to lay their eggs during the cool season from November to February. During this period visitors can see them on the beach at night and also in the surrounding waters. Although the authorities are maintaining a careful watch over the area, the efforts are slightly belated and the number of turtles visiting Hat Mai Khao has started to diminish. Every year from the beginning of the Songkran festival *(see p38)*, baby turtles bred in tanks are released into the sea.

Hat Mai Khao is also home to sea cicadas, a kind of crustacean which is prepared as a delicious snack around this area. The beach is great for sunbathing, but it shelves steeply into the sea, and only strong swimmers

Tall trees lining the walking trails at Sirinath National Park

should venture in, especially during the rainy season from June to September. Visitors can try the seafood at the beach shacks or splurge on any of the restaurants at the upscale Marriott Resort and Spa.

🚇 Hat Nai Thon
หาดในทอน
Sirinath National Park. 🎫 📷

One of the more secluded beaches on Phuket, Hat Nai Thon is set along a picturesque bay. This half-mile (1-km) long beach served by the Nai Thon fishing village is gradually adapting to Phuket's tourism industry. Improved roads to this

beach have brought in some development. However, Hat Nai Thon retains its untouched charm with small, inexpensive bungalows as well as a handful of restaurants, cafés, bars, and shops at the northern end. Both the northern and southern extremities of the bay are protected by large granite outcrops. These rocks shield the bay, providing a home to many species of marine flora and fauna, and are ideal spots for fishing. A few hundred meters south beyond a low headland lies Ao Hin Kruai, a quiet and deserted bay for travelers seeking solitude.

Azure waters surround the long sandy beach, Hat Mai Khao

Exploring Phuket's East Coast

Overlooking the calm waters of the Andaman Sea, Phuket's east coast is divided into the southeast, facing Ao Chalong and lying to the south of Phuket town, and the northeast, stretching north of Phuket town right up to the mainland. The island's good roads and availability of different modes of transportation such as buses, cars, and boats make traveling easy. Visitors can choose among options ranging from watersports to exotic cuisine, national parks to deserted beaches, and ancient temples to museums. The northeastern coast is undeveloped, yet the main road between Phuket town and the mainland passes through it, making the region crucial to the island. Ao Chalong and Thalang are other well-developed areas.

Showcasing Phuket's history and artifacts, Thalang National Museum

Thalang
ถลาง
11 miles (18 km) N of town center.
🖉 📷
Located in the center of the island, Thalang was once the capital of Phuket; in fact the island itself was called Thalang till the late 19th century. With the emergence of Phuket town further to the south, Thalang was soon eclipsed and, today, serves more or less as a junction town. However, it is still one of the larger settlements on the island astride the central north-south Highway 402, leading from Phuket town to the mainland. The town has quite a few cultural attractions which draw visitors here. Notable sights include two highly revered temples – Wat Phra Nang Sang and Wat Phra Thong – both of which house very old Buddha images. Apart from this, there are a few simple restaurants serving local cuisine, and a

busy and interesting market for fresh produce. The town is a good base for exploring the nearby beaches and islands.

🏛 Thalang National Museum
พิพิธภัณฑ์สถานแห่งชาติถลาง
Rte 4027, 5 miles (8 km) SE of Thalang. **Tel** 0-7631-1426. **Open** 8:30am–4pm daily. 🖉 📷
Phuket's main museum, the Thalang National Museum, is worth a visit for a fairly comprehensive insight into the island's history. There are five exhibition halls that cover various aspects of the history, ethnic diversity, economy, and ecology of Phuket.

The museum also has displays on the island's tin-mining history as well as on ancient art. A 9th-century image of Vishnu, part of the Hindu holy trinity, discovered at Takua Pa *(see p212)* in the early 20th century, is impressive. However, the original head has long been lost and has since been replaced by a substitute in gray sandstone. The exhibits showcasing the famous Battle of Thalang where Burmese invaders were repulsed by Khun Chan and Khun Muk are also noteworthy.

Heroines' Monument
อนุสาวรีย์วีรสตรี
5 miles (8 km) SE of Thalang. 🖉 📷
This life-sized monument, built by the locals, is dedicated to two sisters – Khun Muk and Khun Chan – for driving Burmese invaders out of Phuket in 1785. They rallied the women of Phuket together and convinced them to dress in men's clothes and carry fake weapons to drive the Burmese army out. As a reward for their bravery, they were given titles by Rama I (r.1782–1809).

🛕 Wat Phra Nang Sang
วัดพระนางสร้าง
3 miles (5 km) S of Thalang. **Open** dawn to dusk daily.
This temple was supposedly founded in the 19th century by a charitable local lady and is also known as Phra Nang Sang, literally "Built by the Revered

Mural representing myths from Buddhist cosmology, Wat Phra Nang Sang

Main *wihan* containing Budhha image at Wat Phra Thong

Lady". Legend says that after a pilgrimage to Sri Lanka, she wanted to express her gratitude for her safe return. Thus, she sponsored the construction of this temple. Later, however, she somehow came into conflict with a local ruler who condemned her to death. At the beheading her blood apparently flowed white, reflecting her purity. Today, the temple is famous for its collection of religious statuary as well as the murals in the main *wihan*.

Wat Phra Thong

วัดพระทอง

Rte 402, 3 miles (5 km) N of Thalang. **Open** dawn to dusk daily.

Thalang's other well-known Buddhist temple is Wat Phra Thong, or the Temple of the Golden Buddha. This unusual temple is named after the gilded Buddha image that is half buried within the temple precincts so that only its head and shoulders are visible above ground. According to an ancient legend, a local cowherd attempted to tether one of his charges to an outcrop he mistook for a tree stump. This actually was the *ushnisha* (topknot) of a buried Buddha image. Both boy and buffalo unfortunately died for the unintentional heresy. Later, the boy's father had a dream in which he saw that his son

had achieved *nirvana* instead of being punished for his deed. Upon hearing this story, a local landowner ordered the image to be excavated and installed in a temple. However, despite the villagers' best efforts, the image could not be fully dug out, and remained buried from the shoulders down. Thereafter, a roof was erected to shelter the exposed head and shoulders, and since then the temple has become an important site of worship for both local Thais as well as Chinese migrants. The latter believe that the image was brought from Tibet and installed on the island of Phuket after a shipwreck.

Today, the *wat* is among the most venerated Buddhist sites not just in Phuket, but in all of southern Thailand and attracts devotees from as far afield as Trang *(see p268)* and Krabi *(see p248)*.

Khao Phra Taew National Park

อุทยานแห่งชาติเขาพระแทว

3 miles (5 km) E of Thalang. Park HQ (0-7631-1998). **Open** dawn to dusk. Gibbon Rehabilitation Center: **Tel** 0-7626-0491. **Open** 9am–4pm daily. donations. gibbonproject.org

The last of Phuket's once ubiquitous rainforest is preserved at the Khao Phra Taew National Park. Within the park lies the island's largest and grandest waterfall, **Bang Pae**, which is best seen in its full glory during the southwest monsoon from June to September.

The 1-mile (2-km) long hiking trail winds its way right through the forest which is home to *Kerriodoxa elegans* – a species of palm which is unique to this forest. Visitors should dress appropriately to avoid being bitten by insects. The **Gibbon Rehabilitation Center**, a project set up in 1992 by Phuket's Royal Forest Department, is also located within Khao Phra Taew. The main initiative teaches gibbons reared in captivity to survive in the wild. The center also aims to stop the illegal use of these animals as tourist attractions. Visitors are encouraged to donate money and "adopt a gibbon" to help the cause.

Gibbon learning to survive in the wild, Gibbon Rehabilitation Center

Boats lined up in front of a popular bar, Ao Chalong

🪷 Ao Chalong
อ่าวฉลอง
6 miles (10 km) SE of Phuket town.
🚗 🏠

A dominant geographical feature of this region, Ao Chalong is located between Laem Promthep and Laem Phanwa. Sheltered from the Andaman Sea by the hilly Ko Lon, the bay has clusters of bungalows, hotels, and restaurants stretching from Ao Chalong pier to Hat Rawai along Phuket's western shore. The nearby Chalong Yacht Club organizes weekly races and yachting events. The shoreline along the bay is quite muddy and unsuitable for swimming. However, Ao Chalong is an ideal base for fishing, diving, and swimming to the offshore islands.

🪷 Wat Chalong
วัดฉลอง
6 miles (10 km) SE of Phuket town.
🏠 🎪 Temple fair (Dec).

The best-known temple in Phuket, Wat Chalong dates back to the early 19th century. Also known as Wat Chaiyataramit, the temple was granted royal status in 1846. Luang Pho Saem, the celebrated abbot of the temple, was a noted local healer who died in 1908. His successors have maintained his reputation for healing. The most striking structure in the temple is its tall gilded *chedi*, constructed in 2001 and built in the style of the Tat Phanom *chedi* – northeast Thailand's famous temple which

houses relics of the Buddha. The extensive temple grounds and buildings include a cruciform *mondop* containing images of former abbots, photographs, local historical and religious paraphernalia, and an *ubosot* – a cremation hall – as well as a funeral *sala* (open pavilion). A lifelike waxen image of Luang Pho Saem in saffron robes is on display in the *kuti* (monks' quarters). Wat Chalong attracts many pilgrims and is busiest during the annual temple fair held in mid-December.

⛴ Phuket Aquarium
ภูเก็ตอะควาเรียม
51, Moo 8, Sakdidet Rd, Cape Panwa. **Tel** 0-7639-1126.
Open 8:30am–4:30pm (last entry 4pm) daily. 🚗 🚗 🚗 🏠
🌐 phuketaquarium.org

Located on Laem Panwa and part of the Phuket Marine Biological Center, the

Phuket Aquarium houses over 150 different species of marine life. The interactive display covers endangered coral reefs, mangrove swamps, tidal estuaries, rivers, and lakes. The most popular attraction, however, is the long walk-through glass tunnel tank which houses electric eels, stingrays, cuttlefish, and a host of other marine life. The idea is to provide visitors with a fun experience as well as create awareness about the coastal environment.

Ko Hai
เกาะไห
13 miles (21 km) S of Phuket town.
🚤 from Hat Rawai. 🚗 🏠

A picturesque and deserted island, Ko Hai, also known as Coral Island, is an idyllic spot. Visitors can enjoy modern amenites at the upscale Coral Island Resort, with its swimming pool and dive center, or try out the cafés and restaurants in the vicinity. Swimming, snorkeling, windsurfing, and parasailing are other attractions on this island. Day trips to Ko Hai can be organized by any travel agent or dive center in Phuket town or Ao Chalong. This is a good dive spot with high visibility. The small fishing village at Ko Lon makes an interesting stopover en route.

Ko Kaeo Pisadan
เกาะแก้วพิสดาร
12 miles (19 km) S of Phuket town. 🚤 from Hat Rawai.
🚗 🏠

An idyllic little island, Ko Kaeo Pisadan, also known as

Ornate gilded *chedi* housing the Buddha relic at Wat Chalong

Palm trees cover the headland overlooking a wide expanse of sea at Laem Promthep

Ko Kaeo Yai, is located off Phuket's southern headland, in the clear blue waters of the Andaman Sea. Day trips to this island are possible from Hat Rawai on the east coast, and Hat Nai Harn *(see p232)* on the west coast. Boat rides from both spots offer fine views of Laem Promthep on the way.

Ko Kaeo Pisadan is a tiny island with a single, fine 642-ft (196-m) long beach. The whole island can be traversed on foot and its shallow waters and offshore coral reefs make it an ideal snorkeling spot. Visitors can also kayak right around the island. There is a small resort offering simple and comfortable accommodations with a restaurant specializing in seafood and Thai specialties. Smoking is banned at the resort, and elsewhere on the island. The resort also offers camping facilities.

The island also has an isolated monastery – Wat Ko Kaeo Pisadan – which attracts Thai Buddhist pilgrims. The *wat* sustains a small number of monks, who are permanent inhabitants of this island. Visitors should dress appropriately at this sacred spot.

Hat Rawai
หาดราไวย์

10 miles (16 km) from Phuket town. Phuket Seashell Museum: 12/2, Moo 2, Wiset Road, Hat Rawai. **Tel** 0-7661-3666. **Open** 8am–6pm daily.

One of the main beaches of southeastern Phuket, Hat Rawai was once a major attraction of Phuket, but has since been replaced by the more appealing west coast beaches. Today, it is better known as an out-of-town dinner destination for those staying in Phuket town, and is justly celebrated for its seafood restaurants and upscale bars. Visitors can experience a little of the bustling excitement and entertainment of Hat Patong here. One of the local attractions here is the **Phuket Seashell Museum**, with a large collection of seashells from Thailand and around the world. Those eager to explore nearby islands rather than look for entertainment in restaurants and bars tend to skip Hat Rawai and go directly to Laem Promthep.

A small community of *chao lae*, or sea gypsies *(see p208)*, also live here, but they are rather shy and keep to themselves. Visitors often travel to Laem Promthep to see the spectacular sunset, before stopping at Hat Rawai for a rather appropriately named "sundowner" and dinner and then heading back into town.

Laem Promthep
แหลมพรหมเทพ

11 miles (18 km) S of Phuket town. An imposing rocky headland, Laem Promthep projects southwest into the Andaman Sea. Locally known as Laem Jao, or Cape of the Gods, this place offers the island's most famous sunset view and is popular with Thais and foreigners alike. There are food and drink stalls, shops, and a car park. A lighthouse marks the southwestern extremity of the island and visitors can get a 360-degree view across the sea. A rocky path leads down to the water, and offers good views of Ko Kaeo Pisadan. However, the surrounding waters are not good for swimming, as the currents get quite fierce.

Fishing boats belonging to the *chao lae* community, Hat Rawai

Exploring Phuket's Outlying Islands

There are about 39 islands scattered across the Andaman Sea, mainly on Phuket's east coast. These are either uninhabited or home to small communities of Thai fishermen and coconut farmers. Despite relative isolation and tranquility, change is slowly approaching these islands. Some, such as Ko Racha Yai, have already attracted exclusive and luxurious resorts, while others, such as Ko Yao Yai, remain off the tourist track, catering mainly to backpackers. These islands can be visited on a day trip or on weekend trips by taking fishing boats, ferries, or longtailed speedboats from various harbors and piers on and around Phuket. However, Ao Chalong still remains the most popular jumping-off point to reach these islands.

Thai Muslim fisherman perched on his boat, Hat Yao Noi

Ko Yao Yai

เกาะยาวใหญ่

9 miles (14 km) E of Phuket. 🚌 from Bang Rong. 🚤 📷

Located within the boundaries of Phang Nga province, Ko Yao Yai is the larger, albeit less crowded, of the two Ko Yao islands. The island is characterized by a long and irregular coastline, small fishing villages, coconut and rubber plantations, and small areas of rice paddy. Ensconced in a rural setting, it is a far cry from the bustling beaches on Phuket's west coast and an excellent place to sit back, relax, and enjoy a bit of authentic Thai rural life.

There are, as yet, no major resorts on Ko Yao Yai, so its infrastructure remains quite basic with poor and undeveloped roads. It is possible to hire a motorcycle on the island, but many visitors prefer to bring one across with them on the boat from Phuket. Guesthouses and bungalows are simple and

laid-back, as are the few restaurants and cafés. Most of the population – and most activities – are centered in the south of the island, especially around Lohjak pier, which is served by boat from the Phuket town pier. Small boats also ply on a regular basis between Chonglad pier on the island's northeast coast and Manok pier near the southern tip of neighboring Ko Yao Noi.

Ko Yao Noi

เกาะยาวน้อย

12 miles (19 km) E of Phuket. 🚌 from Bang Rong. 🚤 📷

Located in the Andaman Sea almost equidistant from the beach resorts of Phuket, Phang Nga *(see p220),* and Krabi *(see p248),* Ko Yao Noi is about 8 miles (13 km) long. This island is a quiet getaway, with an indigenous population of over 3,000, many of them Thai Muslims, who make a living by fishing and coconut farming.

Its main beach, Hat Yao, or Long Beach, is located on the eastern shore facing the mainland.

The interior of the island provides plenty of opportunities for short treks between the small villages, past patches of forest, shrimp farms, green rice fields, and unfrequented coves. Another popular pastime is sea-kayaking along the island's irregular and indented coast as well as to other offshore islets.

Accommodations are plentiful and cheap. There are several restaurants and bars along the east coast, as well as at Tha Kai, the island's tiny capital.

Ko Racha Yai

เกาะราชาใหญ่

9 miles (14 km) S of Phuket. 🚌 from Ao Chalong. 🚤 📷

Also known as Ko Raya Yai, Ko Racha Yai's chief attractions are the two beaches at Ao Patok and Ao Siam as well as the good offshore diving. The island also has several resorts offering comfortable bungalow accommodations. The largest and most luxurious of these, the Racha, dominates Ao Patok.

Just 5 miles (8 km) farther south is **Ko Racha Noi**, also a fine diving spot. The island is under the aegis of the Royal Thai Navy, which sometimes restricts access, but permits offshore diving among the unspoiled coral reefs.

In fact, both islands have fine, hard coral reefs which are suitable for all grades of divers.

Breathtaking expanse of sand and sea at Ko Racha Yai

Pearls of the Andaman Sea

Chanthaburi may have its rare gems, and Bangkok's Yaowarat District *(see p76)* may be dotted with gold shops, but Phuket is justly famous for its spectacular *mook andaman* (Andaman Sea pearls). Originally, they were a natural product, harvested from the shallow waters around the island on a purely ad hoc basis, but this is not the case anymore. Over the past three decades, Phuket has emerged as a major player in the cultured pearl business, growing to compete internationally with other established major sources such as Japan and the Persian Gulf. Cultured pearls now play a very important role in the island's economy, and the island has several pearl companies. Some of these companies allow visitors to tour their pearl farms and also give demonstrations of pearl culture and harvesting. The 2004 tsunami, however, adversely affected the industry by causing large numbers of oysters to be washed away.

Cultivating Pearls

Pearl cultivation involves raising oysters in a tank until they are large enough to be placed in the sea. These oysters are then injected with an artificial irritant. After 3–4 years, sometimes longer, a cultured pearl is produced. However, this is not an error-free process since only five percent of the nucleated pearls ever become jewelry.

Pearl oysters are made by planting a nucleus or core inside their shells. This is harvested after a few years.

Pearl extraction is carried out with the help of chemicals and machines which remove the pearl by tearing open the pearl sac. Harvested pearls are then washed, polished, and graded for sale purposes.

Pearl farms are generally located in shallow waters, making the Andaman Sea off the east coast of Phuket an ideal place for the process.

Jewelry stores in Phuket sell pearls that are locally produced, cultured, and polished. Visitors can choose from a wide and sparkling range of products, including necklaces.

Visitors to pearl farms can ask for guided tours. Such trips include seafood, dining, and visits to showrooms selling locally produced pearls.

LOWER ANDAMAN COAST

Long regarded as the lesser developed counterpart of the Upper Andaman Coast, the Lower Andaman Coast is now a region of limitless possibilities. From the verdant islands of Ko Phi Phi and Ko Lanta to the idyllic beaches around Krabi and Trang, it has become popular for its diving, snorkeling, and rock climbing. Further south, however, both the Malay-Muslim fishing port of Satun and the pristine Ko Tarutao are still off the beaten track and relatively quiet.

The long, serrated coastline of the Lower Andaman Coast, extending from Krabi to the Malaysian frontier, is a lush, fertile region. Blessed with stunning natural beauty, it is a heady mix of white or golden sand beaches and towering limestone outcrops. The vegetation comprises tall, swaying casuarina trees and coconut palms, dense rain forests and rubber plantations, as well as green paddy fields.

Gorgeous and unspoiled, the region is frequented by travelers who head for towns such as Krabi and Trang, popular destinations for watersports and rock climbing. Home to a substantial Chinese ethnic population, both towns offer visitors – in addition to the Sino-Thai architecture – an exciting variety of eating options including *dim sum*, which is a specialty in many restaurants in Trang. Ko Phi Phi, with its romantic environs and truly outstanding scenic beauty, offers some of the best diving in the area, and is now firmly on the tourist trail. Visitors wanting sand and sun without the crowds head for relatively undeveloped islands such as Ko Lanta.

Few venture as far south as Satun, a peaceful and laid-back town with the highest number of Thai Muslims in the country. Satun also serves as the gateway to the spectacular Ko Tarutao Marine National Park and its outlying islands, within easy sight of Pulau Langkawi and the west coast of Malaysia.

The southwest monsoon, which lasts from June to September, however, makes outlying islands such as Ko Lipe and Ko Rawi inaccessible.

Macaques grooming each other on the grounds of Wat Tham Seua, near Krabi

◀ The famous twin bays on Ko Phi Phi Don, each side of a narrow isthmus connecting the island's two land masses

Exploring the Lower Andaman Coast

Breathtaking natural beauty, verdant rain forests and stunning beaches beckon visitors to the Lower Andaman Coast. The tropical mangrove forests, home to a variety of land and water animals, are one of the region's best kept secrets. Quiet Krabi combines fine beaches with spectacular cliff landscapes. The idyllic island scenery of Ko Phi Phi and Ko Lanta is also accessible from Krabi. The Trang coast and Tarutao archipelago, with sandy beaches and fine corals, still remain relatively untouristed due to undeveloped facilities. National parks such as Hat Chao Mai, Thale Ban, and Ko Phetra are a haven for all kinds of marine animals and wildlife, besides providing ideal trails for trekking and nature walks. Visitors will also find plenty of opportunity for sea-kayaking, diving, and snorkeling from the islands of Ko Hai, Ko Kradan, and Ko Muk.

Longtail boats anchored in the waters off Ko Muk

Getting Around

Most visitors to the Lower Andaman Coast make use of the airports at Trang and Krabi. Reliable air-conditioned buses link these towns with Bangkok and farther south with Satun, where boats depart for Malaysia's Langkawi archipelago and on to Penang. Trang has a rail link to Surat Thani, where you can join the main north–south line, or take a boat to Ko Samui. Both Krabi and Trang make good bases for exploring the region by hired car. Ko Phi Phi, Ko Lanta, Ko Tarutao, and Ko Bulon Leh are all on ferry routes. Longtail boats are the best way to explore the smaller bays and waterways.

Sights at a Glance

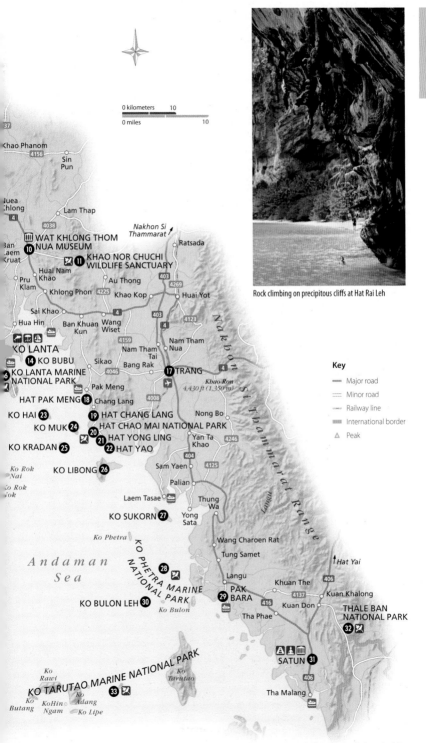

Rock climbing on precipitous cliffs at Hat Rai Leh

Khao Phanom
4156
Sin Pun
37

Juea Chlong
4
Lam Thap
4038

Nakhon Si Thammarat

🏛 WAT KHLONG THOM
10 NUA MUSEUM
Ban aem Kruat

🗹 11 KHAO NOR CHUCHI
WILDLIFE SANCTUARY

Ratsada

Pru Klam
Huai Nam Khao
Au Thong
403

Khlong Phon
4225
Khao Kop
4269
Huai Yot

Sai Khao
4
403

Hua Hin
Ban Khuan Kun
Wang Wiset
4123
Nam Tham Nua
4
Nakhon

🏨🗹⚓
4159
Nam Tham Tai

14 KO LANTA
Sikao
Bang Rak

🏛 KO BUBU
4046
17 TRANG ✈
Si

6 KO LANTA MARINE
2 NATIONAL PARK
Pak Meng
Khao Ron
4,430 ft (1,350 m)
4
Thammarat

HAT PAK MENG 18
Chang Lang
4008
Nong Bo

KO HAI 23
19 HAT CHANG LANG

KO MUK 24
🗹 20 HAT CHAO MAI NATIONAL PARK
Yan Ta Khao
4246
Range

KO KRADAN 25
21 HAT YONG LING
22 HAT YAO

Ko Rok Nai
KO LIBONG 26
404
Sam Yaen
4125

Ko Rok ok
Palian

Laem Tasae 🏨
Thung Wa
Lansu

KO SUKORN 27
Yong Sata

Ko Phetra
Wang Charoen Rat
Hat Yai

Andaman
Sea
KO
PHETRA
28 🗹
Tung Samet
406

MARINE
NATIONAL
PARK
Langu
Khuan The
Kuan Khalong

KO BULON LEH 30
29 PAK BARA
416
Kuan Don
4137

Ko Bulon
Tha Phae
THALE BAN
NATIONAL PARK
32 🗹

🅰🏕🏛
SATUN 31

Ko Rawi
Ko Tarutao
406

KO TARUTAO MARINE NATIONAL PARK

Ko Butang
Ko Adang
KoHin Ngam
Ko Lipe
33 🗹
Tha Malang
🏨

Key

▬ Major road
▭▭ Minor road
▬▬ Railway line
▮▮ International border
△ Peak

For keys to symbols *see back flap*

Twin peaks of Khao Khanap Nam forming a picturesque backdrop for Krabi

❶ Krabi
กระบี่

Road Map B5. 478 miles (770 km) SW of Bangkok. 🚝 68,000. 🚌 🚤 10 miles (16 km) NE of Krabi. ℹ️ TAT, Krabi (0-7562-2163). 🚢 daily.

A small town and provincial capital, Krabi is an important embarkation point for ferries to Ko Lanta, Ko Phi Phi, and Ao Nang. Set on the banks of the Krabi estuary, the town takes its name from a *krabi*, or sword, allegedly discovered here. This quaint and bustling market town is the administrative center of the province, with banks and other facilities. Surrounded by

tall limestone outcrops similar to those in Phang Nga Bay *(see pp216–21)*, it is a scenic spot in its own right. The twin limestone peaks of **Khao Khanap Nam** are among the most notable outcrops, standing like sentinels on each side of the river. The eastern side is flanked by mangroves. Both the limestone karsts and the mangroves can be visited by renting a longtail boat from the Khong Kha pier in the center of town. Although Krabi itself is generally used as a departure point for the nearby islands, it is fast developing, with several bars, restaurants serving eclectic cuisine, and a burgeoning nightlife. There is

also a busy market at Thanon Sukhon, a tourist center, and a good foreign-language bookshop on Thanon Utarakit.

❷ Wat Tham Seua
วัดถ้ำเสือ

Road Map B5. 5 miles (8 km) N of Krabi. 🚌 ℹ️ TAT, Krabi, (0-7562-2163). **Open** dawn to dusk daily. 🅿️ 📷

Built into a limestone cave, Wat Tham Seua, which means Tiger Cave Temple, is regarded as one of southern Thailand's most renowned forest temples. It is named after a rock formation that resembles a tiger's paw. The *wat*'s main *wihan* (assembly hall) is built inside a deep limestone cave which contains various *memento mori* – grim symbols depicting the forsaking of worldly desires. At the rear of the *wihan*, a flight of stairs leads up to the main cave of the *wat* where visitors can see a much-venerated Buddha footprint on a gilded rock platform. The *wat* complex also has a large statue of the highly revered *bodhisattva* Avalokitesvara, in its Chinese manifestation as Guan Yin, the Mahayana goddess of mercy. It is sheltered by a newly built Chinese-style pagoda nearby. A circular path in the nearby forest hollow offers a pleasant walk among towering trees and *kutis* (monks' quarters). The landscaped grounds have a 1,272-step pathway which leads to a Seated Buddha image. Although

Devotees kneeling in front of the Buddha statue in Wat Tham Seua

a strenuous climb, the view from the top is worth the effort. Wat Tham Seua is also famous for its Vipassana Meditation courses.

❸ Than Bok Koranee National Park
อุทยานแห่งชาติธารโบกขรณี

Road Map B5. Park HQ off Hwy 4039, 28 miles (45 km) NW of Krabi. 🚌 🚍 ⓘ Park HQ (0-7568-1071). **Open** dawn to dusk daily. 🅿 🌀 📷 Ⓦ dnp.go.th

Covering an area of 47 sq miles (122 sq km), Than Bok Koranee National Park is characterized by a series of limestone outcrops, evergreen rainforest, mangroves, peat swamps, and several islands. A part of the national park is being developed as a botanical garden. The park headquarters, set amid a series of small streams and dark green pools, is a popular picnic spot. It is possible to camp here by arrangement with park authorities.

Than Bok Koranee is also famous for its cave systems. **Tham Lot** is a cave complex full of winding passages and stalactites and stalagmites, and can be reached by boat from the Bho Tho pier in Ao Luk. The nearby **Tham Hua Kalok**, is well known for its 70-odd ancient cave paintings depicting humans and animals and dating back over two millennia. Other well-

Huay To Waterfall at Khao Phanom Bencha National Park

known caves in the area include **Tham Sa Yuan Thong**, which has a natural spring; **Tham Phet**, or Diamond Cave, which derives its name from its shimmering rock walls; and **Tham Song Phi Nong**, where skeletal remains of humans, ancient pottery, bronze tools, and earrings were discovered.

Than Bok Koranee can be easily reached by bus or car. The best way to explore the park's mangrove swamps is by longtail boat as they are virtually impassable on foot, apart from some places where a boardwalk has been constructed. Visitors can also hike along marked trekking trails.

A clouded leopard cub

❹ Khao Phanom Bencha National Park
อุทยานแห่งชาติเขาพนมเบญจา

Road Map B5. Park HQ off Hwy 4, 12 miles (19 km) N of Krabi. 🚌 🚍 ⓘ Park HQ (0-7566-0716). **Open** dawn to dusk daily. 🅿 🌀 📷 📷 Ⓦ dnp.go.th

This 20 sq mile (52 sq km) national park comprising tropical rainforest is named after the five-shouldered peak of Khao Phanom Bencha, which rises to a height of 4,470 ft (1,397 m).

Despite illegal logging and poaching, the park's rain forest still holds at least 156 species of birds, including the white-crowned hornbill and the striped wren-babbler. Other wildlife includes the Asiatic black bear, wild boar, clouded leopard, and smaller mammals such as the binturong and serow. The thundering Nam Tok Huay To, or Huay To Waterfall and Nam Tok Huay Sadeh, or Huay Sadeh Waterfall, are located less than 2 miles (3 km) from the park headquarters and are worth seeing. Park authorities can arrange treks to the Khao Phanom Bencha peak. The difficult climb is compensated for by the lovely view.

Visitors admiring limestone formations inside the extensive cave system in Than Bok Koranee National Park

❺ Tha Pom
ท่าปอม

Road Map B5. 21 miles (34 km) NW of Krabi. 🚌 ℹ️ TAT, Krabi (0-7562-2163).
Open dawn to dusk daily. 📷 📹

A peat swamp and forest, Tha Pom runs from various sources which originate from a pool called Chong Phra Kaew, along a natural waterway. This waterway is locally referred to as Khlong Song Nam, meaning "two types of water canals". Here, freshwater meets seawater at high tide, and Lumphi palms *(Eleiodoxa conferta)* grow alongside thick mangroves. The area is best explored by hired riverboat, although a raised wooden walkway has also been built through parts of the forest, running a circular course for some 2,250 ft (686 m). Signs along the way, in English and Thai, explain the natural ecology of the region. Wooden chairs are placed at intervals for visitors to sit back and take in the pristine beauty of the area. Another way to explore the area is in a hired canoe.

❻ Mangroves
สวนรุกขชาติกระบี่

Road Map B5. 3 miles (5 km) W of Krabi. 🚐 🚌 ℹ️ TAT, Krabi (0-7562-2163). 📷

Home to several types of birds, fish, crabs, shrimps, and mollusks, the mangroves of Krabi are easily accessible and among the most

Longtail boats frequenting the waterway along the mangroves of Tha Pom

beautiful tracts of forest in Thailand. These mangroves have remained remarkably intact and are important nesting grounds for hundreds of species of bird, including localized specialties such as the mangrove blue flycatcher. These are among the most frequently visited areas by enthusiastic bird-watchers. They also provide shelter for a variety of land and marine animals.

A visit to the Krabi mangrove swamps is easily organized; half-day boat tours to nearby estuaries are also widely available. Boats frequent the area almost every hour from Krabi and are available for hire.

Fortunately, the ecological significance of the Krabi mangrove forests has been recognized by the Thai people and plans for further development of Krabi as a deep-water

port are currently under regular review. These reviews are aimed at protecting this unique environment.

❼ Ko Klang
เกาะกลาง

Road Map B5. 2 miles (3 km) S of Krabi. 🚌 from Krabi. ℹ️ TAT, Krabi (0-7562-2163). 🚲 📹

Among the few remaining non-commercialized islands in Thailand, Ko Klang, or Central Island, is situated across the Krabi River estuary a short distance from Krabi. Clearly visible from the town, the island is a pristine tropical paradise ringed by thick mangrove swamps and can be easily reached by a hired riverboat or longtail boat from Krabi. There are a few beautiful coral reefs off the shore, although they have been damaged by traffic in the water. Offshore swimming is another good option for visitors. Quite a few of the local mangrove swamp tours stop by at the island for an hour or so, but those interested in learning more about Krabi fishermen, boatmen, and their families, can arrange a homestay visit through one of the many travel agencies in Krabi. There are three small fishing villages on this predominantly Thai Muslim island and locals offer homestays including accommodations, food, and hired bicycles or motorcycles.

Fishing farm owned by local fishermen on Ko Klang

Mangrove Ecosystems

The coastal estuaries of southern Thailand are home to dense mangrove forests – a natural haven for all kinds of wildlife. These ecosystems once covered much of the coast, but over the past five decades, many have been destroyed. Those that survive are now being brought under conservation programs. Mangrove species are the only trees to have adapted to the inhospitable conditions of these muddy intertidal zones. However, this vital ecosystem is home to many fish, crabs, mollusks, shrimps, and wild birds such as the ruddy kingfisher, the mangrove pitta, the white-bellied sea eagle, and the masked fin-foot. Larger animals living in the swamps include the dugong or sea cow, macaque monkeys, lizards, and endangered sea turtles.

Cross Section of a Mangrove Levee

This is a typical gradation of trees in a mangrove forest. At high tide, small fish and invertebrates feed in the nutrient-rich waters around the roots. At low tide, when the roots are exposed, crabs and wading birds scour the mudflats for trapped fish and decaying matter.

The soil in this region is rich in nutrients and away from direct wave action.

Pneumatophores or finger-like projections are used for "breathing".

Excess salt is excreted via the shedding of leaves.

Stilt roots grow down from the trunk and absorb oxygen.

Yellow-ringed cat snakes are adept swimmers and tree climbers. They rest by day and hunt for fish, frogs, and other small game by night.

Small-clawed otters are common to this area. They eat mollusks and crustaceans such as crabs.

Crab-eating macaques inhabit mangroves and are good swimmers. They forage for crabs at low tide and also subsist on seeds.

Male fiddler crabs use their one enlarged claw to select tiny organic particles to eat. Their colorful claws are also used in courtship displays.

Destruction of Mangrove Forests

Despite a national management program, some 60 percent of Thailand's mangroves have been cleared since the 1960s, making way for human activities such as shrimp farming, charcoal production, and road and harbor construction. This loss of habitat has decimated marine life, and is also accelerating coastal erosion. Mangrove swamp plays a vital role in natural flood control, and in fact saved much of this area, including the Ko Lanta islands, from total destruction by the 2004 tsunami.

Fish farm in a mangrove area

❽ Krabi Coast

ชายฝั่งกระบี่

Located on the peninsular mainland to the east and south of Phuket, Krabi province comprises more than 1,800 sq miles (4,662 sq km) of forested hills along with more than 62 miles (100 km) of coastline and an estimated 200 islands, all facing the aquamarine waters of the Andaman Sea. Much of the coastline is studded with steep, impenetrable, and uniquely shaped karst outcrops which offer caving, trekking, and some of the finest rock-climbing in the world. The area is also known for its fantastic snorkeling, scuba diving, and sea-kayaking opportunities. Despite rapid development, the Krabi Coast is still largely off the beaten track.

Visitors sunbathing on the pristine sands at Hat Rai Leh West

Display of fossilized seashells in limestone slabs, Susaan Hoi

🚇 Susaan Hoi

สุสานหอย

13 miles (21 km) SW of Krabi.

Located on the southeastern extremity of the Krabi Coast, Susaan Hoi is easily accessible by longtail boat from Krabi. Also known as the Shell Cemetery, this spot is a fantastic agglomeration of thousands of seashells that date back at least 75 million years. It was originally a large freshwater swamp, home to a variety of mollusks. These have petrified over the passage of time due to changes on the earth's surface and fused into large limestone slabs that now project into the sea. A small museum by the site explains the history of these fossils. There are also some souvenir shops selling shells and other local handicrafts. Visitors to this spot can enjoy the secluded stretches, offering good views of islands.

🚇 Hat Rai Leh East

หาดไร่เลย์ตะวันออก

7 miles (11 km) SW of Krabi.

Hat Rai Leh comprises two separate beaches – Hat Rai Leh East and Hat Rai Leh West. Both can be easily accessed by longtail boat from Krabi. The eastern stretch is attractive at high tide, but less appealing at

Climbers scale the bolted outcrops along Hat Rai Leh East

low tide, when wide muddy flats are exposed. The more developed of the two beaches, Hat Rai Leh East offers a wide range of accommodations, including beach bungalows. Visitors can explore the mangroves or practice rock-climbing on the limestone outcrops on the beach. Many travelers prefer to stay at this beach and walk over to Hat Rai Leh West and Hat Tham Phra Nang during the day.

🚇 Hat Rai Leh West

หาดไร่เลย์ตะวันตก

10 miles (16 km) SW of Krabi.

A gently curving stretch of white sand, Hat Rai Leh West faces west across the Andaman Sea offering spectacular sunset views. More attractive but somewhat more expensive than the eastern flank, the beach has little by way of budget accommodations and, although it attracts visitors from all over the coast, most choose not to stay here. For those willing to splurge, there are plenty of mid-range and upscale places, as well as some excellent seafood restaurants and bars. It is also the main landing point for longtail water taxis from Ao Nang. The rocky limestone outcrops particular to this region extend into Hat Rai Leh West, offering opportunities for climbers of all levels. There are plenty of local companies that rent out guides and equipment. Sea-kayaking around the limestone cliffs is another very popular sport.

🚩 Hat Tham Phra Nang
หาดถ้ำพระนาง

9 miles (14 km) SW of Krabi. 🏖 🗺 📷

Located at the southern end of the small peninsula that divides Hat Rai Leh East from Hat Rai Leh West, Hat Tham Phra Nang is considered one of the loveliest spots in southern Thailand. The white-sand beach is sheltered by a variety of karst outcrops.

The limestone cliffs that surround this area have made it a world-famous rock climbing destination. The forbiddingly sheer **Taiwand Wall** and its extensions dominate Hat Tham Phra Nang and have hundreds of routes – from the simple to truly demanding. They are marked by bolts fixed in the rock where climbers can attach their ropes. However, corrosive weather

Fertility shrine dedicated to Phra Nang, Tham Phra Nang

conditions may threaten the integrity of the bolts, thus visitors should take suitable safety precautions. These spectacular outcrops are the highlight of the Krabi experience, offering unparalleled climbing opportunities as well as stunning views.

Longtail boats functioning as makeshift restaurants, Hat Tham Phra Nang

Tham Phra Nang
ถ้ำพระนาง

9 miles (14 km) SW of Krabi.
🏖 🗺

Located along the eastern end of Hat Tham Phra Nang is Tham Phra Nang, which means "Cave of the Revered Lady". This cave is dedicated to the memory of an Indian princess who supposedly drowned offshore centuries ago. A fertility cult has developed around her and locals have set up a small shrine within Tham Phra Nang. Packed with red-tipped phalluses placed here by fishermen praying for a good catch, the shrine is also revered by women, especially expectant mothers and those who want to be blessed with a child. Near the cave is a marked path leading to the small lagoon of Sa Phra Nang, which means "Lady's Bathing Place"; it offers a good view across Hat Rai Leh East.

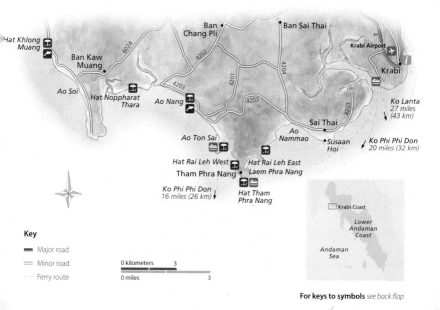

Key

━━ Major road

╍╍ Minor road

- - Ferry route

0 kilometers 3

0 miles 3

For keys to symbols *see back flap*

Limestone karsts and thick scrub dominating the isolated beach at Ao Ton Sai

🔖 Ao Ton Sai

อ่าวต้นไทร
11 miles (18 km) SW of Krabi.
🚌 ⚋ 📷

The least developed of the beaches around Ao Nang, Ao Ton Sai is also the least expensive. It is possible to reach Ao Ton Sai from the western end of the coast on foot, but visitors should be prepared to walk through sticky mudflats. There is also access from Hat Rai Leh West to the south, but this is made uncomfortable and potentially dangerous by jagged rocks studded with sharp-shelled clams. Like the nearby beaches of Hat Rai Leh East, Hat Rai Leh West, and Hat Tham Phra Nang, Ao Ton Sai can be best reached

by boat. Hat Ton Sai is not a standout beach like Hat Rai Leh West or Hat Tham Phra Nang; it is often littered with flotsam and the bay is backed by mangroves rather than the more common coconut palms. However, the view from the bay is quite magnificent and includes sheer karst outcrops. Accommodation options as well as drinking and dining facilities on this beach are appreciably cheaper than at the more upscale Hat Rai Leh West. Many travelers often stay here, heading out to the nearby beaches, such as Hat Tham Phra Nang, during the day and returning to eat and enjoy the fine sunset views across the Andaman Sea.

🔖 Ao Nang

อ่าวนาง
13 miles (21 km) W of Krabi.
🚌 ⚋ 📷

A beautiful and busy bay, Ao Nang is just west of Hat Tham Phra Nang, and is separated from Ao Ton Sai by a rocky headland. Originally a small fishing hamlet popular with the backpacking crowd, the bay has grown into prominence in recent times. Easily accessible by road from Krabi, Ao Nang is extremely popular during peak season with many overseas visitors, especially Europeans. This beach is one of the liveliest spots on the Krabi Coast. The huge tourist influx has led to the development of all kinds of facilities including a variety of accommodations ranging from upscale resorts to budget guesthouses, as well as many restaurants, bars, travel agents, and dive operators.

Visitors looking for a quieter beach can make their way to Hat Rai Leh West, a 10-minute boat ride from Ao Nang. For an island day trip, take a longtail boat from Ao Nong beach to nearby Ko Poda and Chicken Island, both great for snorkeling. Ko Poda has a beautiful beach, ideal for picnicking, while it's hard to miss the extraordinarily shaped rock formation that gives Chicken Island its name.

Massage huts and restaurants along the beach road at Ao Nang

🔳 Hat Noppharat Thara
หาดนพรัตน์ ธารา
11 miles (18 km) W of Krabi. 🖊️ 📷

A popular picnic spot that is just around the corner from Ao Nang, Hat Noppharat Thara is a less-developed extension of the beach at Ao Nang and can be easily accessed on foot from the bay. This quiet 2-mile (3-km) long casuarina-lined beach offers magnificent views of the area's massive karst outcrops. Formerly called Hat Khlong Haeng, meaning Dried Canal Beach, Hat Noppharat Thara derives its name from a canal which divides the beach into two and dries up at low tide.

The beach is similar to that at Ao Nang without its resorts, bars, or crowds. However, Hat Noppharat Thara's proximity to the latter beach means that it is a matter of time before this area develops as a commercial spot. At low tide the waters are too shallow for swimming, but ideal

Coconut palms along the sheltered beach at Hat Khlong Muang

Colorful longtail boats anchored off Hat Noppharat Thara

for walking across to the tiny island of Ko Khao Pak Khlong for a good view of the bay. This area is famous for its seafood especially *hoi chak teen* (wing shells), a local delicacy whose shells are also sold as souvenirs.

🔳 Hat Khlong Muang
หาดคลองม่วง
14 miles (22 km) W of Krabi.
🚌 🖊️ 📷

Shielded from Ao Nang and Laem Phra Nang by a long, rocky headland, Hat Khlong Muang presents the luxurious side of the Krabi Coast. This beach can be easily reached by longtail boats from Ao Nang or *songthaews* or hired cars from Krabi. Once a backpackers' destination, the development

of the luxurious Krabi Sheraton has transformed this pristine stretch on the Andaman Sea into an upscale resort offering all kinds of facilities. The palm-lined beach is interspersed with rocky boulders and a portion of the reef is exposed at low tide; the offshore islands only add to the visual appeal of staying here. Dive schools and travel agents abound in Hat Khlong Muang and can arrange scuba diving, snorkeling, and sea-kayaking trips to the offshore islands. Places to eat include sundowner bars, beach cafés, and noodle bars. In sharp contrast, the resorts offer luxurious restaurants serving international cuisine as well as gourmet Thai food.

The Legend of Phra Nang

According to legend, Phra Nang was an Indian princess who drowned in the Andaman Sea many centuries ago. Her spirit supposedly inhabited the cave that is now known as Tham Phra Nang *(see p253)*. In the past, locals created a simple shrine here and left offerings in the form of carved *lingas* (phallic symbols). Over time, the status of this shrine rose, becoming associated with fertility and good fortune, and the cave itself became a symbol of the female sexual organ. Residents of this area believe that any carved wooden *linga* cast into the sea off the Krabi Coast will eventually find its way to Tham Phra Nang. A minor deity in this region, Phra Nang is the patron saint of women who want to conceive as well as of fishermen out for a good day's haul. She is believed to be capable of great anger and, according to popular belief, insults to her shrine cause damage to those involved. Thus, locals and outsiders generally seek her blessings before undertaking any project in the area.

Phallic symbols as offerings at the shrine of Phra Nang

❾ Ko Phi Phi

เกาะพีพี

This archipelago comprises six islands set like scattered jewels amid the azure waters of the Andaman Sea. Ko Phi Phi Don is the main island, comprising two land masses joined by a narrow palm-fringed isthmus lined with restaurants, bars, and guesthouses. The beautiful and uninhabited Ko Phi Phi Leh lies to its south, while the other islands are just tiny limestone outcrops. Nature lovers will find a haven in the surrounding coral beds teeming with marine life. Tall cliffs and underwater reefs protect the islands from the rough seas. Ko Phi Phi is renowned for its beauty, drawing visitors from all over the world.

Locator map

☐ Area illustrated

Ban Laem Thong

Hat Laem Thong

Ao Lo Bakao

KO PHI PHI DO

Ao Lo Dalum

Ao S

★ **Twin Bays**
There are spectacular views of Ko Phi Phi Don and the twin bays of Ao Lo Dalum and Ao Ton Sai from the famous viewpoint at the eastern end of the island. The best views are during sunrise and sunset.

Beach Activities
Ko Phi Phi is renowned for diving and snorkeling among its superb corals and vibrant marine life. Sea-kayaking and rock-climbing are also popular.

KEY

① **Hiking trails** cut through the eastern half of Ko Phi Phi Don.

★ **Ban Ton Sai**
The largest settlement on Ko Phi Phi, Ban Ton Sai also serves as a ferry port. Once a small Muslim fishing village, today it is a hive of restaurants, bars, and hotels.

Danny Boyle's *The Beach*

Hollywood director Danny Boyle decided upon Ao Maya in Ko Phi Phi Leh as the perfect location for filming Alex Garland's *The Beach* (2000). The movie, about a commune of young people living on a secret island, shows them partying and living a hedonistic life. The film, however, ran into trouble with accusations of environmental damage

and profiteering during its making. 20th Century Fox and their local agents were sued by Thai courts for alleged damage to the bay. Nonetheless, the movie was instrumental in bringing Ao Maya into the limelight, and has led to a substantial increase in the number of visitors.

Taking a shot of Ao Maya during the filming of Danny Boyle's *The Beach*

VISITORS' CHECKLIST

Practical Information
Road Map B5. 25 miles (40 km) S of Krabi. 7,700. TAT, Phuket (0-7621-1036). Chinese New Year (Feb), Songkran (Apr). **phi-phi.com**

Transport
from Phuket or Krabi.

Key

- - Trail
--- Ferry route

0 km 1
0 mile 1

Colorful Coral Reefs
Ko Phi Phi's surrounding waters have several renowned dive sites with a variety of soft corals, anemones, and even sharks.

Hat Ranti

Hat Yao

Krabi
25 miles (40 km)

Phuket
26 miles (42 km)

Viking Cave
This cave has ancient carvings of Chinese junks resembling Viking-style vessels. These petroglyphs, dating back a few centuries, confirm the legends of Viking boats visiting the Andaman coast.

KO PHI PHI LEH

Ao Maya

★ Ao Maya
Popularized by the movie *The Beach*, Ao Maya is one of the most beautiful bays in Ko Phi Phi, sheltered by cliffs on three sides, with excellent snorkeling in the surrounding coral reefs.

For keys to symbols see back flap

Exploring Ko Phi Phi

Although Ko Phi Phi consists of six islands, most of them, including Ko Phi Phi Leh, are uninhabited and undeveloped limestone outcrops. Ko Phi Phi Don, the main island with some settlements is small enough to be explored on foot. There are no motorized vehicles or proper roads, and visitors have to hike to get to the remote parts. However, it is possible to access most of the coast by longtail boats or ferries from the Ban Ton Sai pier. Ko Phi Phi Leh, on the other hand, has no walking paths or marked trails and the only means of accessing this island is by boat from Ban Ton Sai.

Ban Ton Sai
บ้านต้นไทร

As the only settlement of any size on the archipelago, Ban Ton Sai is the de facto capital of Ko Phi Phi as well as the commercial hub of the island. Having developed out of a small Muslim fishing village, this is the only ferry port with links to the mainland. Located along Ao Ton Sai, the village covers the narrow isthmus connecting the two parts of Ko Phi Phi Don. Ban Ton Sai is a crowded hive of small streets packed with foreign visitors as well as Thais from the mainland. Although it was badly damaged by the 2004 tsunami, the village has bounced back, busier than ever. Despite promises from the authorities to control unrestricted building, new resorts keep springing up on this island, which is part of an ecologically sensitive zone.

Everyone visiting Ko Phi Phi passes through Ban Ton Sai, and many choose to stay here for its facilities including hotels, restaurants, and bars. The village

A narrow street lined with shops and restaurants, Ban Ton Sai

is also home to a bank, a police station, a post office, and a clinic. This is an ideal place for visitors to set up base to explore the rest of Ko Phi Phi.

Ao Lo Dalum
อ่าวโละดาลัม

Immediately north of Ban Ton Sai, Ao Lo Dalum is a gorgeous bay fringed by a fine beach with lush green coconut palms. Within a stone's throw of bustling Ban Ton Sai, this beach is busy, attracting day-trippers and visitors on a tight schedule. Holiday-makers on long stays usually have more time to explore the less accessible beaches on the other islands. Ao Lo Dalum is picturesque at high tide but somewhat less appealing at low tide, when the mudflats stretch out endlessly. A steep trail at the eastern end of the bay follows a path across the island's spine and leads up to the island's famous viewpoint. Located at a height of 610 ft (186 m) above sea level, the viewpoint offers a vista spanning the narrow isthmus and its twin bays.

Hat Yao
หาดยาว

Located on the southeastern shore of Ko Phi Phi, Hat Yao is sheltered by a small, rocky promontory to the east. A world-class destination, this beach is a place of exquisite beauty – the sand is fine, white, and powdery, and the surrounding waters are shallow and warm, swarming with all kinds of colorful fish, which live in the rich coral reef. Hat Yao attracts many travelers and the beach is generally quite crowded. Also present are numerous vendors selling everything from cold drinks to a Thai massage. It is easily reached by boat from Ban Ton Sai or on foot via a narrow track leading east from the village.

Hat Ranti
หาดรันตี

Tucked away from the busy Ban Ton Sai, Hat Ranti is one of three linked beaches on the east coast of Ko Phi Phi Don. It offers basic accommodations and affordable restaurants, and is well suited for the budget traveler. Hat Ranti is slightly off the beaten track, and can be reached by a 45-minute walk on the trail across the spine of the main island, or by longtail boats from Ban Ton Sai. This beach with its rocky outcrops and calm waters is a peaceful getaway which is perfect for a picnic or a day trip. However, visitors should bring their own diving gear and other supplies, as this beach has minimal facilities.

Limestone cliffs rising from the calm waters of Ao Lo Dalum

🚋 Ao Lo Bakao
อ่าวโล๊ะบาเก

Located on the eastern coast of Ko Phi Phi Don, Ao Lo Bakao is a long, curved bay facing the mainland. This bay, which is about half a mile (1 km) north of Hat Ranti, is separated from Ban Ton Sai and the rest of the island by a rocky spine. Ao Lo Bakao is only reached on foot via a single narrow trail. Yet its beach has developed as an upscale spot, characterized by expensive, well-appointed resort accommodations. The lovely 2,880-ft (878-m) white-sand beach is well served by restaurants and bars without being overcrowded. This rather exclusive bay attracts upper-class Thais, and is a popular honeymoon spot.

Snorkeling among the corals off Hat Laem Thong

🚋 Hat Laem Thong
หาดแหลมทอง

A lovely strip of sand on Ko Phi Phi Don's northernmost tip, Hat Laem Thong is a jumping-off point for nearby offshore islands. This area is also among the best diving spots in the archipelago. Thus, despite being quite far from Ban Ton Sai, Hat Laem Thong is busy with a constant flow of divers who come to explore the rich coral reefs. The beach is easily accessed by boat from Ban Ton Sai. Hat Laem Thong has quite a few upscale resorts including the Zeavola *(see p301)*, as well as shops, restaurants, and diving agencies. Visitors can go deep-sea fishing or even take cookery courses.

Cave paintings depicting ancient ships at Ko Phi Phi Leh

Pirates of the Andaman Coast

Rock paintings of Arab, Chinese, and European vessels in Ko Phi Phi Leh's caves may be evidence of the existence of pirates on the Andaman Coast. Studies suggest that these paintings were made by the pirates while hiding in these remote spots to escape bad weather, transfer their cargo, or avoid authorities. The drawings are believed to date back at least a few centuries. The Andaman Coast with its many islands, coves, and inlets is a perfect vantage point and hideout. The theory is further proven, as the nearby Straits of Malacca continues to be plagued by piracy even today.

Ko Phi Phi Leh
เกาะพีพีเล

Only a quarter of the size of Ko Phi Phi Don and much less accessible, Ko Phi Phi Leh is a 25-minute boat ride from Ban Ton Sai. Completely uninhabited ,with pristine coves and bays and rich offshore coral reefs, the island's main attraction is its startling beauty and isolation. However, this has changed since Danny Boyle put the island on the world map with his movie *The Beach* (2000), starring Leonardo DiCaprio. Since then a number of visitors have come here to experience this tropical paradise as captured on celluloid. The island's greatest attraction is Ao Maya, located along the southwestern coast.

This exquisite bay offers fine swimming and snorkeling. Apart from tourists, Ko Phi Phi Leh also has regular local visitors. These are the daring climbers who engage in the swiftlet nest trade. This is a coveted ingredient used to make bird's nest soup, an exotic delicacy and among the most expensive animal products. Intrepid climbers scale sheer rock faces and caves on the island to gather these rare products.

In ancient times, Ko Phi Phi Leh was a mooring spot for fishermen and possibly pirates. The Viking Cave on the northern coast has petroglyphs of Chinese-style junks on its walls, which visiting Europeans likened to Viking ships.

Visitors enjoying a boat ride in the pristine waters off Ko Phi Phi Leh

Canopied longtail boats for hire in the Ao Maya lagoon, Ko Phi Phi Leh ▶

Excavated pottery displayed at Wat Khlong Thom Nua Museum

⑩ Wat Khlong Thom Nua Museum
พิพิธภัณฑ์คลองท่อมเหนือ

Road Map C5. 26 miles (42 km) SE of Krabi. *i* TAT, Krabi (0-7562-2163). **Open** 8:30am–4:30pm daily.

Southeast of Krabi along Highway 4, the small town of Khlong Thom is the site of one of the earliest human civilizations in Thailand yet discovered. Excavations in this town, set amid rice paddies and orchards, have revealed stone and bronze tools, metal coins, shards of pottery, and colored beads dating back almost five millennia. These exhibits are now on display in the Wat Khlong Thom Nua Museum in Tambon Khlong Thom Tai, about half a mile from the Khlong Thom district office. Ideal for history lovers, the museum is popular with visitors to the area.

⑪ Khao Nor Chuchi Wildlife Sanctuary
เขตรักษาพันธุ์สัตว์ป่าเขานอจู้จี้

Road Map C5. 38 miles (60 km) SE of Krabi. 🚌 *i* TAT, Krabi (0-7562-2163). **Open** 8am–5pm daily. 🅿

One of the largest and most important wildlife sanctuaries in the Krabi province, Khao Nor Chuchi Wildlife Sanctuary lies to the southeast of Krabi town in a small area of lowland tropical forest. This area, which extends to nearly 71 sq miles (184 sq km), is surrounded by lush green rice paddies, palm oil and rubber plantations, and other arable crops. Popular with bird-watchers, the Khao Nor Chuchi Wildlife Sanctuary is home to the Gurney's pitta, an endangered species once thought to be extinct, but rediscovered in very small numbers both here and across the border in remote parts of southern Myanmar. Other resident birds include the vernal hanging parrot and the Chinese pond heron. There are several wooded walking trails within the forest, the most popular being the 2-mile (3-km) long **Tung Tieo Forest Trail**. This trail winds through the thick woods, leading to two freshwater pools, one of which is called Sra Morakot, or Emerald Pool. These pools are ideal for swimming and make great picnic spots.

Wooded Tung Tieo Forest Trail, Khao Nor Chuchi Wildlife Sanctuary

⑫ Ko Si Boya
เกาะสีบอยา

Road Map B5. 19 miles (31 km) S of Krabi. 🚕 1,000. 🚌 🚢 from Ban Laem Kruat. *i* TAT, Krabi (0-7562-2163). 🚲 📷

Located just off the Krabi coast and accessible by boat from Ban Laem Kruat, Ko Si Boya is an escape-from-it-all retreat. Of the 1,000 people living on the island, most are local Muslims working as fishermen or on rubber plantations. There are about five small settlements on the island, all connected by narrow, unpaved tracks, ideal for bicycling or walking. The

Taking a refreshing dip in the freshwater pool, Sra Morakot, Khao Nor Chuchi Wildlife Sanctuary

For hotels and restaurants in this region see pp300–301 and pp316–17

main attractions, however, are the isolated, undeveloped beaches and mangrove forests. The island offers a few simple and reasonably priced bungalows, and some restaurants and shops. Ko Si Boya has little to offer by way of nightlife, but visitors have plenty of quieter options to choose from – swimming, sun-bathing, reading, or relaxing. There is limited electricity on the island and almost every bungalow establishment has its own generator-powered electricity supply. Snorkeling enthusiasts can kayak to a small island called Ko Kah just offshore from Ko Si Boya, where the clear waters make snorkeling an exciting and rewarding experience.

Expansive green cover on isolated Ko Si Boya

the best beaches are on its western shore. Visitors to Ko Jum must remember to dress appropriately on the beach, keeping in mind the sentiments of the resident Muslims.

More developed than Ko Si Boya, Ko Jum has better accom-modation facilities, although electricity supply on this island too is limited. Most bungalows manage their own supply through generators. An island getaway without the touts and go-go bars, Ko Jum's low-key attractions include swimming, reading, and sunbathing during the day and enjoying a quiet meal and drinks at one of the few beachside bars at night. Transport around the island is by foot, bicycle, or on hired motorcycle taxis.

Brightly colored longtail boat docked in the waters off Ko Jum

⓭ Ko Jum
เกาะจำ

Road Map B5. 24 miles (39 km) S of Krabi. 🚶 3,000. 🚌 🚢 from Ban Laem Kruat. ℹ TAT, Krabi (0-7562-2163). 🚗 📅 ☑ kohjumonline.com

Yet another quiet retreat, the beautiful island of Ko Jum is divided into two, with the mountainous and rugged northern part being referred to as Ko Pu, or Crab Island, by the locals. Ko Jum, with its small population of 3,000, has an overwhelming majority of Thai Muslims, although there are also some small and isolated sea gypsy settlements. The main settlement is at Ban Ko Jum on the island's southern tip, while

⓮ Ko Bubu
เกาะบูบู

Road Map C5. 44 miles (70 km) SE of Krabi. 🚢 from Ko Lanta. ℹ TAT, Krabi (0-7562-2163). 🚗

A privately owned islet covered by thick woods and little more than half a mile (1 km) across, Ko Bubu can be easily traversed in about half an hour on foot. This pretty island, however, is closed during the height of the rainy season from June to September. Ko Bubu's only resort, Bubu Island Resort, offers basic albeit comfortable accom-modations in its bungalows, as well as simple food. Longtail boats are available from Ko Lanta (see pp264–7), but reservations must be made in advance.

Bubu Island Resort, set in thick woods on the private islet of Ko Bubu

⑮ Ko Lanta

เกาะลันตา

A group of 50 islets dominated by two main islands – Ko Lanta Yai, or Big Ko Lanta, and Ko Lanta Noi, or Small Ko Lanta – Ko Lanta has only recently developed as a holiday spot. An erstwhile destination for hippies and backpackers, the island is now rapidly becoming an upscale resort. On offer are miles of sandy beaches, sapphire waters, reasonably priced accommodations, and good restaurants and watering holes. While Ko Lanta Noi remains largely deserted for the present, by comparison the more developed island of Ko Lanta Yai has a good surfaced road which runs down most of the island's western coast. Although the eastern coast, with thick forests and mangrove swamps, is less accessible, it is a great place for bird-watching and kayaking.

Main street in Ban Sala Dan, packed with tour agents and utility stores

Ban Sala Dan

บ้านศาลาด่าน

Located near the northern tip of Ko Lanta Yai, Ban Sala Dan is the main town in the Ko Lanta archipelago. The ferry arrival and departure point for destinations such as Ko Phi Phi, Phuket, Krabi, and Trang, boats also leave here for island-hopping day trips, the highlight of which is usually Ko Muk's exciting Emerald Cave (see p270). Ban Sala Dan is also the main tourist center for the entire district. Visitors will find a number of tour agencies, vehicle rentals, banks, ATMs, medical clinics and pharmacies, Internet cafés, and shops here, along with a post office, reasonable accommodations, and restaurants. Even so, few people opt to stay in Ban Sala Dan, preferring to relax on the long row of beaches further south, and coming to the village only for necessities.

🏖 Hat Khlong Dao

หาดคลองดาว

1 mile (2 km) S of Ban Sala Dan.

The longest and most popular beach on Ko Lanta, Hat Khlong Dao is blessed with golden sands that rise into low, vegetation-covered dunes. The beach itself is wide and a perfect place for sunbathing and swimming, which is quite safe here. Hat Khlong Dao, relatively uncrowded and friendly, draws vacationing families seeking a relaxing stay within walking distance from town. There are plenty of mid-range as well as some budget accommodations available, and the beach strip is home to numerous restaurants, cafés, and small bars. While there are no diving or snorkeling opportunities in the immediate vicinity of the beach, dive shops at Hat Khlong Dao arrange

diving trips offshore, as well as visits to the area's many mangrove forests and local *chao lae* or sea gypsy communities.

🏖 Ao Phra-Ae

อ่าวพระแอะ

2 miles (3 km) S of Ban Sala Dan.

Located just south of Hat Khlong Dao, beyond a small headland, the beach at Ao Phra-Ae is 3 miles (5 km) long. Blessed with crisp white sand and backed by casuarina trees, it was once a backpackers' retreat. Today, however, Ao Phra-Ae is well developed and quite similar to Hat Khlong Dao, although a longer walk from Ban Sala Dan. The beach offers inexpensive accommodations, guesthouses, restaurants, and cafés for the budget traveler. However, more upscale resorts are under construction here. Ao Phra-Ae can be easily reached on hired *songthaews* that ply the route on the island's west coast road, running behind the row of casuarina trees marking the end of the beach. Motorcycles and bicycles are also available at rental shops near the beach.

🏖 Hat Khlong Khong

หาดคลองโขง

4 miles (6 km) S of Ban Sala Dan.

A fine stretch of crisp white sand, Hat Khlong Khong is nearly 3 miles (5 km) long. Located close to two small fishing villages, Ban Phu Klom and Ban Khlong Khong, the beach is ideal for budget

Beautiful beach at Ao Phra-Ae, fringed by palms and swaying casuarina trees

One of the Viewpoint Hill restaurants, offering lovely views of the area

travelers, as it offers cheap bungalow accommodations and simple, friendly bars and restaurants. At the same time, its distance from Ban Sala Dan ensures the beach's tranquility. While Hat Khlong Khong is perfect for sunbathing, the offshore waters are rather shallow and rocky, and only suitable for swimming during high tide. There are also good snorkeling opportunities when the tide is in.

Viewpoint Hill
จุดชมวิว
6 miles (10 km) SE of Ban Sala Dan.

Set in the middle of Ko Lanta Yai, close to its geographical center, Viewpoint Hill marks the highest point on the island. It is reached by the road running between Hat Khlong Nin on the west coast and **Ban Si Raya** on the east coast. The views from this vantage point are stunning; they encompass the mangrove-fringed east coast of

Ko Lanta Yai as well as the many smaller islets scattered across **Ko Lanta Marine National Park** (see p267) and the Trang (see p268) coastline in the distance. Viewpoint Hill is a popular spot to watch mesmerizing sunrises and sunsets over the Andaman Sea. Visitors can enjoy a meal while taking in panoramic views across the sea at any of the two picturesquely located Viewpoint Hill restaurants nearby.

Hat Khlong Nin
หาดคลองนิล
6 miles (10 km) S of Ban Sala Dan.

A delightful stretch of beach with soft white sand, Hat Khlong Nin has a distinct appeal for youngsters. The beach is lined with palm trees, casuarinas, and the occasional frangipani. Although less developed than the beaches to the north of Ko Lanta, Hat Khlong Hin offers reasonably priced accommodations and food. The nightlife, focused on a number of small and unpretentious bars playing music till late, draws revelers to the beach. Swimming is safe here and visitors often stay at Hat Khlong Nin for days at a time, alternating between regular beach activities and attending one of several Thai cooking schools operating in the area.

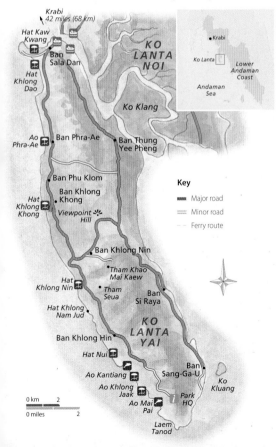

Krabi
42 miles (68 km)
Hat Kaw Kwang
Ban Sala Dan
Hat Khlong Dao
KO LANTA NOI
Krabi
Ko Lanta
Lower Andaman Coast
Andaman Sea
Ko Klang
Ao Phra-Ae
Ban Phra-Ae
Ban Thung Yee Pheng
Ban Phu Klom
Ban Khlong Khong
Hat Khlong Khong
Viewpoint Hill

Key
━━ Major road
═══ Minor road
- - Ferry route

Ban Khlong Nin
Tham Khao Mai Kaew
Hat Khlong Nin
Tham Seua
Ban Si Raya
Hat Khlong Nam Jud
KO LANTA YAI
Ban Khlong Hin
Hat Nui
Ao Kantiang
Ban Sang-Ga-U
Ko Kluang
Ao Khlong Jaak
Park HQ
Ao Mai Pai
Laem Tanod

0 km   2
0 miles   2

Sunbathing on quiet but well-equipped Hat Khlong Nin

For keys to symbols see back flap

Exploring the jungle trail to Tham Khao Mai Kaew

Tham Khao Mai Kaew

ถ้ำเขาไม้แก้ว

7 miles (11 km) SE of Ban Sala Dan.

Located in the wooded interior of Ko Lanta Yai, Tham Khao Mai Kaew is a complex of caverns and tunnels. The caves are reached by a 1-mile (2-km) long narrow track leading east through a rubber plantation on the road between Hat Khlong Nin and Ban Si Raya. The cave complex is extensive and potentially confusing, and can only be explored with the help of a guide. There are chambers filled with stalactites and stalagmites; small cavities which can be reached only by crawling on all fours; and a cave pool that offers a cool dip. Visitors have a choice of 1- or 2-hour tours. The tour operator in charge of the caves also offers half-day and full-day jungle treks in the area.

Tham Seua

ถ้ำเสือ

7 miles (11 km) SE of Ban Sala Dan.

A smaller and less visited cave complex, Tham Seua, or Tiger Cave, is located about 1 mile (2 km) east of the coastal road between Hat Khlong Nin and Laem Tanod. The caves can be reached by a narrow trail that also leads to the headquarters of the Ko Lanta Marine National Park. Since Tham Seua is not as well organized as nearby Tham Khao Mai Kaew, visitors are free to wander through the passages at will, where several caves with stalactites, stalagmites, and still pools wait to be explored. The interior of the caves is quite cool, making them an excellent place to visit during the heat of the day.

Hat Nui

หาดนุ้ย

10 miles (16 km) S of Ban Sala Dan.

An attractive and fairly isolated beach, Hat Nui, also known as Hat Khlong Nui, is located along Ko Lanta Yai's west coast, south of Hat Khlong Nin and the junction east leading to Viewpoint Hill and Ban Si Raya. The beach is distinguished by the ecologically conscious Narima Bungalow Resort *(see p301)*. The buildings in the resort are all constructed from local, natural materials and have a quaint, rustic feel. Lush tropical jungle sweeps down to the beach from the hills behind, providing an idyllic setting for a quiet holiday.

An upscale resort nestled among the trees at Ao Kantiang

Ao Kantiang

อ่าวกันเตียง

11 miles (18 km) S of Ban Sala Dan.

A lovely bay with a perfect white sand beach, Ao Kantiang is home to a number of upscale resorts which fight for space with other more reasonably priced budget accommodations. Although some distance away from Ban Sala Dan, Ao Kantiang is well equipped with facilities, varying from travel agencies and Internet access to motorcycle and jeep rentals. The casuarina-lined beach also has a good selection of restaurants as well as a few bars. While the beach and the bay are ideal for sunbathing and swimming, there is also a small coral reef near the northern end of the bay considered quite good for snorkeling, especially when the tide is in. These are the only activities to indulge in, other than relaxing on the beach, observing the sunset, and enjoying a chilled drink.

Ao Khlong Jaak

อ่าวคลองจาก

12 miles (19 km) S of Ban Sala Dan.

South of Ao Kantiang the surfaced road that runs down the island's west flank deteriorates rapidly, becoming a rutted track that is difficult to negotiate even on a two-wheeler, especially during the

A restaurant perched on a cliff overlooking the sea at Hat Nui

For hotels and restaurants in this region see pp300–301 and pp316–17

rainy season, when the unpaved roads can get very slippery. The bay south of Ao Kantiang, known as Ao Khlong Jaak, offers a varied selection of accommodations – from upscale resorts to simple places suited for those on a modest budget. It is rather off the beaten track, but readily accessible by boat from Ban Sala Dan and other points north along the coast. Ao Khlong Jaak is a good place for getting away from it all. A stay here is usually a rejuvenating and relaxing experience with little activity. The days largely involve going for a drink in a sundowner bar, followed by stargazing from the white, sandy beach.

Getting ready for kayaking on the beach at Ao Khlong Jaak

🏖 Ao Mai Pai
อ่าวไม้ไผ่

13 miles (21 km) S of Ban Sala Dan.
🏍 🏕

The southernmost beach on Ko Lanta Yai, Ao Mai Pai marks the end of the unsurfaced and rutted track leading toward the southern part of the island. A little distance inland are the headquarters for the Ko Lanta Marine National Park. The beach here is beautiful, more so because it is not too busy. An offshore coral reef, great for snorkeling especially during high tide, makes up for the lack of other activities on the beach. Ao Mai Pai offers good mid-range resort accommodations and some more reasonably priced bungalows. The shady beach lined with palms, casuarinas, and screwpine is ideal for sunbathing and taking in views across the Andaman Sea.

Ban Si Raya
บ้านศรีรายา

12 miles (19 km) SE of Ban Sala Dan.
🏍 🏕

A surprisingly attractive village, Ban Si Raya, or Old Lanta Town, is the oldest settlement in Ko Lanta, predating Ban Sala Dan by many decades. Once a marine staging post for British flagged ships sailing between Phuket, Penang, and Singapore, the town has hardly kept up with the rapid development elsewhere on the island. It retains a period charm and not much has changed here since the mid-1990s. Nevertheless, a steady trickle of visitors has necessitated the renovation and restoration of its Chinese-style shophouses. There is a small Chinese shrine facing the sea halfway down the main street, and the mosques nearby stand testimony to the presence of a thriving Thai-Muslim community. A few guesthouses cater to visitors staying overnight, but the real appeal lies in the restaurants and bars that have begun to spring up.

Snorkeling in the clear waters off pretty Ko Rok Nok

⑯ Ko Lanta Marine National Park
พิพิธภัณฑ์ทางทะเลเกาะลันตา

Road Map B5. Park HQ 5 miles (8 km) S of Hat Nui, 44 miles (70 km) S of Krabi. 🚌 🛥 *i* Park HQ (0-7562-9018). 🏍 🏕

Extending over 152 sq miles (394 sq km), Ko Lanta Marine National Park includes the southern tip of Ko Lanta Yai, parts of Ko Lanta Noi, and 15 smaller islands and reefs. Other islands in the park include **Ko Rok Nai** and **Ko Rok Nok**, 31 miles (50 km) south of Ko Lanta Yai; Ko Talabaeng to the east of Ko Lanta Noi, with its limestone caves ideal for sea-kayaking; and tiny Ko Ha.

Ko Rok Nok, or Outer Rok Island, and Ko Rok Nai, or Inner Rok Island, are well offshore and best visited as a day trip from Ko Lanta Yai by speedboat. They can also be visited from Trang's Pak Meng pier. The islands are blessed with tropical forest and fine beaches. Visitors can explore the forested interiors and waterfalls, and snorkel over the coral reefs. The fauna and flora include a variety of birds, reptiles, and fish. The reefs off the island are home to beautiful staghorn and starflower corals.

Diving enthusiasts can also head to **Hin Daeng** and **Hin Muang**, two excellent dive sites just 16 miles (26 km) southwest of Ko Rok known for their colorful soft corals.

Tranquil beach lined with shady casuarinas and screwpine trees at Ao Mai Pai

Ferries and boats lined up at the jetty to take visitors to nearby islands, Hat Pak Meng

⓱ Trang

ตรัง

Road Map C5. 82 miles (132 km) SE of Krabi. 🚉 150,000. ✈ 3 miles (5 km) S of Trang. 🚌 🚐 🚆 ℹ TAT, Trang (0-7521-5867). 🏪 daily. 🎎 Vegetarian Festival (Oct).

A trading center since the 1st century AD, Trang grew to prosperity between the 7th and 13th centuries under the Srivijaya rulers. Capital of Trang province, today it is still an important commercial town with rubber, palm oil, and fishing as the mainstays of its economy. Tourism is also becoming an important industry as the beaches, islands, and mountains of this area are becoming popular. Trang has a strong ethnic character due to an influx of migrant labor from China in the latter half of the 19th century. There are some very good Chinese cafés here – a testament to the ancestry of the locals. The architecture in the town is a combination of Western and Sino-Thai designs and includes shophouses as well as Chinese temples. A number of food markets add to the local color. There is a statue dedicated to Khaw Sim Bee Na-Ranong – the much-revered governor of Trang who adopted the title of Phraya Ratsadanupradit. The area is also famous for its Vegetarian Festival.

Chinese architectural motif

Trang's Vegetarian Festival

People thronging the streets during Vegetarian Festival

Trang's long association with southern China, and the Chinese heritage of many of its inhabitants, manifests itself in the annual Vegetarian Festival, held on a full-moon night at the beginning of October. On this occasion, Sino-Thai locals dress in white, and turn vegetarian for nine days to make merit and earn good fortune. Ascetics parade through the town with their followers, accepting offerings from devotees to the accompaniment of drums, cymbals, and firecrackers. They demonstrate extraordinary scenes of self-mortification including body piercing, self-flagellation, walking on fire, and other such feats while possessed by religious fervor. The resulting injuries from these acts are surprisingly minimal.

Environs
Located 14 miles (22 km) southwest of Trang, **Kantang** is the historical site indicating the site of the first rubber tree that was ever planted in Thailand. Visitors can also stop by to see the historical mansion of governer Khaw Sim Bee Na-Ranong.

⓲ Hat Pak Meng

หาดปากเม็ง

Road Map C5. Along Hwy 4162, 25 miles (40 km) W of Trang. 🚐 🚤 ℹ TAT, Trang (0-7521- 5867). 🤿 🏕

A curved stretch of sand, Hat Pak Meng is a peaceful beach with decent accommodations and restaurants that are famous for spicy seafood. Hat Pak Meng is best known as the embarkation point for nearby **Ko Hai** *(see p270)*, a beautiful and deserted island about 30 minutes by longtail boat. The jetty at the northern end of the beach has several travel agencies that organize both snorkeling and boat tours.

⓳ Hat Chang Lang

หาดฉางหลาง

Road Map C5. 28 miles (45 km) SW of Trang town. 🚐 ℹ TAT, Trang (0-7521-5867). 🤿 🏕

Casuarina-lined Hat Chang Lang is a long and beautiful stretch of white sand. The southern end of the beach houses the headquarters for the Hat Chao Mai National Park. The accommodations on this beach are mostly upscale. The Anantara Si Kao near the northern end of the beach is one of the more exclusive resorts in Trang province. However, there are cheaper accommodation options further down the beach. Hat Chang Lang also offers a range of watersports which include sea-kayaking, deep-sea fishing, and windsurfing. Hat Chang Lang is also famous for its oysters; visitors should try the local seafood restaurants scattered along the beach.

A group of sea-kayakers in the waters off Hat Yao

⑳ Hat Chao Mai National Park

พิพิธภัณฑสถานแห่งชาติหาดเจ้าไหม

Road Map C5. Park HQ Hat Chang Lang, 29 miles (47 km) SW of Trang town. 🚌 ℹ️ Park HQ (0-7521-3260). **Open** 6am–6pm daily. 🚫 📷 🌐 dnp.go.th

Established in 1982, the Hat Chao Mai National Park covers an area of 89 sq miles (231 sq km). Located to the west of Trang, the coastal landscape of the park includes mangrove creeks, coastal karsts, and hidden coves. The main beach, Hat Chao Mai, is backed by limestone outcrops with a series of historical caves. These caves have been found to house various prehistoric remains. The most notable

among these caves is **Tham Chao Mai**, a large marine cave filled with stalagmites. These can be easily reached by longtail boat. Nine offshore islands are also protected under this park and include Ko Kradan and Ko Muk *(see p270)*.

Dugongs can sometimes be spotted in the surrounding waters; the park is also home to otters, dolphins, langurs, and wild boars. The best time to visit Hat Chao Mai National Park is during the cool season from November to February.

㉑ Hat Yong Ling

หาดหยงหลิง

Road Map C5. Hat Chao Mai National Park. 🚌 ℹ️ TAT, Trang (0-7521-5867). 🚫 📷

Located immediately south of Hat Chang Lang on the Trang coast is Hat Yong Ling. The two beaches are separated by a jetty

that serves nearby Ko Muk in the Hat Chao Mai National Park. Hat Yong Ling is a curved white-sand beach backed by a pine forest, with rocky outcrops at either end. The larger of these outcrops is pierced with numerous caves and entrances that can be explored on foot at low tide, or by boat, or by swimming during high tide. Some caves lead to small, hidden, and often very beautiful beaches, with low sand dunes forming private nooks. There is nothing much by way of accommodations at this unfrequented spot, and other facilities or places to eat and drink are similarly minimal. Visitors can use the services provided by the Hat Chao Mai National Park headquarters at Hat Chang Lang.

㉒ Hat Yao

หาดยาว

Road Map C5. Hat Chao Mai National Park. 🚌 ℹ️ TAT, Trang (0-7521-5867). 🚫 📷

Continuing south from Hat Yong Ling, the 3-mile (5-km) long Hat Yao, or Long Beach, is a perfect camping spot. The beach, lined with casuarinas and pines, is mostly deserted on weekdays. However, this long and pristine strip of white sand is gradually undergoing development and some bungalow accommodations, as well as a few restaurants and bars, have begun to appear. The warm waters here are ideal for swimming.

Thin strip of beach bordered by casuarinas at Hat Chao Mai National Park

Beautiful resort with a private beach on the island of Ko Hai

㉓ Ko Hai
เกาะไหง

Road Map C5. 36 miles (58 km) SW of Trang. ⛴ from Pak Meng pier. 🛈 TAT, Trang-Satun (0-7521-5867). 🔗📷

A tiny, beautiful island off the southwest coast of Trang, Ko Hai, also known as Ko Ngai, is a verdant, tropical island with just about all the right elements – a shady, green interior, lovely white powdery sand, warm, shallow waters, and excellent coral reefs close to the shore and swarming with fish. It is both possible and pleasant to stay on Ko Hai, but there are no budget range accommodations available. Visitors must be prepared for mid-range prices, but good-quality bungalows and restaurants make this little island an ideal place for families

with children. Apart from sunbathing, swimming, or just relaxing in a hammock, visitors can go sea-kayaking and snorkeling. It is also possible to arrange snorkeling and diving tours to isolated Ko Rok Nok (see p267), about 19 miles (31 km) southwest of Ko Hai, through tour agents on the island.

㉔ Ko Muk
เกาะมุกต์

Road Map C5. Hat Chao Mai National Park. ⛴ from Pak Meng pier. 🛈 TAT, Trang-Satun (0-7521-5867). 🔗📷

Once a remote backpackers' retreat, Ko Muk, or Pearl Island, can be accessed from Ko Lanta and the mainland Kuan Tunku pier. Inhabited by a handful of chao lae (sea gypsies), stunning

Ko Muk, part of the Hat Chao Mai National Park, is becoming an upscale destination. The main beach on the island, **Hat Sai Yao**, is the principal visitors' attraction with white sands and warm waters, which are safe for swimming. There are some good mid-range resorts and restaurants here. Nearby, **Tham Morakot**, or Emerald Cave, is another major local attraction. Visitors have to swim a short distance, at high tide, through a water-filled cavern – part of which lies in virtual darkness – to reach a hong or underwater cave. This cave is otherwise shut off from the outside world. The only other access to the tunnel is over the top of the collapsed dome, which allows sunlight into the depths below. Boats can also enter the lagoon, which has a small beach, at low tide. The east coast, however, is undeveloped and remains the domain of local fisherfolk.

㉕ Ko Kradan
เกาะกระดาน

Road Map C5. Hat Chao Mai National Park. ⛴ from Pak Meng pier. 🛈 TAT, Trang-Satun (0-7521-5867). 🔗📷

A gorgeous island easily accessible by boat from the Pak Meng pier, Ko Kradan is indeed one of the pearls of the Andaman Sea. A part of the Hat Chao Mai National Park, the interior of the island is a mix of

Visitors starting the swim through the dark tunnel of Tham Morakot

dense tropical jungle and rubber plantations, there are fine coral reefs just offshore, offering excellent snorkeling opportunities. A couple of sunken Japanese ships from the World War II era offer another exciting diving site in the waters off the island. Ko Kradan is less developed than Ko Muk, but this may change given the increasing popularity of these offshore islands. At present, however, there are no upscale resorts here, only a couple of bungalow establishments, although camping is permitted. Visitors can also use the Kuan Tunku pier to get here.

㉖ Ko Libong

เกาะลิบง

Road Map B5. 8 miles (13 km) SW of Ko Kradan. **Tel** 0-7525-1932 (Libong Archipelago Wildlife Reserve). 🚌 from Pak Meng pier. 🛈 TAT, Trang-Satun (0-7521-5867). 🛥️ 📷

Lying further to the east than Ko Muk and Ko Kradan, Ko Libong is larger than both and can also be accessed from the nearby Chao Mai pier. Ko Libong so far remains untouched by the hectic commercial activity which seems to have swept across most of the country, and is home to several small Thai-Muslim fishing communities. The main beach on the island is at Ban Maphrao, on the island's east coast. There are several mid-range resorts here, along with a handful of restaurants, small cafés, and bars. While activities such as

Couple showing their marriage license during an underwater wedding

Ko Kradan's Underwater Weddings

Underwater weddings have been taking place in Trang on Valentine's Day each year since 1996. Although begun in a small way, by 2000 it had become a mass event, with groups of Thais and foreigners marrying underwater. The main venue for this event is Ko Kradan. The island entered the *Guinness Book of Records* in 2000 for hosting the largest underwater wedding in the world. Groups of around 40 couples in diving gear swim a short distance to an underwater altar where they are married by a local official, also in dive gear. This event is now part of the Trang Season of Love. Before the ceremony, the brides and grooms sail along the coast in a flotilla of boats. Couples must have PADI diving licenses, or allow some time for the organizers on Ko Kradan to teach them the basics of diving.

swimming and snorkeling keep visitors busy, another attraction is the rich and varied wildlife of the island, under the aegis of the **Libong Archipelago Wildlife Reserve.** Here, explorers will find mangrove swamps and also get a chance to see the endangered dugong, also known as the sea cow. Conservationists estimate that there may be as many as 20 pairs of dugongs breeding in the vicinity. Sea kayaks with guides are available for those who wish to see them in their natural habitat.

㉗ Ko Sukorn

เกาะสุกร

Road Map C5. 14 miles (22 km) SE of Ko Libong. 🚌 from Tasae pier. 🛈 TAT, Trang-Satun (0-7521-5867). 🛥️ 📷

To the east of Ko Libong, just off Laem Tasae and easily accessible by boat from Tasae pier, Ko Sukorn is another gem of the Trang Coast. Smaller than Ko Libong, and more densely populated, the island is home to a community of about 2,500 Thai-Muslims, mainly fishing families and farmers growing coconuts, rice, and rubber. The island has simple bungalow accommodations, as well as shops, restaurants, and cafés, but no upscale resorts. The electricity supply is erratic, and usually limited at night. The locals on the island are friendly but conservative Muslims, whose main income comes from fish and lobster farming. Visitors can go swimming or snorkeling, or even explore the island on hired bicycles. Ko Sukorn can also be accessed from the Pak Meng pier.

Longtail boats of local fishermen anchored at the pier in Ko Sukorn

㉘ Ko Phetra Marine National Park
อุทยานแห่งชาติเกาะเภตรา

Road Map C6. Park HQ off Hwy 416, 48 miles (77 km) S of Trang. **ⓘ** Park HQ (0-7478-3074). 🚌 from Pak Bara. 🏊 🚲 📷 **W** dnp.go.th

Extending across the maritime territory of both Trang and Satun provinces, Ko Phetra Marine National Park comprises more than 30 islands, including the main island of Ko Phetra, which is also the largest in the group. Established in 1984, the park covers nearly 193 sq miles (500 sq km) of marine territory. Almost all the islands are made up of interesting limestone formations. Several of them are frequented by sea turtles during the egg-laying season. The cliffs are home to great colonies of bats and swiftlets. Rich coral reefs surround the islands and are ideal diving sites. The clear waters around the park also support numerous marine species, including the dugong, numerous colorful fish, and starfish. Although it is a national park, this is also an economically viable fishing zone with plenty of crabs, lobsters, and squid. On the islands, the vegetation is generally dense; there are mangroves as well as lush rainforests. Overnight visitors can stay at the park's lodges at Ko Li Di, or at the park headquarters on the mainland. Camping is also allowed in some places.

Common starfish

Idyllic stretch of sand bordered by turquoise waters, Ko Bulon Leh

㉙ Pak Bara
ปากบารา

Road Map C6. 34 miles (55 km) S of Trang. 🚌 🚌 🚌 **ⓘ** TAT, Trang-Satun (0-7521-5867). Ko Tarutao Park HQ (0-7478-3485).

A small seaside town and fishing village, Pak Bara is less a tourist destination and more a jumping-off point for Ko Phetra Marine National Park and Ko Tarutao Marine National Park *(see pp274–9)*. The park headquarters for Ko Phetra Marine National Park is located 3 km (2 miles) from Pak Bara. A visitors' center for Ko Tarutao is also located in this town. However, the town is a pleasant stopover with reasonable accommodation options, good seafood restaurants, and bars. A number of dive shops and travel agencies have been established to serve visitors. They can also arrange sea-kayaking tours in the surrounding waters.

㉚ Ko Bulon Leh
เกาะบุโหลนเล

Road Map C6. 24 miles (38 km) W of Pak Bara. 🚌 from Pak Bara. **ⓘ** TAT, Trang-Satun (0-7521-5867). 🚲 📷

A tiny yet lovely island, Ko Bulon Leh is becoming popular as an offbeat holiday destination with beautiful white-sand beaches and crystal-clear waters. Once a backpackers' hangout, the facilities on the island are turning increasingly upscale as commercial development is already underway. The main beach lies along **Ao Mamuang** or Mango Bay. A small *chao lae* community *(see p208)* lives in the northern part of the island. The local economy depends on fishing and coconut and rubber farming. Visitors can enjoy swimming and snorkeling among the offshore coral reefs. Ko Bulon Leh is best reached by boats that run daily from Pak Bara.

㉛ Satun
สตูล

Road Map C6. 71 miles (115 km) SE of Pak Bara. 🚐 22,000. 🚌 🚌 🚌 **ⓘ** TAT, Trang-Satun (0-7521-5867). 🚢 daily.

A quiet town near the Malaysian border, with boat services to Penang and the Langkawi archipelago, Satun – capital of the Satun province – has the highest Muslim population in Thailand: about 80 percent of the population. Yet Satun is different from the other Muslim majority towns of Pattani

Passengers at Pak Bara waiting to take ferries to nearby national parks

(see p288), Yala, and Narathiwat *(see p289)*. While these latter follow traditional orthodox Islamic practices, Satun is far more culturally and socially liberal; fundamentalist Islam or separatism does not enjoy any support here. This makes Satun the most laid-back of the Muslim-dominated provinces.

The town has quite a few attractions including the **Satung Friday Mosque**, also known as Masayit Mambang, built in Malay-Muslim style with a minaret and dome, and decorated with glazed tiles, glass, and marble. It also has a library in its basement. Housed in a fine Sino-Portuguese-style mansion, the **Satun National Museum** was the residence of the former governor of Satun. This two-story building has a collection of artifacts showcasing the local history and culture. Another important monument is **Wat Chanathipchaloem**, the town's first Buddhist temple, dating back 200 years. The entrance is guarded by two *yakshas* (nature spirits). The *wat* has a distinctive two-story *ubosot* – the first story is a preaching hall and the second is used for religious practices. The **Po Je Kang Chinese Temple** and the bustling fresh food market are other worthwhile sights. Visitors can also try the local cuisine, which is an interesting blend of Malaysian, Thai, Chinese, and Muslim styles.

The colorful façade of Po Je Kang Chinese Temple, Satun

🏛 **Satun National Museum**
Soi 5, Satun Thani Rd. **Tel** 0-7472-3140. **Open** 9am–4pm Wed–Sun. 📷

🔱 **Wat Chanathipchaloem**
Sulakanukoon Rd, Tambon Phiman. **Tel** 0-7471-1996. **Open** 8am–4pm

❸❷ Thale Ban National Park
อุทยานแห่งชาติทะเลบัน

Road Map C6. Park HQ off Hwy 4184, 23 miles (37 km) E of Satun. 🚌 ℹ Park HQ (0-7475-0390). ⬛ 📷 🖥 dnp.go.th

A lush expanse of tropical rain forest, Thale Ban National Park was established in 1980. The park extends over the Banthat Mountains near the Malaysian border, covering an area of 76 sq miles (196 sq km). Located around a valley, Thale Ban has several waterfalls and its limestone hills are dotted with caves. It is home to a variety of wildlife such as tapir, serow, barking deer, fishing cats, and sun bears. Visitors can see rare birds such as bat hawks, which feed on bats and other small prey, consuming them whole in midair. The park's marked trails lead to several pools and two waterfalls – the nine-level **Nam Tok Ya Roy**, 3 miles (5 km) north of the park headquarters, and **Nam Tok Ton Piew**, 6 miles (10 km) north of the park headquarters. There are bungalow accommodations, a campground, and a restaurant. Satun acts as a gateway to the park.

Walkway leading to the quaint viewing platform near headquarters of Thale Ban National Park

㉝ Ko Tarutao Marine National Park

อุทยานแห่งชาติตะรุเตา

Designated as Thailand's second marine national park in 1974, Ko Tarutao comprises 51 islands. Named after the largest island in the group, which is also the site of the park headquarters, Ko Tarutao is part of an ecologically rich area also comprising Malaysia's Langkawi islands, located 5 miles (3 km) to the south. World famous for its pristine diving sites, rich marine life, and outstanding beauty, this 575 sq mile (1,489 sq km) area is home to an incredible variety of flora and fauna. With olive ridley and hawksbill turtles, langurs, several species of squirrels, 25 percent of the world's tropical fish species, and over 100 varieties of birds, Ko Tarutao is a haven for wildlife enthusiasts.

Lower Andaman Coast
Andaman Sea
Pak Bara
Ko Tarutao Marine National Park

Key

☐ Area illustrated

★ Ko Rawi
An ideal spot for snorkeling, beautiful Ko Rawi remains relatively uninhabited. It is blessed with fine beaches, rich coral reefs, and a densely jungled interior.

Lovers' Gate at Ko Khai
The work of wind and waves over millennia, Lovers' Gate is a naturally carved limestone arch, now a famous symbol representing the marine national park.

Ko Bulon Leh
17 miles (27 km)

Ko Klang
Ko Khai
Ko Ta Nga

Ko Rawi
Ko Adang
Ko Yang
Pirate Waterfall
Ko Butang
Ko Dong
Ko Sakai
Ko Hin Ngam
Laem Son
Tammalang
50 miles (80 km)
Ko Sarang
Ko Lipe
Ko Tarang
Hat Pattaya

KEY

① **Ko Adang**, a picturesque isle covered with verdant rainforest, is surrounded by rich coral reefs.

② **Laem Tanyong Hara**, the scenic northernmost point of the park, makes a great swimming spot.

③ **Nam Tok Lu Du**, a lovely picnic spot, is well-known for its refreshing water.

★ Ko Lipe
Small Ko Lipe has emerged as the focus of development in Ko Tarutao. Ko Lipe has a great selection of resorts and restaurants, and offers a variety of activities.

For hotels and restaurants in this region see pp300–301 and pp316–17

Sea Turtles
Four different species of sea turtle – green, hawksbill, olive ridley, and leatherback – find protection in the park. Ao Son, on Ko Tarutao, is a favored breeding and nesting ground for turtles.

VISITORS' CHECKLIST

Practical Information
Road Map C6. Park HQ 51 miles (82 km) W of Satun. ℹ️ Park HQ (0-7478-3485 or 0-7478-3597). 🗺️

Transport
🚤 from Pak Bara; regular crossings mid-Nov to mid-Apr only.

Jungle Treks
Trekking along nature trails makes for an interesting and rewarding alternative to a day at the beach. Trekkers will see an amazing variety of birds and animals.

Key

-- Trail

— Ferry route

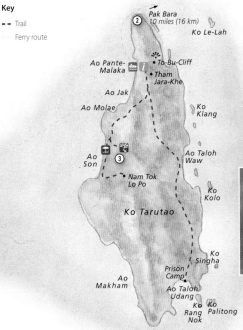

Pak Bara
10 miles (16 km)
Ko Le-Lah
To-Bu-Cliff
Ao Pante-Malaka
Tham Jara-Khe
Ao Jak
Ao Molae
Ko Klang
Ao Son
Ao Taloh Waw
Nam Tok Lo Po
Ko Kolo
Ko Tarutao
Ko Singha
Prison Camp
Ao Makham
Ao Taloh Udang
Ko Rang Nok
Ko Palitong

0 kilometers 5
0 miles 5

★ Dugong Sightings
The waters off Ko Tarutao are famous for sightings of the gentle dugong. These rare mammals graze on verdant sea-grass beds and avoid contact with humans.

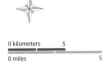

Prison Camp
Also notorious as Prison Island, Ko Tarutao housed several prison camps during World War II. The prisoners, forced to live in inhuman conditions without food or medicine, later took to piracy.

For keys to symbols see back flap

Exploring Ko Tarutao Marine National Park

The largest island of the marine park archipelago is the 16-mile (26-km) long Ko Tarutao, which offers great scenic variety. Tropical rainforests cover most of its surface, which reaches a maximum altitude of 2,300 ft (701 m). Ferries from Pak Bara dock at Ao Pante Malaka, the location of the park headquarters, bungalows, a restaurant, and the island's only store. Just east of Ao Pante Malaka lie the natural attractions of Tham Jara-Khe and To-Bu Cliff. Offshore islands such as Ko Adang, Ko Lipe, and Ko Rawi are popular beach destinations, while there is excellent diving at nearby Ko Kra and Ko Yang.

Bungalow housing the Ko Tarutao park headquarters, Ao Pante Malaka

Ao Pante Malaka

อ่าวพันเตมะละกา

51 miles (82 km) W of Satun. 🚤 from Pak Bara. 🅿 single park fee. 🚲 📷
🌐 dnp.go.th

The site of the Ko Tarutao Marine National Park headquarters, Ao Pante Malaka is a lovely bay on the northwestern shore of Ko Tarutao. The long beach, lined with casuarinas, is great for swimming. Ao Pante Malaka offers more activities for visitors than any other spot on the main island. These include a biking trail and opportunities for sea-kayaking. The bay also serves as the harbor for boats from Pak Bara, 10 miles (16 km) away. A choice of bungalows, long houses, and cabins provide simple accommodations for visitors to the park. Camping is possible here, especially along the beach, but visitors must acquire prior approval of the park authorities.

A good park-run restaurant offers treats and refreshing cooling drinks. Visitors should also see the exhibition on the park's historical and natural background at the tourist service center. Longtail boats from Ao Pante Malaka also make the trip to Tham Jara-Khe, Ao Son, and Ao Taloh Udang nearby.

To-Bu Cliff

ผาโต๊ะบู

1 mile (2 km) E of Ao Pante Malaka.

A 20-minute walk inland from Ao Pante Malaka, through dense evergreen forest, leads visitors to the popular To-Bu Cliff. This 364-ft (111-m) high cliff is clearly visible from the Ko Tarutao park headquarters and offers spectacular views across the archipelago. The trek leading to this site begins close to the headquarters and visitors can stop to read about the large variety of flora and fauna in the forest described on plaques along the way.

To-Bu Cliff is considered to be an exceptionally beautiful and romantic spot from which to watch the sun setting over the Andaman Sea. Visitors, however, must be careful while making the trek to the cliff and head back before it gets dark. There is no electricity in the area and the descent of this rocky outcrop can be quite treacherous once the sun has set.

Tham Jara-Khe

ถ้ำจระเข้

2 miles (3 km) NE of Ao Pante Malaka.

Located near Laem Tanyong Hara, the northern cape of Ko Tarutao, Tham Jara-Khe is a 984-ft (300-m) deep cavern filled with beautiful stalactites and stalagmites. The cave is also notorious as Crocodile Cave because of the dangerous saltwater crocodiles that once inhabited it. Just 20 minutes away from Khlong Pante Malaka in Ao Pante Malaka, Tham Jara-Khe is accessible by longtail boat along the beautiful mangrove-lined canal. Explorers must use rafts to navigate their way within the cave, which is best visited at low tide when navigation is easier; the exploration takes about an hour. Visitors are advised to carry their own supplies, especially flashlights, while visiting the cave, as facilities here are minimal.

Kayakers rowing under the precipitous To-Bu Cliff

Secluded beach at Ao Son, housing a lone ranger station

Ao Jak and Ao Molae

อ่าวจากและอ่าวมอะและ

3 miles (5 km) S of Ao Pante Malaka.

Located to the south of Ao Pante Malaka, Ao Jak and contiguous Ao Molae are two beautiful bays with pristine white-sand beaches, great for walks and picnics. Backed by dense coconut plantations, Ao Jak has no accommodations or other facilities.

Ao Molae, clearly the more developed of the two beaches, lies a little further south of Ao Jak. It can be reached by passing through a small mangrove swamp at low tide. At high tide, however, it is necessary to wade through the incoming seawater for a short distance. There are a few simple bamboo houses belonging to local fishermen here, along with some basic bungalow accommodations and a restaurant. A small ranger camp is also located here and visitors are allowed to camp on the beach.

Ao Son

อ่าวสน

8 miles (13 km) S of Ao Pante Malaka. Situated further down the west coast of Ko Tarutao, Ao Son is a sizable bay with a long, white sandy beach. It offers good swimming and snorkeling opportunities and is best reached by longtail boat from Ao Pante Malaka. However, Ao Son can also be accessed on foot from Ao Molae, 5 miles (8 km) to the north. There is no road here, but a rough track leads south through clumps of wild banana and tall dipterocarp trees and the trek takes about two hours. Ao Son is visited by nesting turtles each year between September and April. The best time to see these gentle creatures is at night. There are no facilities of any kind on the beach, except for a small ranger station. Camping is possible here with the approval of the park authorities.

Treks from Ao Son to the interior of Ko Tarutao lead to two beautiful waterfalls – **Nam Tok Lu Du**, or Lu Du Falls, which is a 1-hour hike away, and **Nam Tok Lo Po**, or Lo Po Falls, which is 2 hours away. Both the waterfalls offer freshwater pools which are good for bathing. Further south is Ao Makham, or Tamarind Bay, which is reached by a long and difficult trek through dense jungle; hiring a longtail boat from Ao Pante Malaka is usually advisable.

Ao Taloh Udang

อ่าวตะโละ อุดัง

15 miles (24 km) S of Ao Pante Malaka.

Situated at the southern tip of Ko Tarutao, Ao Taloh Udang is a deep, sheltered bay facing the tiny offshore island of Ko Rang Nok, home to thousands of swiftlets. Undoubtedly associated with Ko Tarutao's intriguing past, this bay was the site of a prison camp for political captives. Several well-known prisoners, including the author of the first English-Thai dictionary and a grandson of Rama VII (r.1925–35), were incarcerated here. The inhuman prison conditions forced inmates to take to piracy, looting passing ships. This activity was curtailed by the British in 1946. Visitors can go to see the ruins of the prison. However, there are no facilities at Ao Taloh Udang, apart from a ranger station.

Statue at prison camp

Path leading to the remains of the prison camp at Ao Taloh Udang

Enthusiastic snorkelers making the most of the clear waters off Ko Adang

Ko Adang
เกาะอาดัง

26 miles (42 km) SW of Ao Pante Malaka. 🚢 from Ao Pante Malaka. 🏊

About 12 sq miles (31 sq km) in area, Ko Adang is almost completely covered in tropical rainforest. On the island's southwestern side lies Laem Son, passing the much smaller islets of Ko Klang and Ko Khai en route. Ko Adang is famous for its clear waters, fine quartz beaches, and well-preserved coral reefs, which provide a habitat for shoals of brightly colored fish and a host of other exotic marine flora and fauna.

The leafy interiors of Ko Adang are dotted with several beautiful waterfalls cascading from lofty heights of up to 2,300 ft (701 m); perhaps the highest is **Nam Tok Chon Salat**, which has water all year round. Another picturesque spot, **Pirate Waterfall** is reached by a 3-mile (2-km) walkway from near Laem Son. It is said to have been a source of fresh water for pirates living on the island. **Pha Chado**, a cliff located a 30-minute walk from the ranger station at Laem Son to the south of the island, offers fine views across the white sandy cape of Ko Adang.

Other smaller offshore islands, such as Ko Lipe, Ko Dong, Ko Hin Ngam, and Ko Yang, are also great for swimming, diving, sea-kayaking, and sailing, and are easily approached from Ko Adang. **Ko Khai**, or Egg Island, located 11 miles (18 km) from Ko Adang, is too small to stay on, but makes a good diving or snorkeling stopover. The island has a lovely white-sand beach and a beautiful natural rock arch, and is favored by sea turtles for nesting.

Visitors can stay overnight at Ko Adang, although booking in advance is advisable. There is a restaurant serving fine local and Western dishes.

Ko Rawi
เกาะราวี

29 miles (47 km) SW of Ao Pante Malaka. 🚢 from Ko Lipe.

The second-largest island in the Adang-Rawi group, Ko Rawi covers an area of about 11 sq miles (28 sq km). It lies just 6 miles (10 km) to the west of Ko Adang, and is similarly blessed with fine beaches, crystal-clear seas, dense, jungle interior, and rich offshore coral reefs. Like Ko Adang, Ko Rawi has a marine park ranger station at Hat Sai Khao, but there are no accommodations on the island; nor are there any shops, restaurants, or other facilities. Camping, however, is a good option for those who want to get away from it all, but requires permission from the park authorities.

Best visited as a day trip from nearby Ko Adang or Ko Lipe, Ko Rawi offers fantastic swimming, snorkeling, and diving opportunities. The island is also easily accessible by chartered longtail boat from Ko Lipe.

Readying for a splash in the blue waters off Ko Rawi

Ko Lipe
เกาะหลีเป๊ะ
29 miles (47 km) SW of Ao Pante
Malaka. 🚤 from Ao Pante Malaka. 🏊

Located 2 miles (1 km) south of Ko Adang, the much smaller island of Ko Lipe, sometimes called Ko Sipe by locals, has become the most developed and popular destination of the Ko Tarutao Marine National Park. Originally inhabited only by a small community of *chao lae*, or sea gypsies, the island has been seeing rapid development, with a number of resorts and hotels being established on its beautiful beaches. Ko Lipe has just about everything going for it – fine, clear blue waters, good coral reefs, powdery white beaches, and a mountainous, thickly forested interior.

The main focus of development has been at **Hat Pattaya** on Ko Lipe's southern coast, where there are several bungalow-style resorts and a number of laid-back bars and restaurants. The main activities here are sunbathing, swimming, and snorkeling. In fact, the coral reefs, easily visible a short distance from the beach, are home to almost 25 percent of the tropical fish varieties found in the area.

A number of simple tracks, including one leading across the island's narrow center to Sunset Beach on its western coast, can be used to explore the interior of the island. Sunlight Beach, on the eastern side of the island, has bungalow-style accommodations and good views overlooking tiny Ko Kra offshore, yet another popular location. The main *chao lae* settlement is located just south of the beach. The area also houses several shops, a few restaurants, and utility stores such as a medical dispensary. Visitors can take longtail boats, manned by *chao lae*, to other offshore islands nearby.

Ko Yang
เกาะยาง
27 miles (43 km) SW of Ao Pante
Malaka. 🚤 from Ko Lipe.

A tiny but beautiful island equidistant from Ko Adang and Ko Rawi, Ko Yang remains uninhabited, even today. It has a small, perfect white-sand beach, ideal for sunbathing. Ko Yang is surrounded by rich coral reefs, mainly comprising hard corals such as staghorn, leaf, and brain, making the island a popular snorkeling spot. Fortunately, its distance from the mainland and nearby Ko Lipe ensures that it is never crowded.

Ko Yang is best visited as a day trip from nearby Ko Lipe or Ko Adang, by hiring long-tail boats.

Ko Hin Ngam
เกาะหินงาม
27 miles (43 km) SW of Ao Pante
Malaka. 🚤 from Ko Lipe.

Like Ko Yang nearby, Ko Hin Ngam, or Island of Beautiful Stones, is a tiny outcrop set in the immensity of the Andaman Sea. Located about 4 miles

Visitors on the pebbly beach of Ko Hin Ngam

(6 km) northwest of Ko Lipe and about 3 miles (5 km) west of Ko Adang, beautiful Ko Hin Ngam is uninhabited and isolated, making it the perfect snorkeling spot. The most striking feature of the island is its small beach, which is covered with smooth black pebbles in various shapes and distinctive patterns. According to a local legend, Chaopho Tarutao, the guardian spirit of the marine park, curses anyone who dares to take away anything belonging to the park. True or not, visitors should avoid picking up these pebbles as souvenirs.

Ko Hin Ngam is best visited as a day trip from Ko Lipe in a hired longtail boat. It is advisable to combine a trip to Ko Hin Ngam with a visit to nearby Ko Yang before returning to the much more crowded Ko Lipe.

The narrow, jutting strip of the popular Sunset Beach at Ko Lipe

DEEP SOUTH

Among the loveliest and least visited regions of the country, the Deep South has more in common with neighboring Malaysia than with the rest of coastal Thailand. The region's distinct culture, food, history, and religion are a novel experience for travelers, yet political strife keeps many away. The beautiful forested mountains, palm-fringed coastline, and relative isolation make this southern region an alluring and unusual holiday destination.

Despite being a part of Thailand for centuries, the Deep South is culturally different from the rest of the country. The influence of Indian, Chinese, and Malaysian cultures can be seen in the region's architecture and ethnic diversity. Skin tones are noticeably darker than in the rest of the country. The people speak an unusual intonated dialect of Thai and Malay (closely related to the language spoken in Malaysian Kelantan), and even the food is spicier, characterized by bitter curries laced liberally with turmeric. The diverse traditions of this region are especially evident in the town of Songkhla, a cosmopolitan cultural center with *wats*, museums, and an ancient Thai, Muslim, and Portuguese heritage. The area north of Songkhla has a Buddhist majority,

while south of Songkhla, near the coast, most people are Muslim and the minarets of mosques replace the gilded spires of Buddhist temples. Pattani, an important semi-independent Malay kingdom in the 17th century, is now a Thai center of Islamic scholarship. Hat Yai, the commercial capital, has grown from an agricultural and railroad town to a destination for shopping and entertainment, while the fishing villages of the south have a distinct Muslim identity.

However, this complex ethnic mix has also led to violence perpetrated by separatists seeking autonomy. Guerrilla warfare and bombings have disturbed the peace in this area. As a result, tourism has declined although none of the attacks have been directed toward foreign visitors.

A group of Muslim schoolgirls making their way across a bridge over the Songkhla Lakes

◀ A giant Reclining Buddha at *Wat Phranom Laem Phor* on the lake-island of Ko Yo

Exploring the Deep South

Due to its proximity to Malaysia, the Deep South has more in common with its neighbor than the rest of Thailand. Extending over the provinces of Yala, Narathiwat, Songkhla, and Pattani, this southernmost belt of the country covers a huge area. Hat Yai is the commercial capital of the region and is also the main transport hub. The towns of Pattani, Saiburi, and Narathiwat with their large Muslim populations are an ethnic melting pot of Malay-Muslim culture. Songkhla is a charming town with a rich heritage and is regarded as the region's cultural capital. The sprawling Songkhla Lakes form the most significant geographical feature of the Deep South, and are home to a variety of wildlife, especially birds. Although there are fewer natural attractions, this region's historical towns, mosques, and villages give it a unique flavor.

Aquatic plants covering the lake at Thale Noi Waterfowl Park

0 km 25
0 miles 25

Sights at a Glance

Towns and Cities
2 *Songkhla pp284–5*
5 Pattani
6 Saiburi
7 Narathiwat
8 Tak Bai

Beaches and Islands
1 Hat Yai
4 Ko Yo

Areas of Natural Beauty
3 *Songkhla Lakes p286*

Painted *korlae* fishing boats at Khao Seng, Songkhla

Thailand's longest concrete bridge, connecting the mainland to Ko Yo

Key

— Major road

═══ Minor road

∼∼∼ Railway

▬▬ International border

Getting Around

Hat Yai is the main base with direct and frequent road, rail, and air links to Bangkok and the rest of the region. Other ways to get to the Deep South are by road from Nakhon Si Thammarat to Phattalung. All the larger towns are well served by local and long-distance bus services, while Phattalung, Hat Yai, and Yala have railway stations with services to either Bangkok or Malaysia. Cars can be easily hired and driving is the best way to explore this region.

For keys to symbols *see back flap*

Three young devotees praying at a Buddhist shrine, Hat Yai

❶ Hat Yai
หาดใหญ่

Road Map C5. 522 miles (840 km) S of Bangkok. 🚍 70,000. ✈ 7 miles (11 km) W of Hat Yai. 🚉 🚌 ℹ TAT, Hat Yai (0-7424-3747). 🏪 daily. 🎎 Chinese Lunar Festival (Sep/Oct).

The commercial and transport capital of southern Thailand, Hat Yai has grown affluent due to its strategic railroad junction, its discounted products, and the constant flow of travelers from Malaysia on weekends. Various languages and dialects can be heard around the cosmopolitan downtown area.

Hat Yai is Thailand's third-largest city, yet it has few cultural attractions. Most visitors to the city spend their time shopping for bargains. Electrical goods at the Kim Yong market, fruits from street vendors, imported leather goods, and fashionable department stores are some of the popular options. Visitors can also take in a bullfighting bout. This sport, particular to the south, is different from its Spanish counterpart; here bulls fight other bulls and bets are placed on the outcome of the matches.

Wat Hat Yai Nai, near the city center, has the third-largest Reclining Buddha image in the world – 115 ft (35 m) long and 49 ft (15 m) high.

Environs
Ton Nga Chang, 15 miles (24 km) west of Hat Yai, comprises two streams cascading over seven tiers, which is best visited in the cool season from November to February.

❷ Songkhla
สงขลา

Once known as Singora, or Lion City, Songkhla grew to prominence as an important trade center in the 18th century. Located between the Gulf of Thailand and Thale Sap Songkhla, part of the country's largest lake system, it is an important fishing port and an administrative and educational center. A sense of history permeates the city and is evident in its architecture, cuisine, and language. Fringed by beaches, Songkhla is home to museums, bustling night markets, and *wats*. It is a melting pot of Thai and Muslim cultures where trendy bars coexist with fishing villages and old Portuguese-style houses, reflecting the city's multicultural heritage.

Bronze mermaid statue dedicated to Mae Thorani at Hat Samila

🚩 Hat Samila
หาดสมิหลา
Songkhla's main beach, Hat Samila is dominated by a bronze mermaid statue of Mae Thorani, the Hindu-Buddhist earth goddess. This revered statue is an icon for the whole province. Songkhla derives its name from the two lion-shaped islands, which are now called Ko Nu, or Rat Island, and Ko Maeo, or Cat Island. These are among Hat Samila's main attractions.

📷 Khao Noi
เขาน้อย
One of two hills in Songkhla, Khao Noi is located just a short distance south of Hat Samila. It offers great views of the city. There is an old *chedi* and a topiary garden on the hilltop, as well as a park with tennis courts and food stalls at the bottom.

🏛 Songkhla National Museum
พิพิธภัณฑสถานแห่งชาติสงขลา
1 mile (2 km) S of Hat Samila, Wichianchon Rd. **Tel** 0-7431-1728. **Open** 9am–4pm Wed–Sun. 📷
The museum is housed in a beautiful building that is in itself a major attraction for visitors. It was built in 1878, in the southern Thai-Chinese style, as the residence for the then deputy governor of Songkhla – Phraya Suntharanuraksa. This old mansion was renovated and converted into a museum in 1977. A hidden grass courtyard flanks the two spiral staircases that lead to the wood-paneled second story where most exhibits are kept.

Former governor's residence presently housing Songkhla National Museum

Ornate entrance of Wat Chai Mongkhon, Songkhla

The fairly comprehensive collection covers most periods of Thai art and includes Benjarong pottery, 7th- to 9th-century Dvaravati plinths, Buddha images, and remnants of Ban Chiang pottery dating back to 3000 BC.

🗿 Wat Chai Mongkhon
วัดไชยมงคล
2 miles (3 km) S of Hat Samila, Chai-Phet Mongkhon Rd.
Open 8am–4pm daily.

A revered temple in Songkhla, Wat Chai Mongkhon has a *chedi* built to house a Buddha relic brought from Sri Lanka in 1892 by a monk called Na Issaro. The *wat* also houses a Reclining Buddha image.

🏛 Patsee Museum
พิพิธภัณฑ์พัทศรี
2 miles (3km) S of Hat Samila, Wat Matchimawat, Saiburi Rd.
Open Wed–Sun. 🖼

Housed inside the Wat Matchimawat, which dates back 400 years, the Patsee Museum has a wide range of artifacts indicating the importance of Songkhla's former trade links. Exhibits include a 14-in (35-cm) stone image of Ganesha, the Hindu elephant god, dating back to the late 6th century; enamelware from the Chinese Qing dynasty; 15th-century U Thong ware, and 18th-century European plates. However, the arrangement is slightly haphazard.

VISITORS' CHECKLIST

Practical Information
Road Map D5. 16 miles (26 km) NE of Hat Yai. 🚹 86,000. *i* TAT, Hat Yai (0-7424-3747). 🗓 daily. 🎏 Chinese Lunar Festival (Sep/Oct).

Transport
✈ 26 miles (42 km) SW of Songkhla. 🚌 🚍 🚏

Khao Seng
เขาเสง
2 miles (3 km) S of Hat Samila.

A traditional Muslim fishing village, Khao Seng is located on a headland near Hat Samila. Famous for its colorful *korlae* boats (*see p289*), the village also has an information center for the coastal fisheries and is a good place to learn about fishing – the mainstay of coastal Thailand.

Colorful *korlae* fishing boats anchored on the beach, Khao Seng

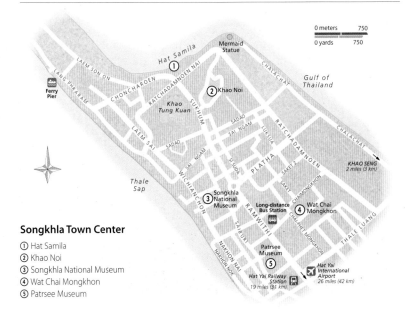

Songkhla Town Center

1. Hat Samila
2. Khao Noi
3. Songkhla National Museum
4. Wat Chai Mongkhon
5. Patsee Museum

For keys to symbols *see back flap*

❸ Songkhla Lakes

ทะเลสาบสงขลา

Road: **Map** C5. 6 miles (10 km) NW of Songkhla. 🚌 🚐 *i* TAT, Hat Yai (0-7424-3747). 🖼 🛋 🏠

The largest natural lake system in Thailand is formed by the Songkhla Lakes. A coastal lagoon, it consists of three interconnected water bodies – Thale Sap, Thale Luang, and Thale Noi. The lakes are separated from the sea by sandy ridges and are fed by water from the forested inland hills as well as seawater. They support an extraordinary biodiversity as the lakes are a feeding ground for thousands of birds migrating from as far as China. They are also home to a small population of the rare Irawaddy dolphin.

Longtail boats navigating through lotuses and other vegetation, Thale Noi

🐦 Thale Sap Songkhla

ทะเลสาบสงขลา

A brackish water lake, Thale Sap Songkhla is the southernmost of the three lakes lying between Phatthalung province to the west and Songkhla province to the east. This lake covers an area of 146 sq miles (378 sq km) and is a haven for bird-watchers. Because it is the closest to the sea, Thale Sap Songkhla is the most salty, and attracts more seabirds than its two northern neighbors.

🐦 Thale Luang

ทะเลหลวง

Located north of Thale Sap, Thale Luang is connected to the former by a narrow channel.

This shallow lake covers an area of 190 sq miles (492 sq km). Although the water has high levels of salinity, it attains freshwater conditions during the rainy season. This lake is part of the protected wetlands area and is dotted with many small islands and surrounded by paddy fields.

The **Khu Khut Waterbird Park** is the star attraction of the area. Established in 1976, this little-visited waterfowl park is home to over 200 species of birds, including a number of bitterns, egrets, and herons. The best time to visit is during early morning or late afternoon, between December and March. The park headquarters can be reached by bus or taxi from Songkhla. Visitors can hire boats from the fisheries department for special bird-watching tours.

A wattled jacana

🐦 Khu Khut Waterbird Park

🚌 🚐 *i* Park HQ (0-7430-4552). **Open** dawn to dusk daily. 🖼 🛋 🏠

🐦 Thale Noi

ทะเลน้อย

The northernmost and smallest of the three lakes, Thale Noi is very shallow and almost entirely covered with aquatic plants with a few scattered islets. Although it is predominantly a freshwater lake, it becomes brackish between May and October. Thale Noi is home to the largest wetland bird sanctuary in Thailand – the **Thale Noi Waterfowl Park** – a resting ground for thousands of exotic migratory birds. The best way to explore the park, which covers 12 sq miles (30 sq km), is by longtail boat.

The best season for bird-watching is between January and April, when over 150 species of birds arrive at the park, swelling its population to about 100,000. There is a viewing platform on the lake and dawn is the best time for visitors to get a glimpse of Thale Noi's birds. Notable inhabitants include the purple swamp hen and the long-legged *nok i-kong*.

Apart from lotuses and lilies, the most common vegetation covering the lake is *don kok*, a reed which the *nok i-kong* birds use to build nesting platforms. There are about 100 families who live in raised wooden houses along the lake and make a living from fishing and weaving reeds into mats.

🐦 Thale Noi Waterfowl Park

🚌 🚐 *i* Park HQ (0-7468- 5230). **Open** 8:30am–4:30pm daily. 🖼 🛋 🛋 🏠 🌐 thailandbirdwatching.com

Restaurant on stilts at the Khu Khut Waterbird Park, Thale Luang

Muay Thai

Muay thai (Thai kickboxing) is the country's national passion. The origins of this unique sport remain uncertain; it is believed to have evolved from *krabi-krabong*, a related technique of self-defense. The traditional form of *muay thai* is further divided – *muay korat* from the northeast, *muay lopburi* from the central region, *muay tasao* from the north, and *muay chaiya* in the south. Although enjoyed throughout Thailand, this sport is immensely popular in the south where the Khon Tai, people of the southern Thai peninsula, are believed to have a fiery nature. The sport's appeal extends from Nakhon Si Thammarat and Hat Yai to Phuket and Ko Samui. Once limited to Thailand and its neighboring countries, such as Cambodia, *muay thai* now attracts an immense following internationally – both as a martial art and a sport.

Thai Boxing

Thai kickboxing uses parts of the body not used in Western boxing, such as the feet and elbows. Thai boxing matches are also faster paced, and are thus limited to five rounds of three minutes each, separated by a short break. Professional boxers, who may start rigorous training as young as six years of age, often retire by 25.

Feet are kept bare in training sessions, although ankle covers may be worn during a match.

Amulets *(see p59)*, worn around the boxer's biceps during the match, are said to offer protection.

Kicks are common in Thai boxing.

Nai Khanom Tom was a legendary Thai boxer who defeated nine Burmese champions in 1774 and won his freedom (he was a prisoner of war).

Before the match, the boxer performs a dance *(wai khru ram muay)* to honor the teacher. The movements involve sweeping arm motions, which are said to draw the power of earth, air, fire, and water into the body.

A ringside *piphat* band is an essential element of *muay thai*. At the opening ceremony, the music is soft, but slowly increases in tempo, adding to the thrill of the match.

In the stadium, the audience becomes excited, shouting encouragement to the boxers. Thais bet furiously, often staking large sums on their favorite fighter. Bouts between famous boxers may be sold out well in advance.

❹ Ko Yo
เกาะยอ

Road Map C5. 9 miles (14 km) SW of Songkhla. 🚌 🚌 ✂️ 📷

A small and secluded island lying near the eastern end of Thale Sap, Ko Yo is best visited on a day trip from Hat Yai or Songkhla. The island is connected to the mainland by the 2-mile (3-km) long Tinsulanond bridge. Built in 1986, this bridge directly links this secluded island with the other southern provinces. It can also be reached by longtail boats.

Ko Yo is covered with lush greenery and its attractions include orchards, two ancient *wats* – Wat Khao Bo and Wat Tai Yo plus Wat Phranom Laem Phor with a reclining Buddha – and the local handwoven cotton fabric available throughout the island. It is also famous for its fisheries and boasts a number of good seafood restaurants on its northern end. Visitors can hire a motorcycle to explore Ko Yo's bylanes. The excellent **Ko Yo Folklore Museum**, established by the Institute for Southern Thai Studies in 1991, was built to preserve and showcase the folk traditions of this region. The museum is located in an attractive series of Thai *sala*-type buildings. It also houses a small café, a souvenir shop, a library of books on the culture of the Deep South, and a series of exhibits that includes *nang talung* puppets *(see p195)*, musical instruments, textiles, basketry, household artifacts,

Aerial view of the floating fish farms around Ko Yo

fishing equipment, jewelry, and weapons. There is also a *suan yaa samunprai*, or a natural herb garden, within the museum's grounds.

🏛 Ko Yo Folklore Museum
Tel 0-7459-1611. 🚌 🚌 **Open** 8.30am–5pm daily. 📷 ✂️ 📷

❺ Pattani
ปัตตานี

Road Map D6. 81 miles (130 km) SE of Songkhla. 🏔 74,000. 🚌 🚌 ℹ️ TAT, Narathiwat (0-7352-2411). 📅 daily. 🎏 Lim Ko Niaw Festival (Mar).

Founded as early as the 15th century, Pattani was once the capital of an independent Malay-speaking sultanate. Capital today of Pattani province, it is a spiritual center of the Malay-Muslim region of the Deep South. About 75 percent of the population are Malay-speaking Muslims. This region has seen rising violence by Islamic extremists against the minority Buddhist population. Apart from the **Matsayit Klang** mosque, there are few buildings of much interest. However, Pattani is lively, especially around the harbor, with its brightly colored *korlae* boats.

Environs
The **Kru Se** mosque, 4 miles (6 km) east of town, was built by a Chinese merchant, Lim To Khieng, who married a local woman and converted to Islam. As a display of his devotion he started building a mosque. His sister sailed from China to protest about his conversion. Although he promised her that he would return to his homeland upon its completion, he never did, and she cursed the building and anyone who attempted to complete it. Her shrine, **Chao Mae Lim Ko Niao**, and the still incomplete mosque draw a number of devotees.

The partially built structure of the 16th-century Kru Se mosque, Pattani

❻ Saiburi
ไทรบุรี

Road Map D6. 29 miles (47 km) SE of Pattani. TAT, Narathiwat (0-7352-2411).

Also called Selindung Bayu, meaning "Wind Shelter", by the local fishing population, the small center of Saiburi is the capital of Saiburi district. This is the second-largest fishing harbor in Pattani province. The highlight of this place is the long stretch of beach, which is more suited for fishing than lounging around on the sands. The nearby **Hat Wa Sukri** is famous for the annual Saiburi Fishing Competition in April, which draws a number of both local and international anglers.

The busy fishing harbor in Saiburi

❼ Narathiwat
นราธิวาส

Road Map D6. 40 miles (65 km) SE of Saiburi. 68,000. TAT, Narathiwat (0-7352-2411). daily. Chao Mae Toe Moe Festival (Apr); Narathiwat Fair (Sep).

Capital of the Narathiwat province and a useful base for exploring the surrounding region, Narathiwat is a laid-back town. However, this province experiences frequent acts of violence carried out by Islamic extremists and Malay-Muslim separatists. Such acts of terrorism are aimed at the Thai-Buddhist administration rather than at Westerners or other visitors.

The nearby port is another good spot to see traditional *korlae* boats. There are also a number of small and secluded

Korlae Fishing Boats

Colorful, painted fishing boats have been built and decorated by Muslim fishermen for hundreds of years all along the east coast of peninsular Thailand. The finest examples of this now declining industry originate in the boatyards of Saiburi district and Pattani province. Originally used as sailboats, *korlae* are now run with engines by local fishermen. Painted with Buddhist and Hindu characters by predominantly

Colorful artwork on a *korlae* fishing boat, Saiburi

Muslim fishermen, the traditional *korlae* designs represent the cultural crossover between Thai Buddhism and Malay Islam.

beaches near Narathiwat, the best of which is Hat Manao. Small beachside shacks sell iced drinks and grilled fish, but alcohol is rarely found here.

Environs
Taksin Palace, to the south of town, is the summer residence of the King and Queen of Thailand. Open to the public when the royal family is not in residence, the palace gardens include an aviary. Khao Kong hill, 4 miles (6 km) southwest of town, has a monastery perched on its top with the tallest seated Buddha image in Thailand. The 79-ft (24-m) high statue is decorated with gilded mosaic tiles in the South Indian style.

 **Taksin Palace**
Off Hwy 4084, 5 miles (8 km) S of Narathiwat. **Open** daily. **Closed** usually Aug & Sep.

❽ Tak Bai
ตากใบ

Road Map E6. 21 miles (34 km) SE of Narathiwat. TAT, Narathiwat (0-7352-2411).

The last point on the southern coast of Thailand, Tak Bai is located right at the border with Malaysia. The main attraction of the town is **Wat Chonthara Sing He**, erected in 1873 by Rama V (r.1868–1910) to stake his claim to a region that the British might have considered incorporating into their Malay colonies. This is an outpost of Thai Buddhism in a predominantly Muslim area. Interestingly, even today, Thai-Buddhist communities called Orang Syam in Malaysia live peacefully among their Muslim neighbors across the border, as they have for many centuries.

Mural depicting a busy rural scene, Wat Chonthara Sing He, Tak Bai

TRAVELERS' NEEDS

WHERE TO STAY

Accommodations in Thailand come in all price ranges, although the distribution of hotels is uneven in coastal areas. The developed beach resorts contrast with basic bungalows in rural areas. All the major cities have at least one hotel matching international standards, while Bangkok boasts some of the best hotels in the world. Mid-range lodgings are available in most towns. A number of luxurious spas, resorts, and villas with stylish decor have appeared all over coastal Thailand, while guesthouses provide budget accommodations. Other alternatives are designated campgrounds, or bungalows inside national parks.

The lavishly decorated Conrad Room at The Mandarin Oriental, Bangkok *(see p294)*

Hotel Grading and Facilities

Hotels in Thailand are not officially graded, although some are registered with the Thai Hotels Association. Price is therefore the only indication of what to expect. Often the best value is found in the once-luxury establishments that have been downgraded since the arrival of international chains. These hotels offer first-class facilities at a fraction of the cost. The **Thailand Tourism** (TAT) offices can be contacted for hotel information.

Resort Hotels

The resort hotels of Thailand are unsurpassed in style, comfort, and elegance by the majority of their international counterparts. Resorts such as the Chiva Som Resort in Cha-am *(see p298)* and the Banyan Tree Resort in Phuket *(see p300)* are luxury designer-built oases of tranquility and opulence. Most resorts offer their guests a wide range of amenities including spas, sports facilities such as golf courses, and cultural performances. They are often situated in isolated locations, but transport is always provided to nearby towns.

Luxury Hotels

Thailand's luxury hotels are on a par with some of the best in the world. Rooms come with every conceivable comfort, from king-sized beds and wide-screen televisions to well-stocked mini-bars and private terrace Jacuzzis. These upscale hotels offer a range of facilities, including business centers, conference rooms, shopping malls, coffee shops, fitness centers, pools, and a number of restaurants serving a wide range of cuisines. However, these hotels are now facing stiff competition from the smaller boutique hotels.

Boutique Hotels

Some of Thailand's latest accommodation choices are super-luxurious boutique hotels that emphasize attention to detail and a more personalized service. These are often located in former private residences and make up for in character what they may lose in facilities provided by the larger properties.

Guesthouses

For those looking for a more authentic stay, guesthouses in Bangkok and bungalows along the coasts offer good value and are usually the cheapest option. In Bangkok, Khao San Road is the primary haunt of the budget traveler. Here accommodations are often unsatisfactory, with some places renting rooms by the hour. Outside the capital, bungalows (sometimes calling themselves "resorts") are a clean, friendly, and cheap option. Some establishments have air-conditioning or fans, and may offer swimming pools and restaurants, for around 500 baht a night. In the cheapest guesthouses and bungalows expect basic amenities, with communal Asian toilets and washing facilities, although the quality of service should still be quite good.

Mid-Range Hotels

Sometimes the traveler seeks nothing more than a clean room for a reasonable price, and Thailand's many modern hotels fit this bill perfectly. Although these hotels have little character, they are secure, efficient, and provide a friendly service.

Swimming pool at a smaller beachside resort, Ko Phi Phi

◀ Tables on the beach at the Grotto restaurant, Hotel Rayavadee, Hat Phra Nang

Tents pitched for campers at Khao Sam Roi Yot National Park

National Parks

Most of the national parks allow camping on designated campsites, although visitors should expect few facilities. Mosquito nets and insect repellent are essential. Most parks have a limited number of bungalows and these should be booked in advance through the **Forestry Department**.

Prices

Tourist accommodations can cost from 1,000 to over 10,000 baht a night in Bangkok, Ko Samui, Pattaya, and Phuket. A comfortable room in a standard hotel costs between 700 and 1,500 baht, depending on season. Prices everywhere are at their peak in the cool season from November to February. In the other seasons, rates fall everywhere except Bangkok. A standard room in a Thai hotel in the capital costs 1,000 baht, falling to 400–750 baht in the provinces. The best deals are at guesthouses and beach bungalows, which cost between 400 and 1,000 baht.

Taxes

All hotels charge seven percent VAT (Value Added Tax), and some luxury hotels will also add a 10 percent service charge on top of their basic rates. Cheaper hotels usually include taxes in the room rates, while top-end hotels generally add the taxes to the final bill, so do check whether the price is inclusive of taxes while booking or before checking in.

Bargaining

It is a good idea to ask about the possibility of a discount. It is not considered impolite to ask, but it is in bad taste to press the point. Many hotels offer special off-season prices.

Tipping

Tipping is not ingrained in Thai culture, but in hotels, it is customary to give bellmen 20–50 baht for delivering your luggage to the room.

Facilities for Children

Very few budget hotels have facilities for children or nursing mothers. However, luxury hotels and resorts may offer babysitting services and free stays for kids as well as special paddle pools.

Disabled Travelers

Even luxury hotels have few facilities for disabled visitors. Wheelchair ramps are making an appearance, and nearly every luxury establishment has an elevator. That, however, is the limit of facilities in most hotels.

Recommmended Hotels

The hotels featured on pages 294–301 are among the best Thailand has to offer in service, ambience, value or location. A range of accommodation options are covered from simple budget hotels and modern rooms, to deluxe beachfront resorts, luxury retreats, and chic boutique hotels. These categories highlight the changes that have taken place along Thailand's coasts in recent years – ultra-luxurious low-rise resorts have found favor over multi-storied buildings. While the high-rise still dominates Bangkok, boutique hotels focusing on classical Thai and Western Colonial-era design have created a new niche. Hotels are listed by area, and within these areas by price. Map references for hotels in Bangkok refer to pages 92–9. For all other map references, see the Road Map at the end of the guide.

For the best of the best look out for hotels featuring the DK Choice symbol. These establishments have been highlighted in recognition of an exceptional feature – be it the decor, service, or a stunning location.

DIRECTORY

National Parks

Forestry Department
Phahon Yothin Rd,
Bangkok.
Tel 0-2562-0760.

Hotel Grading and Facilities

Thailand Tourism Offices
Bangkok
Tel 1672.
w tourismthailand.org
Ko Samui
Tel 0-7728-8818.
Krabi
Tel 0-7562-2163.
Pattaya
Tel 0-3842-8750.
Phuket
Tel 0-7621-1036.

Pretty bungalows lining the beach at Ko Chang

Where to Stay

Bangkok

Chinatown

Chinatown Hotel ⓑ
Budget   **City Map** 6 F2
526 Yaowarat Rd,
Samphan Thawong 10100
Tel *0-2225-0204*
Ⓦ chinatownhotel.co.th
Modern and clean, if somewhat
spartan, this hotel offers
discounts in low season.

Riverview Guesthouse ⓑ
Budget   **City Map** 6 F3
768 Soi Phanu Rang Si, Songwat Rd,
behind San Jao Tosuekong 10100
Tel *0-2234-5429*
Ⓦ riverviewbkk.com
Stay in basic rooms with superb
views of vibrant Chinatown.
Dorms are also available.

Grand China
Princess Hotel ⓑⓑ
Modern   **City Map** 6 E1
215 Yaowarat Rd,
Samphan Thawong 10100
Tel *0-2224-9977*
Ⓦ grandchina.com
Rooms are stylish and carpeted,
and a restaurant on the 25th
floor has live music nightly.

Shanghai Mansion ⓑⓑ
Boutique   **City Map** 6 F2
479–481 Yaowarat Rd, Samphan
Thawong 10100
Tel *0-2221-2121*
Ⓦ shanghaimansion.com
Lavish rooms showcasing
beautiful, traditional Chinese
decor. Enjoy the good food and
fine service.

Downtown

Lub-d ⓑ
Modern   **City Map** 7 B4
4 Decho Rd, Bang Rak 10500
Tel *0-2634-7999*
Ⓦ lubd.com
A hip backpacker favorite,
located in an area known for its
nightlife. Private en-suites and a
ladies-only dorm are available.

Baan K Residence ⓑⓑ
Modern   **City Map** 8 D4
12/1 Soi Sathorn 2, Sathorn
Nua Rd 10500
Tel *0-2633-9911*
Ⓦ baankresidence.com
Studios and suites, with fully
equipped kitchens, make this
accommodation perfect for a
stay with the family. Ideal
location next to Lumphini Park.

City Lodge ⓑⓑ
Budget
137/1–3 Soi 9, Sukhumvit Rd 10110
Tel *0-2253-7705*
Ⓦ mosaic-collection.com
A good-value choice right beside
Nana BTS. Opt for a quiet room in
the back.

Silom Convent Garden ⓑⓑ
Modern   **City Map** 7 C4
35/1 Soi Pipat 2, Convent Rd 10500
Tel *0-2667-0130*
Ⓦ silomconventgarden.com
These non-smoking serviced
apartments come with kitchens.
Elegant decor and a roof garden.

Anantara Baan
Rajprasong Suites ⓑⓑⓑ
Luxury   **City Map** 8 D2
3 Soi Mahatlek Luang 3,
Ratchadamri Rd 10330
Tel *0-2264-6464*
Ⓦ rajprasong-bangkok.
anantara.com
Luxurious, well-appointed suites
come with private balconies.
Great views and location, close
to Rajadamri BTS station.

Ariyasomvilla Boutique
Hotel ⓑⓑⓑ
Boutique   **City Map** 8 F1
65 Soi 1, Sukhumvit Rd 10110
Tel *0-2254-8880*
Ⓦ ariyasom.com
This delightful 1940s family
mansion is a serene urban oasis.
It boasts a lovely garden and pool.

The Banyan Tree ⓑⓑⓑ
Luxury   **City Map** 8 D4
21/100 Sathorn Tai Rd, Pathum
Wan 10120
Tel *0-2679-1200*
Ⓦ banyantree.com
Mostly suites with Asian decor, plus
great views from the restaurant
on the 61st floor. Excellent spa.

Sumptuous surroundings at Shangri-La
Hotel, Bangkok

Price Guide
Prices are for a standard double room
per night during high season, including
taxes and service.

ⓑ   up to 1,000 baht
ⓑⓑ   1,000 to 4,000 baht
ⓑⓑⓑ   over 4,000 baht

The Eugenia ⓑⓑⓑ
Boutique
267 Soi 31, Sukhumvit Rd,
Wattana 10110
Tel *0-2259-9011*
Ⓦ theeugenia.inetasiapreview.com
Twelve stylish suites in a 19th-
century Colonial-style house
with a top-notch spa and
gourmet dining.

The Mandarin Oriental ⓑⓑⓑ
Luxury   **City Map** 6 F4
48 Oriental Ave, Soi Charoenkrung
41, Charoen Krung Rd 10500
Tel *0-2659-9000*
Ⓦ mandarinoriental.com
This elegant mid-19th-century
hotel offers a great riverside
location, impeccable service,
and delicious food.

Metropolitan by COMO ⓑⓑⓑ
Boutique   **City Map** 8 D4
27 Sathorn Tai Rd, Thungmahamek
10120
Tel *0-2625-3333*
Ⓦ comohotels.com
Large, bright rooms with avant-
garde design. Good pool and
spa, plus the award-winning
restaurant Nahm.

Plaza Athenee ⓑⓑⓑ
Luxury   **City Map** 8 E2
61 Wireless Rd 10330
Tel *0-2650-8800*
Ⓦ plazaatheneebangkok.com
Operated by Royal Meridien,
this is an ultra-modern hotel
that offers superb rooms and
sumptuous food.

Shangri-La Hotel ⓑⓑⓑ
Luxury   **City Map** 6 F5
89 Soi Wat Suan Plu,
Charoen Krung Rd 10500
Tel *0-2236-7777*
Ⓦ shangri-la.com
Gorgeous views, an excellent spa,
and a private butler service. Close
to river boats and the Skytrain.

Siam Kempinski ⓑⓑⓑ
Luxury   **City Map** 4 D5
991/9 Rama 1 Rd 10330
Tel *0-2162-9000*
Ⓦ kempinski.com
Close to the shopping areas,
this stylish hotel offers elegant
rooms, landscaped gardens, and
multiple saltwater pools.

The St. Regis ⓦⓦⓦ
Luxury   **City Map** 8 D2
159 Ratchadamri Rd 10330
Tel *0-2207-7777*
ⓦ stregisbangkok.com
Contemporary high-rise hotel
oozing European elegance.
Friendly staff.

Swissôtel Nai Lert Park ⓦⓦⓦ
Luxury   **City Map** 8 E1
2 Wireless Rd, Pathum Wan 10330
Tel *0-2253-0123*
ⓦ swissotel.com
Low-rise, plush hotel set in
spacious tropical gardens, right
in the center of the city.

Colorful ethnic-style decor, Chakrabongse Villas, Bangkok

Dusit

Hotel de Moc ⓦⓦ
Boutique   **City Map** 2 E3
*78 Prachathipathai Rd, Phra
Nakhon 10200*
Tel *0-2629-2100-4*
ⓦ hoteldemoc.com
Spacious rooms with retro 1960s
decor near Khao San Road. There
is a pool plus spa facilities.

The Siam ⓦⓦⓦ
Boutique   **City Map** 2 E1
*3/2 Khao Rd,
Vacirapayabal 10300*
Tel *0-2206-6999*
ⓦ thesiamhotel.com
Superbly designed suites at this
beautiful riverfront gem. Several
restaurants and bars.

Old City

Lamphu Tree House ⓦⓦ
Boutique   **City Map** 2 E4
*Soi Baan Pan Thom, 155 Wanchat
Bridge, Prachathipathai Rd, Phra
Nakhon 10200*
Tel *0-2282-0991-2*
ⓦ lamphutreehotel.com
Tranquil oasis in a residential
neighborhood. Lots of teakwood
decor and an outdoor pool.

Navalai River Resort ⓦⓦ
Boutique   **City Map** 2 D3
*45/1 Phra Athit Rd, Banglamphu
10200*
Tel *0-2280-9955*
ⓦ navalai.com
Ideal breezy riverside hotel with
Colonial- and Thai-themed
rooms. Close to Khao San Road.

New Siam Riverside ⓦⓦ
Budget   **City Map** 2 D3
*21 Phra Athit Rd, Banglamphu
10200*
Tel *0-2629-3535*
ⓦ newsiam.net
Located right on the waterfront, close to the Khao San
entertainment area but quieter,
and with a small pool.

Arun Residence ⓦⓦⓦ
Boutique   **City Map** 5 C1
*36–38 Soi Phatu Nokyung, Mahathat
Rd, Rattana Kosin Island 10200*
Tel *0-2221-9158*
ⓦ arunresidence.com
Sino-Portuguese mansion on the
river, in the heart of historic
Bangkok. Good split-level rooms
with balconies.

DK Choice

Chakrabongse Villas ⓦⓦⓦ
Boutique   **City Map** 5 B1
*396 Mahathat Rd, Phra Nakhon,
Tha Tien 10200*
Tel *0-2222-1290*
ⓦ thaivillas.com
On the banks of the Chao
Phraya River, within walking
distance of the Grand Palace,
this unique boutique hotel was
once the residence of a Thai
prince. The four free-standing
suites and three rooms are
furnished in Thai, Chinese,
and Moroccan motifs. The
Thai Royal cuisine served on the
terrace is unrivalled. A luxurious
introduction to old Bangkok.

Thonburi

Anantara Bangkok
Riverside Resort & Spa ⓦⓦⓦ
Luxury
257/1–3 Charoen Nakhon Rd 10600
Tel *0-2476-0022*
ⓦ bangkok-riverside.anantara.com
Low-rise, with expansive riverside
gardens, a great spa, and several
restaurants. Suitable for families.

Ibrik Resort on the River ⓦⓦⓦ
Boutique   **City Map** 1 B5
*256 Soi Wat Rakhang, Arun Amarin
Rd, Bangkok Noi 10700*
Tel *09-7995-5636*
ⓦ ibrikresort.com
Three homey non-smoking
rooms with a Mediterranean vibe
in a residential neighborhood.

The Peninsula ⓦⓦⓦ
Luxury   **City Map** 6 F5
*333 Charoen Nakhon Rd,
Khlong San 10600*
Tel *0-2861-2888*
ⓦ peninsula.com
Waterfront rooms with superb
views and an elegant ambience,
plus several dining options.

Farther Afield

Amari Don Muang Hotel ⓦⓦ
Modern   **Road Map** D1
333 Chertwudthakas Rd 10210
Tel *0-2566-1020*
ⓦ amari.com
Good location near the old Don
Muang Airport. Clean, affordable,
and well-equipped rooms.

Bangkok Tree House ⓦⓦⓦ
Resort   **Road Map** D1
*60 Moo 1, Petch Cha Heung Rd, Bang
Namphueng, Phra Padaeng 10130*
Tel *08-2995-1150*
ⓦ bangkoktreehouse.com
Popular eco-resort accessible
only by boat or on foot. Delicious
organic food on offer.

Novotel Suvarnabhumi
Airport Hotel ⓦⓦⓦ
Luxury   **Road Map** D1
*Moo 1, Nongprue, Bang Phli,
Samut Prakarn 10540*
Tel *0-2131-1111*
ⓦ novotel.com
Very high standards for an
airport hotel. Plush rooms, an
excellent spa, and good food.

Eastern Seaboard

CHANTHABURI:
River Guesthouse ⓦ
Budget   **Road Map** E2
3/5–8 Sri Chan Rd 22000
Tel *0-3932-8211*
This guesthouse with friendly
staff is close to the Chanthaburi
River and gem-dealing district.

For more information on types of hotels *see page 292*

CHANTHABURI:
Faa Sai Resort ⓑⓑ
Resort   Road Map E2
Hat Kung Wiman, 26/1 Moo 7,
Sanamchai, Nayaiarm 22170
Tel *08-1342-6234*
Ⓦ faasai.com
This off-the-circuit eco-resort, with
beach activities and an organic
garden, is ideal for families.

JOMTIEN:
Fifth Jomtien Pattaya ⓑⓑ
Resort   Road Map E2
75/316 Moo 12 Thanon Nongprue,
A Banglamung, Chonburi 20150
Tel *0-3805-9522*
Ⓦ fifthjomtien.com
A family-friendly hotel near the
beach, with gardens, pool, mini
golf, restaurant and cycle rental.

KO CHANG: Garden Resort ⓑⓑ
Resort   Road Map E2
98/22 Moo 4, Kai Bae 23170
Tel *0-3955-7260*
Ⓦ gardenresortkohchang.com
A 30-minute drive from the ferry,
this resort offers thatched
bungalows with a lovely pool.

KO CHANG: Kai Bae Hut Resort ⓑⓑ
Budget   Road Map E2
Hat Kai Bae 23170
Tel *0-3955-7142*
Ⓦ kaibehutresort.com
Well-run option with a variety of
room and bungalow choices.
Friendly staff and good food.

KO CHANG: Nirvana ⓑⓑ
Modern   Road Map E2
Ao Bang Bao 23170
Tel *0-3955-8061*
Ⓦ nirvanakohchang.com
A splendidly isolated getaway on
the island's southern tip. Two pools,
a rock waterfall, and a restaurant.

KO CHANG:
Siam Beach Resort ⓑⓑ
Resort   Road Map E2
100/1 Moo 4, Lonely Beach 23170
Tel *08-1922-4495*
Ⓦ siambeachresort.in.th
Located away from the busy

beach area, this resort has
bungalows built on a hillside.
Good food.

KO CHANG:
White Sand Beach Resort ⓑⓑ
Resort   Road Map E2
Hat Sai Khao 23170
Tel *08-1863-7737*
Ⓦ whitesandbeachresort.net
Situated at the north end of Hat
Sai Kaew, the liveliest beach on
the island, this resort offers a
quiet getaway.

KO CHANG:
Aiyapura Resort ⓑⓑⓑ
Luxury   Road Map E2
Ban Khlong Son 23170
Tel *0-3955-5111*
Ⓦ aiyapura.com
Expansive beachfront location,
with organic gardens and an
amazing pool. Good for families.

KO CHANG:
Amari Emerald Cove ⓑⓑⓑ
Luxury   Road Map E2
Hat Khlong Phrao 23170
Tel *0-3955-2000*
Ⓦ amari.com
Well-managed plush hotel with
large rooms, a pool, an Italian
restaurant, and kids' activities.

KO CHANG:
Sea View Resort and Spa ⓑⓑⓑ
Resort   Road Map E2
Hat Kai Bae 23170
Tel *0-3955-2888*
Ⓦ seaviewkohchang.com
Guests here enjoy a beautiful
garden and a fantastic spa.
There is a variety of accom-
modation types and prices.
Great value.

KO KUT: Koh Kood Resort ⓑ
Resort   Road Map E2
Ao Bang Bao, Ko Kut 23120
Tel *08-7785-7695*
Ⓦ kohkoodresort.in.th
This resort offers a peaceful stay
in both bungalows and villas.
Activities include sea-kayaking
and trekking.

DK Choice

KO KUT: Soneva Kiri ⓑⓑⓑ
Luxury   Road Map E2
Ko Kut 23000
Tel *08-2208-8888*
Ⓦ soneva.com
This spectacular villa resort is
original in both design and
service. The owners operate on
an ethos of sustainability and
the "Slow Life". There are many
family-oriented activities on
offer. A private plane brings
guests from Bangkok Airport
to the island.

KO MAK: Good Time Resort ⓑⓑ
Resort   Road Map E2
Ko Mak 23120
Tel *0-3950-1000*
Ⓦ goodtime-resort.com
Well-managed accommodations
– from double rooms to three-
bedroom villas. Cooking classes,
kayaking, and diving trips on offer.

KO MAK: Lazy Day –
the Resort ⓑⓑ
Resort   Road Map E2
Ko Mak 23120
Tel *08-1882-4002*
Aptly named beachside resort
with pleasant, clean bungalow-
style accommodations.

KO SAMET: Jep's Bungalow ⓑ
Budget   Road Map D2
Ao Hin Khok 21160
Tel *0-3864-4112*
Ⓦ jepsbungalows.com
Set on one of the best beaches
on the island. Rooms vary in style.
Good food and welcoming staff.

KO SAMET: Tub Tim Resort ⓑ
Resort   Road Map D2
Ao Tubtim 21160
Tel *0-3864-4025*
Ⓦ tubtimresort.com
Set at the southern end of a
pretty bay. The wooden huts
range from basic to very well
equipped.

KO SAMET: Samed Villa ⓑⓑ
Modern   Road Map D2
Ao Phai 21160
Tel *0-3864-4094*
Ⓦ samedvilla.com
Lovely, well-appointed bungalows
run by a Swiss/Thai family. Ask for
a room with a sea view.

KO SAMET:
Sang Thian Beach Resort ⓑⓑ
Resort   Road Map D2
Ao Thian 21160
Tel *0-3864-4255*
Basic but clean rooms on one
of the island's quieter beaches.
Staff speak limited English.

Shaded poolside seclusion at Soneva Kiri, Ko Kut

Key to Price Guide *see page 294*

KO SAMET: Le Vimarn ⑧⑧⑧
Luxury Road Map D2
Ao Phrao 21160
Tel *0-3864-4104*
W levimarncottage.com
The teak villas at this opulent resort are furnished in bamboo and woven fabrics. Private Jacuzzis.

KO SAMET: Paradee ⑧⑧⑧
Luxury Road Map D2
Ao Kiu Na Nok 21160
Tel *0-3864-4285-7*
W kohsametparadee.com
Boasts two private beaches in a splendidly isolated location at the southeast tip of the island.

PATTAYA: Ice Inn ⑧
Budget Road Map D1
528/2–3 Pattaya 2 Rd 20260
Tel *0-3872-0671*
W iceinnpattaya.com
A safe, clean, no-frills hotel just a block from the beach. The quietest rooms are at the back.

PATTAYA: Lek Hotel ⑧
Budget Road Map D1
284/5 Soi 13, Pattaya 2 Rd 20260
Tel *0-3842-5550*
W lekhotelpattaya.com
Excellent-value, high-rise hotel close to the beach, with a pool and roof garden.

PATTAYA: Southern Star Resort ⑧
Resort Road Map D1
Soi 12, Naklua Rd 20260
Tel *0-3822-5593*
W southernstarresort.net
Clean and quiet, single-story, with a pool. Superior rooms have a balcony, and all have free Wi-Fi.

PATTAYA:
Royal Cliff Beach Resort ⑧⑧⑧
Resort Road Map D1
353 Moo 12, Pratumnak Rd 20150
Tel *0-3825-0421*
W royalcliff.com
Sitting atop the cliff south of Pattaya, this top resort has many amenities, plus a private beach.

PATTAYA:
Sheraton Pattaya Resort ⑧⑧⑧
Luxury Road Map D1
437 Pratumnak Rd 20150
Tel *0-3825-9888*
W sheratonpattayaresort.com
On a picturesque headland, with a small private beach and pools. Superb spa and gourmet dining.

PATTAYA: Sugar Hut ⑧⑧⑧
Luxury Road Map D1
391/18 Moo 10, Thabpraya Rd 20260
Tel *0-3825-1686*
W sugar-hut.com
Traditional Thai-style villas with superb gardens, away from the beach. Elegant and relaxing.

A legend in Pattaya luxury, Royal Cliff Beach Resort

RAYONG: Wang Gaew ⑧⑧
Boutique Road Map D1
214 Pae-Klaeng Rd, Charkpong 21110
Tel *0-3863-8067*
W wangkaew.co.th
This eclectic collection of beach houses with kitchens on a private bay offer a true Thai feel. Recommended for longer stays.

TRAT: Ban Jaidee ⑧
Budget Road Map E2
67 Chaimongkhon Rd 23000
Tel *0-3952-0678*
Ban Jaidee is an excellent budget choice en route to Ko Chang. Friendly atmosphere and helpful travel advice.

Upper Western Gulf Coast

CHA-AM: Beach Terrace ⑧
Budget Road Map C1
854/4 Suksamer Rd, Bang Saiyoy
Tel *0-3225-8502*
W beachterrace-chaam.com
Peaceful beachfront place, with friendly, efficient management. Best value in the region.

CHA-AM:
Hotel de la Paix ⑧⑧⑧
Luxury Road Map C1
115 Moo 7, Tambol Bangkao 76120
Tel *0-3270-9555*
W hoteldelapaixhh.com
Contemporary rooms surround a huge pool and the rooftop restaurant serves tasty food.

CHUMPHON: Euro Hotel ⑧
Budget Road Map C3
73/3 Kromluang Rd 86000
Tel *0-7750-2300*
W euroboutique-hotel.com
In the center of town, this pleasant hotel offers free Wi-Fi in each of its air-conditioned rooms.

CHUMPHON: Novotel
Chumphon Beach Resort ⑧⑧
Resort Road Map C3
110 Moo 4, Hat Paradonpab 86160
Tel *0-7752-9529*
W novotel.com
A large but low-rise hotel on the coast with superb rooms, two restaurants, and a nine-hole golf course. Terrific value.

HUA HIN:
Jings Guesthouse ⑧
Budget Road Map C2
Soi Selakam 77110
Tel *0-3251-6594*
W jings.in.th
Great value in the heart of town, close to nightlife and beaches. Rooms come in various sizes, and there is a small garden courtyard.

HUA HIN: Anantasila Villas ⑧⑧
Resort Road Map C2
35/15 Phet Kasem Rd, Nongkae 77110
Tel *0-3251-1879*
W anantasila.com
Beachfront resort south of town, next to a fishing village. Large pool and lots of activities for kids.

HUA HIN:
Araya Residence ⑧⑧
Boutique Road Map C2
15/1 Chomsin Rd 77110
Tel *0-3253-1130*
W araya-residence.com
Centrally located hotel, with an intimate, Asian minimalist style, teak furniture, and Thai decor.

HUA HIN:
Anantara Resort & Spa ⑧⑧⑧
Luxury Road Map C2
45/1 Phet Kasem Rd 77110
Tel *0-3252-0250*
W anantara.com
Lagoon- or sea-facing rooms with private pools. Expansive gardens, an excellent spa, and good dining choices.

For more information on types of hotels *see page 292*

DK Choice

HUA HIN: Chiva Som ⓑⓑⓑ
Resort **Road Map** C2
73/4 Phet Kasem Rd 77110
Tel 0-3253-6536
Ⓦ chivasom.com
Chiva Som offers serious wellness programs focusing on wholesome diets and a variety of holistic practices, including massage and yoga. Expect attentive service and an incredibly luxurious experience.

PHETCHABURI: Sun Hotel ⓑ
Budget **Road Map** C1
43/33 Moo 5, Baan-mor 76000
Tel 0-3240-0000
Ⓦ sunhotelthailand.com
Basic, simple, and clean accommodations, with bicycles available for hire.

PHETCHABURI: Fisherman's Resort ⓑⓑⓑ
Luxury **Road Map** C1
170 Moo 1, Hat Chao Samrin 76000
Tel 0-3244-1370
Ⓦ thefishermansresort.com
Beachfront villas set in a fishing village. Activities include water sports, hiking, and bird-watching.

PRACHUAP KHIRI KHAN: Banito Beach Resort ⓑ
Resort **Road Map** C2
283 Klang Ao Rd, Ban Krut 85000
Tel 0-3269-5282-3
Ⓦ banitobeach.com
On a long beach far from busier resort areas. Quiet spot, good for families. Excellent seafood.

PRACHUAP KHIRI KHAN: Sailom Resort ⓑⓑ
Modern **Road Map** C2
299 Moo 5, Mae Rumpeung, Bang Saphan 85000
Tel 0-3269-1003
Ⓦ sailombangsaphan.com
A wonderful beachside restaurant and a kids' pool feature at this family-friendly hotel.

PRANBURI: Aleenta Resort & Spa ⓑⓑⓑ
Luxury **Road Map** C2
183 Moo 4, Pak Nam Pran 77000
Tel 0-3261-8333
Ⓦ aleenta.com
Minimalist and refined resort on a pretty beach south of Hua Hin. Gorgeous infinity pool with stunning ocean views.

PRANBURI: Evason Resort ⓑⓑⓑ
Resort **Road Map** C2
9 Moo 3, Hat Pak Nam Pran 77000
Tel 0-3263-2111
Ⓦ evason.com
A family-friendly resort featuring free-standing villas with private pools. Award-winning spa.

Lower Western Gulf Coast

KO PHANGAN: Chokana ⓑ
Budget **Road Map** C4
Ao Bang Charu 84280
Tel 0-7723-8085
This hotel offers simple but spacious and airy bungalows. Friendly atmosphere with regular seafood barbecues and parties.

KO PHANGAN: Blue Ocean Garden Resort ⓑⓑ
Boutique **Road Map** C4
Hat Chaophao 84280
Tel 08-7086-2697
Ⓦ blueoceangarden.com
Well-managed resort in a stunning beachside setting. Serves Italian and Thai cuisine. Thai cooking classes are available.

KO PHANGAN: Green Papaya ⓑⓑⓑ
Luxury **Road Map** C4
Hat Salad 84280
Tel 0-7737-4239
Ⓦ greenpapayaresort.com
An intimate hotel with stylish, spacious pavilions set around a pool in a quiet beachside garden. Friendly and helpful staff.

KO PHANGAN: Panviman Resort ⓑⓑⓑ
Resort **Road Map** C4
22/1 Moo 5, Ao Thong Nai Pan Noi 84280
Tel 0-7744-5101
Ⓦ panviman.com
Set in an isolated location on a hill, with shuttles to the beach and a daily speedboat from Petcharat Pier on Ko Samui.

KO PHANGAN: The Sanctuary ⓑⓑⓑ
Modern **Road Map** C4
Hat Thian 84280
Tel 08-1271-3614
Ⓦ thesanctuarythailand.com
Enjoy a relaxed atmosphere, with yoga, detox, massage, and meditation. Accommodations range from dorms to villas.

KO SAMUI: Free House ⓑ
Budget **Road Map** C4
175/7 Moo 1, Bophut 84140
Tel 0-7742-7516
Ⓦ freehousesamui.com
Great-value beachside spot with a restaurant in relatively quiet Bophut. Accommodation is in wooden cottages with fans or air-conditioning.

KO SAMUI: Chaweng Budget Hotel ⓑⓑ
Modern **Road Map** C4
17/4 Moo 3, Hat Chaweng 84140
Tel 0-7742-2703
Ⓦ kohsamuibudgethotel.com
Quiet, clean, and contemporary rooms in a central location. Kids' pool and a private beach.

KO SAMUI: Code ⓑⓑ
Boutique **Road Map** C4
55/13 Moo 6, Bang Por Soi 4, Maenam 84140
Tel 0-7760-2122
Ⓦ samuicode.com
Suites or villas with minimalist modern design; hillside location, superb views and service.

KO SAMUI: Coral Cove Chalet ⓑⓑ
Boutique **Road Map** C4
210 Moo 4, Hat Thong Ta Khian 84140
Tel 0-7742-2260
Ⓦ coralcovechalet.com
Attractive chalets on a palm-covered hill with a private white-sand cove. Good for snorkeling.

KO SAMUI: Hacienda ⓑⓑ
Boutique **Road Map** C4
98/2 Moo 2, Hat Bophut 84140
Tel 0-7724-5943
Ⓦ samui-hacienda.com
Bright, airy suites all come with private terraces. The rooftop pool offers great views of Bhoput Bay.

Outdoor swimming pool at health resort Chiva Som, Hua Hin

Panoramic view from a villa bedroom, Six Senses Hideaway, Ko Samui

KO SAMUI: Jungle Club ⓑⓑ
Boutique   Road Map C4
Soi Panyadee School, Hat Chaweng 84140
Tel *08-1894-2327*
Ⓦ jungleclubsamui.com
Uniquely designed lodgings set on a hill above Chaweng beach. The restaurant serves Thai and French cuisine.

KO SAMUI: Lamai Wanta ⓑⓑ
Modern   Road Map C4
124/264 Moo 3, Hat Lamai 84140
Tel *0-7742-4550*
Ⓦ lamaiwanta.com
Well-managed hotel at the quieter end of Lamai, with an infinity pool. Popular restaurant.

KO SAMUI: The Saboey ⓑⓑ
Modern   Road Map C4
51/4 Moo 4, Big Buddha Beach 84140
Tel *0-7743-0450*
Ⓦ saboey.com
Located on Bangrak Beach, with excellently designed suites and villas. Infinity pool with Jacuzzi.

KO SAMUI:
Anantara Bophut ⓑⓑⓑ
Luxury   Road Map C4
99/9 Moo 1, Ao Bophut 84140
Tel *0-7742-8300*
Ⓦ anantara.com
Boasts Thai architecture, Zen minimalist rooms, and tropical gardens. Unsurpassed service.

KO SAMUI: The Library ⓑⓑⓑ
Boutique   Road Map C4
14/1 Moo 2, Hat Chaweng 84140
Tel *0-7742-2767*
Ⓦ thelibrary.co.th
The theme of this boutique hotel is books. Free-standing villas with sleek decor, and original artworks.

KO SAMUI: Napasai ⓑⓑⓑ
Boutique   Road Map C4
65/10 Moo 5, Maenam 84140
Tel *0-7742-9200*
Ⓦ napasai.com
Sumptuous Thai-style villas with private plunge pools. Spa and tennis courts on site.

DK Choice

KO SAMUI:
Six Senses Hideaway ⓑⓑⓑ
Luxury   Road Map C4
9/10 Moo 5, Ban Plai Laem, Bophut 84140
Tel *0-7724-5678*
Ⓦ sixsenses.com
Set on a hillside overlooking the Gulf of Thailand, on Ko Samui's quiet north coast, this collection of villas offers ultimate luxury in an unrivalled setting. Each villa has either a Jacuzzi or a private infinity pool. Superlative service.

KO TAO:
In Touch Resort ⓑ
Budget   Road Map C3
Hait Sai Ri South 84360
Tel *0-7745-6514*
Ⓦ intouchresort.com
Well-appointed, spacious bungalows at the quiet end of a busy beach. Excellent restaurant.

KO TAO: Nangyuan Island Dive Resort ⓑⓑ
Resort   Road Map C3
Ko Nang Yuan 84000
Tel *0-7745-6088*
Ⓦ nangyuan.com
Located on a tiny, picturesque islet, there is a variety of bungalows available, all with sea views. Scuba-diving facilities for guests.

KO TAO:
Jamahkiri Resort & Spa ⓑⓑⓑ
Luxury   Road Map C3
Ao Thian Ok 84000
Tel *0-7745-6400*
Ⓦ jamahkhiri.com
Located on a hillside, close to a secluded beach, this resort offers excellent spa facilities, plus a PADI diving club.

NAKHON SI THAMMARAT:
Grand Park Hotel ⓑ
Budget   Road Map C4
1204/79 Pak Nakhon Rd, 80000
Tel *0-7531-7666*
Ⓦ grandparknakhon.com
Clean, modern, and comfortable rooms in a central location. Good rest stop en route to the islands.

NAKHON SI THAMMARAT:
Racha Kiri ⓑⓑ
Resort   Road Map C4
Hat Nai Phlao, Ao Khanom 80210
Tel *0-7530-0245*
Ⓦ rachakiri.com
A pleasant resort out of town on the coast; worth a stop if a trip to the islands is not possible.

SURAT THANI:
Papangkorn House ⓑ
Budget   Road Map C4
456/295 Moo 1 39 Talad Mai Road 84000
Tel *09-1516-5161*
Ⓦ papangkornhouse.com
Rooms are bright and clean here, and there is free coffee in the reception area every morning.

Upper Andaman Coast

PHANG NGA BAY:
Pasai Bungalows ⓑ
Budget   Road Map B5
Ko Yao Noi 82160
Tel *0-7659-7064*
Basic bungalows, but a great vibe and excellent local food.

PHANG NGA BAY:
Thaweesuk Hotel ⓑ
Budget   Road Map B5
79 Petchkasern Rd, Taichang 82000
Tel *0-7641-2100*
The central colonial-style hotel offers tours to Phang Nga Bay and the rubber plantations.

PHANG NGA BAY:
Yao Yai Resort ⓑ
Budget   Road Map B5
Moo 7, Baan Lo Pareh, Pru Nai, Ko Yao Yai 82160
Tel *08-1968-4641*
Ⓦ yaoyairesort.com
On a beach with superb sunset views. Diving trips offered. All bungalows have a private garden.

PHANG NGA BAY:
Six Senses Yao Noi ⓑⓑⓑ
Luxury   Road Map B5
56 Moo 5, Koh Yao Noi 82160
Tel *0-7641-8500*
Ⓦ sixsenses.com
Villas come with a private infinity pool and personal staff at this lavish resort with a superb spa.

For more information on types of hotels *see page 292*

Room with private balcony at Mom Tri's Villa Royale, Phuket

PHANG NGA COAST: Poseidon Bungalows ⓑ
Budget **Road Map** B4
1/6 Khao Lak, Lam Kaen 82210
Tel *0-7644-3258*
ⓦ similantour.nu
Relaxed accommodations on the beach. The owners offer diving tours of the Similan Islands.

PHANG NGA COAST: Golden Buddha Beach Resort ⓑⓑ
Resort **Road Map** B4
Ko Phra Thong 82210
Tel *08-1892-2208*
ⓖ goldenbuddharesort.com
Activities at this resort with cottages include trekking, water sports, and yoga. Closed May–Oct.

PHANG NGA COAST: Aleenta ⓑⓑⓑ
Luxury **Road Map** B4
33 Moo 2, Khok Kloy 82210
Tel *0-7658-0333*
ⓦ aleenta.com
Secluded hotel with chic and minimalist decor. Spa packages in the wellness center.

PHUKET: Casa Brazil ⓑ
Boutique **Road Map** B5
9 Moo 3, Soi Luang Por Chuan 1, Hat Karon 83000
Tel *0-7639-6317*
ⓦ phukethomestay.com
Lively decor at this homestay and gallery. Most rooms have air-conditioning and a private balcony. Courtyard with a garden.

PHUKET: Shanti Lodge ⓑ
Modern **Road Map** B5
1/2 Soi Bangrae, Choafa Nok Rd, Ao Chalong 83000
Tel *0-7628-0233*
ⓦ shantilodge.com
Located above Chalong Bay, this good-value guesthouse has a restaurant serving Thai and Western cuisine. Thai massages and cooking classes are among the activities on offer.

PHUKET: Square One ⓑ
Budget **Road Map** B5
241/34 Ratuthit Rd, Hat Patong 83150
Tel *0-7634-9909*
ⓦ square1.biz
Great-value accommodation in a central beach location. Family-friendly and clean.

PHUKET: Baan Krating Resort ⓑⓑ
Boutique **Road Map** B5
11/3 Moo 1, Wiset Rd, Ao Sane, Rawai 83130
Tel *0-7628-8264*
ⓦ baankrating.com
Secluded hotel in a unique jungle setting on a steep hillside. A short walk from the private beach.

PHUKET: Baipho ⓑⓑ
Boutique **Road Map** B5
205/12–13 Ratuthit Rd, Hat Patong 83150
Tel *0-7629-2074*
ⓦ baipho.com
Centrally located chic hotel, with colorfully decorated rooms. Serves good European food.

PHUKET: Benyada Lodge ⓑⓑ
Modern **Road Map** B5
106/52 Moo 3, Cherng Talay, Hat Surin 83110
Tel *0-7627-1777*
ⓦ benyadalodge-phuket.com
This five-story hotel has elegantly designed, spacious rooms. Its restaurant offers creative meals.

PHUKET: Blue Ocean Resort ⓑⓑ
Modern **Road Map** B5
210/23 Soi Kepsap, Hat Patong 83150
Tel *0-7629-8800*
ⓦ blueoceanresort-phuket.com
A modern hotel with large rooms with free Wi-Fi and DVD player. Pool, spa, and sauna.

PHUKET: Sino House ⓑⓑ
Boutique **Road Map** B5
1 Montree Rd, Phuket town 83000
Tel *0-7623-2495*
ⓦ sinohousephuket.com
Rooms here are named for Chinese cities and feature basic cooking facilities, like microwaves.

PHUKET: Sugar Palm Resort ⓑⓑ
Modern **Road Map** B5
20/10 Kata Rd, Hat Kata 83160
Tel *0-7628-4404*
ⓦ sugarpalmphuket.com
Stylish and lively hotel with rooms that surround a black tiled pool. Short walk to the beach.

PHUKET: Amanpuri ⓑⓑⓑ
Luxury **Road Map** B5
118 Moo 3, Sri Sunthorn Rd, Ao Pansea 83110
Tel *0-7632-4333*
ⓦ amanresorts.com
Phuket's original six-star resort, with a private white-sand beach, wellness center, and tennis courts.

PHUKET: Banyan Tree Resort ⓑⓑⓑ
Luxury **Road Map** B5
33/37 Moo 4, Sri Sunthorn Rd, Cherng Thalae 83110
Tel *0-7637-2400*
ⓦ banyantree.com
Part of a top hotel group, this resort has lavish pool villas on a lagoon. Superb food and spa.

PHUKET: Indigo Pearl ⓑⓑⓑ
Luxury **Road Map** B5
Hat Nai Yang, adjoining Nai Yang National Park 83110
Tel *0-7632-7006*
ⓦ indigo-pearl.com
Sumptuous rooms with striking industrial chic design. Very convenient for the airport.

DK Choice

PHUKET: Mom Tri's Villa Royale ⓑⓑⓑ
Boutique **Road Map** B5
12 Kata Noi Rd, Hat Kata Noi 83100
Tel *0-7633-3569*
ⓦ villaroyalephuket.com
An oasis of good taste and luxury. Choose from sumptuous suites or free-standing villas. The food is famous throughout Phuket, and there is an on-site gourmet Thai cooking school.

RANONG AREA: Vijit ⓑ
Budget **Road Map** B4
Ko Phayam 85000
Tel *0-7783-4082*
Basic, clean, and well-maintained bungalows on a picturesque island near Ranong.

RANONG AREA: Tinidee Hotel ⓑⓑ
Modern **Road Map** B3
41/144 Tamuang Rd, Tambol Kao Nives 85000
Tel *0-7783-5240*
ⓦ tinideeranong.com
This central six-story hotel is clean and cool, with a swimming pool and a shuttle to the beach.

Lower Andaman Coast

KO LANTA: Lanta Pearl Beach Resort ⓑ
Budget **Road Map** B3
233 Moo 3, Sala Dan 81150
Tel *0-7568-4204*
ⓦ lantapearlbeach.com
Family-run resort with spacious bungalows and free transfers from the Saladan ferry pier.

KO LANTA: Narima Resort ⓑⓑ
Boutique   **Road Map** B5
98 Moo 5, Khlong Nin 81150
Tel *0-7566-2668*
Ⓦ narima-lanta.com
Well-designed eco-friendly resort
with attentive owners. There is a
dive shop and a jazz bar on site.

KO LANTA:
Pimalai Resort & Spa ⓑⓑⓑ
Luxury   **Road Map** B5
99 Moo 5, Hat Ba Kan Tiang 81150
Tel *0-7560-7999*
Ⓦ pimalai.com
Deluxe pavilion suites and villas.
There are two infinity pools,
complimentary bicycles, water
sports, excursions, and cruises.

KO PHI PHI: Phi Phi Hill Resort ⓑ
Budget   **Road Map** B5
Hat Yao 81000
Tel *0-7561-8203*
Ⓦ phiphihill.com
Basic bungalow-style accommo-
dations with superb views.
Closed from May to October.

KO PHI PHI:
Phi Phi Natural Resort ⓑⓑ
Resort   **Road Map** B5
Moo 8, Laem Thong 81000
Tel *0-7581-9030*
Ⓦ phiphinatural.com
Activity-based hotel in a secluded
location offering snorkeling,
hiking, and boat trips to islands.

KO PHI PHI: Zeavola ⓑⓑⓑ
Luxury   **Road Map** B5
11 Moo 8, Laem Thong 81000
Tel *0-7562-7000*
Ⓦ zeavola.com
Charming teak villas with a rural
Thai decor. Excellent service and
food. Good spa.

KRABI: Chan Cha Lay ⓑ
Budget   **Road Map** B5
55 Uttarakit Rd 81000
Tel *0-7562-0952*
Ⓦ chanchalay.com
Centrally located, modern hotel
with a small garden. Cheerful,
bright, and spotless rooms.

KRABI: Peace Laguna Resort ⓑⓑ
Resort   **Road Map** B5
49/3 Moo 2, Ao Nang 81000
Tel *0-7563-7544*
Clean rooms a 10-minute walk
away from the beach. Owned by a
helpful, knowledgeable family.

KRABI: Phra Nang Inn ⓑⓑ
Modern   **Road Map** B5
119 Moo 2, Ao Nang 81000
Tel *0-7563-7130*
Ⓦ vacationvillage.co.th
Beachside location, near pubs
and restaurants. A good base for
exploring the islands off Krabi.

KRABI: Railei Beach Club ⓑⓑⓑ
Luxury   **Road Map** B5
Hat Pai Leh West 81000
Tel *0-6685-9359*
Ⓦ railaybeachclub.com
Beautiful, eco-friendly private
houses with kitchen facilities.
Stunning location.

DK Choice

KRABI: Rayavadee ⓑⓑⓑ
Luxury   **Road Map** B5
214 Moo 2, Tham Hat Phra Nang,
Ao Nang 81000
Tel *0-7562-0740*
Ⓦ rayavadee.com
From the luxury speedboat
trip to one of Thailand's most
stunningly beautiful beaches
to its villas filled with antiques,
the Rayavadee is superb
and has a price tag to match.
Exquisite attention to detail,
an excellent on-site spa, and
two fine restaurants.

SATUN:
Castaway Beach Resort ⓑⓑ
Resort   **Road Map** C6
Sunrise Beach, Ko Lipe 91000
Tel *08-3138-7472*
Ⓦ castaway-resorts.com
Rustic, solid teak bungalows on
an island three hours by boat
from Satun. PADI dive school.

SATUN: Gleam Resort ⓑⓑ
Resort   **Road Map** C6
61 Sathiyuthitham Rd 91000
Tel *08-1899-8565*
Ⓦ thegleamboutiqueresort.com
Located in a residential area a
short walk away from restaurants.
Beautiful garden and a pool.

TRANG: Sri Trang Hotel ⓑ
Budget   **Road Map** C5
20 Sathani Rd 92000
Tel *0-7521-8122*
Ⓦ sritranghotel.com
Classic, well-kept small-town
Chinese hotel since 1952. Near the
train station and night market.

TRANG: Koh Mook
Sivalai Beach Resort ⓑⓑⓑ
Luxury   **Road Map** C5
211/1 Moo 2, Ko Muk 92000
Tel *0-8876-0999*
Ⓦ komooksivalai.com
Thai-style villas with breathtaking
views and lots of water-based
activities. A great place to relax.

Deep South

HAT YAI: Centara ⓑⓑ
Modern   **Road Map** C5
3 Sanehanusorn Rd 90110
Tel *0-7435-2222*
Ⓦ centarahotelsresorts.com
The Centara boasts an enviable
position in the heart of the city,
within a shopping complex.
Good-sized, well-furnished
rooms and a rooftop pool.

SONGKHLA:
BP Samila Beach Hotel ⓑ
Budget   **Road Map** D5
8 Ratchadamnoen Nok Rd 90000
Tel *0-5322-2099*
Great beachside location, yet
conveniently close to the center
of town. Boasts a large pool.

SONGKHLA: Aloha Hotel ⓑⓑ
Modern   **Road Map** D5
120-124 Niphatuthit 1 Rd 90110
Tel *0-7423-5999*
Ⓦ alohahatyai.com
Clean and functional, the Aloha
Hotel is situated close to the
railway station and main
shopping area.

SONGKHLA: Rajamangkala
Pavillion Beach Resort ⓑⓑ
Modern   **Road Map** D5
1 Ratchadamneon Nok Rd 90000
Tel *0-7444-0222*
Ⓦ pavilionhotels.com
Tasteful decor is the trademark of
this well-appointed hotel close to
the Songkhla coast. Facilities
include a fitness room, Thai
massage, and karaoke.

Nature-themed decor plus all mod cons at the Rayavadee, Krabi

For more information on types of hotels *see page 292*

WHERE TO EAT AND DRINK

Thailand is fortunate in being a land of plenty. Much of the land is fertile and, since the population has always been small relative to the size of the country, famine has been all but unknown. In the 13th century, King Ramkhamhaeng of Sukhothai, the first Thai kingdom, recorded: "This land is thriving … in the water are fish, in the fields there is rice."

He might also have mentioned the wide range of tropical fruits, vegetables, and spices, to which have been added, since his day, a wealth of imports from South America, thriving in their new Old World setting. The range of dishes, as well as the variety and freshness of the ingredients, make for one of the world's great cuisines.

An elaborate buffet at an upscale hotel in Bangkok

Restaurants

Bangkok's dining scene is one of the most cosmopolitan in Southeast Asia. Italian and French cuisines have long been part of the culinary landscape, but now diners can also enjoy Japanese restaurants, Mexican and Tex-Mex bars and grills, and Sunday brunches at upscale hotels, in addition to traditional Thai food. Most urban restaurants, especially those serving Western food, open at about 11am and close between 10pm and midnight. This can mean that finding a Western-style breakfast is difficult, in which case a regular Thai omelette may have to serve as a substitute.

Virtually every major city has at least one free tourist listings magazine which lists restaurants by cuisine and specialty. These can be picked up in hotel receptions, at banks, money changers, and restaurants. Away from the tourist destinations, the main hotels in every town will have air-conditioned restaurants offering a mixture of Thai and Chinese cuisine.

Thais have taken to Italian and Japanese food with enthusiasm, and the most popular imports are pasta and sushi, found in some of the larger towns. Pizzas are another favorite, while outlets of McDonald's and Burger King are constantly popping up in new locations.

Coffee Shops

A coffee culture has increasingly been taking hold in Thailand, with excellent, reasonably priced, and locally run coffee shops opening on every other street. Popular with Thais and foreigners alike, they do not include expensive Western franchises except in some larger cities. Local coffee shops are still favored by older citizens, who prefer a strong, sweet coffee, filtered through a cotton bag. Served with condensed milk, the coffee is excellent for dunking a traditional deep-fried Chinese breakfast doughnut.

Roadside and Market Food Stands

Some of the best and most reasonably priced food in Thailand can be found at any of the numerous roadside food stalls. Such establishments are usually clean and unpretentious.

The ingredients are openly displayed behind glass panels. Fast cooking processes, such as flash-frying, grilling over charcoal, or boiling are often used. So the fare, invariably fresh, should also be well cooked and safe to eat.

A sure way of measuring a stall's popularity, as anywhere in the world, is by its patrons. If there are plenty of locals sitting at the tables most stalls provide, chances are that the food is good. Visitors should not be surprised to find a businessman with a Mercedes parked nearby sitting at the same stall as a tuk-tuk driver. Thais from all sections of society know how to appreciate good, cheap food.

Menus are rarely in English, so it is a good idea to memorize the names of some of the tastier dishes from the food glossary (see pp306–7). Alternatively, point at a dish and ask to taste it before ordering.

Prices

Buying meals is one of the cheapest aspects of a visit to Thailand. Prices are usually

A beach bar and restaurant at Hat Tha Nam, Ko Chang

Bright neon signs announcing various diners in Pattaya

displayed – menus invariably list them next to each dish. The prices for shellfish are often given by weight. The cost of alcohol, however, can often be more than the meal itself. In larger establishments and hotels of international class, a service charge and tax will usually be levied. These extra costs will be clearly detailed on the check.

Even at establishments which are small, prices are usually fixed and marked on a board. Bargaining is limited to bulk purchases in local markets selling fresh food.

Seafood

Thailand offers some of the best seafood and it does not come any fresher than in the kingdom's coastal regions. Visitors can choose from an excellent range, absolutely fresh and generally on display. Everything from swordfish steak to lobster and giant crabs is available, but for conservation reasons, turtle and turtle's eggs are no longer on the menu. Visitors should also avoid eating shark's fin soup.

Tipping

Tipping was once unknown, but its popularity is increasing as Thais grow accustomed to tips from tourists. Avoid applying a percentage: 10 percent of 50 baht may be appropriate, but 10 percent of an expensive meal would be far too much.

Eating Habits in Thailand

The Thai philosophy of nutrition is simple – eat if hungry. Most Thais, moreover, eat little but often, sometimes snacking six or seven times a day. The concept of three meals simply does not apply in Thailand. Although people do indeed eat breakfast, lunch, and dinner, they may also stop for a bowl of noodles, a fried snack, or a sweet at any time during the day.

Eating is a simple pleasure and does not involve complex rituals of etiquette, although visitors should note a few rules. Thais eat with a fork held in the left hand and a spoon held in the right hand. The fork is usually used only to push food onto the spoon; eating straight from a fork is considered crude. Since food, especially meat, is cut into pieces before it is cooked, knives are not needed.

Thai noodle dishes are often strongly influenced by Chinese culinary traditions, and they are eaten using chopsticks and a spoon. Another exception to the general rule is *khao niaw* (sticky rice), which is eaten delicately using the fingers.

Food in Thailand is usually served communally in a series of large bowls. Only small rice bowls are reserved for individual use. Rice is traditionally served first, and then a spoon is used to ladle two or three spoonfuls from the communal bowls on top of the rice. Feel free to take more if necessary, but note that overloading the plate is regarded as uncouth since there is no need to hurry, and there's always plenty more in the kitchen.

A roadside stall displaying fresh mandarins and apples for sale

Recommended Restaurants

The restaurants on pages 308–317 have been selected to give a cross section of options available along the coast of Thailand and in Bangkok, from cheap street food and lively, bistros to Thai and European cuisines prepared to a world-class standard, as well as places serving international favorites. While the Thais take huge pride in their own food, other cuisines are not only available here, but also prepared to a high standard to satisfy the locals' discerning tastes. To Thais, "fast food" means something completely different than in the West: a dish may be quickly prepared – for example, a bowl of noodles – but the skills and techniques particular to each vendor make for never-ending variations on the theme, and freshness is always a priority.

Establishments highlighted as DK Choice have been selected in recognition of a special feature – this could be excellent value, exceptional cuisine, a fantastic atmosphere, or a combination of these.

Visitors enjoying a meal at one of the many street food stalls in Thailand

The Flavors of Thailand

Thai food is famous for its aromatic and spicy qualities. Chili peppers were first imported to Thailand from the New World in the 16th century by European traders and were adopted into Thai cuisine with great enthusiasm. However, mildly spiced dishes are also easily available. Although influences from China and India can be noticed in stir-fries and curries, Thai creativity has yielded a wide range of dishes unique to the country. The cuisine is full of distinctive flavors and complementary textures, nutritionally balanced and delightfully presented.

Phrik nam pla

A wide variety of fresh seafood for sale at Chinatown in Bangkok

Rice and Noodles

In common with all its Southeast Asian neighbors, the Thai diet is based on the staples of rice and noodles. The most popular type of rice is the long-grained *khao hom mali* (fragrant jasmine rice), which is usually steamed. However, in the north and northeast, locals prefer *khao niaw* (sticky rice), which is

eaten with the fingers, rolled into little balls, and dipped in sauces. *Jok* (rice porridge) is a typical breakfast dish, with egg, chilies, and rice vinegar.

Kuaytiaw (rice noodles), *bami* (wheat and egg) or *wun sen* (mung beans), are usually served fried or in a soup. The most well-known Thai noodle dish among foreigners is *phad thai* (which literally means Thai fry). This delicious mix of noodles fried with fresh or

dried shrimp, egg, beancurd (tofu), and bean sprouts competes with *tom yam kung* for the title of Thailand's national dish.

The Four Flavors

All Thai dishes strike a balance between the four flavors – sweet, sour, salty, and hot – although the balance varies from dish to dish. While Thai cuisine is liberal with its use of

Lemongrass   Ginger   Shallots   Thai basil   Chilies

Kaffir lime leaves   Turmeric   Galangal

Selection of typical Thai herbs, spices, and flavorings

Regional Dishes and Specialties

Food in central Thailand has been strongly influenced by Chinese cuisine and these dishes feature on menus nationwide, including the country's signature dish *tom yam kung*. Northern Thai cuisine takes much of its inspiration from Burma and the Yunnan province in China. Examples include *khao soi*, a delicious dish of boiled and crispy noodles in a mild curry broth, and *kaeng hang le*. Northeastern Thais like their food with a kick, and one of their best-known imports from nearby Laos is the tangy, crunchy *som tam* salad. Southern food is the most fiery of the lot, where creamy coconut, turmeric, and sharp tamarind feature in typical dishes as the spicy and sour *kaeng leung pla*.

Pea eggplants (aubergines)

Tom Yam Kung uses chili, lemongrass, galangal, and kaffir lime to flavor this hot and sour shrimp broth.

Traders selling their fresh produce at one of Bangkok's floating markets

chilies, it also features a variety of subtly flavored dishes that make use of different aromatic herbs and spices such as galangal, lemongrass, kaffir lime leaves, basil, and coriander (cilantro) to enhance aroma and taste. Pastes using these ingredients are pounded in a mortar to ensure the freshest flavor. However, the real key to Thai cuisine is *nam pla* (fish sauce), which adds its typical piquancy to most dishes. Mixed with chilies, garlic, and lemon it becomes the popular condiment *phrik nam pla*.

The Thai Meal

A typical Thai meal consists of a soup, a curry, a stir-fry, and a spicy Thai salad, as well as side dishes of raw or steamed vegetables, served with a big bowl of rice. The meal is rarely divided into formal courses. Westerners who do not realize this often order a soup or a salad as a starter although they are supposed to complement the main dish. The spiciness of these dishes is intended to be toned down by eating them

Expertly carved melons in Thai style for use as table decoration

with rice. However, Thai restaurant staff are likely to serve all dishes ordered at the same time anyway. The only concession that Thais make to courses is with dessert, which is usually a plate of mixed fruit intended to clear the palate after the savory dishes. Many foreign visitors also like to indulge in the national favorite – *khao niaw mamuang* (mango with sticky coconut rice).

WHAT TO DRINK

Fruit juices Thailand's wealth of luscious fruits, such as watermelon, mango, lychee, and papaya, are blended into refreshing juices, shakes, and smoothies. Coconut water, drunk through a straw straight from the nut, is a perfect drink for a hot day on the beach.

Beers There is a good range of beers available. Popular choices are the full-bodied local Singha and Chang.

Wines and spirits As well as locally made rice wine, wines from Europe and the New World are widely available. Thai vineyards are also starting to produce acceptable varieties. The local spirits, Mekong and Sang Som, are very palatable when mixed with ice and soda.

Coffee and tea While not traditional Thai drinks, excellent varieties of both are now grown in the northern hills.

Kaeng Hang Le is a dry, mild curry of pork with ginger, peanuts, and garlic, served with rice and Chinese greens.

Som Tam is shredded unripe papaya and other vegetables, with lime juice, chili, fish sauce, and dried shrimps.

Kaeng Leung Pla is a spicy fish soup with bamboo shoots, flavored with tamarind, chili, garlic, and palm sugar.

A Glossary of Typical Thai Dishes

Thai cuisine is famously innovative and varied. Even street vendors delight in their culinary skills, and it is not uncommon to see food being encased in a banana leaf as delicately as if it were being gift wrapped. Such artful presentations and the sheer range of dishes can be bewildering for first timers as it may not even be obvious what is savory or sweet. This glossary covers typical dishes; phonetic guidance for food words is on page 366.

Visitors enjoying a meal in an open-air beach shack in Ko Chang

Choosing Dishes

Restaurant menus in tourist areas may include descriptions in English, and sometimes other languages. The Thai names of dishes are often derived from the main elements – for instance, the dish *khao mu daeng* translates literally as "rice", "pork", and "red." Thus, the basic components of any dish can often be worked out with only a little knowledge of Thai. If there is no menu, the dishes of the day will be on display. If one does not recognize the dish, pointing and saying *ni arai mai* (what is this?) should elicit a list of ingredients.

Vegetarians should find it easy to order *mai ao nua* (food without meat), but ought to be aware that fish sauce is used in many dishes. Dairy products feature rarely in Thai cuisine, so vegans should not fare worse than vegetarians. Foreigners often ask *phed mai?* (is the dish spicy), or request *mai ao phet na* (a non-spicy meal). To enliven any dish, diners can use the ubiquitous condiments of chilies in vinegar, chili flakes, sugar (for savory dishes), and fish sauce usually placed on most tables.

Snacks

Thais love to eat. Almost every popular beach and street corner in Bangkok and other towns and cities has a selection of food stalls selling raw and freshly cooked snacks.

Bami mu daeng
บะหมี่หมูแดง
Egg noodles with red pork.

Khai ping
ไข่ปิ้ง
Charcoal-roasted eggs.

Kai yang
ไก่ย่าง
Charcoal-grilled chicken.

Khanom beuang
ขนมเบื้อง
Stuffed sweet pancakes.

Khanom krok
ขนมครก
Coconut pudding.

Khao tom mat
ข้าวต้มมัด
Sticky rice served in banana leaves.

Kluay ping
กล้วยปิ้ง
Charcoal-grilled bananas.

Look chin ping
ลูกชิ้นปิ้ง
Meatballs with a chili sauce.

Po pia tod
ปอเปี๊ยะ
Deep-fried spring rolls.

Sai krok
ไส้กรอก
Thai beef or pork sausages.

Satay
สะเต๊ะ
Slivers of beef, pork, or chicken grilled on a stick; served with peanut sauce and cucumber.

Tua thod
ถั่วทอด
Roasted cashews or peanuts.

Noodles

Rice noodles come as *sen yai* (broad), *sen lek* (medium), and *sen mi* (thin). *Bami* are egg noodles. *Wun sen* are thin, transparent soy noodles.

Bami nam
บะหมี่น้ำ
Egg noodles in a broth with vegetables, meat, or fish.

Kuaytiaw haeng
ก๋วยเตี๋ยวแห้ง
Rice noodles served dry with vegetables, meat, or fish.

Kuaytiaw nam
ก๋วยเตี๋ยวน้ำ
Rice noodles in a broth with vegetables, meat, or fish.

Kuaytiaw look chin pla
ลูกชิ้นปลา
Fishballs with noodles.

Phad thai
ผัดไทย
Rice noodles fried with egg, beancurd, dried shrimp, bean sprouts, peanuts, and chili.

Vendor selling an array of snacks from his boat-cum-restaurant in Krabi

Rice Dishes

Rice is the staple food. A familiar Thai greeting, *kin khao mai?* (how are you?), literally translates into "have you eaten rice?"

Khao man kai
ข้าวมันไก่
Chinese-style chicken with rice cooked in chicken stock.

Khao mok kai
ข้าวหมกไก่
Thai-style chicken biryani.

Khao mu daeng
ข้าวหมูแดง
Chinese-style red pork served on a bed of fragrant rice.

Khao na ped
ข้าวหน้าเป็ด
Roast duck served on a bed of fragrant rice.

Khao phad mu/kung
ข้าวผัดหมูหรือกุ้ง
Fried rice with pork *(mu)* or shrimp *(kung)*.

Soups

Thai soups, whether mild and comforting or spicy and energizing, are very inventive. Some, such as *jok*, are eaten for breakfast. The word *"sup"* is widely recognized.

Jok
โจ๊ก
Ground rice porridge with minced pork and ginger.

Khao tom
ข้าวต้ม
Rice soup with a selection of meat and vegetable side dishes.

Tom jeud tao hu
ต้มจืดเต้าหู้
Mild broth with beancurd and minced pork.

Tom kha kai
ต้มข่าไก่
Chicken soup with galangal, coconut milk, and lemongrass.

Tom yam kung
ต้มยำกุ้ง
Shrimp, mushrooms, lemongrass, galangal, and coriander.

Curries

Curries are served either *rat khao* (on a plate of rice) or in a bowl as an accompaniment to a central bowl of rice.

Kaeng kari kai
แกงกะหรี่ไก่
Indian-style chicken and potato.

Kaeng khiaw wan
แกงเขียวหวาน
Slightly sweet green curry.

An extensive selection of wines at the Shades restaurant in Ko Samui

Kaeng matsaman
แกงมัสมั่น
A mild curry from the Deep South with chicken, peanuts, potatoes, and coconut milk.

Kaeng phanaeng
แกงแพนง
Southern-style creamy curry with coconut milk and basil.

Kaeng phed
แกงเผ็ด
A hot curry with red chilies, lemongrass, and coriander.

Kaeng som
แกงส้ม
A hot and sour curry, usually with fish.

Seafood

A wide variety of seafood is available at reasonable prices, particularly in the Deep South.

Hoi malaeng pu op
หอยแมลงภู่อบ
Steamed green mussels.

Hoi thod
หอยทอด
Oysters fried in an egg batter, served on a bed of bean sprouts.

Kung mangkon phao
กุ้งมังกรเผา
Grilled lobster.

Pla meuk yang
ปลาหมึกย่าง
Roasted sliced squid.

Pla nung khing
ปลานึ่งขิง
Steamed fish with ginger, chili, and mushrooms.

Pla thod
ปลาทอด
Crispy deep-fried fish which is combined and served with various sauces.

Pu neung
ปูนึ่ง
Steamed crab which is served with a pungent and spicy sauce.

Regional Dishes

Kaeng hang le
แกงฮังเล
A northern delicacy, pork curry with peanut and ginger.

Khao soi
ข้าวซอย
Chicken or beef curry served with wheat noodles, fresh lime, and pickled cabbage. A northern specialty.

Larb ped
ลาบเป็ด
Northern spicy minced duck.

Som tam
ส้มตำ
Green papaya salad with peanuts, from the northeast.

Yam thalay
ยำทะเล
Southern spicy seafood salad.

Desserts

Known as *khong wan* or sweet things, these are mostly coconut or fruit based.

Foy thong
ฝอยทอง
Sweet, shredded egg yolk.

Khao niaw mamuang
ข้าวเหนียวมะม่วง
Fresh mango served with sticky rice and coconut milk.

Kluay buat chi
กล้วยบวดชี
Bananas in coconut milk.

Mo kaeng
หม้อแกง
Thai-style egg custard.

Drinks

Bia
เบียร์
Beer. Usually served in bottles.

Cha ron
ชาร้อน
Tea with condensed milk.

Kafae
กาแฟ
Coffee, often instant.

Nam cha
น้ำชา
Chinese-style tea without milk.

Nam kuad
น้ำขวด
Bottled water.

A coconut seller at a Floating Market

Where to Eat and Drink

Bangkok

Chinatown

Nai Sow ⓑ
Chinese/Thai   **Map** 6 F1
3/1 Maitri Chit Rd, Pom Prap Sattru Phai 10100
Tel *0-2222-1539*
Humble surroundings, serving excellent Chinese and Thai food. Favorites include *hoi thod* (oysters fried in egg batter) and *tom yam kung* (shrimp soup). Popular with office workers at lunchtimes.

Thip Samai ⓑ
Thai   **Map** 2 E5
313 Maha Chai Rd, Samramrat, Pra Nakhon 10220
Tel *0-2221-6280*
The Thai noodle dish *phad thai* is famous worldwide, but come here for the original, said by some to be the best in the world. Try the "Superb" – with extra shrimp, wrapped in a paper-thin omelet.

Harmonique ⓑⓑ
Chinese/Thai   **Map** 6 F3
Soi Wat Muang Khae, Charoen Krung Rd 10100
Tel *0-2237-8175*
Superb atmosphere, a quiet off-street garden, and ramshackle decor inside. Good Thai food prepared to Western tastes. Delicious pastries as well.

Hua Seng Hong ⓑⓑ
Chinese   **Map** 6 E2
371–373 Yaowarat Rd 10100
Tel *0-2222-0635*
Classic, large Chinese-style place with an extensive menu. Try the duck, the clay-pot prawns, or the tasty dim sum. Efficient service.

Seven Spoons ⓑⓑ
American   **Map** 2 F4
22–24 Chakkaphatdi Phong Rd 10100
Tel *0-2629-9214*   **Closed** *Mon*
This unique spot serves delicious and inventive cuisine. Lots of vegetarian specialties (the quinoa salad is a must-try) plus good cocktails and steaks. Book ahead.

T & K Seafood ⓑⓑ
Seafood   **Map** 6 F2
49–51 Phadung Dao Rd 10100
Tel *0-2223-4519*
Choose from a variety of fresh seafood displayed on ice here, where all items are sold by weight. The whole-steamed fish and crab curry are particularly good. Gets busy late in the evening.

Downtown

Hai Somtam ⓑ
Regional   **Map** 7 C4
2/4–5 Convent Rd, Silom 10120
Tel *0-2631-0216*   **Closed** *Sun*
Great place for northeastern Thai food, known as *aharn Issan*. An open-fronted restaurant, packed at lunchtimes and early evenings with locals eating spicy *som tam* (green papaya salad), grilled chicken, sun-dried pork, sticky rice, and other Issan favorites.

Lamyai ⓑ
Regional   **Map** 8 D2
Soi 6, Lang Suan Rd 10330 **Closed** *Sat & Sun, evenings*
A fine choice for lunch. Try *khao soi*, the famous northern Thai curried noodles, at this foodie favorite. The wheat noodles with chicken or pork and fragrant spices are excellent too.

Suda ⓑ
Thai
6–6/1 Soi 14, Sukhumvit Rd 10110
Tel *0-2229-4664*
Inexpensive and delicious fare: Thai office workers flock here for lunch. Popular dishes include tuna with chilies and cashews, and green curry with rice.

Bua ⓑⓑ
Thai   **Map** 7 C4
Siwadol Building, 1/4 Convent Rd, Silom 10120
Tel *0-2237-6640*
Popular with both locals and visitors, Bua serves up an extensive menu of delicious, keenly priced dishes from four of Thailand's main culinary regions. Try the *pla neung mannao* – steamed sea bass in lime juice.

Charley Brown's Mexican Cantina ⓑⓑ
Mexican
1/23 Soi 11, Sukhumvit Rd 10110
Tel *0-2651-2215*   **Closed** *Mon*
With its colorful decor and poster art on the walls, this is a great spot to sample some of Bangkok's best Mexican cuisine, including tacos and burritos, as well as delicious *chili rellenos*. Wash it down with a sangria or margarita. No children after 8pm.

Eat Me ⓑⓑ
International   **Map** 7 C4
1/6 Soi Phiphat 2, Convent Rd, Silom 10120
Tel *0-2238-0931*
The exposed beams give a loft-style look – which is fitting as Eat Me is both a restaurant and an art gallery. Try pan-seared sea scallops with green mango, chili and coriander, or the spicy *nduja* sausage tartine with duck egg and pecans.

Indus ⓑⓑ
Indian
71 Soi 26, Sukhumvit Rd 10110
Tel *0-2258-4900*
The light, simple dishes at Indus place an emphasis on health without sacrificing flavor. The dining room decor draws on northern India's cultural heritage, with stunning results. Lovely bar and café add to the ambience.

American cuisine with healthy choices at Seven Spoons

Krua Nai Baan
ⓑⓑ
Thai   **Map** 8 E2
94 Soi Lang Suan
Tel *0-2253-1888*
Tricky to find and not exciting decor-wise, but the wide menu of classic Thai dishes is delicious and comes at reasonable prices. Seafood is the specialty; try the *kaeng liang*, a peppery soup with shrimp and pumpkin. Sit outside if the weather allows.

Le Dalat
ⓑⓑ
Vietnamese
57 Soi 23, Sukhumvit Rd 10110
Tel *0-2259-9593*
Run by a French-Vietnamese family, Le Dalat is renowned for the culinary blend of these two cultures, also reflected in the decor. Try the angel hair noodles sautéed with crab meat, shiitake mushrooms, and bean sprouts.

Mrs. Balbir's
ⓑⓑ
Indian
155/1–2 Soi 11/1, Sukhumvit Rd 10110
Tel *0-2651-0498*   **Closed** *Mon*
Classy restaurant serving good northern Indian favorites. The owner, Mrs Balbir, is a local TV personality who runs Indian cooking classes. Of several branches in the city, this, the original, is still the best.

Thanying
ⓑⓑ
Thai   **Map** 7 A5
10 Pramuan Rd, Silom 10500
Tel *0-2236-4361*
A Thai title for ladies of nobility, the name Thanying reflects the type of aristocratic but traditional fare on offer here. Located in a lovely old house off Silom – the ambience is good, and the food even better.

Biscotti
ⓑⓑⓑ
Italian   **Map** 8 E1
Anantara Siam Hotel,
Ratchadamri Rd 10330
Tel *0-2126-8866*
In a swish hotel, Biscotti is a stylish but warm and friendly bistro with an open kitchen. The menu features pizza, pasta, and other comfort foods. Top-quality ingredients and attentive service make this a good value place.

Bo.lan
ⓑⓑⓑ
Thai
24 Sukhumvit Soi 53 10110
Tel *0-2260-2962*   **Closed** *Mon*
An Australian chef and his Thai wife have brought the slow food movement to Thai dishes, made with authentic spices and seasonal ingredients. Warm and relaxing atmosphere. Excellent desserts.

Beautifully cool and stylish decor at the Indian-themed Indus

Issaya Siamese Club
ⓑⓑⓑ
Thai   **Map** 8 F5
4 Soi Sri Aksorn, Chuaphloeng Rd 10120
Tel *0-2672 9040-1*
Located in a quiet old home with a lovely garden, Issaya serves Thai food with just enough fusion elements to make it unique. Try the *mu manao* (thinly sliced pork topped with lime and edible flowers), glazed pork ribs, and *pla ob prik* (baked fish with chili glaze).

Koi
ⓑⓑⓑ
Japanese
26 Soi 20, Sukhumvit Rd 10110
Tel *0-2258-1590*
Well established in the city's increasingly eclectic dining scene, Koi attracts Bangkok's celebrities, who come for delicious sushi and sashimi and the excellent cooked dishes. Warm and intimate decor.

Le Beaulieu
ⓑⓑⓑ
French   **Map** 8 F2
Athenee Office Tower,
63 Wireless Rd, 10330
Tel *0-2168-8220*
A long-time Bangkok favorite, Le Beaulieu serves elegant yet rustic cuisine, such as *terrines de campagne* pâté, *bouillabaisse*, roasted Bresse chicken, and *côte de boeuf* (rib-eye steak).

DK Choice

Le Normandie
ⓑⓑⓑ
French   **Map** 6 F4
Mandarin Oriental Hotel,
48 Oriental Ave, Charoen Krung Soi 41, Charoen Krung Rd 10500
Tel *0-2659-9000*
Said to be Asia's finest French restaurant, Le Normandie boasts a river-view setting, impeccable service, and an exceptional wine list. Serving à la carte seafood and meat dishes, menu highlights include breast of Bresse pigeon with *foie gras*.

Naj
ⓑⓑⓑ
Thai   **Map** 7 C4
42 Convent Rd, Silom 10120
Tel *0-2632-2811-3*
Set in an elegant Colonial-style house, Naj serves excellent dishes gently tuned to foreign palates. Try coconut-milk soup with chicken and galangal, wing bean salad with pork and shrimp, or a sizzling seafood hot plate.

The China House
ⓑⓑⓑ
Chinese   **Map** 6 F4
Mandarin Oriental Hotel,
48 Oriental Ave, Charoenkrung Soi 41, Charoen Krung Rd 10500
Tel *0-2659-9000*   **Closed** *Mon*
In a beautifully restored house in the Art Deco style of 1930s Shanghai, China House serves classic Cantonese cuisine with a contemporary twist. Try the delicious home-made tofu and oven-roasted Peking duck.

Vertigo Grill and Moon Bar
ⓑⓑⓑ
International   **Map** 8 D4
Banyan Tree Hotel, 21/100 Sathorn Tai Rd 10120
Tel *0-2679-1200*
This open-air restaurant on the 61st floor offers stunning views, and a meal or an evening cocktail here is a highlight for many. Barbecue dishes include red mullet *en papillote* with thyme, and scallops with coriander butter.

Dusit

Krua Apsorn
ⓑ
Thai   **Map** 2 E1
503–505 Samsen Rd 10200
Tel *0-2241-8528*   **Closed** *Sun*
Authentic, excellent food served in a simple but clean setting. This is the first and best of three branches in the city. Try the mussels fried *phad cha* style, with basil, yellow chili, wild ginger, and green peppercorn, or one of the southern Thai curries.

For more information on types of restaurants *see page 302*

Pacific Rim cuisine and decor, Trader Vic's

May Kaidee
Thai/Vegetarian   ⓑ   **Map** 2 B3
33 Samsen Rd 10200
Tel *0-2281-7699*
An institution for Bangkok's vegetarians, May Kaidee serves mostly Thai dishes, with some Western choices. Delicious spring rolls, green curry with tofu, and *phad thai*. Good buffet.

Old City

Roti Mataba
Indian/Malay   ⓑ   **Map** 2 D3
*136 Phra Athit Rd,
Chanasongkram 10200*
Tel *0-2282-2119*   **Closed** *Mon*
Enjoy a classic Indian/Malay *roti* (a fried flatbread), stuffed with various fillings and served with a bowl of *dhal* or curry sauce for dipping. Good curries too.

Aquatini
Thai   ⓑⓑ   **Map** 2 C3
*45/1 Phra Athit Rd,
Chanasongkram 10200*
Tel *0-2280-9955*
With its large, breezy riverside terrace beside the Phra Athit Pier, this is a convenient place to enjoy a seafood dish or a curry on a hot day, washed down with a cold beer.

Deck by the River
Thai   ⓑⓑ   **Map** 5 C1
Arun Residence, 36–38 Soi Phatu Nokyung, Mahathat Rd 10200
Tel *0-2221-9158*
The food served at Deck by the River is largely Thai fare, prepared with skill and good-quality ingredients. There are also a few Western dishes. Enjoy views of the Wat Arun across the river.

Jay Fai
Thai   ⓑⓑ   **Map** 2 E5
327 Maha Chai Rd 10200
Tel *0-2223-9384*
Jay Fai is a no-frills local cult favorite because of its *phad khii*

mao, literally drunkard's noodles, a spicy fried noodle dish with chicken and basil. Other Thai standards are also available.

Kai Yang Boran
Northeastern Thai   ⓑⓑ   **Map** 2 D5
474–476 Tanao Rd, Banglamphu 10200
Tel *0-2622-2349*
An excellent place to sample the food from Thailand's northeastern Issan region. It may cost more here than street-side, but cleanliness is guaranteed. The place takes its name from the region's signature dish, *kai yang*, or roasted marinated chicken.

Sala Rattanakosin
Thai/Fusion   ⓑⓑⓑ   **Map** 5 B1
39 Mahathat Rd 10200
Tel *0-2622-1388*
The perfect spot to watch the sun set behind Wat Arun is on the deck of this restaurant, or in its bare-brick, air-conditioned interior while enjoying a tikka-spiced salmon fillet or a roasted whole baby chicken. Then head up to the rooftop bar for drinks.

Thonburi

DK Choice

Supatra River House   ⓑⓑ
Thai   **Map** 1 B4
266 Soi Wat Rakhang, Arun Amarin Rd 10700
Tel *0-2411-0305*
With superb views of the Grand Palace and Wat Arun, this riverside dining venue offers not only authentic Thai food, such as pineapple curry with prawn, but an evening to remember with dance performances on Saturday adding to the experience. Guests are picked up by boat from the Maharaj Pier in the Old City.

Prime
Steakhouse   ⓑⓑⓑ   **Map** 6 F3
*Millennium Hilton,
123 Charoen Nakhon Rd 10600*
Tel *0-2442-2000*
Considered one of the city's best steakhouses, Prime has excellent imported beef as well as seafood and side dishes. A contemporary and relaxing ambience, with a fine view of the river.

Trader Vic's
Asian   ⓑⓑⓑ
Anantara Riverside Resort & Spa, 257 Charoen Nakhon Rd 10700
Tel *0-2476-0022*   **Closed** *Sun pm*
A unique experience, with Polynesian decor, fine Asian food, and delicious cocktails on the riverside deck. Go for the Sunday Mai Tai jazz brunch, a fabulous spread of gourmet international cuisine.

Farther Afield

Dream Section
Thai   ⓑ
Chatuchak Market, Mo Chit 10300
Closed *Mon & Fri*
The best place for a break from shopping in Bangkok's Chatuchak market, Dream Section feels more like a food court, with many different cuisines and Thai specialties on offer. Try the delicious barbecued chicken.

Cedar
Lebanese   ⓑⓑ
Soi 49/9, Sukumvit Rd 10110
Tel *0-2714-7206*
A long-standing favorite, Cedar is known for its delicious Middle Eastern fare. Choose from over 30 types of meze appetizers, as well as hearty main dishes and sublime desserts. Friendly service.

Taling Pling
Thai   ⓑⓑ
25 Soi 34, Sukhumvit Rd 10110
Tel *0-2258-5308-9*
In a converted family home with contemporary design, Taling Pling serves home-style Thai food. Since many of the dishes are uncommon, the picture menu, with lucid descriptions, is useful.

Eastern Seaboard

CHANTHABURI:
Chanthorn Pochana   ⓑⓑ
Thai   **Road Map** E2
102/5-8 Benchama-rachutit Rd 22000
Tel *0-3931-2339*
Centrally located restaurant with a tempting variety of curries, spicy salads, and delicious stir-fries on

the menu. Try the local specialty, *sen mi phad pu* – egg noodles topped with crab meat.

CHANTHABURI: Muen Baan ⑧⑧
Thai/Western   **Road Map** E2
Saritidet Rd 22000
Translating roughly as "just like home," Muen Baan serves up home-cooked favorites, including lots of vegetarian options. Handily located next to the bus station. Friendly service.

KO CHANG: Chow Lay ⑧
Seafood   **Road Map** E2
Pier, Bang Bao 23170
This is one of several seafood restaurants located on the pier in this picturesque fishing village. Good food served in a rustic atmosphere, and a wide range of delicious cocktails.

KO CHANG: Oodie's Place ⑧
Thai/French   **Road Map** E2
Hat Sai Khao 23170
Tel *0-3955-1193*
A lively place where the owner and his band play classic rock covers after 10pm most evenings. There is a good variety of food and drink on the menu. A great spot to relax and sing along.

KO CHANG: Invito Al Cibo ⑧⑧
Italian   **Road Map** E2
Hat Sai Khao 23170
Tel *09-0132-3583*
Enjoy great views from this restaurant's hilltop perch above White Sand Beach. The food is excellent – from simple pizzas to fine-dining choices that cover all the regional cuisines of Italy.

KO CHANG: Paddy's Palms ⑧⑧
Irish/Thai   **Road Map** E2
Hat Sai Khao 23170
Tel *0-3961-9085*
Ko Chang's Irish pub, Paddy's pours out draft Guinness and Kilkenny to go with its authentic Irish food. Try the shepherd's pie and beer-marinated beef. They also do an excellent Sunday roast.

KO CHANG: Tonsai ⑧⑧
International   **Road Map** E2
Hat Khlong Phrao 23170
Tel *08-9895-7229*
Excellent Thai and Western food, with many vegetarian choices. Try the stir-fried fish with ginger. Especially good for large groups. Relaxed atmosphere.

KO SAMET: Naga ⑧
Thai/Western   **Road Map** D2
Ao Hin Khok 21160
Tel *0-3865-2448*
Using techniques passed down from the former British owner,

Naga continues to serve up hearty fare using baked goods from their famous bakery. Good vegetarian curries and Thai stir-fries.

KO SAMET: Ao Prao Resort ⑧⑧
International   **Road Map** D2
Ao Phrao 21160
Tel *0-3864-4100*
Chic and fancy by local standards, this resort's restaurant serves beautifully prepared seafood and other Thai dishes adapted to Western tastes. Located on the west side of the island, with great sunset views.

KO SAMET: Ploy Talay ⑧⑧
Seafood   **Road Map** D2
Hat Sai Kaew 21160
Tel *0-3864-4212*
Of the many beach restaurants that set up in the evening along Hat Sai Kaew, this is the best. Sit on cushions surrounding candle-lit table and enjoy fresh seafood. Prices fluctuate according to supply, so check beforehand.

KO SAMET: Red Ginger ⑧⑧
International   **Road Map** D2
Moo 4, Samet Village 21160
Tel *0-4383-4917*
A great alternative to the standard Thai curries and seafood found on the beaches. Red Ginger's imaginative international cuisine is prepared by a Canadian chef in a quiet, intimate atmosphere. Near the ferry landing.

KO SAMET: Tubtim Resort ⑧⑧
Seafood   **Road Map** D2
Ao Tubtim 21160
Tel *0-3864-4025*
This restaurant promises excellent seafood, prompt service, and views of the beach. Try the *hor mok talae*, a spicy soufflé with seafood steamed in a banana leaf.

Decadent dining setting at Mantra restaurant and bar, Pattaya

PATTAYA: Food Wave ⑧
Food Court   **Road Map** D1
Top Floor, Royal Garden Plaza, Pattaya Beach Rd 20260
This food court offers a wide range of cuisines, including Thai, Vietnamese, Indian, Japanese, Turkish, and Western, all at reasonable prices. Good bay views.

PATTAYA: Ali Baba ⑧⑧
Indian   **Road Map** D1
1/13–14 Central Pattaya Rd 20260
Tel *0-3836-1620*
Good range of high-quality North Indian cuisine, including tandoori and curry dishes, with several vegetarian options. Favored by local Indians – a good sign.

PATTAYA: blue Olive ⑧⑧
Mediterranean   **Road Map** D1
62/147 Moo 12, Thep Prasit Soi 8 20150
Tel *0-3841-6285*
While not located in the heart of the action, blue Olive is worth the trip for its excellent Italian, Spanish, and Greek specialties and its famous steaks.

PATTAYA: Lobster Pot ⑧⑧
Seafood   **Road Map** D1
228 Pattaya Beach Rd 20150
Tel *0-3842-6083*
Atmospherically perched on the fishing pier in South Pattaya, the Lobster Pot is a few steps but also a world away from the wildness of Walking Street. Try the lobster thermidor or grilled tiger prawns.

DK Choice

PATTAYA: Mantra ⑧⑧
International   **Road Map** D1
Pattaya Beach Rd 20150
Tel *0-3842-9591*
This restaurant fits Pattaya perfectly: excessive, outrageous, and lots of fun. Seven open kitchens prepare Japanese, Chinese, Indian, and Western dishes – everything except Thai. With two levels of seating, including private alcoves with names like The Sultan's Table or Opium Den, Mantra is as much an event as a restaurant. Dress code – no shorts or sandals.

PATTAYA: The Grill House ⑧⑧⑧
International   **Road Map** D1
Rabbit Resort, Hat Dongtan, Jomtien 20150
Tel *0-3825-1730*
A romantic restaurant in Jomtien, The Grill House serves a wide range of Thai and Western dishes, from a massive buffet breakfast to steaks and seafood skewers from the evening beach grill.

TRAT: Kluarimkhlong Café ⓑ
Thai/Western **Road Map** E2
Soi Rimkhong 23000
Tel *0-3952-4919*
Enjoy simple and authentic Thai food in modern and comfortable surroundings. Popular with locals. Some Western dishes available.

TRAT: Sang Fah Restaurant ⓑ
Thai/Bakery **Road Map** E2
Soi Sukhumvit 23000
Tel *0-3952-3373*
A smart establishment near the night markets, Sang Fah also sells pies, cakes, coffee and soft drinks. Try the Thai chicken curry, or a shrimp and pineapple dish.

Upper Western Gulf Coast

CHA-AM:
Beachside seafood stands ⓑ
Seafood **Road Map** C1
Ruamchit Rd 76120
These stands often have just a few tables and a portable kitchen, but the seafood is super-fresh and cheap. Find out what is best that day, and ask for a price before ordering.

CHA-AM: Aree Restaurant ⓑⓑ
Indian **Road Map** C1
225/52 Ruamchit Road 76120
Tel *08-0267-9213*
An expat favorite for great Indian food, Aree also has some Thai and European standards: try the specialty, chicken tikka masala. Clean, friendly, and efficient.

CHA-AM: Poom Restaurant ⓑⓑ
Thai **Road Map** C1
274/1 Ruamchit Rd 76120
Tel *0-3247-1036*
Sample fresh seafood dishes in a more comfortable atmosphere than the nearby stalls. Popular with Thai families. Friendly and efficient service.

Dinner with splendid water views at Let's Sea, Hua Hin

CHA-AM: Da Vinci's ⓑⓑⓑ
Western **Road Map** C1
274/5 Ruamchit Rd 76120
Tel *0-3247-1871*
The best place in Cha-am for European food, with excellent seafood choices. The Italian dishes are particularly good. Run by a Swedish chef.

CHA-AM: inAzia ⓑⓑⓑ
International **Road Map** C1
Sheraton Resort, 1573 Phetkasem Rd 76120
Tel *0-3270-8000*
Located midway between Cha-am and Hua Hin, this superb restaurant offers a choice of well-prepared Thai, Japanese, Chinese, and Indian dishes. Elegant decor and outstanding service.

CHUMPHON: Khrua Pagsod ⓑ
Vegetarian **Road Map** C3
10/32 Paradorn Rd 86160
Tel *0-7757-1731*
Excellent-value Western and Asian fare, made with farm-fresh vegetables, is served at this clean, modern establishment. The curries are delicious.

CHUMPHON:
Papa Seafood ⓑⓑ
Seafood **Road Map** C3
188/181 Krom Luang Rd 86160
Tel *0-7751-1972*
This indoor/outdoor seafood emporium lets diners choose from the tank and serves up delectable fresh meals. Good service, attention to cleanliness, and a vibrant atmosphere.

HUA HIN: Chatchai Market ⓑ
Seafood **Road Map** C2
Soi 72, between Phetkasem and Sasong Rds 77110
Definitely "street food", but with a higher standard of cleanliness than some. Try the classic *phad thai* with fresh shrimps, *hoi thod* (fried oyster omelet), one of the many noodle soups, or hearty portions of fresh fish.

HUA HIN: I Rice ⓑ
Thai/Western **Road Map** C2
Rot Fai Rd, Soi 68–70 77110
Tel *08-9137-6009*
Head to this no-frills homely restaurant for good-value Thai food prepared to Western tastes, although it can be made more authentic on request. I Rice also serves European main dishes and cheap beer.

HUA HIN: Ketsarin Seafood Restaurant ⓑ
Seafood **Road Map** C2
17/1 Naretdamri Rd 77110
Tel *08-9682-4965*
This mainly outdoor restaurant on a wooden pier is a favorite with tourists as well as local families. Thai seafood specialties are made using the freshest produce available. Very busy on weekends.

HUA HIN: Baan Itsara ⓑⓑ
Thai **Road Map** C2
7 Naep Khehat Rd 77110
Tel *0-3251-1673*
A seaside spot north of Hua Hin, Baan Itsara is a casual, lively place that was once the home of a Thai artist. The menu offers standard Thai takes on seafood, but is prepared with exceptional skill.

HUA HIN: Cool Breeze ⓑⓑ
Mediterranean **Road Map** C2
62 Naretdamri Rd 77110
Tel *0-3253-1062*
Located in a Colonial-style seafront house, Cool Breeze is a good choice for a light meal. The restaurant serves an excellent selection of sandwiches, tapas, dips, and salads, as well as hearty mains.

Cool Breeze in Hua Hin, offering authentic Mediterranean flavors

Key to Price Guide *see page 308*

HUA HIN: Let's Sea
Ⓑ Ⓑ
Thai　　　　　　　Road Map C2
83/155 Soi Talay 12, Khao Takiab Rd 77110
Tel *0-3253-6888*
Let's Sea serves delicious seafood in Thai style with an international twist. Try the fish cakes wrapped in mini-croutons and lobster carpaccio. Gorgeous sea views, in a lovely spot south of town.

HUA HIN: Royal Indian Restaurant
Ⓑ Ⓑ
Indian　　　　　　Road Map C2
Damnoen Kasem, Prachuap Khiri Khan 77110
Tel *08-7528-8640*
This tiny eatery near the Centara Hotel serves Burmese and Nepalese fare, as well as Indian. Try the tandoori chicken with a choice of rice types and naans.

HUA HIN: Hagi
Ⓑ Ⓑ Ⓑ
Japanese　　　　Road Map C2
Centara Grand Resort and Villas, 1 Damnoen Kasem Rd 77110
Tel *0-3251-2021*
Beautifully executed and presented dishes. The 16-seat teppanyaki kitchen turns cooking into theater and makes for a dramatic dining experience.

> ### DK Choice
>
> **HUA HIN: Salathai** Ⓑ Ⓑ Ⓑ
> Thai　　　　　Road Map C2
> *Centara Grand Resort and Villas, 1 Damnoen Kasem Rd 77110*
> **Tel** *0-3251-2021*
> Outstanding dishes prepared with top-notch ingredients are served here. Lovely outdoor seating in a garden with an adjacent pool. The service and ambience are well worth the price. Book ahead.

HUA HIN: White Lotus
Ⓑ Ⓑ Ⓑ
Chinese　　　　　Road Map C2
Hilton Hua Hin Resort & Spa, 33 Naretdamri Rd 77110
Tel *0-3253-8999*
On the 17th floor of the Hilton Resort, White Lotus enjoys views of the town and coastline. The contemporary menu focuses on Sichuan and Cantonese styles, with a great *dim sum* lunch.

PHETCHABURI: Ban Khanom Thai
Ⓑ
Thai　　　　　　Road Map C1
130 Phet Kasem Rd 77110
Tel *0-3242-8911*
This place serves both sweet and savory dishes. Of the sweets, do not miss the *khanom mo kaeng*, a firm custard of mung bean, egg, coconut, and sugar.

Japanese elegance and precision at Hagi, Hua Hin

PHETCHABURI: Rabieng Rim Nam
Ⓑ Ⓑ
Thai　　　　　　Road Map C1
1 Chisa-in Rd 76000
Tel *0-3242-5707*
Choose from a range of tasty and good-value dishes served in this guesthouse-based restaurant. Centrally located with a pleasant garden setting next to the river.

PRACHUAP KHIRI KHAN: Pan Pochana
Ⓑ
Thai　　　　　　Road Map C2
11 Suseuk Rd 85000
A lively place in a sleepy town, with unpretentious but excellent food. A good place to try shellfish, cheaper and fresher here than in many other places.

PRACHUAP KHIRI KHAN: Phloen Samut
Ⓑ Ⓑ
Thai　　　　　　Road Map C2
44 Beach Rd 85000
Tel *0-3260-1866*
Phloen Samut is a good place to try the local specialty, *pla samli daet diaw* – flash-fried, sundried cotton fish, served with a green mango salad. The other Thai and seafood dishes are also excellent.

Lower Western Gulf Coast

KO PHANGAN: Om Ganesh
Ⓑ
Indian/Thai　　　Road Map C4
Hat Rin 84280
Tel *0-7737-5123*
A New Age atmosphere but the Indian curries are authentic. Tasty *thali* platters and cooling *lassis*. Meat dishes and Thai food also available. Backpackers recover from late nights here.

KO PHANGAN: Cucina Italiana
Ⓑ Ⓑ
Italian　　　　　Road Map C4
Ban Chalok Lam 84280
Closed *Mon*
A longtime favorite run from home by an Italian family. Go for the famous pizza, or try the home-made pasta or slow-cooked lamb stew. Good beach location, and a friendly atmosphere. Book ahead.

KO PHANGAN: Luna Lounge
Ⓑ Ⓑ
International　　Road Map C4
Ao Thong Nai Pan Noi 84280
Tel *0-7744-5035*
Considered by many to be the best place to eat on the island, Luna Lounge offers a wide choice of Western and Thai food served in a comfortable and sophisticated atmosphere. Try the Massaman lamb curry or barbecued kingfish.

KO SAMUI: Imchai Thaifood
Ⓑ
Thai　　　　　　Road Map C4
173/17 Moo 4 , Hat Lamai 84310
Tel *08-1266-5526*
A local favorite for classic fare, Imchai is renowned for its fresh ingredients, good prices, and large portions. A smart building has replaced the previous wooden shack, but the friendly owner and staff remain.

KO SAMUI: Will Wait
Ⓑ
International　　Road Map C4
Main Rd, Hat Lamai 84140
Tel *0-7742-4263*
With Thai, Chinese, Western, and even Japanese dishes on the menu, Will Wait has something for everyone. The food is well priced, with good home-made bread and pastries. Contrary to the name, their service is quick.

For more information on types of restaurants *see page 302*

KO SAMUI: Barracuda ⓑⓑ
Mediterranean **Road Map** C4
The Wharf Samui 62/9 Moo 1,
Tambon Bophut 84320
Tel *0-7792-1663*
Barracuda's German chef prepares
imaginative Mediterranean
cuisine with a nod to Thai flavors.
The understated decor belies the
quality food and service. Good
daily specials, but the lamb is
always a great choice.

KO SAMUI: Rocky's Bistro ⓑⓑ
Fusion **Road Map** C4
Rocky's Resort, Hat Lamai 84140
Tel *0-7723-3020*
This resort's casual dining venue
gets excellent reviews for its
fusion cuisine, but its international
dishes are also noteworthy. Thai
decor with poolside seating.

KO SAMUI: The Islander ⓑⓑ
International **Road Map** C4
167–169 Beach Road, Chaweng
84140
Tel *0-7723-0836*
In a good spot on the Chaweng
Beach Road, this is a great place
for Western meals such as
burgers, fish and chips, and pasta
dishes. The drinks, including
cocktails, are reasonably priced.

DK Choice

KO SAMUI:
Dining on the Rocks ⓑⓑⓑ
Asian **Road Map** C4
Six Senses Hideaway, Baan Plai
Laem, Bophut 84140
Tel *0-7724-5678*
This sophisticated restaurant is
spread over 10 terraced decks
perched on boulders, with
incredible views. It serves
unique interpretations of a
range of Asian dishes. The Thai
staple *tom yam* is served with a
tangy foam, scallops, and a
cracker of Parmesan cheese.
Impeccable service. Promises a
memorable dining experience.

KO SAMUI: H Bistro ⓑⓑⓑ
Thai/Western **Road Map** C4
Hansar Resort, Ban Bophut 84140
Tel *0-7724-5511*
Amid modern stone-and-wood
decor, H Bistro offers a menu that
includes European, Thai, fusion,
and vegetarian specialties.
Excellent service. One of the best
restaurants on the island.

KO SAMUI: Le Napoleon ⓑⓑⓑ
French **Road Map** C4
Lamai 4 Rd, Hat Lamai 84140
Tel *08-5478-4571*
Consistently well-rated for its
classic French food, Le Napoleon

Tables with a view at Dining on the Rocks, Ko Samui

features traditional decor. Be sure
to try the gratinéed mussels and
tournedos flambé in Cognac.
Excellent set menus.

KO SAMUI: Tree Tops ⓑⓑⓑ
International **Road Map** C4
Anantara Lawana Resort,
Hat Chaweng Noi 84140
Tel *0-7796-0333*
With individual pavilions built in
a rainforest, this is a cool and
green respite from the beach.
The menu includes sophisticated
interpretations of Thai and
Western dishes. Knowledgeable
and friendly staff.

KO SAMUI: Zazen ⓑⓑⓑ
French/Thai **Road Map** C4
Zazen Resort, Hat Bophut 84140
Tel *0-7743-0345*
Dine in a relaxed yet opulent
atmosphere right on the beach.
The chef prides himself on his
interpretations of French and
Thai classics. Try their famous
lobster set menu.

KO TAO: Porto Bello Bistro ⓑ
Italian **Road Map** C3
Hat Sai Ri 84000
Tel *0-7745-7029*
Excellent Italian cuisine made
using lots of local seafood, plus
good home-made pastas and
mouthwatering desserts. Friendly
atmosphere and service.

KO TAO: Starlight ⓑⓑ
International **Road Map** C3
Charm Churee Resort, Ao Jansom
84000
Tel *0-7745-6394*
In a lovely resort south of the
busier beaches on the island.
Offers not only great sunset
views and a pleasant dining
atmosphere, but also delicious
Thai and Western dishes,
including imported steaks.

KO TAO:
The Gallery Restaurant ⓑⓑⓑ
Thai/Western **Road Map** C3
10/29 Moo 1, Ban Sai Ri 84000
Tel *0-7745-6547*
A refreshing break from the beach
scene, The Gallery offers gourmet
food in an inventive setting with a
fine art display. Relaxing and chic.
Very popular so book in advance.

NAKHON SI THAMMARAT:
Krua Wang Derm
Restaurant ⓑⓑ
Regional **Road Map** C4
Ratchadamnoen Rd 80000
A great place to sample southern
Thai curries, which are ordered
from steaming pots. Alternatively
choose from a range of stir-fried
dishes cooked to order. Krua also
offers tasting platters.

SURAT THANI: Mouth 2 Mouth ⓑ
Thai/International **Road Map** C4
Amphur Road 84000
Tel *0-7796-9099*
Mouth 2 Mouth is popular with
both locals and travelers. The
menu includes interesting
crossovers of Thai and Western
food, but there are also steaks
and burgers, plus imported beers.

Upper Andaman
Coast

PHANG NGA BAY:
Cha Leang ⓑ
Thai **Road Map** B5
Phetkasem Rd 82000
Tel *0-7641-3831*
A no-frills joint where the spicy
and well-prepared seafood
dishes are the highlights. Try *hor*
mok thalay, spiced chunks of
seafood mixed in a savory
custard and steamed. Lovely
balcony seating out back.

PHANG NGA BAY: Je t'aime Ⓑ
International **Road Map** B5
21/1 Moo 1 Market, Ko Yao Noi 82160
Tel *0-7659-7495* **Closed** *Fri*
Je t'aime's Danish owner-chef
prepares a wide variety of tasty
dishes including fresh fish,
excellent lobster, and baked
goods, all at reasonable prices.

PHANG NGA BAY: Duang ⒷⒷ
Thai/Chinese **Road Map** B5
122 Phetkasem Rd 82000
Tel *0-7641-2216*
This place serves both Chinese
and southern Thai fare. Try the
tom yam talay (spicy seafood
soup) or *yam pla duk fu*, a twice-
cooked catfish topped with
freshly shredded green mango.

PHANG NGA COAST:
Stempfer Café Ⓑ
International **Road Map** B4
*Phetkasem Rd, Baan La On,
Khao Lak 82210*
A long-standing favorite for its
very filling German breakfasts,
as well as its cakes, pastries,
sandwich lunches, and beer.

PHANG NGA COAST: Enzo ⒷⒷ
Japanese **Road Map** B4
62/2 Moo 5, Kukkhak, Khao Lak 82210
Tel *0-7648-6671*
A stylish place serving traditional
and modern organic Japanese
food. The attached Azzuro Wine
Bar has great wines by the glass
and serves fusion tapas.

PHANG NGA COAST:
Pizzeria ⒷⒷ
Italian **Road Map** B4
*Phetkasem Rd, Baan La On,
Khao Lak 82210*
Tel *0-7648-5271*
Delicious home-made gnocchi
and other pastas on offer in
addition to the best pizzas north
of Phuket. The wine is reasonably
priced by local standards.

PHUKET: Angus O'Tools Ⓑ
Irish **Road Map** B5
*516/20 Patak Rd, Soi Islandia,
Karon 83100*
Tel *0-7639-8262*
Known for one of the most
generous breakfasts in all of
Phuket, Angus also has excellent
nightly specials and a Sunday
roast. Guinness on tap available.

PHUKET:
Bangkok Burger Company Ⓑ
American **Road Map** B5
Bangla Mall, Patong 83100
Tel *0-7629-2347*
Top-quality gourmet burger
joint with a menu of interesting
side dishes, milkshakes, and
cocktails. Pleasant environs.

PHUKET:
Kan Eang Seafood II Ⓑ
Seafood **Road Map** B5
9/3 Chofa Rd, Ao Chalong 83110
Tel *0-7638-1323*
A seafood institution for over
30 years, Kan Eang started as
a street-side stand, but is now
a lovely restaurant with a garden.
Well-priced meals and a play
area for children on the adjacent
sandy beach.

PHUKET: Natural Restaurant Ⓑ
International **Road Map** B5
*66/5 Soi Phuthon, Bangkok Rd,
Phuket town 83000*
Tel *0-7622-4287*
This garden restaurant is full of
hidden nooks and crannies and
even little waterfalls. There is a
selection of world cuisines, from
Japanese to German and Thai.

PHUKET: Red Duck Restaurant Ⓑ
Thai **Road Map** B5
*Khoktanod Rd, 88/3 Kata Beach,
Kata 83000*
Tel *09-1163-8022* **Closed** *Mon*
Standard Thai fare prepared with
an attention to quality and
served in a no-frills, comfortable
dining space. Excellent curries
that can be tuned to different
tastes, from mild to super spicy.

PHUKET: Red Onion Ⓑ
International **Road Map** B5
486 Patak Rd East, Karon 83160
Tel *0-7639-6827*
A bit basic in appearance, but
the standard Western food is
substantial and tasty. Try the
chicken steak with fries and the
Wiener schnitzel. Popular with
locals, so get there early.

PHUKET: Somjit Noodles Ⓑ
Thai **Road Map** B5
214/6 Phuket Rd, Phuket town 83000
Tel *0-7625-6701*
A daytime noodle shop with an
excellent range of Hokkien and

Thai noodle dishes. Try the island's
best-known noodle dish, *khanom
chin nam ya Phuket* (Chinese
noodles in a curried fish sauce).

PHUKET:
Sugar Reef Ⓑ
International **Road Map** B5
*100/35 Sri Suthorn Rd,
Cherng Talay, Bang Thao 83110*
Tel *08-7898-9160*
This sports bar offers a good
choice of burgers, fish and chips,
and other Western comfort food,
including delicious pies. There are
a few Thai options on the menu,
and kids' meals too.

PHUKET: Baluchi ⒷⒷ
Indian **Road Map** B5
*Horizon Beach Resort, Soi Kepsap,
Patong 83100*
Tel *0-7629-2526*
Considered by many to be
the best Indian restaurant in
Phuket, Baluchi serves top-notch
North Indian specialties. The
chefs are from the subcontinent
as is a large proportion of the
loyal clientele. Good choices
for vegetarians.

PHUKET: China Inn Café ⒷⒷ
Thai/Chinese **Road Map** B5
20 Thalang Rd, Phuket town 83000
Tel *0-7635-8239*
Housed in a Sino-Portuguese
building, this café resembles a
tasteful antique shop. Mainly Thai
dishes and some Western choices.
Great for breakfast; closes early.

PHUKET: Ka Jok See ⒷⒷ
Thai **Road Map** B5
26 Takua Pa Rd 83000
Tel *0-7621-7903* **Closed** *Sun & Mon*
Hidden down a small side-street
in the center of town, Ka Jok See
is famous throughout Thailand for
its lively atmosphere. Enjoy Thai
dishes prepared with flair along
with live music, dancing, and a
cabaret show. Reserve ahead.

Enzo, a Japanese dining option in Khao Lak

For more information on types of restaurants *see page 302*

Upscale dining in Phuket: The Boathouse Wine & Grill

PHUKET: Lair Lay Tong
Seafood   **Road Map** B5
Soi Dr Wattana, Patong 83100
Tel *0-7634-1140*
A lively little oasis amid the raucous Patong scene, serving both Thai and international fare at reasonable prices. Try *pae sa*, a whole steamed fish in a tangy broth with cabbage and other vegetables, served on a brazier.

PHUKET:
Paan Yah Thai Restaurant
Thai   **Road Map** B5
249 Prabaramee Rd, Patong 83110
Tel *0-7634-4473*
Excellent choice in Patong for its reasonably priced fare and beautiful views. Classic Thai seafood and noodle dishes are carefully prepared with fresh ingredients. Outdoor deck with shaded seating.

PHUKET: Salvatore's
Italian   **Road Map** B5
15 Rasada Rd, Phuket town 83000
Tel *0-7622-5958*   **Closed** *Sun lunch; Mon*
Typical trattoria-style place, with the food cooked to perfection and served with a swing in a tasteful, laid-back atmosphere. There is also a separate pizzeria next door.

PHUKET: Tatonka
Fusion   **Road Map** B5
Sri Suthorn Rd, Bang Thao 83110
Tel *0-7632-4349*   **Closed** *Wed*
A consistently well-reviewed restaurant, Tatonka offers "globetrotter cuisine," with influences from various countries the owner has lived in. Diners can choose from the many tasty, unique creations, such as the sashimi spring rolls.

PHUKET: Black Ginger
Thai   **Road Map** B5
Indigo Pearl Resort, Hat Nai Yang 83110
Tel *0-7623-6550*
A black-painted traditional Thai pavilion, built on stilts over a lake and reached by boat. The fun design aside, the dining experience is elegant, with superb renditions of Thai classics on offer.

DK Choice

PHUKET: The Boathouse
Wine & Grill
French/Thai   **Road Map** B5
West Patak Rd, Kata 83100
Tel *0-7633-0015-7*
Thailand's aristocratic hotelier and restaurateur Mom Tri introduced the high life to Phuket, and the Boathouse was his first project here. The menu offers Thai and Mediterranean fare, with innovative interpretations of classic dishes. The beachside setting is superb, the service impeccable, and the wine list unparalleled. Hosts many special events including cooking classes.

PHUKET: La Gaetana
Italian   **Road Map** B5
352 Phuket Rd, Phuket town 83000
Tel *0-7625-0523*
An intimate venue known for its haute cuisine. Go for the mixed carpaccio of salmon, tuna, beef, and smoked duck breast followed by a course of baked portobello mushrooms in Gorgonzola sauce.

PHUKET: Lim's
Thai   **Road Map** B5
28 Soi 7, Phra Baramee, Kalim 83100
Tel *0-7634-4834*
Effortlessly chic restaurant located away from the beach crowds on a hill above Hat Kalim, just north of Patong. Savor authentic and modern cuisine prepared with superb attention to detail. Charming adjacent lounge bar. Popular with locals.

PHUKET:
Siam Indigo
International   **Road Map** B5
8 Phang Nga Rd, Phuket town 83000
Tel *0-7625-6697*
Elegant yet relaxed place, located in a historic downtown building decorated with original artworks. Thai-Chinese fusion dishes on offer, as well as good Western steaks and seafood grills. Lovely indoor courtyard seating.

RANONG AREA:
Buono@Ranong
Italian   **Map** B3
1/12 Chonraru Rd, Khao Niwet 85000
Tel *08-9587-1250*
Come to Buono for solid Italian comfort food such as pasta and pizzas, along with burgers and some Thai fare. Rustic ambience and friendly staff. Great location near the main thoroughfare.

RANONG AREA:
Ranong Hideaway
Thai/International   **Map** B3
323/7 Ruangrat Rd, Ranong 85000
Tel *0-7783-2730*
Formerly called Sophon's, this is still the primary tourist hangout in Ranong, and a good place to gather travel tips. The menu includes a wide choice of both Western and Thai dishes. Lovely garden and a pool table.

Lower Andaman Coast

KO LANTA: Red Snapper
Fusion   **Map** B5
Ao Phra-Ae 81150
Tel *0-7885-6965*
The restaurant at this guesthouse gets good reviews, not only for the food, but also for its cool leafy garden and friendly staff. Daily changing menu.

KO LANTA:
Time for Lime
Thai   **Map** B5
Hat Khlong Dao 81150
Tel *0-7568-4590*   **Closed** *Sun*
Beachside cooking school, great cocktail bar, and restaurant; come for the excellent tasting menu, or to learn how to cook before your meal. The Norwegian owner uses the proceeds to fund an animal welfare charity on the island.

Key to Price Guide *see page 308*

KO LANTA: Seven Seas ⓑⓑⓑ
International **Road Map** B5
Pimalai Resort, Ao Kantiang
81150
One of the few smart places on
the island, offering great seafood,
some fusion dishes, and a superb
view over the ocean. There is a
wine bar attached.

KO PHI PHI: Ciao Bella ⓑ
Italian/Thai **Road Map** B5
Ao Lo Dalum 81150
Tel *08-1894-1246*
Dine in a romantic beachside
location with candle-lit tables.
Pizzas and pastas are excellent,
as are the grilled seafood and
Thai dishes. Delicious cocktails.

KO PHI PHI: Le Grand Bleu ⓑⓑ
French **Road Map** B5
Ban Ton Sai 81000
Tel *08-1979-9739*
French country cuisine and
some fusion dishes served in a
beautiful Thai-style house. Try
the duck breast or shrimp ravioli.
Extensive wine list.

KO PHI PHI: Ruan Thai ⓑⓑ
Thai **Road Map** B5
Outrigger Resort, Ao Lo Bakao 81150
Tel *0-7562-8944* **Closed** *Wed*
Located on a hill above Outrigger
Resort, Ruan Thai is a good place
to enjoy quality Thai food. The
resort's van provides transport.

DK Choice

KO PHI PHI: Tacada ⓑⓑⓑ
International **Road Map** B5
Zeavola Resort, Hat Laem Thong
81000
Tel *0-7562-7000*
A special occasion restaurant
where guests may choose to
dine in the grounds of the
lovely resort, or be taken to an
uninhabited island. The kitchen
serves dishes from Western and
Thai menus, with imaginative
interpretations of both cuisines.

KRABI: Tamarind ⓑ
Thai/International **Road Map** B5
27/29 Chao Fa Rd 81000
Family-run place in a restored old
shophouse. The food here
satisfies all tastes – from pizzas,
steaks, and sausages and mash to
hearty Thai curries. Good milkshakes and cocktails. Popular
with locals.

KRABI: Viva ⓑ
Italian **Road Map** B5
29 Pruksa Utit Rd 81000
Tel *0-7563-0517*
A favorite of those seeking good
Italian food in Krabi that goes
beyond pizzas. The Italian/Swiss
owner/chef does a good job,
offering home-made ravioli and
risotto, Australian steaks, and
tiramisu. Interesting wine list.

KRABI: Anchalee ⓑⓑ
Thai **Road Map** B5
315 Maharat Rd 81000
Tel *0-7563-1797*
Set in a beautiful garden, close
to downtown Krabi. The menu,
while inevitably seafood-focused,
offers a wide selection of Thai
curries which are renowned for
their authentic preparation.

KRABI:
Sala Bua & Lo Spuntino ⓑⓑ
Italian/Thai **Road Map** B5
Beach Rd, Ao Nang 81000
Tel *0-7563-7110*
Separate Italian and Thai
kitchens and menus in one
venue. Efficient service and a
superb beachfront location amid
the hustle of Seafood Street.

KRABI: Lae Lay Grill ⓑⓑⓑ
International **Road Map** B5
89 Moo 3, Ao Nang 81000
Tel *0-7566-1588*
Lae Lay's hilltop location
provides stunning views and a
cool breeze. The restaurant's
menu offers a good Thai
selection, seafood dishes, and
imported steaks. Good service.

SATUN: Time ⓑ
Thai **Road Map** C6
43 Satun Thani Rd 91000
Tel *0-7471-2286*
Time has an extensive picture
menu covering everything –
from roasted duck to banana
blossom salad and ice cream
desserts. Air-conditioned, with
pleasant decor.

TRANG:
Baan Suan Sudaporn ⓑⓑ
Thai **Road Map** C5
66/25 Thanon Rakchan
Thap Thiang 91000
Tel *0-7522-6070*
A great selection of dishes
served in a verdant garden setting
with a fountain. Try the *somtam
phonlamay*, a spicy but sweet
fruit salad, or the *khaa mu thot*,
the fried pork leg dish that this
place is famous for.

Deep South

HAT YAI: Sumatra ⓑ
Indonesian **Road Map** B5
55/1 Ratthakan Rd 90110
Tel *0-7424-6459*
This modest place serves good
clean halal food. Try typical dishes
such as the *mee goreng* – fried
yellow noodles mixed with eggs
and shrimp; *rendang* curry; or
rojak, a filling spicy salad with a
peanut sauce. No alcohol.

HAT YAI: Basil ⓑⓑ
International **Road Map** B5
9 Soi 2 Punnakun Rd 90110
Tel *0-8191-9321* **Closed** *Mon*
Surprisingly good Western
food in a place not usually
associated with international
cuisine. Good pizzas, grills, and
salads served up in a congenial
atmosphere. The tuna with
sesame sauce is a must-try.

HAT YAI: Kaopan ⓑⓑ
Japanese **Road Map** B5
1/51 Thanon Jiranakorn 90110
Tel *0-7423-3156* **Closed** *Mon*
A good place for their specialty
super-fresh sushi, as well as other
Japanese dishes. Fans prefer it
over the Japanese chain restaurants for the quality and value.

SONGKHLA: Khao Noi ⓑ
Regional **Road Map** D5
14/22 Wichianchon Rd 90000
Tel *0-7431-1805*
This unassuming place is
well-known for its curries, both
central and southern varieties.
A clean establishment with
congenial staff that do their
best with limited English.

Pizza and more with good wines at Viva in Krabi

For more information on types of restaurants *see page 302*

SHOPPING IN THAILAND'S BEACHES AND ISLANDS

Thailand is well-known as a country that offers good shopping. The high quality, wide variety, and low prices of many Thai goods are a major attraction. Arts and crafts are probably the most tempting buys. These range from inexpensive wicker rice steamers to valuable antiques, and include many typically Thai items such as triangular cushions, colorful hill-tribe artifacts, and finely crafted silver jewelry. Thai silk has an international reputation and comes in a variety of designs. The country is renowned for its rich supply of gems, and towns such as Chanthaburi are major gem trading centers. With shopping malls sharing space alongside vibrant markets, Thailand offers shoppers an appealing mix of the traditional and contemporary.

Opening Hours

Most small stores open from about 8am to 8pm or 9pm, while department stores, shopping malls, and tourist shops open from 10:30am until 9pm or 10pm. Business days are normally Monday to Saturday, but most shops in Bangkok, tourist areas, and resorts also open on Sundays and public holidays. During the Thai New Year *(see p38)* and the Chinese New Year *(see p41)*, many shops shut for several days. Market hours are usually dawn to mid-afternoon for fresh produce, and late afternoon to midnight, or even later, for tourist souvenirs.

How to Pay

The Thai baht is relatively stable. The baht will always be accepted throughout the country. Credit cards can be used in many stores in Bangkok as well as in island resorts, and increasingly so in provincial towns such as Songkhla. VISA and MasterCard are the most widely accepted credit cards followed by American Express. Upscale places usually take all major cards. Many shops will add a surcharge of up to 5 percent on payment by credit card.

Rights and Refunds

Visitors should ask for a *bai set* (receipt) with the shop's address and tax number when buying costly items. Shops usually fill out a form for visitors who wish to reclaim the 7 percent sales tax. This form must be presented to customs at the airport. If arranging to have goods shipped home, visitors must ensure that they confirm all the costs involved with the supplier in advance.

Refunds are almost unheard of, but exchange of faulty or poorly fitting non-sale goods from reputable stores should be possible.

Bargaining

The trend in cities, especially Bangkok, is toward chain stores with fixed prices and endless discount sales. However, the Thai love of bargaining means visitors can often negotiate at

Swanky interiors of the popular Siam Paragon in Bangkok

small shops, specialty retailers, and market stands. Visitors should be aware of the going rate for items so as not to offer embarrassingly low sums. Learning the Thai for numbers may restrain the vendor's initial bid. Faking lack of interest if the seller's bids remain high also works and is better than enthusiastically bargaining and then deciding not to buy once the vendor agrees.

Department Stores and Malls

International-style department stores are the mainstay of shopping in Bangkok and larger resorts such as Pattaya and Phuket. However, many stores fill their aisles with bargain stands. The main Thai chains are **Robinson's**, with a branch in Phuket, and the more upscale **Central Department Store**. Residents of Bangkok already have countless downtown malls, such as **Peninsula Plaza**, to choose from, as well as luxury shopping complexes such as **Emporium**, **CentralWorld Plaza**,

Stalls selling a variety of items at a busy street market in Bangkok

Asia Books, one of the most popular bookstores in Thailand

and **Siam Paragon**. But the trend is for big malls out of the center of the city – such as **Fashion Island**.

Some of these outlying malls are enormous. **Seacon Square** on Srinakharin Road, southeast of the city, extends for over 1 mile (2 km). A few modern malls are also situated in other large towns and resorts. These include the **Jungceylon Shopping Complex** in Phuket and **CentralFestival** in Pattaya.

English-Language Bookstores

Thailand has three English-language book and magazine chains: **Asia Books**, which has several branches in Bangkok, **Kinokuniya**, and **Bookazine**, also with several branches in the country. The best bet for second-hand books is **Dasa Books** on Sukhumvit. Second-hand books are also widely available in Pattaya, Ko Samui, and Phuket.

Markets and Street Vendors

There is a market at the heart of every Thai town and even the smallest will offer a good range of fresh produce. Larger markets sell everything – local crafts, fruits, vegetables, and household items.

Mobile roadside stands are also found across the country. Some sell items such as jasmine rings, while others are good for souvenirs. Pattaya and Patong in Phuket have many such stands. They are also seen on Silom and Sukhumvit roads in Bangkok.

Thai Silk

The ancient art of Thai silk-weaving was revived by an American, Jim Thompson *(see p81)*, after World War II and is now a booming export business. Silk can be patterned, plain, or in the subtle *mut mee* style made from dyed thread. This heavy, bright, and slightly rough cloth is now used for ties, dresses, shirts, skirts, and other Western outfits. It also makes excellent cushion covers and hangings, as well as sundry ornaments.

Most silk comes from the north and northeast, but some is woven in and around Bangkok. Surawong Road in Bangkok is a reliable place from where such items can be bought. **Jim Thompson**, and **Shinawatra** on Sukhumvit Road, however, are among the best. Jim Thompson also has outlets in Hua Hin, Ko Samui, Pattaya, and Phuket.

Clothes

Thai tailors can make suits and dresses to order for low prices. It is advisable to assess the designs, fabric, and cut beforehand and insist on a couple of intermediate fittings. In Bangkok, Chinese and Indian tailors advertise in tourist magazines and outside their shops along Sukhumvit, Charoen Krung, and Khao San roads. Designs are usually copied, often with great skill, from magazines or catalogues of famous brands such as Armani and Hugo Boss. The

An array of wooden and bronze carved items at a local shop

A dazzling selection of swatches of colorful Thai silk

quality of workmanship can vary considerably, so make sure to ask around for recommendations.

Other popular items of Thai clothing include baggy fisherman's pants, batik sarongs (especially in the Deep South), and vests and trousers made from hill-tribe silk and other northeastern fabrics.

Arts and Crafts

Although most Thai handicrafts are produced in the north and northeast, these are available in Bangkok and throughout the coastal regions, albeit at slightly higher prices.

High-quality ethnic crafts at fixed prices are available from boutiques in upscale hotels – **Silom Village**, **River City Shopping Center**, and the less expensive **Narai Phand** in Bangkok. In the south, **That's Siam At Jungceylon** in Phuket town is a good bet.

Hill-Tribe Artifacts

The costumes and artifacts of the hill tribes make fascinating souvenirs. Items might include Akha coin headdresses, Lahu geometric blankets and cushion covers, Hmong red-ruffled black jackets, and brightly colored Lisu tunics.

A wide range of hill-tribe souvenirs and clothing is on sale at markets and in arcades throughout the south, especially in the markets of Bangkok and Phuket.

Ceramics

Delicate Benjarong pottery used to be made in China and sent to Thailand to be decorated with intricate floral patterns using five colors. Today, the work is done entirely in Thailand. Visitors can buy dinner services in Benjarong in myriad designs, including the more typical spherical pots. In Bangkok, Chatuchak Market is cheaper and offers a wider choice than the downtown shops.

The heavier celadon pottery style is distinguished by its etched designs under a thick, translucent green, brown, or blue glaze with a cracked patina. It is available in Bangkok at **Siam Ceramic Handmade** as well as in many other craft shops, such as those on Silom and Charoen Krung roads.

Lacquerware

Lacquerware usually has floral, flame, or portrait designs in black and gold on bamboo and wood. More common is the Burmese style of red ocher on bamboo and rattan with pictorial scenes or floral patterns. Traditional items include boxes for food and jewelry and are available in Bangkok as well as in Phuket.

Nielloware and Pewterware

Nielloware, the intricate process of silver (or at times gold) inlay in a black metal amalgam, makes for beautiful items such as cufflinks, pill boxes, and jewelry. Some of the finest items are from Nakhon Si Thammarat. Southern Thailand has significant tin deposits, so pewterware is a major craft there. Typical items include vases, tankards, plates, and jewelry boxes.

Masks, Puppets, and Musical Instruments

Musical instruments including *khaens* (northeastern pan pipes), *piphat* ensemble gongs, and drums make impressive souvenirs. They are available at Silom Village, Narai Phand,

Colorful puppets, inspired by the Ramakien, for sale in Bangkok

Chatuchak, and Nakorn Kasem markets in Bangkok as well as in the local markets of Ko Samui and Phuket. These places are also good sources of classic *khon* masks, *hun krabok* puppets, and *nang talung* and *nang yai* shadow puppets.

In the south, these can be bought from the **Shadow Puppet Theater**. Guided tours also show visitors how these intricate puppets are made.

Antiques

The delicacy and charm of Thai antiques are so appealing to shoppers that the few remaining antiques in the country are either very expensive, fake, or illegally obtained. Thailand is, in fact, one of the principal outlets for antiques from all over Southeast Asia. Some shops resemble museums, with tapestries, statues, cabinets, puppets, lacquerware, and temple artifacts. The main

Attractive display of fine ceramic products

sources in Bangkok are Charoen Krung Road, River City Shopping Center, and Chatuchak Market. Antique auctions are held at River City on the first Saturday of each month.

Recommended shops include **The Fine Arts** and **NeOld** in Bangkok. **Chan's Antique House** in Phuket has an excellent reputation.

Export permits are required for antiques and all Buddha images from the Fine Arts Department, via the **National Museum**, and take at least a week to obtain.

Jewelry

Thai jewelry tends to be large and expressive, often with superb detailing. Necklaces, bracelets, earrings, and Lao-style belts are typical in employing silver thread and filigree detail, often incorporating silver beads and large, plate-like pendants. More affordable modern costume jewelry sells well in Siam Square and Chatuchak Market. Some of Thailand's best jewelry is found in Peninsula Plaza as well as hotels such as the Dusit Thani. Some shops, notably **Uthai's Gems**, will also custom-design jewelry. **Astral Gemstone Talisman** also sells pendants and rings customized according to the buyer's zodiac sign.

Gems

Bangkok is possibly the world's biggest gem-trading center. Local stones include rubies, red and blue spinels, orange and white zircons, and yellow and blue sapphires. Markets also operate around Chanthaburi where gems are cheaper than in Bangkok. Phuket is Thailand's only good source of high-quality pearls; **Mook Phuket** sells very good examples.

The **Asian Institute of Gemological Sciences** is a specialized institute that helps in the grading and identification of gems. It also runs short-term courses on gem recognition and grading. These can help in preventing buyers from buying fake products.

DIRECTORY

Department Stores and Malls

Central Department Store
Silom Complex,
191 Silom Rd, Bangkok.
City Map 7 A4.
Tel 0-2231-3333.
W central.co.th

CentralFestival
333/99 Moo 9,
Banglamung, Pattaya.
Tel 0-3300-3999.
W centralfestival.co.th

CentralWorld Plaza
Ratchadamri Rd, Bangkok.
City Map 8 D1.
Tel 0-2640-7000.
W centralworld.co.th

Emporium
Sukhumvit Rd, Prompong,
Bangkok.
Tel 0-2269-1000.
W emporium.co.th

Fashion Island
5/5 Ramindra Rd,
Bangkok.
Tel 0-2947-5000.
W fashionisland.co.th

Jungceylon Shopping Complex
181 Rat-U-Thit 200 Pee
Rd, Patong, Phuket.
Tel 0-7660-0111.
W jungceylon.com

Peninsula Plaza
153 Ratchadamri Rd,
Bangkok. **City Map** 8 D1.
Tel 0-2253-9791.

Robinson's
259 Sukhumvit Rd,
Between Soi 17 and 19,
Bangkok.
Tel 0-2252-5121.

36 Tilokutis 1 Road,
Phuket town.
Tel 0-7625-6500-12.
W robinson.co.th

Seacon Square
55 Srinakarin Rd, Bangkok.
Tel 0-2721-8888.
W seaconsquare.com

Siam Paragon
Rama I Rd, Bangkok.
City Map 7 C1.
Tel 0-2610-8000.
W siamparagon.co.th

English-Language Bookstores

Asia Books
221 Sukhumvit Rd,
Bangkok.
Tel 0-2252-7277.
W asiabooks.com

Bookazine
Floor 10, BIC Building,
Bumrungrad Hospital,
Soi 3, Sukhumvit Rd,
Bangkok.
City Map 8 F1.
Tel 0-2667-2769.

Hat Chaweng,
Opposite McDonald's,
Ko Samui.
Tel 0-7741-3616.

Pattaya Avenue,
Jomtien, Pattaya.
Tel 0-3872-3906.

Phuket Airport, Phuket.
Tel 0-7635-1432-4.

Dasa Books
714/14 Sukhumvit Rd,
Bangkok.
Tel 0-2661-2993.

Kinokuniya
3rd Fl, Unit 3B 01,
EmQuartier Shopping
Complex, 689 Sukhumvit
Rd, Klong Toey, Bangkok.
Tel 0-2003-6507.

Thai Silk

Jim Thompson
9 Surawong Rd, Bangkok.
City Map 7 C3.
Tel 0-2632-8100.
W jimthompson.com

Hilton Hua Hin Resort and
Spa, 33 Naresdamri Rd,
Hua Hin.
Tel 0-3253-3486.

Central Festival Samui
Shopping Centre, Room
115-6, 209/1-2 Moo 2,
Bo Phud, Ko Samui.
Tel 0-7741-0404.

Royal Cliff Beach Resort,
353 Moo 12,
Phra Tamnuk Rd, Pattaya.
Tel 0-3825-2292.

Kata Thani Beach Resort
and Spa, 14 Kata Noi Rd,
Hat Kata Noi, Phuket.
Tel 0-7628-4096.

Shinawatra
94 Sukhumvit Rd, Soi 23,
Bangkok.
Tel 0-2258-0295.
W tshinawatra.com

Arts and Crafts

Narai Phand
Ground Floor, President
Tower, 973 Ploenchit,
Bangkok. **City Map** 8 D1.
Tel 0-2656-0398.

River City Shopping Center
23 Trok Rongnamkaeng,
Yotha Rd, Bangkok.
City Map 6 F3.
Tel 0-2237-0077.
W rivercity.co.th

Silom Village
286 Silom Rd, Bangkok.
City Map 7 A4.
Tel 0-2234-4448.
W silomvillage.co.th

That's Siam
Silang Blvd, JungCeylon
Shopping Complex, 181
Rat-U-Thit 200 Pee Rd,
Patong, Phuket.
Tel 0-7660-0111.

Ceramics

Siam Ceramic Handmade
3rd Fl, Room 325-6 River
City Shopping Center (see
above), Bangkok.
City Map 6 F3.
Tel 0-2639-0716.
W thaibenjarong.com

Masks, Puppets, and Musical Instruments

Shadow Puppet Theater
110/18 Si Thammasok Soi
3, Nakhon Si Thammarat.
Tel 0-7534-6394.

Antiques

Chan's Antique House
99/42 Moo 5,
Chalermkiat R9 Rd,
Tambon Rasada, Phuket.
Tel 0-7626-1416.
W chans-antique.com

The Fine Arts
3/F Room 354 River City,
Bangkok.
City Map 6 F3.
Tel 0-2237-0077 ext 354.

National Museum
Fine Arts Department,
4 Na Phra That Rd,
Bangkok.
City Map 1 C4.
Tel 0-2224-1333.

NeOld
149/2-3 Surawong Rd,
Bangkok.
City Map 7 B4.
Tel 0-2235-8919.

Jewelry

Astral Gemstone Talisman
1st Fl, 123-C All Season
Place, 87/208 Wireless Rd,
Bangkok.
Tel 0-2252-1230.
W agt-gems.com

Uthai's Gems
28/7 Soi Ruam Rudi,
Phloen Chit Rd, Bangkok.
City Map 8 F2.
Tel 0-2253-8582.

Gems

Asian Institute of Gemological Sciences
48th Floor, Jewellery
Trade Center,
919/539 Silom Rd,
Bangkok.
City Map 7 A4.
Tel 0-2267-4315.
W aigsthailand.com

Mook Phuket
65/1 Moo1, Chao Fa Rd,
Phuket town.
Tel 0-7621-3766.
W mookphuket.com

ENTERTAINMENT IN THAILAND'S BEACHES AND ISLANDS

Modern Thailand is a melting pot of cultures and, while it may have adopted many foreign pursuits, ranging from Hollywood movies to karaoke bars, traditional forms of Thai entertainment still flourish. Classical *khon* dance dramas still survive and are showcased through cultural programs for visitors. A large number of Thai people still nurture a passion for the popular *muay thai*. A sense of *sanuk* (fun) pervades most activities on the beaches and islands of Thailand, even during solemn religious festivals. Indulging in local passions is essential to understanding and enjoying life here, whether it be live music at a bar, a colorful temple fair, the acrobatic *takraw* game, or watching the latest Thai blockbuster film.

Information Sources

Details of major events and festivals taking place throughout the country are provided in booklets available at TAT offices. Thailand's leading English-language listings and features magazine, *Big Chilli*, is a useful source for events in the capital as well as in the rest of the country. Other Bangkok-based magazines such as *BK Magazine* and *Bangkok 101* are also useful guides to the city.

The major resort areas, Hua Hin, Ko Samui, Krabi, Pattaya, and Phuket, also produce a number of free monthly listings magazines. Free maps, marked with entertainment venues, are available at airports and at big resorts. Even lesser developed islands such as Ko Phangan and Ko Tao produce a few useful maps.

Booking Tickets

Big hotels and travel agents can book tickets for cultural shows and sports events. Alternatively, visitors can buy their tickets directly from venues or through websites offering ticketing services for concerts and other performances.

Puppeteers with a traditional figure at the Joe Louis Puppet Theatre, Bangkok

Traditional Theater and Dance

Watching the stylized masked *khon* performance by graceful male dancers is akin to watching the murals of Wat Phra Kaeo *(see pp60–65)* in motion. Sadly, interest in these dance dramas based on the Ramakien *(see p63)* is waning, and performances of *khon*, and the elaborate if less formal *lakhon*, are becoming increasingly rare. In even greater danger of extinction are the *Hun krabok* marionette shows *(see pp30–31)*.

The most atmospheric place to watch traditional dance is at Sanam Luang during royal ceremonies such as the king's birthday or a funeral when dozens of stages are built to provide night-long entertainment. Complete performances can go on for days, so abridged scenes are chosen for shows at the **National Theater** on the last Friday of every month, and at the **Sala Chalermkrung Theater** in Bangkok.

Countless dinner shows in major cities and resorts offer dance performances from all over the country. Reliable venues in Bangkok include **Silom Village**, while the Mandarin Oriental's Sala Rim Nam restaurant *(see p78)* presents classical dance. *Lakhon* can also be witnessed in Bangkok, at the Lak Muang shrine near Sanam Luang, and the Erawan Shrine. Traditional puppetry can be seen at the **Joe Louis Puppet Theatre** in Bangkok.

The most widespread dance drama is *likay*, commonly featuring in temple fairs, festivals, and television. Its bawdy, slapstick, and satirical elements ensure a strong following. *Manora* is the ancient equivalent from southern Thailand.

A traditional *khon* performance at the National Theater, Bangkok

While *nang talung*, or shadow puppet, shows are still widespread today in Malaysia and Indonesia, they have almost disappeared from Thailand and survive only in the provinces of Phatthalung and Nakhon Si Thammarat. Performances of *nang talung* at local festivals can continue through the night, but are shortened for visitors. Even rarer are performances of *nang yai*, in which enormous, flat leather puppets are manipulated by a team of expert puppeteers.

Illuminations at Siam Niramit's nightly arts and culture spectacle, Phuket

Concerts, Exhibitions, and Modern Theater

Thailand's major concert and exhibition halls are located in Bangkok. The state-of-the-art **Thailand Cultural Center** has excellent facilities and attracts big international names. The German **Goethe-Institut** and the **Alliance Française** host good exhibitions and concerts, and top stars frequently perform in the ballrooms of upscale hotels.

Siam Niramit presents lavishly costumed 80-minute shows in Bangkok and Phuket that focus on history, folklore, and festivals, with entertaining special effects. The **Phuket FantaSea** also puts on an elaborate nightly performance entitled "Fantasy of a Kingdom" which takes visitors through different eras of Thai history in a stunning audio-visual show.

Movies

Thais are avid moviegoers and Bangkok now has a number of multiplexes. These modern theaters coexist with about 2,000 mobile units in the country that offer impromptu open-air screenings in villages. The film industry in Thailand has a long and somewhat erratic history. Despite the production of serious art cinema such as *Luk Isan* (1978), the majority of the films are formulaic melodramas, violent action films, or comedies. Action films from Hong Kong have always been popular, and have been supplemented by Hollywood movies since the early 1990s. In recent years, however, Thai cinema is enjoying a revival and is now regarded as one of the most creative in Southeast Asia. The capital also hosts the increasingly prestigious annual Bangkok International Film Festival.

Many theaters and multiplexes such as **Century – The Movie Plaza** and **Lido** in Bangkok, and **Major Cineplex** and **SF Cinema City** (*see p325*) in both Pattaya and Phuket, show movies with their original soundtracks.

Discos, Bars, Live Music, and Folk Clubs

Despite being challenged by international rock, Thai pop and folk music has retained its popularity and can be heard throughout the country.

The main styles include the exuberant, rhythmic *ram wong*, a folk dance with drums; *look thung*, folk music combining big band music, costumed dance troupes, and singing; and the sentimental *look krung*. Molam music from the northeast has an upbeat sound and uses *khaen* pipes and rap-like vocals. The radical *phleng phua chiwit*, or songs for life, have a protest-based theme and are a mix of traditional Thai folk music with Western rock.

The **Raintree** in Bangkok showcases folk music, while **Saxophone** features jazz and blues, and new rock bands often play at **O'Reilly's Irish**

Dancer in Calypso Cabaret

Pub. The hotels are home to classier venues such as Grand Hyatt Erawan's **Spasso**, Shangri-La's **Angelini**, and Mandarin Oriental's **Bamboo Bar**. These live music haunts are supplemented by karaoke, theme bars, and discos in Bangkok's fashionable districts. There are many large nightclubs in Bangkok including the popular **Narz**. Sarasin Road is a well-frequented strip with restaurants and bars. The gay scene is centered on Silom Soi 2.

Clubs are found in all major resorts in Thailand. In Pattaya, **Club Insomnia** is the hottest nightspot. Phuket's Soi Bangla on Hat Patong is the epicenter of the island's night-life. Ko Samui's burgeoning nightlife is split between Hat Chaweng and Hat Lamai.

Notorious red-light districts such as Patpong, Nana Plaza (Sukhumvit Soi 3), and Soi Cowboy in Bangkok, plus Pattaya and Patong in Phuket, are infamous for their way-out entertainment. Travelers should be wary of getting cheated. It is better to stick to the King's group of bars, which are slightly better than the others. These areas are also home to the famous *kathoeys*, or flamboyant transvestites, who are a part of this industry and put up colorful shows. Cabarets are also popular and the best of these are at **Calypso Cabaret**, Bangkok; **Simon Cabaret**, Phuket; and **Alcazar**, Pattaya.

Visitors enjoying drinks at a colorful theme bar, Bangkok

Thais preparing *krathongs* for the Loy Krathong festival

Temple Fairs and Festivals

The Thai calendar is packed with national holidays and local festivals *(see pp38–41)*. These may be religious festivals or those that honor a local hero, celebrate seasonal changes and harvests, or are dedicated to activities such as boat racing and kite flying.

Apart from hosting other events, most *wats* stage temple fairs. Along with scheduled fairs such as the Golden Mount Temple Fair in Bangkok and Loy Krathong *(see p41)*, there are a number of smaller regional festivals and celebrations. The smaller ceremonies are often as entertaining as the main event itself, with vendors selling food and trinkets, and flamboyantly dressed *kathoeys* adding color. Folk music such as *likay* and *ram wong*, beauty contests, and games add to the general festivities. These also include cockfighting and Siamese fighting fish contests.

Muay Thai and Krabi-Krabong

Muay thai (see p287) is a national passion. Most provinces have a boxing arena, but the top venues are in Bangkok. **Lumpinee Stadium** has bouts every Tuesday, Friday, and Saturday, and there are boxing matches at the **Ratchadamnoen Boxing Stadium** on Mondays, Wednesdays, Thursdays, and Sundays. Krabi's **Ao Nang Krabi Stadium** is the south's largest arena, with bouts every Monday and Friday. Visitors interested in actually learning the skills of this sport should contact the **World Muay Boran Federation**, who should be able to recommend suitable gyms and instructors.

Another revered, long-established Thai martial art is *krabi-krabong*, meaning "sword-staff", after some of the hand weaponry used in this sport. The techniques are taught according to ancient rules and standards, although skill and stamina, rather than injuries inflicted, are now the measure of an accomplished fighter. *Krabi-krabong* is often demonstrated at cultural performances for tourists.

Muay thai fighters enact a bout

Takraw

This acrobatic sport, which is similar to volleyball, is popular all over Southeast Asia and played by young males on any clear patch of ground. The idea is to keep a woven rattan ball in the air using any part of the body apart from the hands. The players' extraordinary agility and speed are a treat for visitors reared on more ponderous sports. There are elaborate versions of this game, but the classic style has a team trying to get the ball into a basketball-like net during a set time frame more times than their rivals. Despite *sepak takraw* (a competitive version of the original *takraw*) being incorporated into the Asian Games and Olympics, professional games of this sport are surprisingly rare.

Soccer, Rugby, and Snooker

Thais have always been enthusiatic about football or soccer and the game was introduced to the country as early as 1897 and came under the king's royal patronage a few years later. In 1996, a professional soccer league – the Thai Premier League, with 18 clubs – was introduced. Rugby has also sparked remarkable interest, with its own league and participation in the Hong Kong Sevens. Matches are held in Bangkok at **National Stadium, Hua Mark Indoor and Outdoor Stadiums, Army Stadium**, and **Royal Bangkok Sports Club**.

Thailand is one of the most successful non-Anglophone countries to adopt snooker. Revived by an Englishman, Maurice Kerr, Managing Director of the Royal Bangkok Sports Club, it was thereafter popularized throughout the country by the world-seeded James Wattana. Since then snooker has become professional and both domestic and world-ranking events are held in Bangkok.

An acrobatic bout of the game of *takraw*

DIRECTORY

Traditional Theater and Dance

Joe Louis Puppet Theatre
Asiatique, 2194 Charoen
Krung, Bangkok.
Tel 0-2688-3322.
W joelouistheatre.com

National Theater
Rachinee Rd, Bangkok.
City Map 1 C4.
Tel 0-2224-1342.

Sala Chalermkrung Theater
66 Charoen Krung Rd,
Bangkok.
City Map 6 D1.
Tel 0-2222-0434.
W salachalermkrung.com

Silom Village
286 Silom Rd, Bangkok.
City Map 7 A4.
Tel 0-2234-4448.
W silomvillage.co.th

Concerts, Exhibitions, and Modern Theater

Alliance Française
179 Witthayu Rd,
Pathum Wan, Bangkok.
City Map 8 D4.
Tel 0-2670-4200.
W afthailande.org

Goethe-Institut
18/1 Soi Goethe,
Sathorn Tai Rd, Bangkok.
City Map 8 E4.
Tel 0-2108-8200.
W goethe.de/ins/th/en/ban.html

Phuket FantaSea
99 Moo 3, Hat Kamala,
Kathu, Phuket.
Tel 0-7638-5000.
W phuket-fantasea.com

Siam Niramit
Ratchada Theater,
19 Tiam Ruammit Rd,
Bangkok.
Tel 0-2649-9222.
55/81 Moo 5,
Chalermprakiet Rd,
Rassada, Muang, Phuket.
Tel 0-7633-5000.
W siamniramit.com

Thailand Cultural Center
Ratchadaphisek Rd,
Bangkok.
Tel 0-2247-0028.

Movies

Century – The Movie Plaza
15 Phaya Thai Rd,
Ratchathewi, Bangkok.
City Map 4 E3.
Tel 0-2247-9940.
W centurythemovieplaza.com

Lido
Siam Square, Bangkok.
City Map 7 C1.
Tel 0-2252-6498.

Major Cineplex
The Avenue, Soi 13,
2nd Rd, Pattaya.
Tel 0-3805-2227.
W majorcineplex.com

SF Cinema City
6th Fl, Central Festival,
333/99 Pattaya Beach
Road, Chonburi, Pattaya.
Tel 0-3300-3222.
W sfcinemacity.com

SFX Coliseum Phuket
3rd Fl, Central Festival,
74–75 Wichitsongkram
Road, Phuket town.
Tel 0-7620-9000
W sfcinemacity.com

Discos, Bars, Live Music, and Folk Clubs

Alcazar
Pattaya 2nd Rd, Pattaya.
Tel 0-3841-0224–7.
W alcazarthailand.com

Angelini
Shangri-La Hotel,
89 Soi Wat Suan Phu,
Bangkok. City Map 6 F5.
Tel 0-2236-7777.
W shangri-la.com

Bamboo Bar
Mandarin Oriental,
48 Oriental Ave, Bangkok.
City Map 6 F4.
Tel 0-2659-9000.
W mandarinoriental.com

Calypso Cabaret
Asiatique, 2194 Charoen
Krung, Bangkok.
Tel 0-2688-1415
W clubinsomniagroup.com

Club Insomnia
Walking Street,
South Pattaya.
Tel 0-3871-1322.
W clubinsomniagroup.com

Narz
112 Sukhumvit Soi 23,
Bangkok.
Tel 0-2258-4805.
W narzclubbangkok.net

O'Reilly's Irish Pub
62 Silom Rd, Bangkok.
City Map 8 C4.
Tel 0-2632-7515.

Raintree
116/64 Soi Rang Nam,
off Phaya Thai Rd,
Bangkok. City Map 4 E4.
Tel 0-2245-7230.

Saxophone
3/8 Soi Ratchawithi,
11 Phaya Thai Rd,
Bangkok. City Map 4 E3.
Tel 0-2246-5472.
W saxophonepub.com

Simon Cabaret
8 Sirirach Rd,
Patong, Phuket.
Tel 0-7634-2011.
W phuket-simoncabaret.com

Spasso
Grand Hyatt Erawan
Hotel, 494 Ratchadamri
Rd, Bangkok.
City Map 8 D1.
Tel 0-2254-1234.
W bangkok.grand.hyatt.com

Muay Thai and Krabi-Krabong

Ao Nang Krabi Stadium
100 Moo 3,
Ao Nang, Krabi.
Tel 0-1606-2888.
W aonang-thaiboxing.com

Lumpinee Stadium
6 Ramintra Rd,
Anusawaree,
Bang Khen, Bangkok.
Tel 0-2252-6843.
W muaythailumpinee.com

Ratchadamnoen Boxing Stadium
1 Ratchadamnoen
Nok Rd, Bangkok.
City Map 2 F4.
Tel 0-2281-4205.
W rajadamnern.com

World Muay Boran Federation
Luk Tup Fah Academy,
5 Onnut 65 Soi 8 Pravet,
Bangkok.
Tel 08-1302-4622.
W worldmuayboran.com

Soccer, Rugby, and Snooker

Army Stadium
Wiphawadirangsit Rd,
Bangkok.
Tel 0-2278-5000.

Hua Mark Indoor and Outdoor Stadiums
2088 Ramkhamhaeng Rd,
Bangkok.
Tel 0-2318-0937.

National Stadium
154 Rama I Rd,
Bangkok.
City Map 7 B1.
Tel 0-2214-0120.

Royal Bangkok Sports Club
1 Henri Dunant Rd,
Pathum Wan,
Bangkok.
City Map 8 D2.
Tel 0-2652-5000.
W rbsc.org

OUTDOOR ACTIVITIES AND SPECIAL INTERESTS

Thailand offers an impressive range of outdoor activities and special interests. The coastal regions are ideal for all kinds of aquatic pursuits from sailing, waterskiing, jet-skiing, and windsurfing to big-game fishing, snorkeling, and diving. Trekking in this spectacular region is also a popular pastime, especially in the forested hills and mountains of southern peninsular Thailand. Coastal Thailand also has an extensive network of national parks. Exciting ways to explore the country's natural wilderness include white-water rafting and kayaking, canoeing, sailing, wildlife watching, and rock-climbing. Visitors can also take advantage of the growing number of excellent golf courses in various resorts such as Phuket and Hua Hin, or learn a variety of cultural skills such as Buddhist meditation forms, traditional Thai massage, and the delicious secrets of Thai food and culinary techniques.

Diving and Snorkeling

Abundant, gorgeous coral reefs, thronging with aquatic life and serviced by countless diving operations, make Thailand one of the world's most accessible and rewarding destinations for underwater exploration. The Andaman coast and islands in particular have some stunning reefs, ocean drop-offs, and submerged pinnacles, as well as visibility that often exceeds 100 ft (30 m). A rich variety of marine life – such as huge whale sharks off the exotic Burma Banks (see p209) – can be spotted in these waters.

Much of the best diving is to be found in national marine parks, such as the Surin, Similan, and Ko Tarutao archipelagos; Ko Tao; and Ko Chang. The once magnificent Ko Phi Phi has not been protected by this reserve status, and has been damaged by anchoring and snorkelers breaking the coral. Reckless fishing with dragnets, harpoons, and explosives has also killed some reefs, while siltation and pollution pose growing threats. Although the tsunami of 2004 caused a tragic loss of life, its effect on the coral reefs of the Andaman Sea was minimal.

Because of rough weather brought on by monsoons, the Andaman sites are accessible only from November to April; the waters of the Western Gulf are best visited between January and October. The Eastern Seaboard, however, is accessible all year round.

Diving trips vary in length from one to several days, and many tours accommodate snorkelers also. The *Asian Diver Scuba Guide: Thailand* (Asian Diver) and *Diving in Thailand* (Asia Books) have comprehensive listings and details of dive sites. Additional information is available online at **Dive Info**, a good source of diving information. PADI-approved diving courses are widely available in Thailand. The main centers offering

Beachside dive shop at Hat Khlong Phrao, Ko Chang

courses are **Dive Asia**, **Santana Diving and Canoeing**, and **Sunrise Divers** in Phuket; **Sea Dragon Dive Center** in Khao Lak; **Crystal Dive Resort** and **Phoenix Divers** in Ko Tao; **Planet Scuba** in Ko Samui; **Haad Yao Divers** in Ko Phangan; **Phi Phi Scuba** and **Blue View Divers** in Ko Phi Phi. Basic diving rules include: inspecting equipment properly, making sure it fits well; only diving after adequate training; diving with a buddy system; making sure the group is not too large; being confident in the abilities of the instructor; and never touching the coral.

Snorkeling is an easy alternative to diving, since all one needs is the ability to swim. **Medsye** offers great snorkeling trips to the Similan Islands. Most hotels and guest-houses located near the reefs rent equipment, but to make the most of the experience, it is best to buy one's own. It is also important to be constantly aware of one's position and not venture too far.

Divers swimming with a leopard shark off the Andaman coast

Sailing

Thailand's dramatic coastline is popular with the yachting fraternity, who come to Phuket every December for the King's Cup Regatta (see p232). Chartering a yacht – with or without a skipper – is possible, although rates for this exclusive activity are not cheap.

Some sailing companies, such as **Gulf Charters Thailand**, operate on the Eastern Seaboard, where sea breezes are often ideal, but the widest choice of sailing companies is in Phuket. Some of the best known are **Phuket Sailing, Yachtpro**, and **Seal Superyachts**.

Watersports

Watersports are popular at many Thai resorts, but the disturbance they cause to the environment has resulted in them being banned in places such as Krabi. However, at most other seaside towns it is possible to rent windsurfing boards and jet skis. Banana boat rides are common, even in places such as Ko Samet.

For the best range of such sports, vacationers should head to Hat Jomtien in Pattaya, or try resorts in Hua Hin, Cha-am, and Hat Patong or Hat Karon in Phuket.

Anglers can make use of the excellent big-game fishing opportunities with **Scuba Dawgs Pattaya** in Chonburi and **Dorado Game Fishing** or **Aloha Tours** in Phuket, but they must pay in excess of 10,000 baht for boat rental. The **Barracuda Bar** in Pattaya also arranges freshwater lake fishing.

Canoeing

Sea-canoeing is not just the most peaceful way to enjoy the unusual karst islets of Phang Nga Bay and the Ang Thong archipelago, but also the only way to explore their collapsed sea caves. Ringed by forest and often containing tiny beaches, many of these spectacular *hongs*, or hidden lagoons, were discovered by **John Gray's Sea Canoe Thailand**, which, along

Kayaking, an adventurous way to explore the mangroves and caves

with **Sea Canoe Thailand**, runs the most responsible tours to these fragile "lost worlds". Another reliable outfit that operates tours around Phang Nga Bay, Ko Tarutao Marine National Park, and the huge reservoir in Khao Sok National Park is **Paddle Asia**.

White-Water Rafting and Kayaking

Sedate bamboo rafting is a popular tourist pastime, particularly in the Phang Nga area where **Sealand Camp** is the acknowledged leader. More exciting, though, is white-water rafting on hardy inflatables. No experience is necessary apart from the ability to swim, since instruction is

Enjoying a game of golf on one of the many courses in Hua Hin

given to paddlers before setting out, and each raft has a crew capable of dealing with any emergency. **The Wild Planet** provides good information on the best times and places. The season for white-water rafting and kayaking lasts from July to December.

Golf

With green and caddie fees cheaper than in the West, it is easy to see why many visitors to Thailand include a round of golf on their itinerary.

Many clubs are open to non-members, and golfing vacation packages are particularly popular at places such as **Laem Chabang International Country Club** in Pattaya, **Blue Canyon Country Club**, **Mission Hills Golf Resort**, and **Phuket Country Club** in Phuket, **Palm Hills Golf Club** in Cha-am, and the **Black Mountain Golf Club** in Hua Hin. Ko Samui also has excellent golfing facilities, such as the **Santiburi Samui Country Club**. Visit the Golfasian.com website to see what is on offer. The best printed guides to courses are the *Thailand Golf Map* and *Thailand Golf Guide*. TAT also publishes a free directory of the country's top 75 courses. The David Leadbetter Academy of Golf at the **Thana City Golf and Country Club** is a great place to reduce handicaps.

Elephant Riding

After the mechanization of logging and its supposed ban in 1989, elephants were no longer used for logging work, and their mahouts were reduced to begging on city streets for a living. Offering elephant rides was an obvious way to generate income and was perceived by many as a positive step toward securing the survival of this national symbol, since the elephants' lowland forest habitat had been largely destroyed.

However, recent research has provided us with greater knowledge of the intelligence and emotions of these animals, and animal welfare groups have expressed serious concerns about the ethics of training and riding elephants, and of forcing them to perform elaborate shows for the amusement of tourists.

There are many ways to enjoy the landscape and wildlife of Thailand without riding an elephant, such as trekking, kayaking, white-water rafting, or taking a river cruise.

Trekking

Thailand offers some ideal terrain for trekking. The precipitous karst forests of Krabi and Khao Sok, in particular, have outstanding hiking trails.

Useful tips include lining backpacks with plastic bags to keep damp out; sleeping in dry clothes (even if it means wearing wet clothes by day); wearing a sun hat and cream for protection against sunburn, and long trousers to protect against

Colorful floating market at Amphawa in Bangkok

leeches; using insect repellent; and wearing worn-in hiking boots or at least supportive athletic shoes. The best time to trek is from November to February and early in the wet season, in June and July. Eco-friendly visitors can try **Evolution Tour**, **Khao Sok Discovery**, **Siam Safari**, and **Phuket Trekking Club**; **Friends of Nature** also organizes ecological treks.

Wildlife Watching

Unfortunately, much of Thailand's large wildlife has been hunted almost to extinction, so there is little point in spending a few days in a hide in the hope of seeing a wild tiger or a bear. However, the country has a wide network of national parks, where some effort has been made to protect pockets of natural beauty. Here, visitors might well see rare and colorful birds, huge butterflies, and foot-long centipedes. The entrance fee to most national

parks for foreigners is 400 baht. Some parks have campsites, and most have log-cabin-style accommodations that can be reserved through the **National Park, Wildlife, and Plant Conservation Department**. The more popular parks, such as Khao Sok, Khao Sam Roi Yot (see pp148–9), and Khao Phanom Bencha (see p249), have well-marked nature trails, but in less popular parks, visitors should ask park rangers to lead them to interesting features.

Boat Trips

Before the arrival of motor cars, boats were the only form of transportation in Thailand, apart from walking. Low-lying areas of the country were criss-crossed by canals that enabled locals to visit friends and do their daily shopping. These days, however, floating markets are strictly for vacationers who can enjoy the colorful spectacle of it all.

Apart from these floating markets, there are several other locations where visitors can go sightseeing by boat. In Bangkok, **Chao Phraya Express Boats** offers short tours with commentary on the main riverside sights. In the south, companies such as **Sayan Tour** organize half- and full-day trips on longtail boats around the limestone stacks in Phang Nga Bay; visitors also have the option of canoeing for an hour.

Cycling

With cycling growing in popularity worldwide, it is no surprise that more and more people consider touring Thailand on a cycle. Not only is it healthy and environmentally sound, it also guarantees meaningful encounters with local people along the way – just put a bike on a bus or train and head for quieter rural areas. The terrain is mostly cyclist-friendly, and several companies organize guided rides along country lanes.

Visitors considering a cycling holiday are advised to consult the websites of the **Thai Cycling**

Trekking through Thailand's beautiful and varied rainforests

Thailand's best rock-climbing at Hat Rai Leh near Krabi

Thailand is from November to February; the worst is in the hot season between March and May. Cycling in the rainy season is also worth considering. **Bike and Travel** and **Spice Roads** are two recommended cycling tour operators with offices in Bangkok and Pathum Thani near Bangkok.

Rock-Climbing

Those looking for an activity that gets the adrenaline flowing will find rock-climbing hard to beat. Thailand is one of the most popular destinations for this sport.

Krabi is the epicenter of rock-climbing, especially at Hat Rai Leh, where several companies offer half- to three-day courses for beginners and rent out equipment to experienced climbers; the more reliable operators include **Tex Rock Climbing**, **King Climbers**, and **Hot Rock**. More than 700 bolted routes in the region offer climbs which are graded according to the French system. Ko Phi Phi has a similar limestone terrain, and a few local companies, such as **Spidermonkey Climbing**, offer instructions for beginners at Ton Sai Tower and Hin Taek.

Bungee Jumping

Visitors who want to go bungee jumping should head to **Jungle Bungy Jump**, a successful company operating in popular tourist locations such as Phuket. A certificate is issued on completion of the jump.

Horse Racing and Riding

As one of the few forms of gambling allowed in Thailand, horse racing attracts a strong local following, and the atmosphere is always vibrant. Races are held on Sundays in Bangkok at the **Royal Bangkok Sports Club** and the **Royal Turf Club**. For a more hands-on equine experience, check out the activities on offer at the **International Riding School** near Pattaya and the **Phuket Riding Club**.

Cultural Study

Courses in meditation can give a valuable insight into Thai culture and also provide invaluable skills to help cope with stress. Participants are required to dress in white and adhere to the fundamental vows of Buddhism – refraining from killing, stealing, lying, and eating after midday. Practitioners are expected to be up before dawn and to plan their day around sessions of walking and sitting meditation, as well as abstaining from entertainment (no TV or music) and idle chat (no mobile phones). Since the Dharma, which means "Way of the Higher Truths", or code of conduct, is given for free, most places suggest that students make a donation to cover their lodging and food. For meditation sessions in English and longer, disciplined retreats, contact the **World Fellowship of Buddhists**. Visitors are welcome to join the 10-day course run by the **International Dharma Heritage** at the beginning of each month at Wat Suan Mokkh *(see p164–5)* near Chaiya. Other options include the famous **Wat Mahathat** *(see p66)* in Bangkok and **Wat Khao Tham** *(see pp181)* on Ko Phangan, as well as the **Dhammakaya Foundation**'s retreats and Sunday sessions. Some locations have facilities for women, while others are only for men.

Visitors can also study Thai massage, a vigorous combination of yoga, reflexology, and acupressure. Courses typically last between one and two weeks, and consist of theory, demonstration, and practice, leading to a certification of competence. Popular training in English is conducted at Wat Pho *(see pp68–9)*.

The technique of preparing Thai food – including fruit and vegetable carving – can be learned at cooking schools in hotels such as the Mandarin Oriental *(see p78)* in Bangkok and Mom Tri's Villa Royale in Phuket *(see p300)*, the **Blue Elephant** restaurant and cooking school and **Baipai Thai Cooking School** in Bangkok, **Happy Chef Cooking School** in Pattaya, **Pat's Home Thai Cooking School** in Phuket, and the **Samui Institute of Thai Culinary Arts** in Ko Samui.

Visitors learning to cook Thai food in the Baipai Thai Cooking School

DIRECTORY

Diving and Snorkeling

Blue View Divers
100 Moo 7, Ko Phi Phi.
Tel 0-7581-9395.
W blueviewdivers.com

Crystal Dive Resort
7/1 Moo 2, Mae Hat,
Ko Tao.
Tel 0-7745-6106.
W crystaldive.com

Dive Asia
24 Karon Rd, Hat Kata,
Phuket.
Tel 0-7633-0598.
W diveasia.com

Dive Info
Ban Chuancheun,
Pattanakarn 57,
Bangkok.
Tel 08-4006-0001.
W diveinfo.net

Haad Yao Divers
84/31 Moo 8,
Ko Phangan.
Tel 08-6279-3085.
W haadyaodivers.com

Medsye
78/46 Moo 5,
Thap Lamu,
Thai Muang,
Phang Nga.
Tel 0-7644-3276.
W similanthailand.com

Phi Phi Scuba
Ao Ton Sai, Ko Phi Phi.
Tel 0-7560-1148.
W ppscuba.com

Phoenix Divers
1 Moo 1, Hat Sai Ri,
Ko Tao.
Tel 0-7745-6033.
W phoenixdivers
kohtao.com

Planet Scuba
Next to Seatran Pier,
Bophut, Ko Samui.
Tel 0-7741-3050.
W planetscuba.net

Santana Diving and Canoeing
11/2 Rat-U-Thit
200 Pi Rd,
Hat Patong,
Phuket.
Tel 0-7629-4220.
W santanaphuket.com

Sea Dragon Dive Center
5/51 Moo 7,
T Khuk Khak,
Khao Lak.
Tel 0-7648-5420.
W seadragon
divecenter.com

Sunrise Divers
269/24 Patak Rd,
Karon Plaza,
Hat Karon, Phuket.
Tel 0-7639-8040.
W sunrise-divers.com

Sailing

Gulf Charters Thailand
Ocean Marina,
167/5 Sukhumvit Rd,
Sattahip.
Tel 0-3823-7752.
W yachtcharter
thailand.com

Phuket Sailing
20/28 Soi Suksan,
Moo 4, Tambon Rawai,
Phuket.
Tel 08-1797-0516.
W phuket-sailing.com

Seal Superyachts
A10 The Royal Place,
96/68 Praphuketkhew Rd,
Kathu, Phuket.
Tel 0-7661-2654.
W seal-superyachts.com

Yachtpro
Adjacent to Yacht Haven
Marina, Phuket.
Tel 0-7633-1615.
W sailing-thailand.com

Watersports

Aloha Tours
Chalong Junction Rd,
Chalong Bay, Phuket.
Tel 0-7638-1220.
W thai-boat.com

Barracuda Bar
157/132–133 Moo 5,
Pattaya-Naklua Rd,
Chonburi province.
Tel 0-3837-0288.
W barracudabar-
pattaya.com

Dorado Game Fishing
46/17-18 Moo 9, Tharue,
Ao Chalong, Phuket.
Tel 0-87889-4588.
W phuket-fishing.com

Scuba Dawgs Pattaya
Bali Hai Pier,
551/2 Moo 10,
Tambon Nongprue,
Banglamung, Chonburi.
Tel 0-3871-0029.
W scubadawgspattaya.com

Canoeing

John Gray's Sea Canoe
86 Soi 2/3 Yaowarat Rd,
Phuket town.
Tel 0-7625-4505.
W johngray-
seacanoe.com

Paddle Asia
18/58 Rasdanusorn Rd,
Phuket.
Tel 0-7624-1519.
W paddleasia.com

Sea Canoe Thailand
125/461 Moo 5,
Baan Tung Ka – Baan
Sapam Rd, Phuket.
Tel 0-7652-8839.
W seacanoe.net

White-Water Rafting and Kayaking

Sealand Camp
125/1 Phang Nga Rd,
Phuket town.
Tel 0-7622-2900.
W sealandcamp.com

The Wild Planet
666 Sukhumvit 24,
Bangkok.
Tel 0-2261-4412.
W thewildplanet.com

Golf

Black Mountain Golf Club
565 Moo 7, Nong Hieng
Rd, Hin Lek Fai, Hua Hin.
Tel 0-3261-8666.
W bmghuahin.com

Blue Canyon Country Club
165 Moo 1,
Thepkasattri Rd,
Thalang, Phuket.
Tel 0-7632-8088.
W bluecanyon
club.com

Golfasian.com
W golfasian.com/golf-
courses/thailand-golf-
courses

Laem Chabang International Country Club
106/8 Moo 4, Beung,
Sri Racha, near Pattaya.
Tel 0-3837-2273.
W laemchabang
golf.com

Mission Hills Golf Resort
195 Moo 4 Pla Khlok,
Thalang, Phuket.
Tel 0-7631-0888.
W missionhills
phuket.com

Palm Hills Golf Club
1444 Phet Kasem Rd,
Cha-am.
Tel 0-3253-7777.
W palmhills-golf.com

Phuket Country Club
80/1 Vichitsongkram Rd,
Moo 7, Kathu, Phuket.
Tel 0-7631 9200.
W phuketcountry
club.com

Santiburi Samui Country Club
12/15 Moo 4,
Baan Don Sai,
Ko Samui.
Tel 0-7742-1700.
W santiburi.com

Thana City Golf and Country Club
100/2 Moo 4,
Bang Na Trat Rd,
off Hwy 34, near Bangkok.
Tel 0-2336-1968.
W thanacitygolf.com

DIRECTORY

Trekking

Evolution Tour
29/18 Moo 4, Baan
Khlong Phrao, Ko Chang.
Tel 0-3955-7078.
W evolutiontour.com

Friends of Nature
133/21 Ratchaprarop Rd,
Bangkok.
City Map 4 E5.
Tel 0-2642-4426.
W friendsofnature
93.com

**Khao Sok
Discovery**
11/36 Moo 5, Chalong,
Phuket.
Tel 0-7652-1857.
W khaosokdiscovery.
com

Phuket Trekking Club
55/779–780 Villa
Daowroong Village,
East Chao Fa Rd,
Tambon Vichit, Phuket.
Tel 0-7637-7344.
W phukettrekking
club.com

Siam Safari
17/2 Soi Yadsanae, Chao
Fa Rd, Chalong, Phuket.
Tel 0-7638-4456.
W siamsafari.com

Wildlife Watching

**National Park,
Wildlife, and Plant
Conservation
Department**
61 Phaholyothin Rd,
Chatuchak, Bangkok.
Tel 0-2561-0777.
W dnp.go.th/index_
eng.asp

Boat Trips

**Chao Phraya
Express Boats**
78/24–29 Maharaj Rd,
Phra Nakhorn, Bangkok.
City Map 2 C1.
Tel 0-2623-6001.
W chaophrayaexpress
boat.com

Sayan Tour
209 Phang Nga Bus
Terminal, Phang Nga.
Tel 0-7643-0348.
W sayantour.com

Cycling

Bicycle Thailand
W bicyclethailand.com

Bike and Travel
802/756 River Park,
Moo 12, Prathum Thani,
near Bangkok.
Tel 0-2990-0274.
W cyclingthailand.com

**Biking Southeast
Asia**
W mrpumpy.net

Spice Roads
45 Sub Soi Pannee, Soi
Pridi Banomyong 26,
Sukhumvit Soi 7, Bangkok.
Tel 0-2381-7490.
W spiceroads.com

Rock-Climbing

Hot Rock
Hat Rai Leh, near Krabi.
Tel 0-7566-2245.
W railayadventure.com

King Climbers
Hat Rai Leh, near Krabi.
Tel 0-7566-2096.
W railay.com

**Spidermonkey
Climbing**
Ton Sai Village, Ko Phi Phi.
Tel 0-7560-1026.
W spidermonkey
phiphi.com

Tex Rock Climbing
Hat Rai Leh, near Krabi.
Tel 08-1891-1528. W tex-
rockclimbing.com

Bungee Jumping

Jungle Bungy Jump
61/3 Moo 6,
Witchitsongram, Kathu,
Phuket.
Tel 0-7632-1351.
W phuketbungy.com

Horse Racing
and Riding

**International
Riding School**
100 Moo 9, Tambon Pong,
Amphur Banglamung,
Chonburi.
Tel 08-3988-7860.
W ridingschool
asia.com

Phuket Riding Club
95 Viset Rd, Rawai, Phuket.
Tel 0-7628-8213.
W phuketriding
club.com

**Royal Bangkok
Sports Club**
1 Henri Dunant Rd,
Bangkok.
City Map 8 D2.
Tel 0-2652-5000.
W rbsc.org

Royal Turf Club
Phitsanulok Rd, Dusit,
Bangkok.
Tel 0-2628-1810.

Cultural Study

**Baipai Thai
Cooking School**
8/91 Ngam Wongwan Rd,
Soi 54, Ladyao,
Chatuchak, Bangkok.
Tel 0-2561-1404.
W baipai.com

Blue Elephant
233 South Sathorn Rd,
Bangkok.
Tel 0-2673-9353.
W blueelephant.com/
cooking-school

**Dhammakaya
Foundation**
40 Moo 8,
Khlong Song, Khlong
Luang, Prathum Thani.
Tel 0-2831-1000.
W dhammakaya.net

**Happy Chef
Cooking School**
81/65 Moo 9, Central
Pattaya Rd, Soi 14, Pattaya.
Tel 08-0809-4453.
W thaicookingschools
pattaya.com

**International
Dharma Hermitage**
Wat Suan Mokkh,
Chaiya, Surat Thani.
Tel 0-7743-5340.
W suanmokkh-idh.org

**Pat's Home Thai
Cooking School**
26/4 Moo 3,
Chao Fa Rd, Phuket town.
Tel 08-1538-8276.
W phuketindex.com/
pathomethai
cookingschool

**Samui Institute of
Thai Culinary Arts**
46/6 Moo 3,
Hat Chaweng,
Ko Samui.
Tel 0-7741-3172.
W sitca.com

Wat Khao Tham
Near Ban Tai, Ko Phangan.
Tel 08-3593-3597.
W kowtahm.com

**Wat Mahathat
(Section Five)**
Maharat Rd, Bangkok.
City Map 1 C5.
Tel 0-2222-6011.

**World Fellowship
of Buddhists**
616 Benjasiri Park,
Soi Medhinivet, off
Sukhumvit 24, Bangkok.
Tel 0-2661-1284.
W wfbhq.org

Spa Breaks

Coastal Thailand has numerous spas offering every kind of treatment possible. Its sultry weather, idyllic landscapes, and sense of tranquillity make it an ideal destination for a spa break. Traditional Thai architecture, serene Zen-minimalist decor, and enchanting gardens blend with the Thai people's gentle and giving nature to make it a memorable experience. Massage has been practiced in Thailand for some 2,500 years, and while it is possible to have a cheap shoulder rub in a backstreet shop, nothing beats the pampering at a luxury resort or an afternoon at a day spa.

Relaxing in the peaceful garden of the Anantara Resort and Spa

Hotel and Resort Spas

Travelers tend to visit a hotel or resort spa as part of a wider holiday, with the main focus being a beach or a cultural experience. However, the luxurious, upscale hotels and resorts in Thailand are home to some of the world's very best spas, offering an enormous range of professional, unique, and blissful treatments.

The greatest concentration of spas is on the islands of Phuket and Ko Samui and in the beach resort towns of Hua Hin and Cha-am. The country's foremost spa resorts include the exotic **Four Seasons Resort**, **Ko Samui**, the popular **Banyan Tree Spa**, **Phuket**, the **Evason Phuket Resort and Six Senses Spa** and the **Evason Hua Hin**, and the **Anantara Resort and Spa**, which has locations in Hua Hin as well as Ko Samui.

Spa treatments are generally an added extra, but many resorts are increasingly offering all-inclusive packages. The Anantara resorts, for example, offer three- and seven-day programs that include between 4 and 10 treatments.

Spa Retreats

Thailand has a number of luxury resorts situated in truly breath-taking settings. Visitors looking for an intimate getaway on a deserted white-sand beach skirted by palm trees should head to the **Aleenta Resort and Spa**, **Phang Nga**. Those who like the idea of retreating into the tropical forests to rejuvenate the body and spirit should visit the **Tamarind Retreat** in Ko Samui. This spa offers two different kinds of treatments – classic and forest spas – with an exotic treat in the form of a herbal steam cave and dipping pool. The aim of staying here is to experience the local culture and lush environment as much as it is to have a spa experience. The

fact that these resorts are often set in remote locations and may be accessible only by speedboat, such as the **Rayavadee Spa** near Krabi, adds to the allure. The **Pimalai Resort and Spa** on Ko Lanta provides treatment rooms named after local flowers and massages with aromatic herbs. The spas at these resorts offer daily treatment programs for those who really want to unwind.

Destination Spas

Revitalizing the mind, body, and spirit is the central purpose of destination spas, with guests rarely leaving the resort once they have checked in. Thailand's first and best, the **Chiva-Som International Health Resort**, in Hua Hin, offers more than 150 treatments focused on relaxation and rejuvenation, stress relief, detoxification, and weight loss. Guests undergo an extensive health consultation upon arrival, and a program is specifically created to match their goals. There is a three-night minimum stay, although most guests stay a week or more, and nutritious spa cuisine, activities, and treatments are included in the rate. Another famous destination spa is the **Kamalaya Wellness Sanctuary and Holistic Spa** in Ko Samui.

Because spa resorts tend to provide an array of non-spa activities too – from elephant and water-buffalo riding to mountain climbing – signature treatments at destination spas also cater to travelers who may be suffering from some painful aftereffects.

A rejuvenating massage at Banyan Tree Spa, Phuket

Day Spas

Travelers can easily find day spas – stand-alone operations not attached to resorts or hotels. Many hotels also offer treatments to non-guests on a per-session basis. Most day spas are in Bangkok and include the stylish **Being Spa**, **Pirom Spa**, the **Harnn Heritage Spa**, and **Spa of Qinera**.

Spa Treatments

Despite Thailand's long history of therapeutic massage and natural healing – including *nuad paen boran* (traditional Thai massage), medicinal herbs, and natural springs – the country offers unique, cutting edge treatments. Thai spa treatments are meant to be both relaxing and rejuvenating, and offer holistic healing which invigorates not just the body, but also the soul. Expect to see anything and everything on a spa menu, from Tropical Sprinkles and Tranquility Mists at the Banyan Tree Spa, Phuket, to their famous four-hand Harmony Banyan treatment, where two

Working out stress through yoga at Chiva-Som International Health Resort

therapists work on the client at once. Other frequently visited spas, such as the Six Senses Spa and Anantara Spas offer versions of this indulgent treatment. While some treatments are indigenous to Thailand – the traditional Thai massage, for example – others such as hydrotherapy, thalassotherapy, aromatherapy, and Ayurvedic treatments, can be found all over the world. Thai masseurs do not make use of any oils or lotions for their massages and a traditional massage is given to the client who is asked to lie on a mat or mattress. Many spas have also developed their own signature treatments. The Four Seasons Spas, for example, have an array of sensual offerings connected to the cycles of the moon, with exotic treatments that should be experienced only during certain lunar phases.

DIRECTORY

Hotel and Resort Spas

Anantara Resort and Spa
Phet Kasem Beach Rd, Hua Hin.
Tel 0-3252-0250.
W anantara.com

99/9 Moo 1, Bophut Bay, Ko Samui.
Tel 0-7742-8300.

Banyan Tree Spa, Phuket
33 Moo 4, Srisunthorn Rd, Cherngtalay, Phuket.
Tel 0-7632-4374.
W banyantreespa.com

Evason Hua Hin
9 Moo 5, Hat Paknampran, Pranburi, Prachuap Khiri Khan.
Tel 0-3263-2111.
W sixsenses.com

Evason Phuket Resort and Six Senses Spa
100 Vised Rd, Moo 2 Tambol Rawai, Phuket.
Tel 0-7638-1018.
W sixsenses.com

Four Seasons Resort, Ko Samui
219 Moo 5, Ang Thong, Ko Samui.
Tel 0-7724-3000, 0-7724-3002.
W fourseasons.com

Spa Retreats

Aleenta Resort and Spa, Phang Nga
33 Moo 5, T Khokkloy, Phang Nga.
Tel 0-7658-0333.
W aleenta.com

Pimalai Resort and Spa
99 Moo 5, Ba Kantiang Beach, Ko Lanta.
Tel 0-7560-7999.
W pimalai.com

Rayavadee Spa
214 Moo 2, Tambol Ao-Nang, Amphur Muang, Krabi.
Tel 0-7562-0740-3.
W rayavadee.com

Tamarind Retreat
205/7 Thong Takian, Ko Samui.
Tel 0-7742-4221, 0-7742-4311.
W tamarind retreat.com

Destination Spas

Chiva-Som International Health Resort
Phet Kasem Rd, Hua Hin.
Tel 0-3253-6536, 0-2711-6900.
W chivasom.com

Kamalaya Wellness Sanctuary and Holistic Spa
102/9 Moo 3, Laem Set Rd, Na-Muang, Ko Samui.
Tel 0-7742-9800.
W kamalaya.com

Day Spas

Being Spa
88 Soi Sukhumvit, 51 Klongton Nua, Bangkok.
Tel 0-2662-6171.

Harnn Heritage Spa
Siam Paragon, 4th Floor, Bangkok. **City Map** 7 C1.
Tel 0-2610-9715.

Pirom Spa
87 Nai Lert Building, Sukhumvit Rd, Bangkok.
Tel 0-2655-4177.

Spa of Qinera
172/1 Soi Phiphat 2, Chong Nonsi, Bangkok.
Tel 0-2638-8306.

SURVIVAL
GUIDE

PRACTICAL INFORMATION

Thailand is well equipped to cater to its growing number of tourists. The millions of people who visit the country each year find one of the biggest and best organized tourism industries in Asia. The headquarters of the helpful, government-run Tourism Authority of Thailand (TAT) is in Bangkok, and there are offices across the country and several overseas branches. The relevant TAT address and telephone number is given for each town and sight throughout this guide. The industry is developing rapidly,

and the adventurous traveler need no longer be restricted to organized tours or just the major tourist destinations such as Bangkok, Pattaya, and Phuket. There are many reputable travel agencies all over Thailand. These agencies can offer valuable advice, book flights and accommodations, and will also organize sightseeing tours. Some pre-travel planning is necessary to avoid the worst of the rainy season and holiday periods such as the Chinese New Year *(see p41)*.

When to Go

Thailand's weather can be tempestuous, with year-round humidity, high temperatures, and heavy rainfall. However, the optimum time to visit is during the cooler months from November to February, which is the peak tourist season. The hot season, from March to June, can be unbearable, while the rainy season, which generally lasts from June to October, is the least predictable of the three periods. Climate and rainfall charts can be found on pages 39–41.

What to Take

As the climate in Thailand is generally hot and humid, it is advisable to dress in cool clothes made from natural fibers. Throughout Thailand, the rainy season brings sudden downpours, so a light raincoat is handy. If visiting temples,

appropriate dress is required *(see p339)*, as is easily removable footwear. Visitors should also carry a basic first-aid kit.

Visa and Passports

Many nationalities, including citizens of most European countries, Australia, and the US, can enter Thailand for up to 30 days without a prearranged visa. However, proof of a confirmed return flight or other ongoing travel arrangements must be presented upon arrival. For those wishing to stay longer, a 60-day tourist visa can be arranged from a Thai embassy or consulate prior to arrival in Thailand.

A 90-day non-immigrant visa must be applied for in the visitor's home country and requires a letter of verification from a Thai source giving a valid reason, such as business or study, for spending three

months in Thailand. This visa is slightly more expensive than the 60-day tourist visa.

With all visas, entry into Thailand must occur within 90 days of issue. Visa extensions are at the discretion of the **Immigration Department** in Bangkok or any other immigration office in Thailand. Overstaying a visa carries a fine of 500 baht per day and can result in serious penalties. Travelers to Thailand should have at least six months' validity left on their passport.

Immunization

There are no immunization requirements unless a visitor is from a country infected with yellow fever. It is recommended that visitors be immunized against polio, tetanus, typhoid, and hepatitis A. In addition, those traveling to remote areas, or who are staying more than three weeks, should get BCG (tuberculosis), hepatitis B, rabies, diphtheria, and Japanese encephalitis vaccinations.

Customs Information

Customs regulations in Thailand are standard. During an inbound flight, travelers will be given a customs form that must be completed and handed over at the customs desk after claiming baggage. Thai customs restrictions for goods carried into the country include 200 cigarettes and one liter of wine or spirits. For complete details

Relaxing under shady beach umbrellas at Hat Kata Noi, Phuket

◀ Fruit sellers at the Damnoen Saduak Floating Market outside Bangkok about export declarations, duty payments, and VAT refunds visit **The Customs Department** website. The carrying of drugs, firearms, or pornography is prohibited.

Antiques and images of the Buddha are not allowed out of Thailand without authorization. If visitors wish to export such items, they must first contact the **Fine Arts Department** of the National Museum in Bangkok at least five days before the date of shipment to fill in a form accompanied by two frontal photographs of the object being purchased. However, contemporary works of art, such as paintings, do not fall under this category. It is also illegal to leave Thailand with more than 50,000 baht without authorization.

Travel Safety Advice

Visitors can get up-to-date travel safety information from the **Department of Foreign Affairs**

Content pages of some popular destinations from TAT's e-brochures

and Trade in Australia, the **Foreign and Commonwealth Office** in the UK and the **State Department** in the US.

Tourist Information

The many branches of the **Tourism Authority of Thailand** (TAT) are very helpful, offering plenty of information on sights and festivals, as well as maps, brochures, guides, and posters. They also have a useful list of reputable travel agents and hotels.

Buddha images wrapped and ready for sale in Bangkok

Admission Charges

Admission charges to sights in Thailand generally range from 10 to 50 baht. National parks, however, charge between 200 and 500 baht. Some museums in Thailand have free entry, but others may charge up to 200 baht. Occasionally, foreigners may be charged a higher admission fee than locals.

Opening Hours

Most destinations in Thailand can be visited throughout the year, although accommodations on, and ferry services to, some of the southern islands are limited in the rainy season. In general, major tourist attractions open at 8am or 9am and close between 3:30pm and 6pm. A few places also shut for lunch between noon and 1pm. Most major sights open daily, but a few museums close for public holidays as well as on Mondays and Tuesdays.

Large department stores are usually open 10am–9pm, and smaller shops are open 8am–9pm. In smaller towns, there are daily markets.

Commercial offices are open 8am to noon and 1–5pm Monday to Friday. Government offices are open 8:30am to noon and 1–4:30pm Monday to Friday. During the Chinese New Year, many businesses may close. For details of banking hours see page 342.

Facilities for the Disabled

There are few facilities for disabled travelers in Thailand. Sidewalks can be uneven and pedestrian bridges are often accessed only by steep steps. Wheelchair access is limited to luxury hotels in major cities. Public transport, including buses and Skytrains, is inaccessible for the disabled and even the Suvarnabhumi International Airport has few elevators or disabled access toilet facilities. The easiest way to travel is to book an organized tour *(see p349)* or contact the **Association of Physically Handicapped People** for information.

Facilities for Children

The larger hotels in Thailand have babysitting services, and TAT offers advice on attractions that have special appeal to kids, such as zoos and amusement parks. Hats and sunblock are a must for children (as well as adults) out in the tropical sun.

Language

It is useful to learn a few Thai phrases *(see pp366–8)*, and Thais will be delighted with the effort. Many local people in popular tourist towns speak some English, as do most hotel receptionists. Sight and road names in these areas are transliterated, and menus are often in English as well as Thai. Prices and road numbers are generally in Arabic numerals.

Tourist information center, Than Bok Koranee

Thai Time System and Calendar

Bangkok time is seven hours ahead of Greenwich Mean Time (GMT), 12 hours ahead of Eastern Standard Time, and 15 hours ahead of Pacific Standard Time.

Two calendars are used in Thailand – the Gregorian (Western) and the Buddhist calendars. The Buddhist Era (BE) starts 543 years before the Gregorian era, thus AD 1957 is the equivalent of 2500 BE.

Electricity

The electric current for the whole of Thailand is 220 volts AC. Dual-prong rounded pin plugs as well as flat-pin plugs can be used in sockets. Major hotels in Bangkok also have 110-volt outlets for electric razors. Adapters can be bought from any department store or electrical store. These outlets also sell power-surge cables, which are vital if one is traveling with a laptop. It is advisable for visitors traveling to smaller towns or villages to keep a flashlight handy.

Conversions

US to Metric
1 inch = 2.54 centimeters
1 foot = 30 centimeters
1 mile = 2 kilometers
1 ounce = 28 grams
1 pound = 454 grams
1 gallon = 3.79 liters

Metric to US
1 millimeter = 0.04 inch
1 centimeter = 0.4 inch
1 meter = 3 feet 3 inches
1 kilometer = 1 mile
1 gram = 0.04 ounces
1 kilogram = 2.2 pounds
1 liter = 2.1 pints

Photography

Digital photography is popular in Thailand. Photography shops are quite easy to find, and they make prints or load digital images onto a disk at very reasonable rates. Those using film may find it slightly harder to obtain, although there are several professional photography stores in the capital Bangkok.

Etiquette

It is not without reason that Thailand is often referred to as "the land of smiles". Thais are exceptionally friendly and helpful people. A few taboos do exist, however, mostly with regard to the monarchy and Buddhism. Visitors should be particularly careful to behave respectfully at *wats* and in front of any image of the Buddha. Confrontation is considered extremely rude. Losing one's temper is seen as an embarrassing loss of face.

Bargaining is quite common, but it is best to avoid getting too loud or aggressive. Tipping, on the other hand, is not as common a practice in Thailand as it is in the West.

Greeting People

The Thai greeting is known as the *wai* and consists of the palms being pressed together and lifted toward the chin. Traditionally, the inferior party initiates the *wai* and holds it higher and for longer than the superior, who returns it according to his or her social standing. Thais use first names to address people. The polite form of address is the gender-neutral title Khun, followed by the first name or nickname. Every Thai

Two Thais addressing each other with a *wai*, the traditional greeting

person has a nickname, usually with a simple meaning, such as Moo, which means "pig", or Koong, which means "shrimp".

Body Language

The head is considered a sacred part of the body by Thais, so touching someone's head, even that of a child, should be avoided. The feet are seen as the lowliest part of the body and to point the feet toward someone or rest them on a table is considered rude. When sitting on the floor, especially inside a temple, it is best to tuck one's legs behind or to the side and avoid stepping over others.

Smoking

Smoking is prohibited in all public areas and on all public transport in Bangkok. It is also banned in restaurants as well as in pubs.

Royalty

The royal family is the most revered institution in Thailand. Defaming it in any way can be considered as an affront to the monarchy. Not only could this mean a jail sentence, but Thai people will nearly always be deeply offended. Coins, bills, and stamps bear the images of Thai kings and should be treated respectfully by visitors.

The National Anthem

The national anthem is played twice daily, at 8am and 6pm, on radio and through tannoys

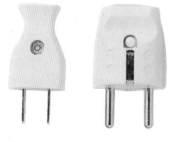

A range of plugs and adaptors that can be used in Thailand

in smaller towns and some public spaces. It is polite to stop and stand still. In theaters, the national anthem is played before all performances. The audience stands in silent respect to a portrait of the king.

Monks

The *sangha* (monkhood) is a respected institution, second only to the monarchy. It is prohibited for a monk to touch a woman or to receive anything directly from her. When traveling by public transportation, women should avoid sitting next to a monk.

Etiquette at Wats

Decorum should be observed when entering any *wat*. Temples

Devotees kneeling before a shrine with their feet facing away

Surin Islands National Park regulations

are quiet places, so visitors should try to avoid disturbing the peace. The clothes one wears must be clean and respectable. Shoes must be removed before entering any *wat*. All Buddha images are sacred, even small, ruined, or neglected ones. Visitors must never sit with their feet pointing toward them.

Suitable Dress

Thais are a modest people, so visitors, especially women, must remember to wear clothes that are not too revealing. Topless sunbathing is frowned upon.

Responsible Travel

Thai authorities are now actively promoting eco-tourism by creating awareness of the need for conservation through various means. They are prohibiting

locals from fishing with dynamite and drag-netting coral reefs, and encouraging tourists to "leave nothing but footprints."

Ecologically aware dive companies visiting marine parks such as Similan and Surin forbid visitors from taking away even a seashell, and in extreme cases will "name and shame" those who violate this basic rule. Similarly, visitors are increasingly discouraged from taking plastic bags and water bottles into national parks. With increasing awareness, the kingdom is already more engaged than its Southeast Asian neighbors in promoting responsible travel.

However, the government's efforts have been thwarted by environmentally destructive shrimp farms, expensive, water-intensive golf courses, the clearing of natural forests for palm oil plantations, and even the breeding of tigers in captivity for their body parts.

Visitors can set an example by carefully disposing off garbage, choosing to boycott noisy and polluting watersports such as jet skis, and refusing to eat food derived from endangered species such as shark's fin soup and sea turtle eggs or meat. Most Thais are sensitive, so setting an example will certainly help kick-start Thailand's nascent eco-tourism industry.

DIRECTORY

Visas and Passports

Immigration Department
Soi Suanphlu, Sathorn Tai Rd, Bangkok. **City Map 8** D5. **Tel** 0-2287-3101.
W immigration.go.th

Customs Information

The Customs Department
1 Sunthornkhosa Rd, Khlong Toey, Bangkok. **Tel** 0-2667-6000.
W customs.go.th

Fine Arts Department
National Museum, 1 Na Phra That Rd, Phra Nakhon, Bangkok.

City Map 1 C4. **Tel** 0-2224-2050.
W finearts.go.th

Travel Safety Advice

Australia
Department of Foreign Affairs and Trade
W dfat.gov.au
W smartraveller.gov.au

United Kingdom
Foreign and Commonwealth Office
W gov.uk/foreign-travel-advice

United States
US Department of State
W travel.state.gov

Tourist Information

Tourism Authority of Thailand
1,600 New Phetchaburi Rd, Bangkok. **Tel** 1672.
W tourismthailand.org

Facilities for the Disabled

Association of Physically Handicapped People
73/7 Soi 8, Thepprasan, Tivanond Rd, Talad Kwan, Nonthaburi. **Tel** 0-2951-0569.

Embassies

Canada
15th Floor, Abdulrahim Place, 990 Rama 4 Rd, Bangkok. **Tel** 0-2636-0540.

Malaysia
33–35 Sathorn Tai Rd, Bangkok. **Tel** 0-2629-6800.

Myanmar (Burma)
132 Sathorn Nua Rd, Bangkok. **Tel** 0-2234-4698.

United Kingdom
14 Witthayu (Wireless) Rd, Bangkok. **Tel** 0-2305-8333.

United States
120-122 Witthayu (Wireless) Rd, Bangkok. **Tel** 0-2205-4000.

Personal Health and Security

Thailand is a fairly safe country, and simple health and safety precautions keep the vast majority of travelers out of trouble. The infrastructure of emergency services for both health and crime is efficient throughout Bangkok and other larger towns. As a rule of thumb, the more remote the area, the higher the health risk and less support available in the event of any mishap. The main hospitals in Bangkok, the main islands, as well as other large cities have modern equipment and well-trained doctors, many of whom speak good English. Even on smaller beaches and islands, medical facilities have improved dramatically.

Tourist policeman wearing a beret, and an ordinary officer

A well-stocked pharmacy in Ban Bophut, Ko Samui

In an Emergency

For English-speaking help, call the **Tourist Assistance Center**, which will contact the appropriate service. Lines are open from 8am to midnight, after which visitors will have to rely on English-speaking hotel staff. During office hours, TAT (see p339) may also be able to help. The **Metropolitan Mobile Police** covers general emergencies in Bangkok. All Bangkok hospitals have 24-hour trauma and emergency departments.

General Precautions

Bangkok and the coastal areas are relatively safe. Usually discretion and sobriety are the best means of avoiding problems. Be on guard at tourist locations (scam artists can direct tourists to pricier, less impressive sights), and at bus and train stations. It is advisable not to flash large amounts of cash or leave luggage unattended. If leaving valuables in a hotel safe, make sure to get a receipt, and do not let credit cards out of

sight. Drugging and robbing tourists on long-distance trains and buses has occurred, so politely decline food or drink from strangers.

Drugs

Thai law absolutely prohibits the sale or purchase of opium, heroin, or marijuana. Charges for possession, smuggling, or dealing can lead to a 2–15 year jail sentence or, in extreme cases, the death sentence.

Danger Spots

In some parts of the Deep South, the militant Malay-Muslim group PULO (Pattani United Liberation Organization) can be dangerous. It is wise to stay away from the remote border areas.

Women Travelers

Female travelers are unlikely to be harassed in Thailand. The coastal areas are quite safe for women, as are hotels. Taxis are readily available.

Tourist Police

There are tourist police stations in Bangkok, Ko Samui, Pattaya, and Phuket. Tourist police officers all speak some

English and are attached to TAT offices. They help with anything from credit card scams to excessive surcharges. They are also helpful in emergencies, and can act as an English-speaking liaison. The Bangkok branch of the tourist police is located close to Lumphini Park (see p78).

Medical Facilities

Medical insurance is advisable when traveling in Thailand. Private hospitals such as **Phuket International Hospital** in Phuket, **Bangkok General Hospital** and **Bumrungrad Hospital** in Bangkok, as well as other public hospitals, are modern, clean, and efficient. Waiting times are longer in public hospitals, but their doctors are trained abroad.

Outside the capital, the best facilities are in the large towns. For dental or eye care, however, it is best to seek treatment in Bangkok.

Pharmacies

There are plenty of pharmacies in Bangkok and the coastal areas. They can all dispense antibiotics over the counter, without a prescription. Most pharmacies are open from 8am–9pm. In small towns, however, pharmacies are less widespread.

Patrol car used by the tourist police, seen mainly in cities

Coping with the Heat

It is advisable to avoid exertion for the first few days. Drink lots of fluids, take plenty of rest in the shade, and avoid being out in the midday sun. Once acclimatized, continue with a high intake of fluids, especially bottled water or formulated electrolyte drinks.

The tropical sun is very powerful; a good sunscreen and a wide-brimmed hat are therefore indispensable.

First-aid Kit

A basic first-aid kit should include: any personal medication; aspirin or pain killers for fevers and minor aches and pains; an antiseptic for cuts and bites; a digestive pill or syrup to soothe an upset stomach; insect repellent; bandages; scissors; tweezers; and a thermometer.

Minor Stomach Upsets

Should diarrhea occur, eat only plain food for a few days and drink plenty of fluids. It is not wise to drink tap water – bottled water is readily available across the country. Ice should be fine in main hotels and restaurants, but crushed iced drinks from street vendors are best avoided.

Drugs such as Lomotil and Imodium can bring relief from diarrhea, but rehydrating solutions, available at pharmacies, are usually the best remedy. For immediate relief, a single 500 mg dose of Ciprofloxacin is safe and effective.

Insect-borne Diseases

Seven of Thailand's 410 mosquito species carry malaria. Symptoms of this serious disease include headache, fever, and violent chills. Visitors experiencing such symptoms should seek medical advice.

The main towns and islands are largely free of malaria-carrying mosquitoes. For the latest information, call a travel clinic or, in the US, the Tourist

Spicy street food, best avoided by those with a delicate stomach

Assistance Center, to obtain information on health matters. Malarial mosquitoes are active from sundown till sunrise, so use plenty of repellent, wear long-sleeved clothing and use mosquito nets and coils.

Another mosquito-borne disease, dengue fever, is also a risk during the daytime. However, few mosquitoes are infected with the virus, and the symptoms, though intense and unpleasant, are rarely fatal. These include fever, headache, severe joint and muscle pains, and a rash. No preventive treatment or vaccination is available.

People- and Animal-borne Diseases

Acquired Immune Deficiency Syndrome (AIDS) is passed through bodily fluids. The high turnover of Thailand's sex industry means that unprotected sex carries a serious risk. Blood transfusion methods in Thailand are not always reliable and it is safest to seek treatment only in the main hospitals. The same goes for inoculations – make sure needles are new or bring a personal supply.

Hepatitis B is also transmitted through bodily fluids. Symptoms include fever, nausea, fatigue, and jaundice, and it can severely damage the liver. A prophylactic vaccine is available. Vaccines are also available for rabies and tetanus.

Food- and Water-Borne Diseases

Dysentery is a severe form of food or water poisoning. Bacillary dysentery, characterized by stomach pain, vomiting, and fever, is highly contagious but rarely lasts longer than a week. Amebic dysentery has similar symptoms but takes longer to develop. Medical help should be sought without delay.

Hepatitis A is passed on in conditions of poor sanitation or contaminated water or food, and can now be prevented with a vaccine. Typhoid is also transmitted through contaminated water or food. Medical attention is essential as complications such as pneumonia can occur. The available vaccine is not always reliable.

Banking and Local Currency

Throughout Bangkok and the main provincial towns such as Krabi and Surat Thani, banking facilities and exchange services are plentiful, well run, and easy to access. In the major centers, tellers often speak some English. Exchange booths are usually located in the central parts of towns, and mobile exchange units are stationed near larger tourist attractions. Automatic Teller Machines (ATMs) can be found in all cities. Smaller towns are less likely to have exchange facilities, but most have banks or ATMs. Rural villages, unless they are tourist spots, might not have banking or currency exchange services.

HSBC, an international bank operating in Bangkok

Banks and Banking Hours

The three main banks in Thailand are the **Bangkok Bank**, the **Kasikorn Bank**, and the **Siam Commercial Bank**. The **Bank of Ayudhya** and **CIMB Thai**, along with several smaller but reliable banks, have branches throughout the country. Foreign banks such as **Bank of America**, **Citibank**, **Deutsche Bank**, **HSBC**, and **Standard Chartered Bank** offer full commercial banking services in Bangkok and operate major branches.

Banking hours are generally 8:30am–3:30pm, Monday to Friday. Some banks have branches in department stores which are open 8am–8pm. Exchange booths are open daily through the day. Apart from providing banking services, the major banks can also organize international money transfers. Most banks in cities have an associated ATM.

Automatic Teller Machines, found in Bangkok and many Thai towns

ATM Services

Most ATMs provide instructions in both Thai and English. Any ATM displaying the VISA or MasterCard sign will accept these cards and dispense cash in baht using the regular PIN. There are surcharges for such transactions.

For visitors planning to stay in Thailand for several months or more, it might be a good idea to open an account at a Thai bank. This would allow access to any ATM or bank without having to worry about exchange rates or inter-provincial charges on Thai ATM cards.

Changing Money

Banks usually offer the best exchange rates, and rates differ little between banks. Hotels usually offer the worst rates, while those at exchange booths can vary greatly. US dollars are the most widely accepted foreign currency when buying baht, although sterling is also accepted. In Bangkok, small exchange booths can be found in most major department stores, shopping malls, and on big roads. Mobile exchange units can often be found near tourist attractions and around market areas. These are generally open every day 7am–9pm. Exchange rates are published in the *Bangkok Post* and the *Nation*.

DIRECTORY

Banks

Bangkok Bank
333 Silom Rd, Bangkok.
City Map 7 C4.
Tel 0-2231-4333.
🆆 bangkokbank.com

Bank of America
CRC Tower, 33rd Floor
Wireless Rd, Bangkok.
City Map 8 E2.
Tel 0-2305-2900.

Bank of Ayudhya
1222 Rama 3, Bangkok.
Tel 0-2296-2000.

CIMB Thai Bank
44 Luang Suan Rd,
Bangkok. **City Map** 8 E2.
Tel 0-2626-7000.
🆆 cimbthai.com

Citibank
399 Sukhumvit Rd,
Bangkok.
Tel 0-2232-2484.
🆆 citibank.co.th

Deutsche Bank
Athanee Tower, Levels
27–29, 63 Wireless Rd,
Bangkok. **City Map** 8 E2.
Tel 0-2646-5000.

HSBC
Rama IV Rd, Bangkok.
City Map 8 D4.
Tel 0-2614-4000.
🆆 hsbc.co.th

Kasikorn Bank
1 Soi Ratburana 27/1,
Ratburana Rd, Bangkok.
Tel 0-2888-8800.
🆆 kasikornbank.com

Siam Commercial Bank
9 Ratchadaphisak Rd,
Bangkok. **Tel** 0-2544-1000. 🆆 scb.co.th

Standard Chartered Bank
90 Sathorn Nua,
Bangkok. **City Map** 7 C5.
Tel 0-2724-6326.
🆆 sc.com/th/en

Credit Cards

American Express
Tel 0-2273-5544.

MasterCard
Tel 001-800-11-887-0663.

VISA
Tel 001-800-441-3485.

Credit Cards

Credit cards are accepted in major hotels, department stores, and upscale shops and restaurants. They can also be used at major banks (and some exchange kiosks) for cash advances. Be aware, however, that a surcharge will be applied. **VISA** and **MasterCard** are the most widely accepted cards; the use of **American Express** cards is more limited.

All Thai commercial banks accept cash withdrawals from both MasterCard and Visa credit or debit cards. Visitors may need to show their passports at these transactions. Credit and debit cards can also be used at local ATMs, but a surcharge will be levied.

As the popularity of plastic money increases, so too does the incidence of credit card fraud and travelers should always carefully check bills before they sign.

Currency

The Thai unit of currency is the baht, usually seen abbreviated to B. There are 100 satang in a baht, but the satang represents such a small sum today that it is scarcely used. A 25 satang coin is sometimes known as a saleung. However, inflation is rendering this colloquial term redundant.

Banknotes come in different sizes and colors. They are available in denominations of 20 baht (green), 50 baht

Bangkok Bank
The Asian International Bank

Logo of one of Thailand's long-established banks

(blue), 100 baht (red), 500 baht (purple), and 1,000 baht (brown). Finding change for large denomination notes in rural areas can be difficult, so be sure to carry change and small notes with you. The coin denominations are 25 satang (or 1 saleung), 50 satang, 1 baht, 2 baht, 5 baht, and 10 baht.

Travelers' Checks

Travelers' checks are the safest way to carry money and can be exchanged for cash at banks, hotels, and bureaux de change. Banks usually provide the lowest surcharge for this service. They also charge a fee per check, so cashing large amounts in one transaction works out the cheapest.

VAT

Thailand imposes a 7 percent Value Added Tax (VAT) on goods and services. Tourists can redeem purchases above 5,000 baht at the customs counter at airports upon production of bona fide receipts.

20 baht

50 baht

100 baht

500 baht

1,000 baht

Coins come in the following denominations:

25 satang

50 satang

1 baht

2 baht

5 baht

10 baht

Communications and Media

Thailand's communication network is becoming increasingly sophisticated. The telephone system is run by the Telephone Organization of Thailand (TOT) under the umbrella of the Communications Authority of Thailand (CAT). It is possible to make international calls and send faxes from all business centers and hotels. Public phones are found on most roads while cell phone networks have penetrated the whole country. The postal system, however, can be erratic and it is advisable to use a courier service for valuables. Major international and local English-language newspapers and magazines are found in hotels, bookstores, and newsstands. Internet and Wi-Fi facilities are available even in the smaller towns.

A branch of Asia Books, which sells books and magazines

International Calls

All major hotels and most guesthouses offer international dialing services, although there is a surcharge levied well above the call charges. Business centers and Internet cafés in small towns usually offer e-mail and phone services. Bangkok's Central Post Office on Charoen Krung New Road and some major post offices around the country have a CAT center that can arrange collect and credit card calls. In Bangkok, these are open from 7am to midnight, with reduced hours in the provinces. To dial from a hotel room, contact the desk, or dial 001 (for an international line) followed by the country code and telephone number. It is also possible to use 007, 008, or 009 to prefix your number, to get cheaper rates. Alternatively, dial the international operator at 100. Blue and yellow international pay phones are found on streets, shopping malls, and airports. The blue phones take credit cards while the yellow phones can be used with stored value cards, sold in post offices and by authorized agents.

Local Calls

Local calls can be made from any public pay phone other than the blue and yellow international pay phones. Domestic calls can be made from blue and silver coin phones or green card-phones. Coin-operated phones accept 1, 5, and 10-baht coins, whereas cards for card phones can be bought at post offices, bookstores, and hotels and come in denominations of 25 baht, 50 baht, 100 baht, and 250 baht. The long-distance domestic service covers calls within different regions of Thailand, as well as to Malaysia and Laos.

Cell Phones

Cell phones are extremely cheap in Thailand. SIM cards can be bought from mobile phone shops, though they are also given away free to tourists arriving at airports. Customers can pay through scratch cards with a dial-in code to top up their credits. Cards range from 50 to 500 baht in value and are sold in mini-marts throughout the country.

In most of Thailand's coastal areas, cell phone coverage is good. Of the several service providers, AIS has the best coverage but is expensive. Any island with an indigenous population now also has good coverage. Weak signals might cause problems within the larger national parks.

Television and Radio

Thailand has many television channels, and programs are mostly in Thai, although in Bangkok, some are broadcast with an English simulcast on FM radio. Satellite and cable networks are fast expanding all over Asia, and most international English-language networks such as BBC, CNN, Al Jazeera, and CNBC are readily available. Many hotels provide satellite and cable television as well as an in-house video channel. Visitors should check the *Bangkok Post* and *The Nation* for details.

There are more than 400 radio stations operating on a nationwide scale. English-

Cell phone networks enabling communication on offshore islands

language stations manned by local DJs are listed in the *Life* section of the *Bangkok Post*. The national public radio station, Radio Thailand, broadcasts English-language programs on 107 and 105 FM 24 hours a day, and listings for shortwave frequencies that receive BBC, VOA, Radio Australia, Radio Canada, RFI (French), and Deutsche Welle are found in the *Focus* section of *The Nation*.

Newspapers and Magazines

The best English-language newspapers in Thailand are the *Bangkok Post* and *The Nation*. Both these publications provide reliable local, regional, and international coverage. The daily supplement *Life*, in both the Bangkok Post and *The Nation*, includes features on lifestyle, travel, human interest, as well as listings for restaurants, films, concerts, and exhibitions in Bangkok. Both are widely sold in news kiosks and shops throughout Bangkok. The *International New York Times* and the *Asian Wall Street Journal* are sold in hotels and English-language bookstores such as Asia Books and Bookazine, which also stock a good selection of international magazines. News weeklies including *The Economist*, *Time*, and *Newsweek* are also widely available.

The Nation, one of Bangkok's leading business newspapers

Among the local English language monthly publications are the useful listings guide *Bangkok 101* with information on city-based events and reviews and the society rag *Thailand Tatler*. In addition to these, helpful free guides are available in restaurants, bars, and bookstores and include *BK Magazine*, *Absolute Thai Lifestyle Magazine* and *Thaiways*.

Mail

Letters and postcards posted in Thailand usually take at least one week to reach Europe and North America. Stamps are available at all post offices and can also be bought at many hotels. Packages and valuable items should be sent by registered mail or via International Express Mail (EMS), which can be a cheaper alternative to international shipping companies. General delivery facilities are available at all main post offices in the country. Letters will normally be held for

Easily identifiable Thai mailbox

up to three months. To claim mail from general delivery, visitors must show their passport and sometimes pay a small fee. Letters should be addressed to the visitor (with the last name written in capitals and underlined), GPO, address, town, and Thailand. Thus for Bangkok's main GPO, correspondents should send mail written as care of GPO, Charoen Krung Road, Bangkok, Thailand. Post offices are usually open 8:30am–4:30pm Monday to Friday and 9am to noon on Saturdays.

Internet Access

Internet access is available all over Thailand. Charges range from 20 baht per hour in a local Internet café to 250 baht per hour in an upscale hotel. Wireless connection hot spots are becoming very common, even in the provinces. Once a monopoly, Internet services are now provided by a number of companies.

Courier Services

Main international courier companies such as **DHL**, **FedEx**, and **UPS** operate at multiple locations in Thailand, so it is easy to send goods by air freight. However, for very large items, such as furniture, shipping is usually more affordable. Many shops or courier companies can arrange this as well as provide the necessary paperwork.

Useful Dialling Codes

- For international calls, dial 001, 007, 008, or 009 followed by country code. To put a call through the international operator, or to report technical problems, dial 100.
- Country codes are: UK 44; Ireland 353; France 33; US and Canada 1; Australia 61; New Zealand 64. It may be necessary to omit the first digit of the destination area code.
- For directory assistance, dial 1133 from anywhere in the country.
- For domestic calls dial a nine-digit number for Bangkok beginning with (02) and a 10-digit number for other provinces. All cell phone numbers start with the digits 08 or 09.
- To speak to the domestic operator, dial 101.
- To make a domestic collect call dial 101.

TRAVEL INFORMATION

For most visitors, flying is the most convenient way of getting to Thailand's beaches and islands – other routes are by ferry, road, or rail from Malaysia and Cambodia. Domestic flights within Thailand are easy and reduce the traveling time considerably, with several provincial airports located around the country. Flights to neighboring countries are often cheaper if they are booked within Thailand. Rail services run on a regular basis between Bangkok and Singapore, via Kuala Lumpur, Butterworth, and some southern Thai towns. Rail travel is both comfortable and efficient. Long-distance and provincial buses run to all towns and most villages. For local transportation, visitors can choose between a variety of taxis, *songthaews*, and tuk-tuks.

Arriving by Air

Thailand is served by many different airlines. Direct flights are available from North America, Europe, Australasia, Africa, and Asia. A flight from the US may entail an overnight stay in Japan or Taiwan. **Thai Airways International** operates direct flights from Los Angeles to Bangkok. **British Airways**, **United Airlines**, and **Delta Airlines** have a connecting service from New York. Some flights from Asia land at Phuket, Hat Yai, Krabi, and Ko Samui. Other international airlines operating in Thailand are **Qantas Airlines** and **Singapore Airlines**. Low-cost carriers operating in the domestic circuit and within Asia include **Bangkok Airways**, **Air Asia**, and **Nok Air**.

Air Fares

The cost of air tickets to and from Thailand varies according to the destination, the airline, and the time of year. In countries in the northern hemisphere, low fares to Thailand are available from September to April, while in the southern hemisphere, cheap tickets can usually be booked between March and November.

Suvarnabhumi International Airport

After years of planning and numerous delays, Bangkok's Suvarnabhumi International Airport opened in 2006. Located 18 miles (29 km) east of the capital, this is one of the busiest airports in Asia. Suvarnabhumi is used for all international flights as well as many domestic ones.

Arriving passengers enter the terminal on the second floor of the concourse buildings. After passing through the passport checkpoints and customs, they can proceed to the arrivals hall, where they will find transportation and accommodation counters as well as a tourist information center. A meeting point on the third floor allows passengers to get to their next destination as well as obtaining any information that they need.

Getting to and from Suvarnabhumi International Airport

Metered taxis are available outside the first floor. A trip into the city will cost roughly 400 baht, including expressway charges, and would take around 45 minutes, depending on

License plates of a taxi with yellow and black registration numbers

Pale green registration plates of an airport limousine

traffic. Passengers may also make use of the shuttle bus.

A rail link connecting the airport to the city center has two services: the SA City Link, which makes local stops into Bangkok and takes 30 minutes, or the SA Express Line which takes 15 minutes and goes to Makkasan City Air Terminal or Phayathai station.

Keep in mind that check-ins, particularly at the Thai Airways International counter, are often subject to delays, and the walk from the passport checkpoint to the flight lounge is also long.

Don Muang Airport

A number of domestic and inter-national flights from Bangkok leave from Don Muang Airport, which serves the domestic flights of all local budget carriers.

Thai Airways International and Bangkok Airways fly to all major domestic destinations such as Hat Yai, Ko Samui, Krabi, and Phuket. Air tickets can be bought through travel agents and hotels, or booked directly through the airlines. On public holidays (see p41) and on

An aircraft displaying the colors and logo of Thai Airways International

Beautiful interiors created out of natural products at Ko Samui Airport

weekends, when there are more people traveling, it can be difficult to get a flight; visitors are advised to book tickets in advance or travel on weekdays.

Green Travel

Travel around Thailand's beaches and islands is easy, convenient, and cheaply priced, but not very eco-friendly. Most visitors travel by train and long-distance buses, these being less polluting. Hired cars are also preferred by many, but they are not very eco-friendly. Thailand's roads are well maintained, although driving may be hazardous at times, especially in remote areas. The rising price of gas and the prevalent pollution in large cities has caused the introduction of the less polluting and environment-friendly Liquid Petroleum Gas (LPG). However, this is still work in progress and few self-driven vehicles use LPG, though there are several LPG stations outside the major cities. Another alternative is to use Gasohol, a gas which combines fuel derived from sugar cane with ordinary benzene. Both LPG and Gasohol are to some extent subsidized by the government to encourage their use. Leaded gas has almost been phased out. Other ways to minimize an individual traveler's carbon footprint include using shared taxis, buses, and ferries rather than flying, and hiring longtail boats. Although motorcycles remain the most common way of getting around on the smaller islands, it is best to avoid the environmentally unfriendly and noisy two-stroke motorcycles. The most green and healthy way to travel and explore the local sights of any area is on foot or by bicycle.

DIRECTORY

Arriving by Air

Air Asia
Tel 0-2515-9999. W airasia.com

Bangkok Airways
Tel 1771. W bangkokair.com

British Airways
Tel (800) 441-5906;
(0844) 493-0787 (UK).
W britishairways.com

Delta Airlines
Tel 0-2660-6900;
(800) 221-1212 (US).
W delta.com

Nok Air
Tel 1318. W nokair.com

Qantas Airlines
Tel 0-2632-6611;
(0845) 774- 7767 (UK).
W qantas.com

Singapore Airlines
Tel 0-2353-6000;
(800) 742-3333 (US).
W singaporeair.com

Thai Airways International
Tel 0-2356-1111;
(800) 426-5204 (US).
W thaiairways.com

United Airlines
Tel 0-2634-1640;
(800) 864-8331 (US).
W united.com

Visitors traveling between various offshore islands on public ferries

Airport	ℹ Information	Distance to Town or Resort	Average Taxi Fare	Average Journey Time
Bangkok: Don Muang	0-2535-1111	City center 12 miles (19 km)	300 baht	Rail: 50 minutes Road: 1–2 hours
Bangkok: Suvarnabhumi	0-2132-1888	City center 16 miles (26 km)	400 baht	Road: 45 minutes
Hat Yai	0-7422-7131	City center 7 miles (12 km)	200 baht	Road: 25 minutes
Phuket	0-7635-1166	City center 18 miles (29 km)	550 baht	Road: 45 minutes
Ko Samui	0-7760-1300	Chaweng 3 miles (5 km)	500 baht	Road: 15 minutes

Local Transportation

After years of traffic congestion, Bangkok finally launched the BTS (Bangkok Mass Transit System) Skytrain in 1999, and an underground network in 2004. This well-maintained service, along with the Chao Phraya Express Pier, has revolutionized travel in the capital. Transportation in the provinces is less frenetic, with a choice of *samlors* (bicycle rickshaws), tuk-tuks (auto rickshaws), and *songthaews* (converted pickup trucks). Bargaining over fares is also a part of the Thai experience.

A *samlor*, a common mode of transportation for short journeys

Getting Around Bangkok

In downtown Bangkok, the efficient Skytrain has two lines – the Sukhumvit route from Morchit Station in the north to Bearing Station in the east, and the Silom route from National Stadium to Bang Wa in Phasi Charoen, with an interchange between the two at the Siam Center. The airport rail link is a direct route to Suvarnabhumi Airport, offering both express and local services. The express service takes just 15 minutes and the local service around 30 minutes.

The MRT (Mass Rapid Transit) underground runs for 12 miles (19 km) from Hua Lampong Station to Bang Sue. Other forms of city transport include riverboats, buses, limousines, and tour buses, along with taxis, and tuk-tuks.

Express riverboats serve the popular piers along the Chao Phraya River. Ferries link the east and west banks, and it is possible to rent a longtail boat at some piers.

One-way bus lanes make for speedy road transport. The BMTA (Bangkok Mass Transit Authority) map, available at most bus terminals, shows the routes. Blue air-conditioned buses and white Metrobuses are comfortable and cover the popular routes. Non air-conditioned buses are cheap, cover all of Bangkok, and run into the night. Buses outside Bangkok are not easy to use for non-Thai speakers, but tuk-tuks, *songthaews*, and taxis are readily available.

Taxis

Metered taxis operate all over Bangkok and Hat Yai, and are distinguishable by the Taxi-Meter sign on the roof. Drivers tend to know the names and locations of only the major hotels and sights. In non-meter taxis (in Bangkok these are now quite rare and not recommended at all), visitors will have to bargain for the fare before getting in. Motorcycle taxis operate in some towns. Drivers tend to congregate near markets and long *sois* and can be identified by their colorful numbered vests. Prices are usually negotiable.

Brightly colored tuk-tuk

Songthaews, Samlors and Tuk-Tuks

Songthaews – literally, "two rows" – are vans or converted pickup trucks with two rows of seats in the back. They are more common than city buses outside

Bangkok and run popular routes for set fares, typically between 20 and 40 baht. There are no fixed schedules for departure or arrival as drivers wait until they are at least half occupied before starting out. Routes are sometimes written in English on the sides of the vans. A *songthaew* can also be rented like a taxi, but they are generally less comfortable.

Samlors are three-wheeled non-motorized vehicles or rickshaws that can transport one or two people up to a few kilometers. Motorized *samlors* are also known as tuk-tuks. Their two-stroke engines, introduced by the Japanese during World War II, are very noisy. In heavy traffic or during the rainy season, tuk-tuks can be uncomfortable and unstable, but are always popular with tourists. For short trips a reasonable price to pay is 50–80 baht. Visitors should do some prior research and negotiate a price before climbing into either of the two.

A Skytrain pulling into a station in Bangkok

Organized Tours

Hundreds of tour companies are based in Bangkok and major resorts such as Phuket and Pattaya. Most hotels throughout the country also offer a variety of tours. Typical excursions range from day-long city tours to more comprehensive itineraries taking in different towns and sights over several days. Costs are generally higher, but using public transport within the city can be time-consuming, especially in congested areas such as Greater Bangkok. The drawback of most organized tours is that there is no freedom of choice and there is rarely any time to linger.

Booking counter for local transportation on the Eastern Seaboard

Booking a Tour

It is often possible to book a tour of Thailand from a prospective traveler's home country and the package usually includes all travel and accommodation arrangements. Such all-inclusive tours typically last between one and two weeks and include a few nights in Bangkok followed by excursions to Hua Hin, Ko Samui, Krabi, or Phuket. Other packages are more specialized, concentrating, say, on visiting Khao Lak or Phuket and trekking in Khao Sok National Park (*see pp210–11*), and may vary from a few days to several weeks in duration. Bangkok-based **Diethelm Travel**, **Thai Overlander Travel & Tour**, **Arlymear Travel**, **NS Travel & Tours**, **Regale International Travel**, **STA Travel**, and **World Travel Service Ltd** are major operators offering packages.

Most regional hotels and many guesthouses also offer tours, or are in contact with local tour companies. The local TAT office will be able to recommend reputable tour companies. Day trips to the most popular sights can be booked just a day in advance. Tours to more distant sights should include arrangements for accommodations, and have at least one departure day each week. Tour companies often pick up visitors from their respective hotels or guesthouses.

Tour Buses and Boats

Many tour operators use VIP or luxury coaches, with reclining seats, refreshments, air-conditioning, and a toilet. Air-conditioned minibuses are also common, as well as jeeps for the remote areas. Most vehicles

Speedboat ready to take tourists to the Similan Islands

are well maintained and quite safe. Boat tours are popular. Day trips to islands often include watersports. Hotel transfers are also part of the deal. Boat trips to remote islands also usually come with onboard accommodations and diving facilities.

Guided Tours

Bilingual guides accompany many tours, especially to cultural sights such as Nakhon Si Thammarat or Phetchaburi. For diving and snorkeling trips, a qualified guide is essential for safety reasons. The quality of guides and tours varies, and listings of reputable tours along with good maps are published by the provincial TAT offices.

DIRECTORY

Booking a Tour

Arlymear Travel
6th Floor, CCT Building,
109 Surawong Rd, Bangkok.
City Map 7 C3. **Tel** 0-2236-9317.
W arlymear.com

Diethelm Travel
12th Floor, Kian Gwan Building II,
140/1 Witthayu Rd, Bangkok.
City Map 8 E3. **Tel** 0-2660-7000.
W diethelmtravel.com

NS Travel & Tours
133/48 Ratchaprarop Rd,
Bangkok.
City Map 4 E4. **Tel** 0-2640-1440.
W nstravel.com

Regale International Travel
191/1-2 Soi Suksaviddhaya,
Sathorn Nua Rd, Bangkok.
City Map 7 B5. **Tel** 0-2635- 2450.
W regaleintl.com

STA Travel
14th Floor, Wall Street Tower
Building, Suriwong Rd, Bangkok.
City Map 7 C3. **Tel** 0-2236-0262.
W statravel.co.th

Thai Overlander
Travel & Tour
407 Sukhumvit Rd (between
Sukhumvit Soi 21 and 23),
Bangkok.
Tel 0-2258-4778.

World Travel Service Ltd
1053 Charoen Krung Rd,
Bangkok.
City Map 7 A4. **Tel** 0-2233-5900.
W worldtravelservice.co.th

Traveling by Train, Bus, and Boat

The State Railway of Thailand (SRT) has four major lines connecting Bangkok with other parts of the country. Although trains are safe and comfortable, they are slow and the number of towns on the network is limited. Phuket, Krabi, and Trang, for instance, do not have train stations. By contrast, long-distance buses connect all major cities to Bangkok, while provincial buses serve smaller towns and villages. Ferry services serve the main islands.

Fountain at the entrance to Hua Lampong Station, Bangkok

Railroad Network

Bangkok's main terminus, **Hua Lampong Station**, which opened in 1916, serves all four major lines and over 130 trains to different parts of Thailand. The first line runs to Chiang Mai via the central plains. A second, which later divides in two, runs to Nong Khai and Ubon Ratchathani in northeast Thailand. A third connects Bangkok to the Eastern Seaboard and Cambodia, and a fourth runs down the peninsula to Malaysia. This station is the principal departure point for trains to the coastal areas.

Window of a first-class coach in a train

Trains

Train services are labeled Special Express (the fastest), Express, Rapid, and Ordinary. Travel times, even on Express trains, can be longer than by road. The trip from Bangkok to **Surat Thani Station**, for instance, takes 11–12 hours.

First-class coaches (available on Express and Special Express trains) consist of individual cabins with air-conditioning.

Second-class coaches have reclining seats and a choice of fan-cooled or air-conditioned coaches. Sleepers in this class have individual seats that are converted into curtained-off beds at night. Toilets (there should be at least one Western toilet) and washing facilities are usually located at the end of the coaches.

Most tourists find that a second-class train compartment is comfortable enough for long distances and it is far more relaxing than a protracted bus journey.

Third-class coaches have wooden benches, each seating two or three passengers: they are cheap but not recommended for long distances. Most trains are clean and well maintained. Uniformed vendors move along the aisles with refreshments, and buffet cars are attached to trains on long-distance routes.

Train Tickets and Fares

A train timetable in English is available from Hua Lampong Station in Bangkok. Visitors should remember that tickets in peak periods (weekends and holidays) can be sold out days in advance. Hua Lampong has an advance booking office with English-speaking staff. Some travel agents also book train tickets.

Fares depend on the speed of the train and the class of the carriage. A second-class ticket between Bangkok and Surat Thani is about 440 baht, with supplements included in the price. Second-class sleeper tickets cost about 850 baht. Shorter trips, for example from Bangkok to Pattaya, cost around 30 baht (third class).

Tourists can also buy 20-day rail passes. These cost 3,000 baht. Information about these passes is available at Hua Lampong Station.

Long-distance Buses

Long-distance buses run from the **Eastern (Ekamai)**, **Northern (Morchit)**, and **Southern (Boromratchonnee Road)** bus terminals in Bangkok. Provincial capitals can be reached directly from Bangkok. **Surat Thani Station** is an important point in southern Thailand with both long-distance and local connections. Buses can be faster than trains and are very comfortable as the vehicles are air-conditioned, with a toilet, reclining seats, and plenty of leg room. "VIP" buses have the best facilities, including free refreshments served by a stewardess. Overnight buses are especially popular. The air-

Double-decker luxury bus for traveling on long-distance routes

Eastern & Oriental Express

The world-renowned Eastern & Oriental Express operates between Bangkok and Singapore. This journey in style takes three days and two nights, including stops at Butterworth and Kuala Lumpur in Malaysia. Its 22 carriages have fabrics and fittings evocative of 1930s luxury rail travel. Double and single cabins come in private and presidential classes, and there are two restaurants, a saloon car, a bar, and an observation deck. Such luxuries are also reflected in the price.

Dining car on the Eastern & Oriental Express

conditioned buses can get quite cold and travelers should dress suitably in long-sleeved shirts and long pants, although blankets are usually provided.

Bus Tickets and Fares

Fares for long-distance bus journeys are similarly priced as second-class train tickets. VIP buses cost about 20 to 50 percent more. Book well in advance through a travel agent or at the bus station if traveling on a weekend or public holiday. Otherwise, just turn up at the coach station at least half an hour before departure. Bus tickets are always bought on a one-way basis.

Provincial Buses

The government bus company is called *Bor Kor Sor* (BKS). The BKS buses are frequent, relatively reliable, and the cheapest form of travel around Thailand. Booking is rarely necessary. On many buses, travelers just need to pay the driver or conductor. Almost every town will have a BKS terminal. *Rot thamadaa* (non-air-conditioned) buses are the cheapest and slowest, and stop almost everywhere along the way. The *rot aer* (air-conditioned) local buses do not always provide blankets, so visitors are advised to take a jacket or sweater, especially for the night.

Traveling on provincial buses is a good way to meet local people and reach the more obscure villages and sights en route. Travelers should beware that refreshment and toilet stops may be infrequent, and buses may be crowded and in poor shape. Local services are nearly always slow and the skills of drivers will vary. Back seats

are reserved for monks, so be prepared to move or stand. Women should especially avoid sitting next to monks.

Boats to the Islands

Scheduled ferries are erratic, since their service is heavily dependent on the weather conditions. Regular services are available to Ko Samui, Ko Phangan, and Ko Tao from Surat Thani. Smaller islands have less regular services that depend on the number of seats filled. These makeshift ferries or longtail boats are run by local fishermen and services often stop in the rainy season.

Ticket counter at Krabi for boats to the nearby islands

Renting a Car, Moped, or Bicycle

Driving in Thailand is definitely not for the faint-hearted. Hazards come in the form of potholed roads, confusing intersections, badly maintained vehicles, and dangerous driving. For many visitors wanting to explore the country off the beaten track, hiring a car and a driver familiar with the roads is by far the best option. International and local car rental firms of varying standards operate all over Thailand. In the resorts, mopeds and jeeps are popular options.

Renting a Car

A valid international driver's license is a necessity for most visitors, while those from ASEAN countries (Association of Southeast Asian Nations) need only have a license from their home countries. International rental agencies offer safe cars and extensive insurance and backup services. **Avis** and **Budget** have desks at some airports and in major cities. Charges range from about 1,800 baht for a day to 35,000 baht for a month. **Siam Express** is another prominent rental agency.

With other less familiar car rental companies, visitors should check the small print on the contract for liabilities. Obtain a copy of the vehicle registration and carry it around.

Hiring a Chauffeur-Driven Car

Hiring an experienced driver with a car is becoming a popular option for visitors to Thailand. The cost is often less

Typical traffic congestion in Thailand's notoriously busy capital

than 50 percent extra on top of the normal price of the car rental. Some drivers know about local sights and suggest interesting spots. Most car rental firms can arrange drivers. Siam Express offers packages including a chauffeur, car, and accommodations in a range of hotels.

Renting a Moped

Mopeds and motorcycles are widely available for rent in resorts, big cities, and other towns as

well as beaches. In areas with a lot of guesthouses, visitors can rent anything from a moped to a heavy-duty dirt bike. Driver's licenses are rarely requested, and few firms bother with insurance. Costs can be as low as 150 baht for a day's rental. Safety precautions are essential. Check tires, oil, and brakes before setting out. Wear a helmet (compulsory in Thailand) and proper shoes. Long sleeves and trousers will minimize cuts and grazes in a minor accident. Take great care on dirt roads and avoid driving alone in rural areas. Visitors should remember that medical help is not always easily available.

Gasoline and Servicing

Gas stations in Thailand are well manned and are located on main roads in towns and along highways. They are modern and most provide unleaded fuel. Attendants will fill the tank, wash the windows, and pump air into the tires. Some garages have a resident mechanic for major jobs, or will at least recommend one. Most of them have a small general store, and all have toilet facilities. Many garages are open 24 hours, while others close at about 8pm. Gas itself is often cheaper in Thailand than it is in the West.

Parking

Multistoried parking lots in Bangkok are usually attached to major hotels and departmental stores. Parking is generally free for hotel guests and visitors for up to a few hours. For general parking, issued entry tickets should be stamped and paid for while exiting. Yet, parking can be difficult in the congested streets of the capital.

Pavements painted with red and white stripes indicate a no-parking zone. In smaller towns, many hotels and guesthouses provide free parking. In quieter towns, visitors can park anywhere that is obviously not going to obstruct passing traffic.

Mopeds for rent at Hat Sai Khao, Ko Chang

Traffic policeman managing the rush at a Bangkok intersection

Roads and Road Signs

Multi-lane national highways exist mostly in and around Bangkok. A toll is charged on the expressways, including the one leading to Bangkok Airport. The fee is indicated above the booth and exact change is required at most manually operated booths.

Expressways are less congested than other roads, but they are still prone to traffic jams. Many roads in Bangkok are one-way, although there are special lanes reserved for buses traveling in the opposite direction.

National highways (also known as routes) such as Highway 4, which runs like a spine from Bangkok down to southern Thailand, are fast and efficient, despite being congested in places. Provincial highways are paved and vary in quality. Smaller roads linking villages are sometimes no more than dirt tracks. Main roads in towns are called *thanons* and numbered lanes leading off these are called *sois* and *troks*. Most roads can get quite flooded in the rains.

Destinations are marked in both Roman and Thai script. Arabic numerals are used for distances, and kilometer markers are placed along all main roads. Road markings and traffic symbols are quite clear and easy to understand.

Rules of the Road

Driving is on the left-hand side of the road. The speed limit is 35 mph (60 kph) within city limits, unless signed otherwise, and 50 mph (80 kph) on open roads. The standard international road rules apply, but are hardly followed by Thai drivers. The only consistent rule is determined by the size of the vehicle one is driving.

The rather eccentric use of indicators and headlights can be unnerving. A left signal can indicate to another driver that it is alright to pass, while a right signal can indicate hazardous oncoming traffic. A flash of the headlights means a vehicle is coming through.

For what it is worth, horns are hardly used, except in emergencies, as it is thought to be impolite. Drivers think nothing of rash driving and it is wise to yield to larger vehicles at unmarked intersections. It is legal to turn left at red lights if there is a blue sign with a white left arrow, or if one happens to be in the left lane. Visitors should be careful of animals that often wander onto minor roads.

Traffic fines are commonly imposed for illegal turns. If a visitor gets a ticket and the license is taken, they should go to the local police station, the address of which will be on the ticket, and pay the fine. Visitors should drive slowly

Visitors cycling through rough terrain on mountain bikes

through army checkpoints in border areas, and be prepared to stop if necessary.

Road Maps

Most Thais rely on memory and see no need for maps. Tourist maps are widely available but cover major roads only. Some foldout maps produced by the Prannok Witthaya Map Center are excellent, showing all roads and reliefs, but are sold at few outlets. The *Thailand Highways Map* by the Auto Guide Company and the *Thailand Highway Map* by the Roads Association are the best atlases, written in both Thai and Roman scripts.

Renting a Bicycle

In the cool season, cycling in the quieter areas is a pleasant way to explore the place. Guesthouses and small rental shops have bicycles for hire for 50–100 baht a day, though the bikes may be rickety. New mountain bikes may be available, but costs could exceed those of mopeds. Taking plenty of water is essential and, of course, great care must be taken riding on busy roads.

General Index

Acknowledgments

Dorling Kindersley would like to thank the many people whose help and assistance contributed to the preparation of this book.

Main Contributor
Andrew Forbes has a Ph.D. in Central Asian History. He lives in Chiang Mai and is an editor with CPA Media. He has authored many books on Thailand and Eastern Asia.

David Henley is a widely published photographer whose work has appeared in *National Geographic*, The *Washington Post* and numerous international publications and travel guides.

Peter Holmshaw has lived in Chiang Mai for more than 20 years, and has contributed to several travel guides on Southeast Asia.

Fact Checker Peter Holmshaw

Indexer Cyber Media Services Ltd

Thai Translator Sulaganya Punyayodhin

Design and Editorial
Publisher Douglas Amrine
List Manager Vivien Antwi
Project Editor Michelle Crane
Editorial Consultants Hugh Thompson, Scarlett O Hara
Project Designer Shahid Mahmood
Senior Cartographic Editor Casper Morris
Managing Art Editor (jackets) Karen Constanti
Jacket Design Kate Leonard
Senior DTP Designer Jason Little
Senior Picture Researcher Ellen Root
Production Controller Vicky Baldwin
Revisions and Relaunch Team Louise Abbott, Claire Baranowski, Sheeba Bhatnagar, Conrad Van Dyk, Ron Emmons, Emer FitzGerald, Cincy Jose, Maite Lantaron, James Marshall, Helen Peters, Neil Ray, Natalie Revie, Ankita Sharma, Rituraj Singh, Tarini Singh, Jaynan Spengler, Rose Teare, David Tombesi-Walton, Nikky Twyman, Ajay Verma, Nikhil Verma, Catherine Waring.

Additional Photography
Rob Ashby, Philip Blenkinsop, Gerard Brown, Jane Burton, Peter Chadwick, Andy Crawford, Philip Gatward, Steve Gorton, Frank Greenaway, Will Heap, David Henley, Stuart Isett, Hugh Johnson, Dave King, Mathew Kurien, Cyril Laubscher, Brent Madison, James Marshall, Alan Newham, David Peart, Roger Phillips, Tim Ridley, Alex Robinson, Rough Guides/ Ian Aitken, /Simon Racken, Steve Shott, Michael Spencer, Kim Taylor and Jane Burton, Karen Trist, Richard Watson, James Young.

Special Assistance
Ruengsiri Sathirakul at Anantara Hua Hin Resort & Spa, Suwan Chakchit at Baipai Thai Cooking School, Fann Kulchada and Joyce Ong at Banyan Tree Phuket, Adam Purcell at The *BigChilli* Magazine, Puritad Jongkamonvivat at Nation Multimedia Group, Sirin Yuanyaidee at The National Museum Bangkok, Toby To at Patravadi Theater, Somchai Bussarawit at Phuket Aquarium, Nam and Prompeth L at Tourism Authority of Thailand.

Photography Permissions
Dorling Kindersley would like to thank the following for their assistance and kind permission to photograph at their establishments:
Abhisek Dusit Throne Hall, The Jim Thompson House, Joe Louis Theater, King Mongkut Memorial Park of Science and Technology, Marine Research Center, Marukhathaiyawan Palace, The National Museum Bangkok, Royal Carriage Museum, Thai Ramakien Gallery, Than Bok Koranee National Park, Under Water World Pattaya. Also all the other temples, museums, hotels, restaurants, shops, galleries and other sights too numerous to thank individually.

Picture Credits
Placement Key- a = above; b = below/bottom; c = center; f = far; l = left; r = right; t = top.

The publisher would like to thank the following individuals, companies, and picture libraries for their kind permission to reproduce their photographs:

Matthias Akolck: 185cr.

Alamy Images: AA World Travel Library 263br; Ace Stock Limited 4br, 19b; Victor Paul Borg 36bl; Paul Brown 100; Pavlos Christoforou 105tr, 208crb; Thomas Cockrem 83tr; Richard Cummins / Destinations 58bl; Jean-Pierre De Mann 322c; Ray Evans 39br; F1online digitale Bildagentur GmbH 25bl; Blaine Harrington 160, David Fleetham 24cl; Mike Goldwater 38b; Ingolf Pompe17 167cr; Norma Joseph 84cr; Paul Kingsley 40c; John Lander 59bl; Antony McAulay 134; Chris McLennan 181br; Robert Harding Picture Library Ltd 219tr; Leonid Serebrennikov 224cl; Neil Setchfield 21tr; Martin Strmiska 208bl; Peter Treanor 28br, 101b; WaterFrame 25tr; Terry Whittaker 210c; Andrew Woodley 27br.

Amari Orchid Pattaya: 311bc.

Anantara Hotels, Resorts & Spas: 310tl, 332cl.

Ardea.com: Jean Paul Ferrero 157br.

Baipai Thai Cooking School: 329br.

Bangkok Airways Co., Ltd: 347tl.

Banyan Tree Bangkok: 87tl.

Banyan Tree Spa Phuket: 332br.

Black Mountain Resort and Country Club Co., Ltd: 327bc.

The Boathouse Wine & Grill restaurant: 316tl.

The Bridgeman Art Library: The King of Siam on his Elephant, from an account of the Jesuits in Siam, 1688 (w/c on paper), French School, (17th century) /Bibliothèque Nationale, Paris, France /Archives Charmet /113cl.

Centara Grand Beach Resort & Villas Hua Hin: 313tr.

Chakrabongse Villas Bangkok: 295tr.

Chiva-Som resorts: 298cl, 333tr.

Cool Breeze Cafe Bar: 312bl.

Corbis: Bettmann 46tr, 48tl, 48bc; Christophe Boisvieux 28clb; John Van Hasselt 30-31c, 322bl; Brooks Kraft 49bc; Luca Tettoni 47bc; Narong Sangnak 39c; Scott Stulberg 52br; Sunset Boulevard 217br; Sygma /Jean Leo Dugast 29cr; Staffan Widstrand 149cra, Xinhua Press / Rachen Sageamsak 49crb.

CPA Media: Oliver Hargreave 213bl; David Henley 28tr, 45tr, 47tl, 47cr, 48c, 81br, 324br; Daniel Kestenholz 74clb; Pictures from Asia/David Henley 74tr.

Gerald Cubitt: 22cl, 22cr, 22crb, 22bc, 23tc, 23cl, 23cb, 23bc, 23br, 24tr, 251crb.

DK Images: Courtesy of the Buddha Padipa Temple, Courtesy of The National Birds of Prey Centre; David Peart 25br, Courtesy of Whipsnade Zoo, Bedfordshire/ Dave King 205, David Henley

13tl, 14tr, 15bl, 123clb, Stuart Isett 12br, Karen Trist 15br, Martin Richardson 13br.

Dreamstime.com: Guido Amrein 10c, Barelkodotcom 167tl, Alex Bramwell 11b, Rene Drouyer 11tl, 124-125, Giuliachristin 323cl, Wisit Kumlerd 146t, Pratchaya Leelapatchayanont 123tl, Jan Łętowski 33cla, 231br, Madrugadaverde 166cl, Noppadol Niyomthai 15tr, Pixattitude 328 tc, Voranat Rajchatan 142cra, Stemoir 14bl, He Tian 113bl, Tzidos 50-51, Vitaly Titov & Maria Sidelnikova 169tr.

ENZO Bistro Fusion Japanese: 315br.

FLPA: Terry Whittaker 22cb.

Getty Images: AFP /Saeed Khan 49t, Peter Parks 243clb; Patrick Foto 2-3; Photographer's Choice /Georgette Douwma 25tl; Stone /David Hanson 195c; Taxi /Hummer 353bc.

The Granger Collection, New York: 155cr.

Indus Restaurant: 309tr.

Istockphoto.com: Rontography 275tl; ShyMan 305c.

The Kobal Collection: 20th Century Fox /Mountain Peter 257tl.

Let's Sea: 312tc.

Lonely Planet Images: Anders Blomqvist 247tr; Austin Bush 175clb, 184br; Felix Hug 35tr; Noboru Komine 41bl; Bernard Napthine 272tr; Bill Wassman 175bc; Carol Wiley 195br.

Mary Evans Picture Library: 45bc, 46cl, 158bl.

Masterfile: Brad Wrobleski 344bl.

Mom Tri's Villa Royale Phuket: 300tl.

The National Museum Bangkok: 43clb, 45cb, 66c.

Nation Multimedia Group: 345tc.

Naturepl.com: Geogette Douwma 24bl, 25cr. Raymond Ong: 199tl.

Neil Ray: 158tl.

Orient-Express Hotels Trains & Cruises: 351ca.

Photobank (Bangkok): 29tl, 29cra, 30tr, 30cla, 30clb, 30bl, 30br, 31tl, 31tr, 31cr, 31crb, 31bl, 31bc, 31br, 33cr, 34tr, 34bl, 34-35c, 35cr, 44tl, 46c, 46-47c, 47tr, 47clb, 73cb, 77cl, 77bl, 113ca, 113cr, 142cl, 153br, 155crb, 159b, 165bl, 165br, 175cl, 191b, 231tr, 243crb, 243br, 267tr, 282cl.

Photolibrary: age fotostock/ Chua Wee Boo 154c, /Alan Copson 264br, /Alvaro Leiva 259tr, /P Narayan 37cr; All Canada Photos/ Kurt Werby 173tr; Alexander Blackburn Clayton 55b; CPA Media 187tl; Imagebroker.net/ Norbert Eisele-Hein 329tl; Imagestate/ Art Media 47c, /Mark Henley 53tr, /Steve Vidler 20bl, 216br, /The British Library 28-29c;

Lonely Planet Images/ Claver Carroll 324tl, Mauritius/ Birgit Gierth 36cl; Oxford Scientific (OSF)/ Splashdown Direct 190bl; Robert Harding Travel/ Gavin Hellier 287cr; WaterFrame - Underwater Images/ Reinhard Dirscherl 24br, 26br.

Private Collection: 155bc, 287cr.
Rayavadee and Tamarind Village: 301br.

Reflexstock: Alamy/ sdbphoto.com 63br.

Robert Harding Picture Library: Gonzalo Azumendi 290-291, 334-335, Stefano Baldini 280, Michael DeFreitas 54, Ingolf Pompe 222-223, 264-265, Otto Stadler 18, Dave Stamboulis 150-151, Thomas Stankiewicz 182-183, Luca Tettoni 8-9, Stuart Westmorland 200.

Royal Cliff Beach Resort: 297tr.

Brian Ng Tian Soon: 199br.

Seven Spoons Restaurant: 308br.

Shangri-La Hotel Bangkok: 294bc.

Six Senses Hideaway: 299tl, 314tr.

Soneva Resorts and Residences: 296bl.

Superstock: Mikel Bilbao 244; Ben Mangor 243cl; Westend61 26-27c.

Thai Airways International Public Company Limited: 346bl.

Tourism Authority of Thailand: 142br, 268bl, 271tr, 326bl, 328bl, 337cl.

Viva Restaurant: 317bl.

Front Endpaper: Left : Robert Harding Picture Library: Michael DeFreitas (t); Stuart Westmorland (c). SuperStock: Mikel Bilbao (b)
Right : Paul Brown (t); Antony McAulay (cr); Blaine Harrington (cl). Robert Harding Picture Library: Stefano Baldini (b)

Cover Images: Front: 4Corners: Tuul & Bruno Morandi / SIME; Spine: 4Corners: Tuul & Bruno Morandi / SIME

All other images © Dorling Kindersley
For further information see: www.dkimages.com

Phrase Book

Thai is a tonal language and regarded by most linguists as head of a distinct language group, although it incorporates many Sanskrit words from ancient India, and some modern English ones, too. There are five tones: mid, high, low, rising, and falling. The particular tone, or pitch, at which each syllable is pronounced determines its meaning. For instance "mâi" (falling tone) means "not," but "maˇi" (rising tone) is "silk."

The Thai script uses one of the most elaborate alphabets in the world, running left to right and using over 80 letters. In the third column of this phrase book is a phonetic transliteration for English speakers, including guidance for tones in the form of accents. This differs from the system used elsewhere in the guide, which follows the Thai Royal Institute's recommended romanization of common names.

Guidelines for Pronunciation

When reading the phonetics, pronounce syllables as if they form English words. For instance:

a	as in "**a**go"
e	as in "**he**n"
i	as in "**thi**n"
o	as in "**o**n"
u	as in "**gu**n"
ah	as in "**ra**ther"
ai	as in "**Thai**"
air	as in "**pair**"
ao	as in "**Mao** Zedong"
ay	as in "**day**"
er	as in "**e**nter"
ew	as in "**few**"
oh	as in "**go**"
oo	as in "**boo**t"
OO	as in "**boo**k"
oy	as in "**toy**"
g	as in "**g**ive"
ng	as in "si**ng**"

These sounds have no close equivalents in English:

eu	can be likened to a sound of disgust – the sound could be written as "**errgh**"
bp	a single sound between a "b" and a "p"
dt	a single sound between a "d" and a "t"

Note that when "p," "t," and "k" occur at the end of Thai words, the sound is "swallowed." Also note that many Thais use an "l" instead of an "r" sound.

The Five Tones

Accents indicate the tone of each syllable.

no mark	The **mid tone** is voiced at the speaker's normal, even pitch.
á é í ó ú	The **high tone** is pitched slightly higher than the mid tone.
à è ì ò ù	The **low tone** is pitched slightly lower than the mid tone.
ǎ ě ǐ ǒ ǔ	The **rising tone** sounds like a questioning pitch, starting low and rising.
â ê î ô û	The **falling tone** sounds similar to an English speaker stressing a one-syllable word for emphasis.

Male and Female Polite Forms

In polite speech, Thai men add the particle "**krúp**" at the end of each sentence; women add "**ká**" at the end of questions and "**kâ**" at the end of statements. These particles have been omitted from all but the most essential polite terms in this phrase book, but they should be used as much as possible. The polite forms of the word "I" are, for men, "**pŏm**" and, for women, "**dee-chún**."

In an Emergency

Help!	ช่วยด้วย	chôo-ay dôo-ay!
Fire!	ไฟไหม้	fai mâi!
Where is the nearest hospital?	แถวนี้โรงพยาบาล อยู่ที่ไหน	ta˘ir-o née mee rohng pa-yah-bahn yòo têe-na˘i?
Call an ambulance!	เรียกรถพยาบาล ให้หน่อย	rêe-uk rót pa-yah-bahn hâi nòy!
Call the police!	เรียกตำรวจให้หน่อย	rêe-uk dtum ròo-ut hâi nòy!
Call a doctor!	เรียกหมอให้หน่อย	rêe-uk mo˘r hâi nòy!

Communication Essentials

Yes	ใช่ or ครับ/ค่ะ	châi or krúp/kâ
No	ไม่ใช่ or ไม่ครับ/ไม่ค่ะ	mâi châi or mâi krúp/ mâi kâ
Please can you …?	ช่วย …	chôo-ay …
Thank you	ขอบคุณ	kòrp-kOOn
No, thank you	ไม่เอา ขอบคุณ	mâi ao kòrp-kOOn
Excuse me/sorry	ขอโทษ (ครับ/ค่ะ)	ko˘r-tôht (krúp/kâ)
Hello	สวัสดี (ครับ/ค่ะ)	sa-wùt dee (krúp/kâ)
Goodbye	ลาก่อนนะ	lah gòrn ná
What?	อะไร	a-rai?
Why?	ทำไม	tum-mai?
Where?	ที่ไหน	têe na˘i?
How?	ยังไง	yung ngai?

Useful Phrases

How are you?	คุณสบายดีหรือ (ครับ/คะ)	kOOn sa-bai dee reu (krúp/kà)?
Very well, thank you – and you?	สบายดี (ครับ/ค่ะ) แล้วคุณล่ะ	sa-bai dee (krúp/kâ) – lâir-o kOOn lâ?
How do I get to…?	… ไปยังไง	… bpai yung- ngai?
Do you speak English?	คุณพูดภาษาอังกฤษ เป็นไหม	kOOn pôot pah-sa˘h ung-grìt bpen mái?
Could you speak slowly?	ช่วยพูดช้าๆหน่อย ได้ไหม	chôo-ay pôot cháh cháh nòy dâi mái?
I can't speak Thai.	พูดภาษาไทย ไม่เป็น	pôot pah-sa˘h tai mâi bpen

Useful Words

woman/women	ผู้หญิง	pôo-yi˘ng
man/men	ผู้ชาย	pôo-chai
child/children	เด็ก	dèk
hot	ร้อน	rórn
cold	เย็น or หนาว	yen or na˘o
good	ดี	dee
bad	ไม่ดี	mâi dee

open	เปิด	bpèrt
closed	ปิด	bpìt
left	ซ้าย	sái
right	ขวา	kwáˇh
straight ahead	อยู่ตรงหน้า	yòo dtrong nâh
on the corner of	ตรงหัวมุม	dtrong hǒˇo-a mOOm
near	ใกล้	glâi
far	ไกล	glai
entrance	ทางเข้า	tahng kào
exit	ทางออก	tahng òrk
toilet	ห้องน้ำ	hôrng náhm

Telephoning

Where is the nearest public telephone?	แถวนี้มีโทรศัพท์ อยู่ที่ไหน ที่นี่ได้ไหม?	taˇir-o née mee toh-ra-sùp yòo têe-naˇi? nêe dâi mái?
Hello, this is… speaking.	สวัสดี (ผม/ดิฉัน) … พูด (ครับ/ค่ะ)	hello (poˇm/dee-chún) … pôot (krúp/kâ)
I would like to speak to…	ขอพูดกับคุณ … หน่อย (ครับ/ค่ะ)	kǒˇr pôot gùp khun … nòy (krúp/kâ)
Could you speak up a little, please?	ช่วยพูดดังๆหน่อย ได้ไหม	chôo-ay pôot dung dung nòy dâi mái?
local call	โทรศัพท์ภายใน ท้องถิ่น	toh-ra-sùp pai nai tórng tìn
phone booth/kiosk	ตู้โทรศัพท์	dtôo toh-ra-sùp
phone card	บัตรโทรศัพท์	but toh-ra-sùp

Shopping

How much does this cost?	นี่ราคาเท่าไร	nêe rah-kah tâo-rài?
I would like …	ต้องการ …	dtôrng-gahn …
Do you have …?	มี … ไหม	mee … mái?
I am just looking.	ชมดูเท่านั้น	chom doo tâo-nún
Do you take credit cards/travelers' checks?	รับบัตรเครดิต/เช็คเดิน ทางไหม	rub but cray-dit/ chék dern tang mái?
What time do you open/close?	เปิด/ปิดกี่โมง	bpèrt/bpìt gèe mohng?
Can you ship this overseas?	ส่งของนี้ไปต่าง ประเทศได้ไหม	sòng khoˇng nee bpai dtàhng bpra-tâyt dâi mái?
cheap	ถูก	tòok
expensive	แพง	pairng
gold	ทอง	torng
hill-tribe handicrafts	หัตถกรรมชาวเขา	hùt-ta-gum chao kaˇo
silver	เงิน	ngern
Thai silk	ผ้าไหมไทย	pâh-maˇi tai
department store	ห้าง	hâhng
market	ตลาด	dta-làht
newsstand	ร้านขายหนังสือพิมพ์	ráhn kaˇi núng-sěu pim
pharmacy	ร้านขายยา	ráhn kaˇi yâh
tailor	ร้านตัดเสื้อ	ráhn dtùt sêu-a

Sightseeing

| travel agent | บริษัทนำเที่ยว | bor-rí-sùt num têe-o |
| tourist office | สำนักงานการ ท่องเที่ยว | suˇm-núk ngahn gahn tôrng têe-o |

tourist police	ตำรวจท่องเที่ยว	dtum-ròo-ut tôrng tee-o
beach	หาด or ชายหาด	hàht or chai-hàht
coral	หินปะการัง	hiˇn bpa-gah-rung
festival	งานออกร้าน	ngahn òrk ráhn
hill/mountain	เขา	kaˇo
historical park	อุทยานประวัติศาสตร์	ÒO-ta-yahn bpra wùt sàht
island (ko)	เกาะ	gòr
temple (wat)	วัด	wút
museum	พิพิธภัณฑ์	pí-pìt-ta-pun
national park	อุทยานแห่งชาติ	ÒO-ta yahn hàirng châht
park/garden	สวน	soˇo-un
river	แม่น้ำ	mâir náhm
Thai boxing	มวยไทย	moo-ay tai
Thai massage	นวด	nôo-ut
trekking	การเดินทางเท้า	gahn dern tahng táo
waterfall	น้ำตก	náhm dtòk

Transportation

When does the train for … leave?	รถไฟไป … ออกเมื่อไร	rót fai bpai … òrk meu-rài?
How long does it take to get to …?	ใช้เวลานาน เท่าไรไปถึงที่ …	chái way-lah nahn tâo-rài bpai těung têe …?
A ticket to … please..	ขอตั๋วไป … หน่อย (ครับ/ค่ะ)	koˇr dtoˇo-a bpai … nòy (krúp/kâ)
I'd like to reserve a seat, please.	ขอจองที่นั่ง	koˇr jorng têe nûng
Which platform for the … train?	รถไฟไป … อยู่ ชานชาลาไหน	rót fai bpai … yòo chahn cha-lah naˇi?
What station is this?	ที่นี่สถานีอะไร	têe nêe sa-taˇhn-nee a-rai?
Where is the bus stop?	ป้ายรถเมล์อยู่ที่ไหน	bpâi rót may yòo têe-naˇi?
Where is the bus station?	สถานีรถเมล์อยู่ที่ไหน	sa-taˇhn-nee rót may yòo têe-naˇi?
Which buses go to …?	รถเมล์สายไหนไป …	rót may saˇi naˇi bpai …?
What time does the bus for … leave?	รถเมล์ไป … ออกกี่โมง	rót may bpai … òrk gèe mohng?
Would you tell me when we get to ..?	ถึง … แล้ว ช่วยบอกด้วย	těung … lâir-o chôo-ay bòrk dôo-ay?
arrivals	ถึง	těung
booking office	ที่จองตั๋ว	têe jorng dtoˇo-a
bus station	สถานีรถเมล์	sa-taˇhn-nee rót may
departures	ออก	òrk
baggage room	ที่ฝากของ	têe fàhk koˇrng
ordinary bus	รถธรรมดา	rót tum-ma-dah
tour bus	รถทัวร์	rót too-a
ticket	ตั๋ว	dtoˇo-a
ferry	เรือข้ามฟาก	reu-a kâhm fâhk
train	รถไฟ	rót fai
railroad station	สถานีรถไฟ	sa-taˇhn-nee rót fai
moped	รถมอเตอร์ไซค์	rót mor-dter-sai
bicycle	รถจักรยาน	rót jùk-gra-yahn
taxi	แท็กซี่	táirk-sêe

Staying in a Hotel

Do you have a vacant room?	มีห้องว่างไหม มั้ย?	*mee hôrng wâhng mái?*
double/twin room	ห้องคู่	*hôrng kôo*
single room	ห้องเดี่ยว	*hôrng dèe-o*
I have a reservation.	จองห้องไว้แล้ว	*jorng hôrng wái láir-o*
Will you spray some mosquito repellent, please?	ช่วยฉีดยากันยุงให้ หน่อยได้ไหม	*chôo-ay chèet yah gun yOOng hâi nòy dâi mái?*
air conditioner	เครื่องปรับอากาศ	*krêu-ung bprùp ah-gàht*
fan	พัดลม	*pùt lom*
key	กุญแจ	*gOOn-jair*
toilet/bathroom	ห้องน้ำ	*hôrng náhm*

Eating Out

A table for two please.	ขอโต๊ะสำหรับ สองคน	*ko·r dtó su·m-rùp so·rng kon*
May I see the menu?	ขอดูเมนูหน่อย	*ko·r doo may-noo nòy*
Do you have …?	มี … ไหม	*mee … mái?*
I'd like …	ขอ	*ko·r …*
Not too spicy, ok?	ไม่เอาเผ็ดมากนะ	*mâi ao pèt mâhk na*
Is it spicy?	เผ็ดไหม	*pèt mái?*
I can eat Thai food.	ทานอาหารไทยเป็น	*tahn ah-ha·hn tai bpen*
May I have a glass of water, please.	ขอน้ำแข็งเปล่า แก้วหนึ่ง	*ko·r núm ka·irng bplào gâir-o nèung*
I didn't order this.	นี่ไม่ได้สั่ง (ครับ/ค่ะ)	*nêe mâi dâi sùng (krúp/kâ)*
Waiter/waitress!	คุณ (ครับ/ค่ะ)	*kOOn (krúp/kâ)*
The check, please.	ขอบิลหน่อย (ครับ/ค่ะ)	*ko·r bin nòy (krúp/kâ)*
bottle	ขวด	*kòo-ut*
chopsticks	ตะเกียบ	*dta-gèe-up*
fork	ส้อม	*sôrm*
menu	เมนู	*may-noo*
spoon	ช้อน	*chórn*
water	น้ำ	*náhm*

Health

I do not feel well.	รู้สึกไม่สบาย	*róo-sèuk mâi sa-bai*
It hurts here.	เจ็บตรงนี้	*jèp dtrong née*
I have a fever.	ตัวร้อนเป็นไข้	*dtoo-a rórn bpen kâi*
I'm allergic to …	(ผม/ดิฉัน) แพ้ …	*(po·m/dee-chún) páir …*
asthma	โรคหืด	*rôhk hèut*
dentist	ทันตแพทย์ or หมอฟัน	*tun-dta-pâirt or mo·r fun*
diabetes	โรคเบาหวาน	*rôhk bao wa·hn*
diarrhea	ท้องเสีย	*tórng sěe-a*
dizzy	เวียนหัว	*wee-un ho·o-a*
doctor	หมอ	*mo·r*
dysentery	โรคบิด	*rôhk bìt*
fever	ไข้	*kâi*
heart attack	หัวใจวาย	*ho·o-a jai wai*

hospital	โรงพยาบาล	*rohng pa-yah-bahn*
injection	ฉีดยา	*chèet yah*
medicine	ยา	*yah*
penicillin	ยาเพนนิซิลลิน	*yah pen-ní-seen-lin*
prescription	ใบสั่งยา	*bai sùng yah*
prickly heat	ผด	*pòt*
sore throat	เจ็บคอ	*jèp kor*
stomach ache	ปวดท้อง	*bpòo-ut tórng*
temperature	ตัวร้อน	*dtoo-ah rórn*
traditional medicine	ยาแผนโบราณ	*yah pa·irn boh-rahn*
vomit	อาเจียน	*ah-jee-un*

Numbers

0	๐ or ศูนย์	*so·on*
1	๑ or หนึ่ง	*nèung*
2	๒ or สอง	*so·rng*
3	๓ or สาม	*sa·hm*
4	๔ or สี่	*sèe*
5	๕ or ห้า	*hâh*
6	๖ or หก	*hòk*
7	๗ or เจ็ด	*jèt*
8	๘ or แปด	*bpàirt*
9	๙ or เก้า	*gâo*
10	๑๐ or สิบ	*sìp*
15	๑๕ or สิบห้า	*sìp-hâh*
20	๒๐ or ยี่สิบ	*yêe-sìp*
30	๓๐ or สามสิบ	*sa·hm-sìp*
40	๔๐ or สี่สิบ	*sèe-sìp*
50	๕๐ or ห้าสิบ	*hâh-sìp*
60	๖๐ or หกสิบ	*hòk-sìp*
70	๗๐ or เจ็ดสิบ	*jèt-sìp*
80	๘๐ or แปดสิบ	*bpàirt-sìp*
90	๙๐ or เก้าสิบ	*gâo-sìp*
100	๑๐๐ or หนึ่งร้อย	*nèung róy*
200	๒๐๐ or สองร้อย	*so·rng róy*
1,000	๑๐๐๐ or หนึ่งพัน	*nèung pun*
10,000	๑๐,๐๐๐ or หนึ่งหมื่น	*nèung mèun*
100,000	๑๐๐,๐๐๐ or หนึ่งแสน	*nèung sa·irn*

Time and Seasons

one minute	หนึ่งนาที	*nèung nah-tee*
one hour	หนึ่งชั่วโมง	*nèung chôo-a mohng*
half an hour	ครึ่งชั่วโมง	*krêung chôo-a mohng*
quarter of an hour	สิบห้านาที	*sìp-hâh nah-tee*
midnight	เที่ยงคืน	*têe-ung keun*
noon	เที่ยงวัน	*têe-ung wun*
a day	หนึ่งวัน	*neung wun*
a weekend	สุดสัปดาห์	*sÒOt sùp-pah-dah*
a week	หนึ่งอาทิตย์	*nèung ah-tít*
a month	หนึ่งเดือน	*nèung deu-un*
a year	หนึ่งปี	*nèung bpee*
cool season	หน้าหนาว	*nâh na·o*
hot season	หน้าร้อน	*nâh rórn*
rainy season	หน้าฝน	*nâh fo·n*
vacation	วันหยุด	*wun yÒOt*

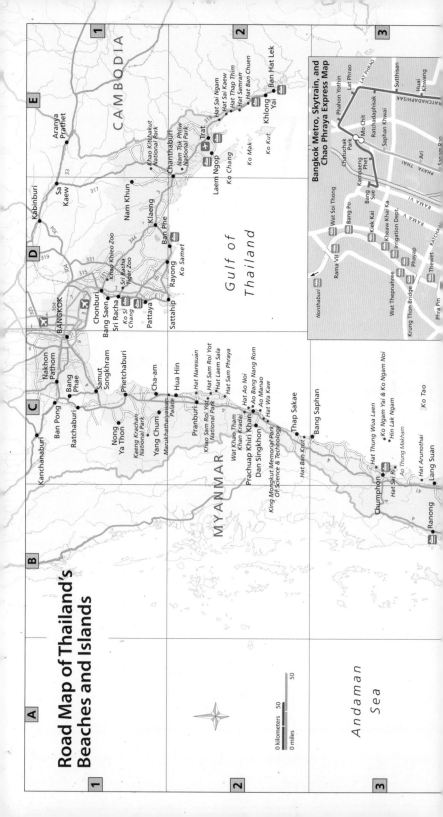